THE STOCK MARKET COURSE

WILEY TRADING ADVANTAGE

Beyond Candlesticks / Steve Nison

Beyond Technical Analysis / Tushar Chande

Campaign Trading / John Sweeney

Contrary Opinion / R. Earl Hadady

Cybernetic Trading Strategies / Murray A. Ruggiero Jr.

Day Trade Part-Time / John Cook and Jeanette Szwec

Encyclopedia of Chart Patterns / Thomas Bulkowski

Expert Trading Systems / John R. Wolberg

Fundamental Analysis / Jack Schwager

Gaming the Market / Ronald B. Shelton

Genetic Algorithms and Investment Strategies / Richard J. Bauer Jr.

Intermarket Technical Analysis / John J. Murphy

Long-Term Secrets to Short-Term Trading / Larry Williams

Macro Trading and Investment Strategies / Gabriel Burstein

Managed Trading / Jack Schwager

McMillan on Options / Lawrence G. McMillan

Neural Network Time Series Forecasting of Financial Markets / E. Michael Azoff

New Market Timing Techniques / Thomas R. DeMark

New Trading Dimensions / Bill Williams

Nonlinear Pricing / Christopher T. May

Option Market Making / Alan J. Baird

Option Strategies, Second Edition / Courtney Smith

Pattern, Price & Time / James A. Hyerczyk

Point and Figure Charting / Thomas J. Dorsey

Profits from Natural Resources / Roland A. Jansen

Schwager on Futures / Jack Schwager

Seasonality / Jake Bernstein

Stock Index Futures & Options / Susan Abbott Gidel

Study Guide for Trading for a Living / Dr. Alexander Elder

Study Guide to Accompany Fundamental Analysis / Jack Schwager

Study Guide to Accompany Technical Analysis / Jack Schwager

Technical Analysis / Jack Schwager

Technical Analysis of the Options Markets / Richard Hexton

Technical Market Indicators / Richard J. Bauer Jr. and Julie R. Dahlquist

THE STOCK MARKET COURSE

George A. Fontanills and Tom Gentile

JOHN WILEY & SONS, INC.
New York • Chichester • Weinheim • Brisbane • Singapore • Toronto

Published by John Wiley & Sons, Inc.

Published simultaneously in Canada.

This publication is designed to provide accurate and authoritative information in regard to
the subject matter covered. It is sold with the understanding that the publisher is not engaged
in rendering professional services. If professional advice or other expert assistance is
required, the services of a competent professional person should be sought.

Designations used by companies to distinguish their products are often claimed as
trademarks. In all instances where the author is aware of a claim, the product names appear
in Initial Capital letters. Readers, however, should contact the appropriate companies for
more complete information regarding trademarks and registration.

Library of Congress Cataloging-in-Publication Data:

Fontanills, George.
   The stock market course / George A. Fontanills and Tom Gentile.—1st ed.
      p.   cm.—(Wiley trading advantage)
   Includes bibliographical references and index.
   ISBN 0-471-39315-0 (cloth : acid-free paper)
   1. Stocks—United States.   I. Gentile, Tom, 1965–   II. Title.   III. Series.
   HG4910.F598   2001
   332.63'22—dc21   00-053368

Printed in the United States of America.
10 9 8 7 6 5

I would like to dedicate this book to
the Optionetics.com staff, writers, and traders.
Their innovative ideas and commitment to excellence,
hard work, and constant good humor are
the reasons Optionetics.com is enjoying
such phenomenal success!

Thank you, one and all.

Acknowledgments

After my first two books on option trading were published, I was approached about writing a comprehensive book on how to trade the stock market. At first the prospect of writing a book on a scope as wide as the stock market shook me to the core. But being the kind of person who loves a challenge, I soon warmed up to the idea. It has been a long, sometimes arduous, journey.

After years of experience teaching people how to trade options, I have learned many things about the process of learning. First and foremost, you can't teach anyone anything unless they have the desire to learn. Second, everyone learns at his or her own speed. Third, you have to break the complexities of trading down into bite-size, understandable pieces that are interesting enough that people naturally continue the learning process because they get it. If it gets too complicated, people give up. Learning involves a feeling of accomplishment with a few epiphanies thrown in here and there to spice things up and keep the process engaging. I am hopeful that this book not only accomplishes these goals, but also helps people to understand the stock market and gives them enough tools to make money in it.

As usual, I could not have written this book without the supreme effort of the Optionetics.com staff and the research team that helped put it all together. I would now like to take the time to acknowledge each one of these brilliant people.

At the top of the list, I want to thank my coauthor for this book, Tom Gentile. As Chief Options Strategist at Optionetics.com and coinstructor at Optionetics Seminars, Tom is one of the most brilliant traders I have ever had the pleasure to know. Although this book is written from a first person perspective, please note that it is the work of two authors. To his credit, Tom put in a phenomenal amount of time and energy researching every aspect of this book while sharing his extensive experience and insightful trading knowledge. His consistency and attention to detail make him the best writing partner I can imagine. Thank you, Tom Gentile, for your supreme effort in the completion of this book.

My deepest thanks go to Richard Cawood, the CEO of Optionetics.com, for his unbiased support and can-do, positive thinking. He is the backbone of this organization, and without him I would not be able to do all the things I love to do as well as

I get to do them. I would also like to acknowledge Amy Morris, our Director of Administration, whose tireless efforts keep the day-to-day running of Optionetics.com a smooth, well-organized process. In addition, I would like to thank Tony Clemendor, our Chief Operating Officer, for his innovative leadership, excellent ideas, and tireless dedication to the expansion of Optionetics.com.

There are also a host of excellent writers on my research team that deserve a big round of applause. Without them, I would not have been able to write such a comprehensive book or finish it on time. Specifically, I would like to thank Mike Keller, Frederic Ruffy, and Phillip Wiegand for their insightful devotion to this project. How they magically found time to help me complete my thoughts I'll never know. My thanks also go to Ed Hecht, Scott Kaye, Chris McLean, and Roy Lindsay for their support. I would like to acknowledge and thank Andrew Neyens and Shelley Souza for their editorial genius, timely commentary, and market expertise. Special thanks also go to Mary Jo Thayer for her in-depth research, last-minute edits, and overall assistance in the completion of this book.

Last, but not least, let me express my deep appreciation to Kym Trippsmith, the Editor-in-Chief of Optionetics.com and the senior editor for this project. She has been absolutely indispensable in the development and coordination of this book. Kym's unconventional approach to life and wild sense of humor serve as an inspiration to all of us.

Good luck and great trading!

—GEORGE A. FONTANILLS

About the Authors

George A. Fontanills Having struggled to overcome a life-threatening illness as a young man, George Fontanills is a true believer in the idea that pursuing your dreams is something that should never be put off until tomorrow. Like many people, George followed the typical educational and work-related path: After high school he went to college, and from college to an accounting job at the prestigious firm of Deloitte, Haskins Sells. Upon receiving his CPA license, George started work with Andersen Consulting. Not quite satisfied with where his life was headed, he left this job to attend Harvard Business School's MBA program.

After receiving his MBA, George decided to get off the treadmill of unsatisfying jobs. In the face of several high-paying job opportunities, George decided that he needed to start his own business. His first business failed. Undaunted, he started a second business that never left the starting gate. A survivor, he kept going. Running low on money, George became a real estate investor buying property with no money down. Finding a business he enjoyed, he quickly began to build a successful track record increasing his assets. Just as he began to feel that he had found his life-long career, the bottom fell out of the real estate market—strike three.

As George pondered his next move, he received a brochure on making money in the markets. After ordering the book, he began trading—and losing money. Rather than concentrating on his own losses, he began studying successful traders to see what they were doing differently. Using the analysis skills he developed at Harvard, George conducted a comprehensive investigation to determine what differentiated the winners from the losers. Risking the money he made in real estate, George tested his conclusions and eventually learned to use managed-risk strategies. This innovative approach uses options to mathematically control risk every time a trade is placed, thereby consistently producing income without the stress of unbridled losses. He called this trading style Optionetics. As his net worth soared, George gained a reputation as one of the world's most respected traders. As an expert in nondirectional, managed-risk options trading, George Fontanills became a regular speaker at trading conferences and investment summits.

Today, Mr. Fontanills is the President of Global Investment Research Corp. and remains an active equity options and stock investor. He currently teaches this strategic approach through his study program, Optionetics: The Science of High Profit and Low Stress Trading. Specializing in delta neutral trading using stocks, options on indexes, and options on stocks, George Fontanills has instructed thousands of traders internationally.

As President of Pinnacle Investments of America, Inc., Mr. Fontanills is a registered investment adviser and hedge fund manager, as well as a consultant to a number of offshore trading organizations, professional trading firms, and large financial institutions. His unique approach to trading and phenomenal success has made him a sought-after speaker at a variety of conferences. His reputation as a pioneer in teaching delta neutral trading has led to numerous guest appearances on television and radio shows across the country. He has been most recently written about in the *Wall Street Journal*, *Barron's*, *Research* magazine, CBS MarketWatch, and TheStreet.com. He is a featured trading expert on CNBC, Bloomberg, and CNNfn, as well as many radio stations across the country. In addition, Mr. Fontanills' two best-selling hardback releases—*The Options Course* and *Trade Options Online*, published by John Wiley & Sons, Inc.—have added to his critical acclaim as one of the best trading instructors in the country.

Tom Gentile   Mr. Gentile was born of steelworker descent in Pittsburgh, Pennsylvania, in 1965. During his childhood, he moved around the country as his family worked on various state government projects. He dubbed himself the "professional new kid" as he wound up in virtually a different school each year. As college approached, Mr. Gentile excelled as a distance runner, and during 1982 and 1983 was rated one of the top distance runners in the state of Georgia. In 1984, Tom went to work for Home Depot, and by 1987 had become one of the youngest managers in the company. By 1990, Gentile progressed to become a regional coordinator in Home Depot's information services. His responsibilities included financial training of executive, regional, and district managers over the entire northeastern United States.

Gentile began his trading career in 1986 and made the jump to full-time trading in 1994, landing a job at the American Stock Exchange. During his tenure on the floor, he met George Fontanills and began teaching the Optionetics Seminars, one of the most successful options seminars in the markets today. Gentile also played a key role in the development of the synthetic straddle, a strategy developed as an off-the-floor trading approach to rebalance a position.

Currently, Gentile serves as the Chief Options Strategist for the Global Investment Research Corp. and Optionetics.com. He is a contributing writer in numerous publications, including *Fortune* magazine, *Barron's*, and the *Wall Street Journal*, as well as many other magazines and publications. Online appearances have been numerous, with regular spots and articles at RadioWallStreet.com, TheStreet.com, Barrons.com, and a host of others. Gentile is currently hard at work on a new book entitled *The Volatility Course*, to be published by John Wiley & Sons. As an up-and-coming market wizard, Gentile's passion for trading and down-to-earth style is a refreshing change. "In trading, the education business is just like any other business," says Gentile. "You either make dust, or you eat it."

Contents

Foreword

Audentis fortuna juvat.
"Fortune favors the bold."
—Virgil, *Aeneid, X*

I remember the first time I got a taste of the markets. I was facing a few personal problems in my life, when I received something in the mail about trading. Without much thought, I decided to take a chance on a home study course on trading the markets using some simple technical analysis techniques. When I received this manual, I completely dove into it and let it consume me for a few weeks while I trained myself. Gradually, I started to understand market concepts, mathematics, and how to enter and exit orders. I quickly became convinced that I was going to be a millionaire in no time.

After finishing the course, I tried paper trading a few times. But the whole time I just kept thinking, "This is just too easy. I can't believe I didn't think of doing this before." Within six months from my initial trade, I blew out my first account completely. I set about blaming everything else except the man in the mirror. In retrospect, I realize that my biggest problem in trading early on was twofold: not having the specialized knowledge about what it was that I was trading, and not having an entry and exit plan for every event that could take place once my trade became reality. I was simply too focused on the dream of becoming a rich, lazy trader who sat in a hammock on some remote island, while gobs of money dropped each day into my bank account.

A lot has changed since the 1980s when yuppies, power lunches, and full-service brokers seemed to dominate the scene. Yuppies have turned into "dot-commers," while the broker arena has turned completely upside down. At this moment in time, 20% of all stock transactions are executed online, and this number is expected to triple within the next five years. Online trading has its pros and cons. The advantages of online trading are many. First, commissions on a stock transaction are quite cheap and getting cheaper every day—as low as a penny a share when placing through a direct access broker. When buying in bulk (5,000 shares), that number can even be less. Another great reason to be trading online is that with the developing technology, executions are becoming split-second fast, allowing very little lag time between placing an order and getting filled. With real-time streaming feeds, you can see bids and offers, as well as size for each, and not have to wonder whether your limit got filled. But drawbacks do exist. The biggest potential problem that comes with all this technology is that the major trading decisions have become the direct responsibility of the individual trader. Without a professional by your side to help you, it has become your job to get educated on the ins and outs of the market, both technically and fundamentally.

Why read this book? One answer: *specialized knowledge*. We are laying the groundwork to help you understand that trading the markets is not like any other corporate career. Specialized knowledge is the best thing you can receive before taking on any venture. This is where a good education in the markets will save you thousands of dollars in mistakes. It amazes me how many people will try to save a few dollars trying to figure this market out on their own, and in the process spend thousands of dollars in losses to learn the markets. Bottom line: You will pay to learn this business one way or another. The biggest problem with learning it the hard way is that it will kill your ego (and your account) very quickly.

This book is designed to satisfy the needs of the novice trader. It provides a comprehensive beginner's education that includes as many of the important aspects of trading stocks that we could fit into one volume. Placing a trade is the easiest part. It takes a mere nanosecond to complete. It's what you do before and after the trade is placed that will determine your outcome. To become a successful investor or trader, you have to start with the basics, develop an understanding of the types of accounts to set up, project your goals as a trader, and accurately assess your time availability. These first steps are crucial to your success in this otherwise hectic business.

In many ways, introducing the world of investing to a beginner is a bit like attempting to explain American culture to an off-world alien. After all, the stock market is a world unique unto itself. It has its own strange rhythms and an infinite number of tiny details that require explanation. To be successful, you need to amass enough weapons to effectively do battle in its highly competitive arenas. Knowing the language of the market is only part of it. In addition, there are a multitude of players, trading strategies, analysis techniques, ordering protocols, and regulations that make or break you as an investor.

In truth, the stock market may hold the key to making your dreams come true or allowing your nightmares to become reality. It can beat you down or make you rich. To sway the delicate balance between the two, every conceivable piece of the puzzle must be used to your advantage. At times, things may turn ugly. Yet, history has shown, there is opportunity in every crisis. As an investor, success lies in turning seemingly dire situations into profitable investment opportunities. In other words, you must learn to master the art of investing to become successful at it.

Just how does one go about mastering the art of investing? Learning to be a profitable investor is an uphill battle. Just figuring out how to get started may seem like an overwhelming challenge. Odds are that you'll lose money before you make any at all. There are neither any get-rich-quick strategies nor foolproof tricks of the trade. Learning to master the art of investing requires knowing the ground rules, being able to filter out unnecessary information, gaining practical experience before you run out of money, and a true passion for the game.

Let's face it: People play the stock market to make money. Although the possibility of loss always exists, investors prefer to concentrate on the triumph of profit-making instead. There's something irresistible about getting more money back from an investment than you originally paid for it. To successfully compete with thousands of market analysts, institutional money managers, professional brokers, and Internet-savvy traders, you have to be able to make accurate and timely decisions. You have to arm yourself with enough knowledge to know whether an investment is worth the risk.

Unfortunately, many novice traders depend on tips from brokers and intuitive hunches. They end up placing impractical trades that often result in disappointing losses. To be successful, you have to stay in the game long enough to make money at it. You need to improve your skills to the point that your investments make consistent profits. Hence, investing seems full of catch-22s: It takes money to foster experience; and it takes experience to make money.

One of the most obvious ways of making money in the stock market is by owning shares of premier U.S. companies. However, with more than 10,000 stocks and 3,000 stock options traded at the major stock exchanges, choosing a winner is not easy. One strategy that has worked well for me has been identifying growth stocks and trying to buy them early in their growth cycle. Basically, for a company to grow, it has to continually expand its business. A company can do this by reinvesting profits toward the development of new products and services. If a company grows and is well managed, the company's revenues and profits increase simultaneously. An increase in a company's profitability and net worth can, in turn, lead to an increase in the value of the company's stock. For me, spotting a company in the early stages of the growth cycle has proved to be an integral part of my investment success. But that's just one piece of the puzzle.

To an extent, this book has three goals. The first is to make stock investing relevant to your particular situation. During my years of teaching trading seminars, investors have continually asked for specific recommendations. Although I always have investment ideas, it's difficult to make specific suggestions because everyone's situation is different. In other words, a trade that seems ideal for me may well be unsuitable for someone with a totally different financial condition, time availability, and risk tolerance. It would be like a doctor prescribing medicine without doing an examination first. So, the first goal of this book is to help you evaluate your current financial situation and to determine if trading stocks fits your lifestyle.

The second goal of this book is to make the case for stocks over any other investment. If successful and appropriate to your individual financial situation, investing in the stock market can be the most important decision you ever make.

Some may object and suggest that the stock market is a risky place. True enough, day-to-day, the stock market moves up and down—sometimes violently. However, over the long haul, stocks have proven themselves to be the most effective way of maintaining one's purchasing power and standard of living. It is an exciting time to be an investor. The world is embracing the market system and that creates opportunities for other entrepreneurs to obtain enough capital to implement their ideas, grow profits, and to ultimately increase shareholder value.

The third goal is to teach you how to filter out unnecessary information so that you can focus on what's really important. The advent of the Internet has opened up a Pandora's box of financial information. But how much of this information is pertinent to the finding of promising investment opportunities? There are a multitude of analysis techniques that can be used to gauge market performance. The trick is to use the techniques that help you find the right kind of stock to fit your financial profile.

The initial chapters of the book provide an introduction to various investment instruments including cash equivalents and bonds as well as stocks, mutual funds, and indexes. All of these instruments are part of a balanced investment portfolio. To dispel the myth that options are risky, an in-depth section on options is included to help you see options for what they truly are, a risk-adjusted instrument.

Once you get an idea of how to diversify your assets, it's time to get educated as to the specifics of stock fundamentals. Screening real-market moving fundamentals will save you thousands of dollars in mistakes. Just knowing what a P/E ratio is doesn't cut it anymore. In this new era of fundamental analysis, investors have to look beyond old-century thinking to adapt to the new-age style of fundamental thinking. Understanding the fundamentals as presented here will clarify for you what to look for and what to avoid in company statistics. The introduction of technical analysis and how it can be combined with fundamental analysis will help you to develop a more precise entry and exit system. From the beginnings of moving averages and trends to advanced techniques such as oscillators and breakout indicators, this section will prepare you to fine-tune your entries and exits in the stock market. No analysis section can be truly complete these days without a section on the psychology of the markets. Sentiment analysis is filling an important gap between fundamental and technical analysis and can be extremely helpful in the development of a contrarian approach. In addition, the Appendixes are filled with all manner of important lists and informational charts. A glossary can be found online at www.optionetics.com.

Investing is such a unique journey for each one of us. George and I have done our best to eliminate the superfluous material and concentrate on those key elements that have really helped us to succeed. Rather than trying to teach you everything you've always wanted to know about trading, this book sets forth a strong stock investing foundation—a stepping-stone if you will—for your own journey.

Since one of the keys to learning is repetition, I have included "Roadmaps to Success " at the end of each chapter to enable readers to have a step-by-step guide to using the information in each chapter. The hardest part of learning to trade is making the transition from theory to real-world trading. The roadmaps are designed to give you a quick rundown of what you need to know and how to get going. There is also an accompanying book, *The Stock Market Course Workbook,* available for those of you up to the challenge of studying this book in greater detail.

With the proliferation of the Internet, it's now up to individual investors and traders to become self-educated on the art of stock speculation. This book will provide you with the tools necessary to begin to make decisions based on more than just a hunch. Trading is a vast realm of uncertainties. I hope this book provides an anchor for you as you weather the storms and enjoy the calmer waters of the investment arena. Knowledge and perseverance are the keys to smooth sailing and eventual trading success. I hope this book provides you with a better understanding of what you're up against and how you can use the tools at hand to enjoy a successful career in the stock market.

TOM GENTILE

1

Welcome to the Stock Market

I'm in love with my job. Every day I wake up raring to go. I turn on my computer and in seconds, I'm ready to take on the world—the new David in a land full of institutional Goliaths. Most days I'm up before the markets open, strategizing my next move and looking for winning trades. The everyday challenges presented by market uncertainty make trading the best job I could possibly imagine. There's none of this "same-old-same-old, day-in-day-out" stuff for me! Each day I wage war on a virtual battlefield and I thrive on the excitement. Fortunately, I win more often than I lose.

Make no mistake: Trading stocks is not for the weak of heart. Every day, the decisions you make potentially affect everything from where you can afford to send your kids to college to where you'll spend your golden years. It's been my experience that to become a proficient trader, you need to be dedicated to learning, and passionate about winning. After all, you're competing with people who want to take your money away from you.

Stocks have consistently outperformed all other forms of investment—period. The surging stock market in the last decade of the millennium has driven the markets higher than ever before—regardless of corrections. It's hard to think of any reason why anyone with a certain level of disposable income wouldn't utilize stocks as an investment vehicle. Investing in stocks has enhanced millions of people's lives. But just because other people have made profitable investment decisions doesn't guarantee the success of your future endeavors.

From the institutional money manager with half a century of experience to the cyber-investing mom placing her first trade, every investor dreams of making a killing in the markets. Why do some succeed and others fail? Is it chance or skill that makes the difference? I have spent years trying to figure out exactly what separates the winners from the losers, and in the process have discovered a few key explanations.

Stocks: Securities or certificates representing fractional ownership of a company purchased as an investment. How much you own depends on how many shares of stock you possess versus how many shares have been issued.

Stock market: A catchall name for the overall facilitation of the buying and selling of shares of ownership in companies.

The first key to winning as an investor is to develop a healthy respect for risk. It's actually quite common for people who do not invest in the markets to consider stock trading a form of gambling. *Webster's New 20th Century Dictionary* defines gambling as "an act that depends solely upon chance." The stock market is anything but a roll of the dice or luck of the draw. Successful investing relies on an investor's ability to reason, weigh risks, spot opportunities, and make quick decisions. And yes, chance can have an effect on performance. Choosing to take an unavoidable risk is simply part of the decision-making process. Neglecting to assess risks before entering any trade is definitely a gamble.

Risk: In terms of an investment, risk represents the maximum potential financial loss inherent in the placement of an investment.

The second task is to develop a low-stress investment plan that will enable you to build your knowledge base systematically. Most investors start the same way. They read a few books, open a small account, and lose a chunk of money in no time. There is one way, however, to differentiate the winners from the losers: Winners persist at learning as much as they can by starting slow and collecting the trading tools necessary to manifest a competitive edge. Successful traders first learn to crawl, then walk; given enough time, they may eventually learn to fly.

Third, beginners need to start by specializing in one or two markets at a time. Specialization allows traders to match winning strategies with recognizable market conditions. Successful traders realize that similar market conditions will recur in the future and the same strategy can then be used to reap rewards.

Specialization: Focusing on mastering one or two stocks or trading strategies at a time before moving on to the next ones.

Fourth, define your limits in terms of the amount of money you can afford to lose. Before investing a single dollar, it is essential you make an honest appraisal of your financial assets and capabilities. Although real estate can be purchased with no money down, an investor needs cash to open a brokerage account. When you put up cash to invest in stocks, you are coming face-to-face with risk. Hopefully, you'll never lose your entire trading account. But you need to be prepared in the event that you do. In short, assess your financial capabilities and pinpoint your risk tolerance. You may think those two simple words—risk tolerance—are heading into oxymoron territory (up there with jumbo shrimp, military intelligence, and rich broker). But in truth, it is vital to assess the level of risk you can afford to take before placing your first trade. Start by determining how much disposable income you earn monthly. How much money do you need to set aside for life's little (and big) emergencies? How much of your savings can you afford to lose?

Brokerage account: A trading account hosted by a firm that acts as an agent for a customer and charges the customer a commission for its services.

Novice investors need to acquire the information necessary to make intelligent investment decisions. Thanks to the advent of the Internet, the abundance of available information has increased tenfold and more. But the burgeoning of information has its downside. Investors now have a profusion of information to sift through and assess for reliability and accuracy. This information glut has driven many investors to choose to leave investment decisions, and hence their financial futures, in the hands of someone else.

The underlying objective of this book is to empower the reader through knowledge. Successful trading involves developing an information filter tailored to meet your financial goals.

My specific experience—as a stock market investor, instructor, and writer—has taught me many lessons. Perhaps the most significant involves developing the ability to discriminate between what information is useful in making investment decisions and what is not. There is little doubt that advances in information technology and communications have provided investors with more power and resources than ever before. In the past, investors were limited to the business section of one or two newspapers and occasional comments on the television news. Today there are financial web sites, e-mail services, and even financial updates delivered via pagers. This abundance of information, ironically, has created a different set of problems: What information is truly valuable and worthwhile? Having access to a lot of information is great, but if it doesn't help make better investment decisions, it's useless. How does one filter out the bad from the good? One of the goals of this book is to help you answer that question by providing a solid foundation in stock market basics.

Bottom line: To play the investment game well, you have to learn the rules by which the game is played!

TAKING RISKS IN THE STOCK MARKET

Risk is easily one of the most misunderstood investment concepts because it comes in many forms, including market risk, opportunity risk, and inflation risk. *Market risk* is a catchall phrase for the inherent risk associated with market forces. *Opportunity risk* involves the economic sacrifice that arises from having to forgo the benefits of alternate investments. For example, if you have $10,000 tied up in one investment, that's $10,000 that can't be used elsewhere. *Inflation risk* affects all investments—some more than others. Inflation refers to the overall economic increase in the general price level of goods and services. Investments have to overcome inflation risk by making a higher return than the rate of inflation (see Figure 1.1). Before you invest a penny, make sure that you assess all of the risks involved. Bottom line—if you can't afford the risk, you can't afford the investment.

My subjective reason for consistently assessing risk is a simple one. Risk is directly tied to what I believe is an investor's worst enemy: stress. Stress produces incomplete knowledge access. This one sentence sums up why trading coupled with stress can produce only one result—loss of capital. It certainly seems ironic that individuals who take up trading in order to reduce the stress of not making enough money from their day jobs often end up creating more. Unfortunately, trading can be an extremely stressful endeavor. If you don't really know what you're doing, stress will be pervasive and the ultimate enjoyment of trading will be greatly diminished. Improper decisions can lead to rapid losses and depletion of your hard-earned cash. This can produce a higher level of stress than you have ever experienced. In today's highly volatile markets, successful trading requires a low-stress trading approach that fits a trader's unique lifestyle and risk tolerance. This book is designed to help you get started on the right foot by showing you what it takes to compete in the investing arena. The number one rule is to assess the risks involved and determine how much risk you can handle.

Serious risk assessment can reduce the stress inherent
in trading and help you to invest intelligently.

On average, almost two billion shares trade hands on the three major U.S. exchanges every day. It really is a fascinating process, considering each trade reflects

Value of Today's $100 after the Impact of Inflation

Rate of	After Number of Years				
Inflation (per Year)	5	10	15	20	25
3.0%	$86.26	$74.41	$64.19	$55.37	$47.76
3.5%	$84.19	$70.89	$59.69	$50.25	$42.31
4.0%	$82.19	$67.56	$55.53	$45.64	$37.51

Figure 1.1　Inflation and the Real Rate of Return

the views or expectations of two particular investors (buyer and seller). Consequently, one of the interesting things about the stock market is its ability to digest information. When information concerning a company is disseminated, the stock price may react favorably (go up) or unfavorably (go down). For example, news that Intel Corp. (INTC) has developed a new and faster computer chip made the stock rise, while news that Microsoft was being investigated by the U.S. Department of Justice sent the stock price of Microsoft (MSFT) down. Many investors choose to sit on the sidelines until the uncertainty dissipates.

When news concerning a company is considered to be unfavorable, the result is a drop in stock price. If you purchased shares in a particular company the day before bad news is released, the value of your stock holdings will fall upon the news. That is the risk of owning stocks—that they can, periodically, decline in value. You hope they recover, but sometimes they don't, and if they do they may take an incredible amount of time to do so. Simply put, in an effort to buy a stock and sell it at a higher price, investors run the risk of seeing the stock price fall instead.

One of the most important lessons to be encountered in trading is the concept of the risk to reward ratio (i.e., there is a certain level of risk and the potential for a certain reward associated with every investment). Calculating this ratio provides essential information as to the viability of the trade.

THE INVESTMENT SETTING

Stock represents an ownership share in a corporation, so when you purchase stock, you become a partial owner in a corporation. The percentage you own depends on the number of shares purchased and the size of the company. For instance, the total number of shares in existence of Intel is roughly 3,349,000,000. If you purchase 100 shares, you become a fractional owner. Your ownership amounts to $1/33,490,000$. As small and insignificant as that might seem, you still have rights as a shareholder:

1. Right to profits

2. Right to vote

3. Right to information

Perhaps the most important right shareholders have is the right to share in the company's net profits. In theory, the value of a company is a direct function of the profits that it is able to generate. Consider, for instance, if someone offered to sell you a corner grocery store in your neighborhood. After looking over the books, you figure out that the store has failed to make any money for the past 10 years. If you decide to buy the store anyway, either you are going to suffer financial losses or you must turn the business around so that it makes money and you can get paid.

Earnings: Net income for the company during a specific period.

Dividends: When a corporation pays a fraction of its profits to its shareholders, those payments are called dividends. The amount is announced before it is paid, and is distributed to shareholders of record on a per share basis.

The same holds true for stock ownership. A profitable company has *earnings*, which are either reinvested back into the company or distributed to stockholders (or a combination of the two). When a company distributes a portion of its earnings, the payment is referred to as a *dividend*. If none of the earnings are being passed on to stockholders as dividends, then they are most likely being reinvested to fuel the company's future success and profitability.

As a stockholder, you also have the right to information. Annual and quarterly reports are provided to all shareholders and are available to the financial public at large. These reports provide information that includes: business developments; updated financials (see Chapter 8 for a closer look at reading financial reports); and an assessment of the business outlook for the coming quarter and year.

Annual report: A report issued by a company to its shareholders at the end of the fiscal year, which contains an income statement, balance sheet, statement of changes in financial position, changes in the stockholder's equity account, a summary of the significant accounting principles used by the firm, the auditor's report, and comments from management about the significant business and financial events of the year, as well as various other data pertinent to the financial health of the firm. A more detailed (and numbers-oriented) version is the 10-K report required to be filed with the Securities and Exchange Commission (SEC) and made available to all stockholders who request it. The 10-K report is also available online and from the SEC to all interested parties.

Stockholders also have the right to vote on major issues facing the company such as the selection of accountants, whether to accept takeover offers from other companies, or authorizing the distribution of additional shares. In most cases, the votes from individual investors on such matters are relatively inconsequential.

THE EXCHANGES

Stocks, futures, and options are traded on organized exchanges throughout the world, or on a computerized system. These exchanges establish rules and procedures that foster a safe and fair method of determining the prices as well as provide an arena for the trading of stocks. Advancements in technology have inspired many of these exchanges to update their systems in order to stay competitive on a global basis.

A stock exchange is an actual physical location (or computerized system) for the organized buying and selling of stocks. There are three main U.S. exchanges for trading stocks: the New York Stock Exchange (NYSE), the American Stock Exchange (AMEX), and the Nasdaq (National Association of Securities Dealers Automated Quotations system). Exchanges are businesses. They provide the public with a place to trade. Each exchange has a unique personality and competes with other exchanges for business. This competitiveness keeps the exchanges on their toes. Exchanges rent booths on the exchange floor to brokerage firms and specialists and must be able to react to the demands of the marketplace with innovative products, services, and technological innovations.

The Securities and Exchange Commission (SEC) regulates U.S. exchanges. The Commission was created by Congress during the Great Depression in 1934 and is charged with making sure that securities markets operate fairly and protect investors. It is composed of five commissioners appointed by the President and approved by the Senate. The SEC enforces, among other acts, the Securities Act of 1933, the Securities Exchange Act of 1934, the Maloney Act of 1938, the Trust Indenture Act of 1939, the Investment Company Act of 1940, the Investment Advisers Act of 1940, the Securities Investor Protection Act of 1970, and the Securities Act Amendments of 1975.

Founded in 1792, the New York Stock Exchange is the largest and most familiar auction-style exchange in the world. It currently lists approximately 3,050 companies trading more than 206.6 billion shares worth approximately $8.9 trillion (as of April 2000). The average daily turnover is roughly one billion shares, which gives an idea of the sheer size of today's markets. The NYSE is a corporation overseen by a board of directors who are responsible for setting policy, supervising Exchange and member activities, listing securities, and overseeing the transfer of members' seats on the Exchange.

Auction-style market: The facilitation of executing trading orders in which buyers enter competitive bids and sellers enter competitive offers simultaneously. The stock market is like a giant garage sale—if you don't like the price listed, you can make your own bid for the item and wait to see if someone is willing to match it.

The American Stock Exchange (AMEX) is the second-largest auction-style equities market in the world. A private, not-for-profit corporation located in New York City, AMEX handles approximately one-fifth of all securities trades within the United States—approximately 1,750 companies trading over 5 billion shares annually worth around $92 billion. Most of the companies AMEX offers are too small to be listed on the New York Stock Exchange.

To be an exchange member at either the AMEX or NYSE requires the purchase of a seat on the exchange that cost upwards of $500,000.

There are six regional exchanges—in Boston, Chicago, Cincinnati, Philadelphia, Los Angeles, and San Francisco. Some of these exchanges use an open-outcry auction-style system where buyers and sellers come together to trade shares of stocks and option contracts. Others are evolving into fully automated systems that electronically match buyers and sellers.

The Nasdaq exchange is not a physical location, but a computerized network that stores and displays stock price quotes. Originally created at the request of the SEC in 1971, it facilitates the trading of stocks over the telephone and via computer directly from brokers all over the country. Nasdaq utilizes a vast telecommunications network to continuously broadcast price fluctuations directly to the computers of market participants. Listing more than 5,540 foreign and domestic companies, the Nasdaq offers more stocks than any other exchange. The Nasdaq has experienced phenomenal growth due to the large number of technology companies listed there.

Each exchange has specific listing requirements—market cap, sales, and so on. The listing requirements vary from exchange to exchange. If you meet the listing requirements for a particular exchange, you can list your stock there. If your company meets the listing requirements, but then later does not, you can be de-listed from the exchange. Once a stock is listed on an exchange, it is assigned a symbol for trading. For instance, the stock symbol for America Online is AOL. These symbols are called *ticker symbols*.

Ticker symbols: Ticker symbols are composed of one to three letters for "listed" shares (those traded on the NYSE or AMEX exchanges) and four or five letters for those on the Nasdaq. This is why Nasdaq stocks are sometimes referred to as "four-letter" stocks.

On June 25, 1998, the National Association of Securities Dealers (NASD)—the parent company of the Nasdaq—and the American Stock Exchange announced that its members approved a plan to combine the AMEX with the Nasdaq system. The merger was completed on November 2, 1998, and created what is now known as the Nasdaq-Amex Market Group. Although the two exchanges still operate under separate managements, their new products and technological developments created a milestone event. One significant development was the creation of a new exchange-traded fund based on the Nasdaq 100. The fund is an average of the 100 largest non-financial stocks listed on Nasdaq and is called an *index share*. Known mainly by its ticker symbol, QQQ, it is one of the most actively traded securities on the American Stock Exchange. The merger also led to the development of one of the most popular financial web sites—www.nasdaq-amex.com. The site offers a host of information including market data, research, and news any investor would find helpful.

National Association of Securities Dealers (NASD): This self-regulatory organization of the securities industry is responsible for the regulation of Nasdaq and the over-the-counter markets.

Index share: A share that secures ownership of a group of stocks traded as one portfolio, such as the S&P 500. Broad-based indexes cover a wide range of industries and companies, and narrow-based indexes cover stocks in one industry or economic sector.

Smaller companies with a limited amount of shares (or *float*) are traded on the *over-the-counter* (*OTC*) market. The OTC market lists more than 30,000 stocks. Brokers who trade these smaller markets receive daily price updates called "Pink Sheets" (the paper they were originally printed on was pink). Today brokers receive the "Pinks" either by fax or electronically.

Float: Refers to the number of shares of a company that are in public hands and are actively traded. Also known as "floating supply," it is the amount of a company's common stock that is traded in the marketplace. To calculate a stock's float, deduct the shares held by insiders and owners, as well as Rule 144 shares from the number of shares outstanding.

Rule 144: A Securities and Exchange Commission (SEC) rule that says a corporate executive or insider who owns a large stake in his or her company—or shares not purchased in the open market—is allowed to sell a portion of that stock every six months after a holding period of two years without reporting it to the SEC. If an insider sells more than the allowable portion in the six-month period or prior to the two-year lock-out, it is known as Rule 144 stock, and the insider must file a formal registration with the SEC.

In addition, exchanges all over the world are linked together regardless of different time zones. The major international exchanges include Frankfurt, Hong Kong, Johannesburg, London, Singapore, Sydney, and Tokyo. Prices shift as trading ends in one time zone and activity moves to the next. This global dynamic explains why stocks close at one price and open the next day at a completely different price at the same exchange. With the increased use of electronic trading in global markets, these price movements are becoming more unpredictable than ever before.

If you've never had the chance to visit an exchange, I highly recommend it. The exchange floor is a mammoth hall filled with representatives from all the major brokerages as well as floor traders, market makers, and specialists who cocreate the investment process. Orders are phoned or electronically communicated from the outside world to *floor traders*, who take them to trading areas, or *trading pits*, to be *executed*. To an outsider's eye, the order process may seem fraught with chaos, but a highly developed, organizational method to the madness actually exists.

> **Floor traders:** Exchange members who execute transactions from the floors of the exchanges for the profits (or to the detriment) of their own accounts.
>
> **Trading pits:** Specific areas on the floors of exchanges where floor traders, market makers, and specialists meet to buy and sell the same security.
>
> **Executed:** The process of completing an order to buy or sell securities.

When investors want to buy or sell shares of AOL, the orders are executed on the floor of the New York Stock Exchange. But don't worry; if you want to buy shares of America Online, you don't have to catch the next flight and go to New York. Instead, you instruct a *broker* to make the transaction for you. Then, the order is routed to the trading floor of the New York Stock Exchange through your broker's firm.

> **Brokerage firm:** Where a trade takes place depends on whether that particular company is listed on the New York Stock Exchange, the Nasdaq, or the American Stock Exchange. One company may be listed on more than one exchange.

THE PLAYERS

When you buy or sell a stock, it is called a *trade*. For instance, if you decide to buy 100 shares of AOL and the stock price is $52, you are trading your money for the stock. In this case, the trade is $5,200 for 100 shares of stock (plus commission). However, many traders prefer to buy shares on *margin*. A trader then needs to put up only *half* the total amount to purchase shares, while the brokerage lends the other half at a small interest rate.

> **Trade:** The actual process of buying or selling a financial instrument in order to attempt to profit from it.
>
> **Margin:** The portion of a trade's value that the customer must pay to initiate the trade, with the remainder of the purchase price being borrowed from the broker.

Regardless of the exchange, each time a trade is executed, the price and number of shares traded is logged. The number of shares, in turn, is referred to as *volume*. Each day, the total volume on each exchange is recorded. At the end of 1999, the average daily volume on the New York Stock Exchange was 809.2 million; on the Nasdaq it was 1.07 billion; and on the American Stock Exchange, 32.7 million. In one day's trading, on the three exchanges, almost two billion shares are being bought and sold! So who's doing all this trading?

The Story Volume Tells: *Keeping an eye on the volume can help you anticipate the degree of price movement. If a stock surges up on heavy volume, it is a very good indicator of further price increases. A stock that sells off on heavy volume is a reliable indicator that further declines are in the offing.*

There are three chief players in the stock market today: the *professional*, the *short-term trader*, and the *individual investor*. The professional—sometimes referred to as an *institutional investor*—trades stocks on behalf of other people. These investors are hired to make buying and selling decisions and are paid for their work. In theory, professional investors have the academic and professional backgrounds necessary to make superior stock selections. In actuality, most professionals fail to deliver superior results. Nevertheless, professional investors buy and sell large quantities of stocks and are important players in today's market environment.

> **Institutional investor:** A person or organization that trades large enough quantities of shares that the trades qualify for preferential treatment and lower commissions. Institutional investors enjoy fewer protective regulations and are usually more knowledgeable and better able to protect themselves from risk. Individual investors often follow sizable stock trades initiated by institutional investors since they can have a significant effect on a stock's price performance, not to mention market sentiment.

The words "trader" and "investor" are used to describe two types of market participants. An *investor* is someone like Warren Buffett—a classic buy-and-hold kind of guy. He keeps an investment through thick and thin, understanding that wealth is created over time, provided the company has solid management and is in an industry that's likely to prosper. The *trader*, on the other hand, is seen as a person who buys and sells often, even intraday, looking for price swings and situations he or she can trade profitably. These are the people who constantly monitor every move the market makes, looking for trends, trend reversals, breakouts, and all manner of stock movements.

> **Trader:** Someone who buys and sells stocks and options frequently with the objective of short-term profit.
>
> **Investor:** Someone who looks at the Big Picture, ignoring the day-to day price fluctuations, focusing instead on making investments for the long haul.

If you decide that you want to trade individual stocks, you have an important decision to make. You have to choose the style of trading (and risk) you want to pursue: long-term or short-term. Long-term investors enjoy a lower risk and reduced stress. Investments are made with the intention of accumulating profits and dividends over the long run. Long-term investors need to do their homework carefully in order to find companies that can potentially double and triple in the decades ahead. Focusing on long-term returns makes long-term investors relatively impervious to day-to-day price fluctuations—a much less stressful way to live.

Short-term trading is a different scene altogether. There are varying degrees of short-term trading—anywhere from mere seconds to several months to a year. Short-term traders are generally speculators looking for advantageous trends and momentum changes in highly volatile stocks to inspire profit-making opportunities. Many short-term traders integrate the use of options into their master trading plans to hedge risk and promote leveraging. Time is a big factor for short-term traders—not just time spent in a trade, but the time required to monitor the market in search of golden opportunities. Short-term trading is an extremely active process. It requires specific tools to do the job right, including real-time streaming quote services, trading analysis software, and plenty of room on your computer's hard drive. If you want to compete in this arena, you have to be prepared. It's more than a matter of tools. You need to have the right kind of psychological stamina to withstand the tests that will come your way.

Until you become an expert investor, you should probably focus more on the buy-and-hold approach; it's far easier on the nerves and less likely to lose money. Pick a few companies that offer solid growth, or mutual funds that meet your own criteria, and then hang onto them for as long as their outlooks and performances remain positive. Later, in Chapter 4, we'll discuss a variety of additional trading approaches that may pique your interest.

THE ORDER PROCESS

Although technology has made the order process take but a few seconds, an extensive number of steps are involved in the execution of a trade (see Figure 1.2). The information superhighway may be revolutionizing the entire operation as we speak, but an order still begins when a trader (or investor) contacts a broker. From there, the order jumps through a series of hoops on its way to execution. The process the order goes through depends on the type of trade you want to execute, the kind of order that is placed, and the overall mood of the market.

A trader places an order with his or broker—electronically or by phone or fax. The broker either submits the order to be executed electronically or transmits it to the exchange floor where a floor ticket is prepared and passed along to a floor broker. The floor broker takes it to the appropriate trading pit and uses the open outcry system to try to find another floor broker who wants to buy or sell your order. If your floor broker cannot fill your order, it is left with a specialist who keeps a list of all the unfilled orders, matching them up as prices fluctuate. In this way, specialists are brokers to the floor brokers and receive a commission for every transaction they carry out. Groups of specialists trading similar markets are located near one another

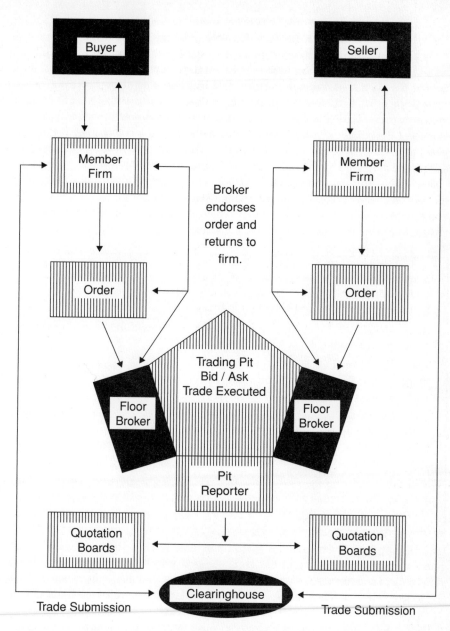

Figure 1.2 How a Trade Is Made

in trading pits. Once your order has been filled, the floor trader contacts your broker, who in turn calls you to confirm that your order has been placed.

In addition to the specialists, there are also market makers who create liquidity by narrowing the spread. *Market makers* trade for themselves or for a firm. Once an order hits the pit, the market makers participate with the other players on a competitive basis. If there isn't much action in the pit, market makers are obligated to make the market happen. Market makers derive the bulk of their profits by mastering the dynamics of the bid/ask spread. The *bid* is the highest price a prospective buyer is prepared to pay for a share of a specified security. The *ask* is the lowest price acceptable to a prospective seller of the same security. These two prices constitute a *quotation* or "quote." The difference between the bid and ask is called the *spread*, and that's where the market maker makes his or her living. This difference may be only $0.25 ($^1/_4$ point) or less, but it accumulates quickly when you're dealing in tens of thousands of shares. Market makers are also experts at *hedging* their positions for protection.

Market maker: An independent trader or trading firm that is prepared to buy and sell shares or contracts in a designated market. Market makers must make a two-sided market (bid and ask) in order to facilitate trading.

Bid: The highest price at which a floor broker, trader, or dealer is willing to buy a security or commodity for a specified time.

Ask: The lowest price at which market makers and floor traders of a specific market are willing to sell a security, and the price at which an investor can buy it from a broker-dealer.

Quotation: Refers to the highest bid and lowest offer (ask) price currently available on a security or commodity. An investor who asks for a quotation or quote on AOL may be told "70 to 70$^1/_2$." This means that the best bid price is currently $70 per share and that the best ask a seller is willing to accept is 70^1/_2$ at that time.

Hedging: Reducing the risk of loss by taking a position through options that balances out or significantly reduces the risk of the current position held in the market.

Nasdaq offers brokers the ability to trade directly from their offices using telephones and continuously updated computerized prices. In this way, they bypass floor traders and the need to pass along a commission to them. This means that they get to keep more of the commission for themselves. There are no specialists, either, but there are market makers.

Day trading has become an important aspect of the stock market today. The market crash of 1987 brought about the creation of the *Small Order Entry System (SOES)*, which overcame early inefficiencies and now permits lightning-fast executions for orders up to 1,000 shares. This system spawned the birth of day trading, because it permitted the little guy to compete with institutional traders, using the SOES system with other, previously unavailable, technology. The day trader sits in front of a computer monitor and takes advantage of the spread on a stock by splitting it. If the spread is a quarter ($^1/_4$ point), the day trader places an order that falls in the middle of it, and in many cases will get an execution, or fill. This new "SOES bandit" began to feast on the market makers' spreads, trading dozens or even hundreds of times daily, taking his or her bite out of spreads that until then had been the sole domain of the market maker. (If you don't think this is much money, consider taking just $^1/_8$ point, or $0.125, multiply that by 1,000 shares ($125), then multiply that by 10, 20, 50, and more. Now you can see why day trading is so appealing!

Although day trading, as it is done today, is relatively new, short-term traders have been around a long time. Traders are simply those individuals who make assessments as to the price change of a stock over the course of a few days, weeks, or months and try to buy a stock at a low price and then sell it back later at a higher price.

The short-term trader and professional have always been an important part of the stock market. Recently, the individual has become more active—some as long-term investors and others as aspiring traders. In fact, due to the strong performance of the stock market throughout the 1990s, droves of individual traders wanting a piece of the action were responsible for the emergence of financial web sites that cater to individual investors. Financial services and investment firms, financial publications, and entrepreneurs have joined in this modern-day gold rush by creating a host of products and sources of stock market information.

Weeding through the profusion of investment information is one of the challenges of the new millennium.

THE NEW ERA

Prior to the great advances in technology and the advent of the Internet, individual investors were limited in the amount of stock market information that was available to them. Financial newspapers like the *Wall Street Journal* and *Investor's Business Daily* have been in existence for some time and provide a wealth of stock market data. Aside from that, there weren't a lot of alternatives available to the retail investor.

Wall Street brokerage firms publish detailed research reports on the stock market and companies, but limit their distribution to existing clients. Other financial publishers such as Standard & Poor's and Value Line produce timely investment research. Unfortunately, for the individual investor, the cost associated with such products has been overwhelming. The alternative was to visit the local library, pull the 10-pound publications off the shelves, and sift through stacks of pages in an effort to find a good investment.

Technology has changed all that. Today it's possible, sitting in the comfort of your own home, to read research reports on individual companies, do searches and screens, obtain market commentary, get price quotes, even trade. The Internet has

The **Wall Street Journal:** With worldwide distribution and an extensive readership, the Wall Street Journal is packed with financial information and has the ability to significantly influence the markets. For a company to get in the Wall Street Journal is news (interactive.wsj.com).

Investor's Business Daily: Founded by William J. O'Neil, the IBD was originally developed to add a new dimension of crucial information to the investment community. The IBD focuses on concise investment news information, sophisticated charts, tables, and analytical tools while adding valuable information that the Wall Street Journal may not provide (www.investors.com).

wired individual investors directly into the market. So there's no longer a need to wait for the morning paper to see what happened in the market. Thanks to the Internet, you can see it as it happens.

In addition to easier access to greater amounts of information, investors today have more investment alternatives. Specifically, stock investors have the choice of buying shares of individual companies or buying groups of stocks through investment vehicles known as *mutual funds* and *index shares*. While mutual funds have been around for a long time, the growing interest in index shares is relatively new. Let's explore both.

Mutual Funds

Mutual funds have become extremely popular. In 1983, for instance, there were a little over 1,000 funds. By the end of 1999, there were over 7,000! One reason for the growth stems from the fact that mutual funds offer a solution to the problem of "smallness." That is, most households do not have sufficient savings to buy a sufficiently diversified portfolio. The pooling of investor capital provides the ability to buy a greater number of stocks, spreading the risk with diversification. If one stock or sector has a bad month or quarter, another portion of the fund will probably do well, mitigating the setback.

*Another reason for the popularity of mutual funds is that,
for many investors, they make life easier. By investing in a mutual fund,
rather than making the buying and selling decisions yourself,
you're hiring a portfolio manager to do that job for you.*

Mutual funds are investment vehicles operated by *investment companies* and are heavily regulated by the Securities and Exchange Commission (www.sec.gov). Specifically, a mutual fund is a pooling of money by a group of people with similar investment objectives and risk tolerances. An investment company is in charge of the mutual fund, which consists of money from a number of like-minded investors.

> **Mutual funds:** An investment company that pools investors' money to invest in a variety of stocks, bonds, or other securities. Each mutual fund's portfolio matches the objective stated in the firm's prospectus; the type of portfolio guides the fund's professional manager to pick appropriate securities for the fund to buy.

The fund is then used to create a diversified portfolio of stocks, bonds, or a combination of the two. Unlike a stock that trades on a stock exchange, mutual fund shares are purchased through the investment company. If you decide to buy the XYZ fund, your money goes to the mutual fund company. A professional investor, hired by the investment company, makes the investment decisions. In essence, investment companies need little or no capital of their own. Through sales and marketing they gather assets from individual investors to be managed.

Mutual funds are divided into two categories: open-ended and closed-end funds. Both varieties have portfolios of stocks (and sometimes bonds) and cash that are professionally managed. The market value of the portfolio is called the *net asset value"* or *NAV*. The NAV is calculated by dividing the number of shares by the market value of the fund's portfolio. This is the main difference between the open-ended and closed-end funds: The closed-end fund has a fixed number of shares, whereas the open-ended fund continually issues new shares (new money is deposited) or redeems shares (money is withdrawn). A closed-end fund trades on an exchange, with a bid and ask like any other shares. The NAV may be greater or less than the market price of the fund at the end of each day.

> **Open-ended fund:** A mutual fund that sells its own new shares to investors, buys back its old shares, and is not listed for trading on a stock exchange. The open-ended fund gets its name because its capitalization is not fixed and it normally issues more shares as demand for the shares increases.
>
> **Closed-end fund:** An investment company that issues a fixed number of shares in an actively managed portfolio of securities. The shares may be of several classes; they are traded in the secondary marketplace, either on an exchange or over-the-counter (OTC). The market price of the shares is determined by supply and demand and not by net asset value.
>
> **Net asset value (NAV):** The value of a fund's investments. For an open-ended mutual fund, the net asset value per share usually represents the fund's market price, subject to a possible sales or redemption charge. For a closed-end fund, the market price may vary significantly from the net asset value.

The open-ended fund never trades at a premium or discount to its NAV. The value is the NAV, not what the market decides it should be. The open-ended fund is subdivided a few more times, the first classification being *load* and *no-load* funds. A no-load fund has no sales charge, or load. Every dollar deposited buys one dollar's worth of shares at the current NAV. The load fund has a sales charge associated with it; that is, a commission is charged to purchase the fund's shares. Load funds have taken a lot of flak for charging a commission, mostly from proponents of the no-load approach. Load funds are sold most often by registered representatives or stockbrokers. They are, after all, in business to make money by dispensing financial advice, and would make nothing for their time and trouble by recommending a no-load fund.

Load fund: An open-ended mutual fund with shares sold at a price including a sales charge—typically 4% to 8% of the net amount indicated. A load implies that the fund purchaser receives some investment advice or other service worthy of the charge.

No-load fund: An open-ended mutual fund whose shares are sold without a sales charge. Although sometimes there are other distribution charges, a true no-load fund will have neither a sales charge nor a distribution fee.

To lessen buyer resistance when selling a load fund (when they're being compared to a no-load), load funds have begun to offer different classes of funds that offer the investor various choices. A description of these classes can be found in Figure 1.3.

Index Funds

A variation of the mutual fund is the *index fund*. An index is simply an average of a group of stocks. Most evenings, reporters cite the daily point movement in the Dow Jones Industrial Average. The Dow Jones Industrial Average is an index that monitors 30 select stocks including Intel, Procter & Gamble, Hewlett Packard, and others. There are also mutual funds that are designed to mirror the performance of an index. In an index fund, investors are pooling their money, but rather than hiring a portfolio manager to make specific buy and sell decisions, the stocks within the fund mirror the index.

Index fund: A group of stocks that make up a portfolio in which performance can be monitored based upon one calculation.

Why would an investor want to mirror an index rather than have a professional make individual buy and sell decisions that reflect the sensitivity of market movement? For one thing, it's less expensive. Mutual funds carry fees in one form or another. A fund that requires a sales charge when money is invested is called a load

Class	Sales Charge
Class A: Sales charge imposed on new deposits	For every dollar invested, the load is charged before the money is invested. If the load is 3%, then $0.97 of every dollar is invested. *Advantage*: Load is paid and forgotten; money can be withdrawn without penalty.
Class B: Sales charge placed on any withdrawals before a certain date	Investors are not charged when they deposit their cash into the fund in exchange for pledging to leave the money in the fund for a certain number of years. The fee is reduced annually on a sliding scale until the time period is complete. Any new deposits are subject to the new time restrictions. Withdrawals are treated (most often) using the FIFO method of accounting (first in, first out). *Advantage*: More dollars are working for you right away; there's no deficit to overcome, as is the case with Class A shares. *Disadvantage*: If you need your money sooner than originally planned, the amount withdrawn might be greater than the amount deposited, meaning the surrender fee is more than the initial sales charge might have been (as in the example of Class A shares).
Class C: One-year surrender period, with early withdrawal charge of 1%.	At first, Class C offers the best of all worlds: no charge going in and only a one-year surrender period. However, annual charges are higher and never go away, so they end up cutting into your rate of return.

Figure 1.3   Description of Classes of Load Funds

fund. So if you invest $10,000 and the load is 5%, $500 will come out of your investment and be paid to either the investment company or the broker who sold you the fund. Index funds have no front-end sales charges and are, therefore, no-load. Mutual funds also have annual management fees that go to pay the fund manager— around 1% or 2%. Index funds, however, have no portfolio manager and therefore pay out no management fees.

In addition to being less expensive, index funds have historically offered superior performance on average. Interestingly, although there is no manager at the helm, index funds have, over the long term, bested the performances of most portfolio managers. Given the superior performance and low cost, index funds have become among the most popular types of mutual funds. In fact, the largest mutual fund as of this writing is the Vanguard 500 Index fund that tracks the performance of the S&P 500 index.

Index shares are relatively new instruments. Similar to index funds, index shares mirror the performance of a market average. In 1993, the American Stock Exchange launched Standard & Poor's Depositary Receipts (SPDRs, pronounced "spiders"), which track the S&P 500 index. Unlike index funds, shares are purchased on the exchange like a stock. The SPDRs proved extremely popular, and as a result, in 1998 the American Stock Exchange launched an index share on the Dow Jones Industrial Average, and in 1999 on the Nasdaq 100 index. Furthermore, the growing popularity of index shares has led a San Francisco-based financial adviser—Barclay's Global Investors—to launch a series of 50 index shares called iShares.

AFTER-HOURS TRADING

The demand for more trading just keeps rising. Unfortunately, the auction-style market is simply ill-suited to providing the additional trading capacity necessary to cater to the ongoing desire for trading after four o'clock eastern time. By the end of a busy workday, floor traders are ready to quit for the day. As stock market fever reaches Middle America, people in later time zones are increasingly interested in getting involved, but in many cases cannot due to working hour conflicts. It seems only logical, then, for the brokerage industry to band together to offer late-afternoon or early-evening trading sessions.

Advances in technology and electronic trading have made after-hours trading possible, filling the demand of the individual investor and extending the revenue stream of participating brokerage houses.

There are a number of ways to trade after hours. Many brokers are offering the ability to trade a limited number of Nasdaq issues beyond four o'clock eastern time. The Nasdaq, as the sole all-electronic exchange, is the only big exchange that can facilitate after-hours trading. But new systems called *electronic communications networks (ECNs)*—such as *Island, Instinet,* and others—provide execution services to the after-hours brokers who funnel their orders through their respective systems.

At this time, other exchanges simply can't sustain around-the-clock pit-trading operations for conducting transactions. Perhaps this may change in the future, but for now this is the state of after-hours trading.

One big reward of after-hours trading is that traders can take advantage of news events such as earnings and other announcements that commonly occur after the markets close. An investor trading during traditional market hours must wait until morning to buy or sell a favorable or unfavorable position. Those investors whose accounts are linked through their brokers to an ECN can make their transaction immediately upon hearing the news (provided that it occurs before eight o'clock eastern time, when after-hours trading ends).

Another version of extra-hours trading is premarket trading, essentially the same as after-hours trading, but commencing at seven o'clock in the morning eastern time. This is convenient for many on the East Coast who wish to trade for an hour or so before heading to work in the morning.

One of the drawbacks to pre- or postmarket trading is that the shares can be fairly thinly traded. This can lead to price swings that may or may not be favorable for those investors trading the shares upon the resumption of regular market hours. For instance, if a company announces earnings after the market closes and the shares trade up several percentage points in after-hours trading, there's no guarantee that they will hold their value into the regular trading session the next day. Subsequent late evening or early morning news commentary may swing the sentiment in the other direction. The stock may even gap down to start the next day. Similarly, if a company makes an announcement and the primarily retail after-hours trading community sees this as a bearish signal, it may drive the stock down several dollars in the evening session. Yet the market may be met with analysts' reiterations of their own "buy" or "hold" recommendations when regular trading resumes the next day. This could bring the price back to the previous day's regular-hours levels. Those who sold a previously entered position in the extended sessions will wish they'd waited to take action, while those who shorted (sold) the stock may be scrambling to cover their losses by exiting the position. (We'll discuss shorting stocks in Chapter 3.)

Gap down: A gap down occurs when a stock price opens much lower than it closed on the previous day. It is most often the result of bad news after the market closed. In looking at stock price charts, a gap (area of empty space) in the price data sometimes occurs. This happens when the opening price on one day is significantly lower than the closing price the day before. For instance, if the stock of Microsoft closes the day at a price of $50 and, due to some news event after the market closes, the next day it opens at a price of $40, there will be a gap in the chart.

Shorting a stock: Selling a security that the seller does not own but is committed to repurchasing eventually. This technique is used to capitalize on a decline in a security's price.

It is interesting to note that companies usually make important announcements after regular trading hours. In many ways, this is a liability issue. Companies are responsible to their shareholders. By making an announcement after-hours (such as earnings), investors and analysts have enough time to analyze the information and decide on an appropriate response by the time the markets open up in the morning.

ALTERNATIVES TO STOCKS

Although investing in stocks can be quite lucrative, it is essential to diversify your money into a variety of investment instruments. Each instrument comes with its own advantages and disadvantages, as well as risk and reward profile. If the markets are in a bearish slump, you may want to consider investing in one or two of these alternatives to avoid losses.

Cash Equivalents

When I have cash I'm not ready to put in the market, I park those funds in *cash equivalents*—certificates of deposit (CDs), Treasury bills (T-bills), and money market funds. Cash equivalents offer investors a slightly lower fixed rate of return without any risk of loss. The advantage of these instruments is that, while they do offer a return, money is not tied up for long periods of time and, in the case of money markets, can be easily converted to cash. In terms of risk and reward, cash equivalents offer little of both. The three most common cash equivalents are:

- *Certificates of deposit (CDs):* Fixed-income debt securities issued by banks usually in minimum denominations of $1,000 with maturity terms of one to six years.

- *Treasury bills (T-bills):* Short-term debt securities issued by the U.S. government (minimum amount $10,000) with maturities of 13, 26, and 52 weeks.

- *Money market funds:* Funds organized to buy short-term high-quality securities like CDs, T-bills, and short-term commercial paper. Investors can buy and sell shares through a mutual fund company.

Debt: A security that represents borrowed money and that must later be repaid. In other words, an IOU.

Commodities

Commodities compose the raw materials used in most retail and manufactured products. The five major categories are: grains, metals, energies, raw foods, and meats (see Figure 1.4). Some are seasonal in nature (heating oil, for instance), which causes demand to fluctuate based on the time of year and climatic conditions. Others react to specific events: A drought in the Midwest can send grain prices soaring. Commodities are also very leveraged investments. A small amount of cash can control many times its face value in commodity contracts. But this works both

Grains	Metals	Energies	Raw Foods	Meats
Corn	Gold	Crude oil	Coffee	Live cattle
Soybeans	Silver	Natural gas	Cocoa	Live hogs
Wheat	Copper	Heating oil	Sugar	Pork bellies

Figure 1.4 Major Commodity Categories and Examples

ways, creating huge potential wins and losses. Due to its high-risk nature, this area of investing is utilized mostly by professional traders.

Commodities are traded as futures contracts. In addition, the futures market consists of a variety of financial instruments, including debt instruments such as bonds and Treasury notes and currencies such as the Canadian dollar and the Japanese yen. A futures contract, then, is an obligation to buy or sell a specific quantity of a commodity, currency, or financial instrument for a predetermined price by a designated date.

> **Futures contract:** An agreement from a buyer to accept delivery (or for a seller to make delivery) of a specific commodity, currency, or financial instrument at a future date.

Farmers and producers initially used futures contracts to lock in the price of a certain crop or product cycle. That's why traders who intend to sell or take delivery of a commodity are called hedgers. For example, if a farmer grows wheat, soybeans, and corn, he (or she) can sell the product with a futures contract before it is actually harvested and ready for sale. In other words, if the farmer believes the price of corn is at an attractive level, he (or she) can sell a corresponding number of futures contracts against the expected production. An oil company can do the same thing. It may want to lock in the price of oil at a certain point to guarantee the price it will receive. For instance, Exxon Mobil Corp. (XOM) may sell crude oil futures, one year away, to lock in that specific price because the company has to know the price in advance to be able to plan production costs accordingly.

Most futures contracts are bought on speculation about future prices, and most futures traders are speculators (i.e., they do not expect to take delivery of the product or lock in a crop price). For example, if you believe corn prices will rise in the next three months, based upon whatever information you may have, you could buy the corn futures a few months out. High-risk speculators have the same objective as stock traders. They intend to buy low and sell high. They make money by forecasting price movement. The primary difference is that futures contracts expire on a certain date. This adds a completely new dimension to the trading process. Speculators not only have to forecast price movement, but they also need to predict *when* a price will be higher or lower. This makes futures trading, although sometimes lucrative, very risky.

Therefore, in terms of risk and reward, futures contracts are at the opposite end of the spectrum from cash equivalents. Figure 1.5 shows how investments fall along a continuum of risk and reward, with futures at one end and cash equivalents at the other. It is also important to note that stocks vary in terms of risk and reward. That is, some stocks with little history and no earnings will be considered high-risk/reward, while a well-established company with a history of dividend payments will be lower-risk/reward.

Bonds

Bonds are highly popular debt obligations that pay periodic interest at a fixed rate and promise repayment of the principal at maturity. Buying bonds is comparable to making a loan at a fixed rate of interest. Each bond pays a fixed interest rate. At the end of a predetermined period, the loan is paid back. The borrower can be the government, a municipality, or a company (see Figure 1.6). Each borrower is obligated to pay back the loan at the end of the bond's term—at maturity.

Although there is a promise of repayment at maturity, the market price of a bond will fluctuate in response to the rise and fall of interest rates. Let's say that you decide to lend me $1,000 for a five-year period of time. I agree to pay you interest at a rate of 8%—$80 per year interest. Shortly afterward, interest rates jump to 10%. Now you could have lent the same $1,000 and received 10% interest—$100 per

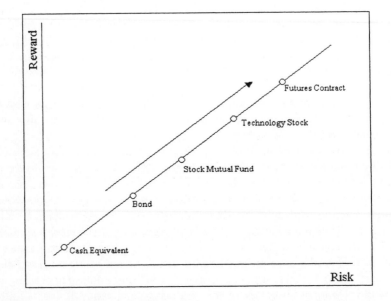

Figure 1.5   Trading Instrument Risk Graph

Bond Issuer	Name	Duration
U.S. federal government	Treasury bonds	Maturity of 10 years or more
	Treasury notes	Maturity of between one and 10 years
	Treasury bills	Maturities of no more than one year and no fixed interest rate
State, city, or municipality	Municipal bonds*	Varies
Corporations	Corporate bonds	Varies

*Interest paid on municipal bonds is not subject to federal taxes, and in some cases not subject to state taxes.

Figure 1.6 Bond Breakdown

year. Did the value of the first loan go up or down with the interest rate rising? The value of the 8% loan went down primarily because you do not have the opportunity to lend it out at the higher rate of interest. Therefore, when interest rates go up, bond (loan) prices fall. Conversely, when interest rates fall below the interest rate guaranteed on a specific bond, that bond increases in value.

> **Interest rate:** The charge for the privilege of borrowing money, usually expressed as an annual percentage rate of the principal amount borrowed.

> *Federal bonds are backed by the full faith and credit of the United States government, and are considered to be the safest investment in the world.*

Municipal and corporate bonds are rated according to the creditworthiness of the issuer, and range from high-grade bonds down to what's become known as junk bonds. The higher the rating, the lower the interest rate paid. Bonds are traded after they are issued; depending on a bond's interest rate (yield), it may be worth more or less than par value (usually $1,000) in the aftermarket.

Interest rates are based on the federal funds rate, which is set by the Federal Reserve Board. The current Fed chairman, Alan Greenspan, is assisted by the Board of Governors in determining what the federal funds rate should be. That decision is based on the health of the economy among other factors. If the economy gets too hot (i.e., U.S. economic growth is robust and jobs are plentiful), *inflation* begins to accelerate. Inflation lessens the purchasing power of money over time. The Fed increases interest rates, making it more expensive to borrow money, in order to slow the economy. If the economy begins to lag, rates are lowered, which theoretically spurs expansion of the economy. So, bond traders study the economic data and buy and sell bonds accordingly. Sharp drops in the prices of bonds and companion increases in interest rates have, on occasion, triggered sharp drops in stock prices.

The Fed: Nickname for the Federal Reserve Board (FRB), a seven-member group that directs the operations of the Federal Reserve System (FRS). Board members are appointed by the president and are subject to approval by Congress. The FRS supervises the printing of currency and the regulation of the national money supply, examining member banks to ensure they meet various regulations and acting as a clearinghouse for the transfer of funds for the government's finances.

Inflation: Increase in the general price level of goods and services (i.e., your dollar won't buy as much as it used to). Inflation is commonly reported using the Consumer Price Index (CPI) as a measure. Inflation is one of the major risks to investors over the long term, as savings may actually buy less in the future if they are not invested with inflation as a consideration. The inflation rate refers to the rate of change in prices.

The Treasury bond market is important for stock market investors to understand. When investors talk about the bond market, they are referring to the 30-year bond market. It serves as a barometer of the expectations as to future trends within the U.S. economy. That is, sophisticated professionals, who spend an inordinate amount of time studying economic data, trade Treasury bonds. Their chief aim in life is to determine the future direction of interest rates. Recall that when interest rates rise, bond prices fall, and vice versa. If these traders begin to fret about the prospect of higher interest rates, they sell bonds.

The determination of the state of the economy and thus interest rates has a powerful effect on the stock market. Sometimes negative economic news will come out and the markets will climb in reaction. Why the curious reaction to what appears to be bad news? Simple: If the economy is slowing, interest rates must either come down or stay down longer to keep the economy from going into a recession. Lower rates mean investors need to move further out on the risk/reward scale to get a good rate of return (as compared to the 30-year bond). If economic news is good, this could be interpreted as bad for interest rates (meaning they'll rise). This sends bond yields up as investors anticipate rate hikes by the Fed to slow the economy down. If investors can get relatively good rates of return with little risk, they'll take money out of the stock market. So even if you're interested in stocks, you have to learn about the bond market to understand why the markets behave as they do.

The economy affects bond prices, which in turn affect stock prices. Economic reports can sometimes have a profound effect on bond prices. This is why the markets get a little jittery before an economic report is due to be released. Analyzing economic data is the only way the Fed can determine how the economy is faring, and thus provide a basis for interest rate policy.

WHY TRADE STOCKS?

Without question, there are specific risks associated with owning stocks. If a country goes to war, it might have a direct effect on the profitability of companies and send their prices down until peace prevails. Assassinations or political events can be a risk to the market. Some stocks also have a *liquidity risk* (i.e., they are easy to buy but difficult to sell because of an absence of buyers). As you try to sell, the market makers keep moving the price lower, and by the time you finally succeed in selling it, its price has dropped far lower than you care to remember. Therefore, before buying a stock, look at the daily volume. If volume is light, there may be a liquidity risk. This kind of stock is said to be thinly traded, and should be carefully considered before you purchase it. In addition, the fewer shares outstanding, the more volatile the stock might be.

Liquidity: The ease with which an asset can be converted to cash in the marketplace. A large number of buyers and sellers and a high volume of trading activity provide high liquidity.

With any company, there is *business risk*. Companies continually face new competition and difficulties that, if not effectively addressed and dealt with, will eventually have an adverse effect on earnings and the stock price. This might even lead to a company going out of business—and your stock certificates becoming your only reminder of an investment turned worthless.

A company may have a lot of shares outstanding (issued), but a major percentage is held by insiders (management, family-owned, etc.). The remaining shares traded by outside investors are called the float. For example, a company may have 3 million shares outstanding, but 1 million shares are closely held, which would make the float 2 million shares.

Given the myriad of risks, why bother trading stocks? Because stocks have historically offered the best returns of any investment vehicle over time. Well-managed companies have been able to grow their earnings, and shareholders have been well rewarded. Without question, there are periods when stocks drop. When you measure market performance over the course of several years, the trend is up, easily outdistancing any other investment.

If the prospect of a high rate of growth is appealing, you're able to withstand price fluctuations, and your time horizon is suitably long, then stock investing will most likely be your primary investment choice. Once you feel that you meet these criteria, recall that there are three basic methods of stock investing: buying/selling individual stocks, owning a mutual fund, or trading index shares. Figure 1.7 provides a general overview of the advantages and disadvantages associated with each.

Methods of Stock Investment		
Individual Stocks	*Mutual Funds*	*Index Shares*
Advantages • Highest potential return on investment. • Allows traders to customize their portfolios to meet their investing needs. • Easy to adjust the portfolio mix without disrupting the whole account. *Disadvantages* • Takes more time to manage than other choices. • Extremely volatile and susceptible to bad news from a company, sector problems, and the whims of the market in general. • Have to know how to pick a winning stock opportunity. • Have to learn how to filter out unnecessary information.	*Advantages* • Professional money managers watch your money. They have more time and resources than most individuals who try to manage their own investments. • Offers excellent diversification. • Can benefit from up moves in a basket of stocks, and protects investors from company risk associated with investing in individual stocks. • The safest way to invest overseas, because funds have managers watching international companies on which individual investors would find it difficult to gather information. *Disadvantages* • Tax considerations. Investors may have to pay taxes on capital gains even if their portfolios are down. • It is difficult to follow what stocks make up the mutual fund portfolio. • If a team manages the fund, the members who created a good performance record last year may have left the fund unbeknownst to you. • Fund will likely produce only average market gains unless it concentrates in aggressive sectors, thus losing some of the advantages of diversification.	*Advantages* • Allows investors to diversify their holdings with one decision by investing in a group of stocks as opposed to just one. • If one stock is going down, it won't hurt the overall fund too much. The poorly performing stock will be balanced out by others that are advancing. • Requires little time to manage. *Disadvantages* • Indexes represent a set group of stocks in a fixed proportion. This selection may exclude companies that you want to invest in. You may also be forced to invest in companies that you don't want to invest in just because these companies are part of the index. • Index shares are traded on the exchanges, and sometimes the market price will fall below the actual value of the index. • Fees and commissions.

Figure 1.7 Advantages and Disadvantages of the Three Basic Stock Investments

Risks and rewards are associated with all investments, and stocks are no exception. For some people, they just aren't suitable, either for emotional reasons (they cannot tolerate any price fluctuations) or because their time horizons are too short. For most people, however, they are the best vehicles for preserving the purchasing power of their capital.

Inflation erodes your purchasing power, and that's why beating inflation is the main reason to invest in the first place.

The growing popularity of the mutual fund industry is as much a result of convenience as diversification. The toughest part is picking the right fund. To build and manage your own portfolio is a much more daunting challenge, but it can be done. This book seeks to show you how.

ASSESSING YOUR OWN NEEDS

Before you do anything, you need to consider your own personal financial situation. Many people think that all you have to do to start trading is open an account with a brokerage firm, buy a few shares of a volatile high-tech stock, and watch the profits roll in. I can't tell you how many times I've been asked for a specific recommendation, as if knowing which stock is about to take off translates into an easy million and early retirement. Before you begin looking for a broker, opening an account, or placing your hard-earned money in a high-flying stock, there are several things you can do to maximize your chances of long-term success.

First, you have to figure out how much money you can safely afford to invest. An adequate time horizon is critical, because if you are forced to sell, the market may not be at an opportune place, forcing you to sell at a loss. Therefore, be certain you have enough money in reserve to meet any financial emergency or unforeseen expense without having to access your equity account. Things have a habit of going wrong at the worst possible time, so be prepared.

To determine your financial capabilities, take a discerning look at your liquid assets by objectively assessing how much cash you have readily available. You can do this by calculating your cash on hand and placing a value on any assets that can be readily converted into cash. *Never* invest your rent or mortgage funds, food money, or any dollars critical to your current lifestyle or your family's immediate future. I recommend that you leave a three- to six-month cushion in your savings account, just in case. By using funds that are above and beyond your immediate needs, you will make the investing process less stressful and be able to invest with far less stress and apprehension.

To determine exactly how much money you can afford to invest, you need to assess your financial condition. To help accomplish this task, we have included three useful templates in Appendix A:

1. Personal balance sheet

2. Monthly income statement

3. Risk tolerance and investment goals worksheet

A balance sheet is designed to help you figure out exactly where you stand financially. A monthly income report can help to track how you spend your money each month. Although it is tempting to skip over these tables, think of the process as part of your investment education. Filling out this information will help you to determine how much money can be safely put into your investment plan. If you are learning how to break into the world of investments, this is your first step.

The final worksheet provides for a method of detailing your personal risk tolerance and investment goals. Once again I highly recommend you take the time to fill this form out. The findings are an important clue to analyzing your trading approach. As far as I'm concerned, anything that helps beginners to define their goals is a thoroughly worthwhile pursuit.

ROADMAP TO SUCCESS

Objective	Course of Action
Stocks	A security or certificate representing fractional ownership of a company purchased as an investment.
Stock Market	An all-encompassing name for the overall facilitation of the buying and selling of shares of ownership in companies.
Risk and the Market *Do I have to take "chances" in order to make money in the stock market?*	**The Risk of Inflation** • Inflation erodes the purchasing power of money. • Cash in a mattress is certain to decline in value due to its loss in purchasing power caused by inflation. • Investments must overcome inflation. • Inflation should be calculated at 3% to 5% per year. • "Real rate of return" is the annual return (realized or unrealized) minus inflation. This is how much your investment grew in *purchasing power.* • "Safest investments" may not grow faster than inflation—real rate of return is actually negative! • Breaking even after inflation is a long-term losing strategy—higher returns are necessary.
Investments: The Spectrum of Risk Categories	**Risk/reward ratio: The lower the risk, the smaller the rate of return that can be expected; the greater the risk, the higher the expected rate of return.** • Lowest-risk (safest) investments: Cash and equivalents; U.S. Treasury notes: lowest return—virtually no risk. • Moderate-risk investments: Blue-chip stocks; investment-grade bonds.

	• Growth investments: Possible to achieve high return on investment. Risk is time, business, possible liquidity risk.
The first task is to understand risk.	**What types of risks exist and understanding how to manage them.** • **Inflationary risk:** The erosion of purchasing power. • **Business risk:** Investing in a company that goes out of business altogether; loss of most if not all of investment. • **Timing risk:** Liquidating an investment at an inopportune time; for example, the market is in a down cycle. • **Market risk:** (1) There is an extended down (bear) market that exceeds your initial investment time estimate; or (2) you lose money in a trade due to market conditions that were unforeseeable or somehow misinterpreted.
The second task is to develop a low-stress investment plan that will enable you to build your knowledge base systematically.	**When you buy a stock, you are 100% at the mercy of market conditions and direction.** • Market goes through up and down cycles. • Bull market: Trend is up; increasing prices. • Bear market: Trend is down; decreasing prices. • "Directional" decisions are 50/50 propositions. • Investments work or don't work. • Often time is required to allow investment to work out. **What if I'm right? What if I'm wrong?** • Develop a strategy to reduce stress. • Risk is minimized. • Return is still attractive.
Third, beginners need to start by specializing in one or two markets at a time.	**To become successful, in-depth knowledge and understanding of an industry is a big advantage.** • Understand that anything is possible. • Your learning curve limits you. • Developments may occur too fast to track effectively. • Watch for ample opportunity to invest successfully in one or two sectors. • Different sectors perform differently, even at the same time. • By specializing, it is possible to take advantage of new product developments, mergers, and acquisitions. • Long-term vision is attained by asking: What kind of growth will this sector experience? Who will be the winners and losers? • Long-term outlook reduces stress of day-to-day market fluctuations. • Better information leads to better investment decisions (and results!).
Fourth, define your limits in terms of the amount of money you can afford to lose.	**Stress avoidance comes from a clear picture of your financial condition.** • Net monthly income. • Subtract rent/mortgage, car payment, groceries, and miscellaneous expenses.

- Entertainment allowance! (If you don't leave money for the fun stuff, you'll end up resenting your budget, and you'll stop following it.)
- Three–six months of cash reserves.

Now you know how much you can invest!

Becoming Familiar with "Performance Reporting" from Public Companies	**SEC requires full disclosure.** - Annual reports. - Quarterly reports (known as 10-Qs). - Quarterly earnings released at end of each quarter. - "Warnings" issued if company is experiencing a slowdown to alert that results will be below analysts' expectations. - Financials are required to be audited.
Trading Locations: Exchanges and the Nasdaq	**Stock exchanges—Physical locations for the organized buying and selling of stocks.** - New York Stock Exchange (NYSE). - American Stock Exchange (AMEX). - Pacific Exchange. - Regional exchanges. - Auction style. - Membership required. **The Nasdaq (National Association of Securities Dealers Automated Quotations system)** - Decentralized; trades done electronically by telephone and computer. - Must be licensed broker-dealer for membership. - Trading permitted by "registered representative" (a stockbroker) only. - Created in 1988, operates separately. - Created new "fund stocks." - Nasdaq 100 (QQQ) index shares. - Internet Index (HHH). - Check out this great web site for answers to Nasdaq questions: www.marketdata.nasdaq.com/mr_section2.html#8 **Over-the-counter stocks** - Too small to be traded on the Nasdaq. - Includes penny stocks; low-priced stocks whose quotes are found in the Pink Sheets.
Company Identification	**Ticker symbol—Assigned to each company's stock for easier identification.** - NYSE and AMEX—one, two, or three symbols. - Nasdaq/OTC—four–five symbols.
Regulatory Agencies	**Securities and Exchange Commission (SEC)** - Oversees all exchanges, including the Nasdaq. **NASD (National Association of Securities Dealers)** - Oversees Nasdaq and OTC markets. - Overseen by SEC.

A Roster of People Involved with Stock Trading	• **Broker:** Also known as a "registered representative," a broker is licensed to dispense investment information, recommend investments, determine suitability of an investment for an investor, and to enter an order on behalf of an investor. • **Floor trader:** An exchange member who executes orders from the floor of the exchange only for his or her own account. • **Specialist:** A trader on the exchange floor assigned to fill bids/orders in a specific stock out of his or her own account. • **Market makers:** An independent trader or trading firm that is prepared to buy and sell shares or contracts in a designated market. Market makers must make a two-sided market (bid and ask) in order to facilitate trading.
Terminology Used Most Often in Trading	• **Trade:** To buy or sell a stock, bond, or option. • **Margin:** The use of borrowed funds to purchase a stock; the (security) capital required to adequately pay for the risk on an option transaction. • **Volume:** The total number of shares traded in a particular time period on a specific stock. • **Bull market:** A market with a strong upward bias; stock is being accumulated. • **Bear market:** A market with a downward bias; distribution of stock is occurring. • **Short sell:** To sell short means that a person believes a stock will soon decline in value, so he or she borrows it from a brokerage firm and sells it, in hopes of repurchasing it at a lower price. Upon repurchase, the stock is returned to the brokerage firm it was borrowed from. • **Fill:** The term applied to the price at which a trade is executed.
The Three Faces of Stocksmiths	**Traders on the floor of the NYSE fall into three categories:** • **The "professional"**—Also known as an "institutional investor," professionals typically trade stocks on behalf of other people. They are hired to make buying and selling decisions and are paid for their work. • **The short-term trader**—A person who buys and sells often, even intraday, looking for price swings and situations one can make money on. • **The individual investor**—Retail investor dealing in 1,000-share lots at the most, and generally much less. Prone to "rookie" mistakes, the individual investor is often seen as a contrary indicator: when he's buying, it's a sign of a market top. Odd-lot sales are his identifying mark.
Putting in the Order: Terms You Need to Know!	**To buy or sell a stock, these terms and phrases will be very helpful to understand:** • **Bid**—What a buyer is willing to pay. If you are selling a stock, the best or highest bid is the easiest price at which to get a fill.

- **Ask** (or "Offer")—If you're buying a stock, the lowest "offer" or "asking price" is the easiest price to get an order filled.
- **Inside quote**—Used to describe the best bid and lowest offer. Also known as a "current quote."
- **Market order**—When buying or selling, a market order will get your trade executed at the lowest offer or best bid at that particular time!
- **Limit order**—This indicates the minimum or maximum price you're willing to buy or sell a stock (or option) at.

Research—Finding the Information You Need	**Research information abounds. Finding pertinent data is the key.** **Newspapers** • *Wall Street Journal* (interactive.wsj.com). • *Investor's Business Daily* (www.investors.com). **Web Sites** • **EDGAR Online** (www.edgar-online.com). • **Microsoft Investor** (www.investor.msn.com). • **Motley Fool** (www.fool.com). • **Quote.com** (www.quote.com). • **TheStreet.com** (www.thestreet.com). • **Wall Street City** (wallstreetcity.com). • **Yahoo! Finance** (quote.yahoo.com). • **Zack's Investment Research** (www.zacks.com).
Mutual Funds	**Where to find their records and ratings:** • *Investor's Business Daily*—"Making Money with Mutuals" (second half of paper). • **Multex** (www.multex.com). • **Morningstar.com** (www.morningstar.com). • **Value Line** (www.valueline.com). • **VectorVest** (www.vectorvest.com).
Mutual Funds— What's Important	**You're picking a manager, not the fund!** • Open-ended or closed-ended? • Load or no-load fund? • Look at past earnings performance. • Is the same portfolio manager still there? • If not, what's the manager's past record? • What fund did he or she come from? • Portfolio turnover indicates how much the fund trades. A reading of 50% indicates it traded half of the portfolio away and replaced it with new stocks. A high percentage here indicates an aggressive stance. • Biggest positions: What are the fund's largest holdings?
Mutual Fund Classes of Shares	**Load funds have different classes; three ways to pay your load:** • **Class A—Pay up front.** If the load is 3%, for every dollar invested, three cents is taken off the top, leaving $0.97 actually invested.

- **Class B—Pay when you withdraw the money.** This probably is more expensive, because the amount you withdraw will (hopefully) be greater than the amount deposited. Which would you rather pay?
- **Class C—Pay as you go.** No initial charge, but rather a "trailing" commission is assessed. Also known as a 12(b)-1 fee (look at prospectus), this is deducted from your account, meaning you'll end up paying a lot of commission and achieving a lesser rate of return overall.

Index Funds	**A portfolio of stocks that mirror the composition of a major index or sector. Reasons they've grown in popularity:** • Lower fees. • Historically better performance than managed funds. • SPDR (SPY). • HOLDRs—Merrill Lynch products—sector-specific.
After-Hours Trading	**New venues facilitate expanded trading hours.** • Electronic communications networks (ECNs). For example, Island and Instinet. • Anonymity (no one can tell who the buyers and sellers are). • People who trade there are "for real"; no tactics are used to manipulate market price. **Advantages** • Trade on news releases after the NYSE/Nasdaq close. • Greater flexibility for those unable to trade during market hours. **Disadvantages** • No guarantee the markets will agree with your decision when they reopen. • Could be buying at top. • Could be selling at bottom. • Liquidity not 100% proven.
The Economy and the Market	**Interest Rates, the Economy, and the Market** • Risk/reward: The lower the rate of interest, the more attractive stocks become. • Interest rates are set by the Federal Reserve Board. • If economy gets too hot, rates are increased to cool it down. • If economy gets too sluggish, rates are lowered to stimulate it. • Good economic reports will sometimes send the market down, because traders fear the Fed will hike interest rates. • Higher interest rates means investors have to move further out on the risk/reward curve to beat what they can get with little or no risk. • Investors can see where interest rates are by looking at the bond market, specifically the 30-year Treasury bond.

2

Solving the Broker Dilemma

Today's *brokerage firms* have evolved from a time when "the market" was the sole domain of powerful businessmen, their workings shrouded in mystery from the public at large. To own stock most often signified wealth beyond the average person's means. The stock market itself had little to do with everyday life for the vast majority of Americans. Today it's a whole new ball game, with more people owning equities, either directly or indirectly vis-à-vis mutual funds and pension funds, than at any time before. The bull market that began in 1982 with the Dow below 1,000 has now soared tenfold from that level, fueled in part by the entrance of the small investor.

> **Brokerage firm:** A firm that charges commissions for executing buy and sell orders submitted by individuals or other firms.

But as common as it is today, many people still view the world of *public offerings*, stockbrokers, leveraged buyouts, and analyst recommendations like they would the engine in a car: "I know it's there but I don't know exactly how it works." Let's first take a look at the reasons brokerages exist, and then investigate how they work and why we need to have a basic knowledge of their universe.

> **Public offering:** The sale of securities by an issuing corporation to the general investing public.

WAY BACK WHEN

Brokerage firms can trace their heritage back to when America was just getting started. Their principal purpose was to raise capital (money) to help finance America's growth. Those early years saw companies like General Electric, Ford, Standard Oil, and the like emerge as they took an active part in the creation of the infrastructure we take for granted today. Few people could spare the money to own stock, and the ones who did saw their portfolio values skyrocket as the country grew. Tremendous fortunes were amassed by names synonymous with power and wealth: Rockefeller, Carnegie, DuPont, and so on. *Investment bankers* worked closely with corporations to access public markets. Prior to the stock market crash of 1929, the world of investment bankers and the stock market in general was a wild and untamed place. Huge price swings and shady manipulations were the order of the day. As the industry matured, increased scrutiny was placed on the industry. The boom-bust cycles were significantly mitigated, but not vanquished. Many new requirements were implemented, designed to protect the investing public and to prevent fraud.

> **Investment bank:** A financial institution in the business of raising capital for corporations and municipalities through initial public offerings, secondary offerings, and debt (bond) offerings.

Following World War II, the United States entered what arguably was the most significant growth era we have ever known. This period saw the birth of the baby boom generation, whose mind-set altered everything from the way we styled our hair to the way we saved money.

The wealth created in the postwar era made the demand for goods and services soar. Investment bankers were more than happy to assist the companies that made and provided them. Firms with names like Merrill Lynch, Morgan Stanley Dean Witter, Reynolds Funds, and Salomon Brothers provided valuable expertise in funding our growth, and in turn made great strides in educating a greater number of investors about the possibility of equity ownership.

THE ROLE OF THE BROKER

In the first half of the twentieth century the stockbroker emerged as the intermediary between investment bankers and the investing public. Initially the stockbroker's role and image in society was on a par with the family attorney, physician, and neighborhood banker. Brokers studied companies and monitored price movement from the comfort of luxurious offices through the use of the ever-mysterious *ticker-tape machine*. These brokers would "read the tape" as it came out on long ribbons, and would then convey this information to their clientele at opportune moments. The stockbroker was a valuable and trusted financial adviser, and was well compensated for his services.

> **Ticker-tape machines:** Glass-domed machines of yesteryear that reported stock transactions on the various exchanges using stock symbols and prices.

As technology improved, an electronic tape replaced the ticker tape. Eventually desktop monitors were introduced, greatly enhancing the efficiency of price dissemination and lowered the learning curve required to enter the brokerage community. This, of course, fueled the expansion of brokerage firms as their charter soon evolved from one of investment bankers to marketing entities. Not only could *Wall Street* firms finance public offerings, they now had the ability to sell the stock quickly and profitably. The overall wealth of our country increased, and in turn the number of households that owned securities—be it stocks or bonds—also rose. Fees charged for buy or sell orders were much higher than what we see today, and the income potential attracted many ambitious people to a career as a stockbroker.

Wall Street: Specifically refers to the financial district at the lower end of Manhattan in New York City where the New York and American Stock Exchanges as well as various brokerages are located. In general, the term "Wall Street" describes the investment community as a real-world entity that receives and reacts to information on a daily basis.

THE BROKERAGE INDUSTRY TODAY

The brokerage business was so profitable it began attracting more participants, customers and brokers alike. As World War II veterans began to reach retirement age, many of them sought out stocks and bonds as a way to ensure comfortable retirements. Brokerage firms began growing more quickly than ever, so new brokers were hired and trained. Their compensation was, and is, primarily commission-based; therefore, the new stockbroker needed to develop a "book" of clients to avoid starving. How do you create a new client base after you've contacted all your family and friends? The answer was the *cold call*.

Telemarketing is a nice word given to a decidedly unpleasant task: cold calling people at home or work to offer "valuable" investment services and products to those with the means and proclivity to take advantage of them. A good stockbroker meant large commission revenues to the brokerage firm. A hardworking and persistent cold caller could build a valuable book of business in a year or two. Branch managers of brokerage firms began separating the wheat from the chaff in search of the Next Big Producer. A parade of likely candidates materialized, their appearance seeming to coincide with the great bull market of 1982. Novice brokers began attracting novice investors as well as experienced ones. But how would the broker know what to recommend? A poor recommendation could result in a loss, not only investment-wise, but also the loss of the customer as well.

The need for solid ideas and strategies spelled the emergence of the analyst, a person who would study and analyze a particular industry and generate reports that foretold of tremendous opportunities or potential disasters. These reports were crafted either for the public in general or for "internal use only" to keep the brokers informed. This financial food chain meant the broker could be educated relatively quickly and easily, as well as kept abreast of changing market conditions. This was extremely critical to all concerned because as a broker developed relationships with investors, the broker's recommendations had better be right the majority of the time or clients would take their accounts to another firm down the street, meaning a loss of revenue to both the broker and the brokerage firm.

A DISTRIBUTION SYSTEM

Once the retail base was established, the other half of the brokerage firm, the investment bankers, not only were able to structure complex transactions—such as *initial public offerings*, *secondary offerings*, and debt (bond) offerings—but also could ensure the stock was sold, too, meaning they made money two ways: underwriting the offering and selling it to investors. The better they did at both sides of the deal, the more attractive they were to companies that sought to enter the public arena. This vertical system of marketing has become the hallmark of most of the big investment houses today.

Initial public offering (IPO): The first sale of common stock by a corporation to the public at large. IPOs usually represent young, small companies seeking outside equity capital as well as a public market for their stock. Investors purchasing stock in IPOs must be prepared to accept very large risks for the possibility of big gains.

Secondary offering: A sale of securities that occurs when one or more major stockholders in a company sell all or a large portion of their holdings. Such an offering primarily occurs when the founder or one of the original financial backers of a business determines that there is more to be gained by going public than by staying private.

The amount of money made was astonishing. Stories abounded of huge paychecks being earned by 20-somethings fresh out of school. Alluring profits heightened competition among all levels of investment firms. The relationship between broker and customer was important to the firm's success, and the role of the investment banker side of the firm was even more critical.

The role of the aforementioned analyst in this situation began to get complicated. Suppose Don Doe is an analyst for XYZ Investments. Mr. Doe covers the semiconductor sector, and sees a big slowdown coming. The investment bankers are close to signing a contract with Chips America, the largest chipmaker in the world. If they get the deal, it will mean huge profits for XYZ Investments. The analyst knows the slowdown is coming, and it will be very bearish for the sector. If he downgrades the group, it will hurt the chances of XYZ getting Chips America as a client. If he doesn't tell XYZ's clients of the slowdown, they'll be caught in what will certainly be a drastic sell-off when another firm does make the announcement.

This is not a true story, but the conflicting interests are very real. This is why we hear analysts say anything but "sell" if they feel a slowdown is coming. Investors need to learn how to interpret these softened downgrades, to read between the lines if you will. An "outperform" gets dropped to "market perform." An "aggressive buy" gets dubbed "accumulate." This way everyone saves face. The clients get the warning message without offending the company the analyst is following.

It is wise for any investor or trader to become familiar with the analysts covering the sector they're invested in. Some analysts clearly have a better grasp of what's happening within a company or sector, and others miss it badly. In the summer of 2000, one analyst called for a slowdown in the semiconductor sector, and it caused a sell-off in the semiconductor stocks. It was worth noting that this analyst was singular in his opinion. Semiconductor analysts at other firms defended their estimates, and the sector went on to post very impressive gains. It is virtually impossible for one analyst to specifically call a top or bottom in a sector (or the market overall).

A FIELD GUIDE TO BROKER IDENTIFICATION

The new millennium brought with it several types of brokerage firms that fall into the following categories:

- *Full-service brokers:* Offering stocks, bonds, mutual funds, options, and investment advice.
- *Discount brokers:* Offering stocks, bonds, mutual funds, and options without, or with very little, investment advice.
- *Deep-discount brokers:* Offering stocks, bonds, mutual funds, options, and no advice.
- *Online brokers:* Offering stocks, bonds, mutual funds, options, with no advice but various levels of electronic help files to help educate the investor.

Let's examine each category in depth.

Full-Service Brokers

The full-service brokerage firm is the most influential entity on Wall Street today. Sometimes referred to as "wire houses," these venerable institutions have built vast distribution networks of brokers in offices anywhere they think large sums of money reside. Their brokers actively market ideas and strategies to their clients and prospective clients in an effort to win their trust, confidence, and most if not all of their investment capital. Companies such as Merrill Lynch, Paine Webber, Salomon Smith Barney, Morgan Stanley Dean Witter, Goldman Sachs, and Donaldson, Lufkin & Jenrette (DLJ) are almost household names these days.

These firms do their level best to deliver accurate investment advice to their customers, and offer a dizzying array of financial products including checking accounts, *money market accounts*, their own mutual fund families, and of course stocks, bonds, mutual funds, and advice aplenty. In some cases they've even invented their own indexes that keep track of particular market sectors.

> **Money market account:** A securities market that primarily deals in short-term debt instruments that mature in less than one year and are very liquid. The fund's main objective is to earn interest while maintaining a stable net asset value of $1 per share.

The analysts hired by these "houses" are extremely bright and well-educated over-achievers with heads for numbers and business models. They investigate companies and generate investment reports that are disseminated regularly to their clients and brokers. They even have "market analysts" whose recommendations have the ability to move the financial markets with their public opinions. Some have been around a long time, achieving almost mythical status. (Peter Lynch, the man who made the Magellan Fund so successful, is one such person.) Others labor in relative obscurity as they research every aspect of a sector or company in an effort to give their clients a trading edge.

But just because you're on the phone with a top firm's broker doesn't necessarily imply he or she is going to give good advice on any given day, much less on a consistent basis. Why? Because to become a broker you need only have a license—called a *Series 7*, which can be obtained after studying for a short period—and a somewhat pleasant demeanor that will appeal to total strangers.

Most brokers are salespeople learning to become market gurus. A percentage of them eventually evolve into good brokers, able to dispense solid investment advice that truly is in your best interest and capable of reading market conditions accurately. But it's difficult to determine where the broker is in this curve, so great care must be taken in the early stages of a relationship.

> **Series 7:** A specific license (General Securities Registered Representative License) issued by the National Association of Securities Dealers (NASD) that entitles the holder to sell all types of securities products, with the exception of commodities futures.

In many cases, these brokers are paid strictly on commission. This isn't exactly a situation that prevents conflicts of interest, is it? To illustrate a point, let's imagine it's the end of the month, and the broker (whose paycheck comes once a month and is determined by "production," or commissions generated) is having a poor month. Needing some sales in a hurry, he (or she) looks through his (or her) book for an account with idle cash to invest or stocks that can be sold to capture profits. Portfolio laggards also get jettisoned at this point, the proceeds reinvested into the latest "great idea." Some brokers use *fear* and *greed* to motivate a client to issue a "sell" or "buy" order. These brokers, fortunately, don't last too long in the business, for

> **Churning:** Excessive trading in a customer's account by a registered representa-
> tive who ignores the customer's interests and seeks only to increase commis-
> sions; this violates the NASD Rules of Fair Practice.
>
> **Commission:** A service charge assessed by a broker in return for arranging the
> purchase or sale of a security. The amount of the commission varies depending
> on whether it's a fixed cost or a percentage charged on the transaction's value.

they aren't placing the clients' interests ahead of their own. But the potential for
needless transactions or *churning* exists nonetheless.

Full-service brokers also collect much higher commissions as a rule, and rightly
so. They are charged with "overseeing" portfolios for investors who are often too
busy making money to effectively be a watchdog over them. The full-service broker
also provides timely research opinions and recommendations, as well as attractive
security offers such as a hot IPO.

---

*A word of caution: Just because someone is licensed to take an order doesn't
mean that individual has the knowledge to invest your money wisely.*

With little effort a customer could unearth many stories of excessive trading
(called churning) in an account—ill-timed recommendations either to buy or sell, and
recommendations that are not suitable for the investor. Suitability is of paramount importance when a broker recommends an investment. The potential customer should be
asked to convey an accurate picture of his or her assets and investment expertise, as
well as goals and risk tolerance, before a recommendation is made. This is why some
securities are termed *widow and orphan* investments, which is another way of indicating safety instead of high risk. A good, experienced broker is worth his or her weight
in gold as well as every penny received in commissions. As a novice, it is your challenge to seek out a good broker. The best way to meet this challenge is by paying attention to what others are saying about their investment advisers.

> **Widow and orphan stock:** A safe stock that typically pays high dividends, offers
> a low beta coefficient, and is often associated with noncyclical businesses.

So how can you determine whether the person asking for a portion (or all) of
your available investment dollars will truly be an advocate (consistently placing
your needs first) or a selfish rookie more concerned with production? Here are some
questions to ask:

- How long has the broker been in the business?
- What are his or her biggest positions and why?
- What is the broker's specialty? Where does the bulk of his or her commission
  dollars come from? Some brokers specialize in government bonds while oth-

ers fancy themselves to be stock pickers. Stick to the ones that most closely reflect your philosophy.

- When a recommendation is made, what is the expected "hold time"? That is, how long can you expect to have it in your portfolio? If a sudden move up occurs (which is always nice), will you be urged to capture the quick profit or will you risk riding it back down, focusing more on the Big Picture of long-term growth?

A real eye-opener is to contact the National Association of Securities Dealers (NASD), the governing body of brokerage firms. Inquire as to any disciplinary action or complaints against the broker in question. In addition, always ask in advance for a sample monthly statement. Some firms have relatively easy ones to read, while others are more difficult to decipher than the Dead Sea Scrolls.

If possible, ask for referrals. Nothing sells like word of mouth. While you're at it, ask around! Who are your friends using? What do they think of the firm itself? If you do this long enough, the same broker's name will keep popping up. Be proactive and contact him or her to set an initial interview date.

When you begin a relationship with a broker, by all means be patient. Many customers determine the future of their relationship based on the first trade or two. Market circumstances can unexpectedly move against both of you, and this should be taken into consideration. But be wary if the broker's first idea is not suitable for you, or you just aren't comfortable with it. This is a signal your risk tolerance or investment goals were either ignored or forgotten, and doesn't bode well when you're considering a long-term relationship.

Another approach some brokers take is to suggest a strategy for buying a basket of stocks, or to ask you to deposit a lump sum that will be invested as conditions warrant. In many ways this is a much fairer method of determining the value and expertise of the broker. Ask the potential adviser, "How would you invest X amount of money in today's market? Which stocks do you like, and at what price?" Track the recommendations closely using the newspaper or by going online. This is a risk-free method of broker evaluation.

When Should You Change Brokers?
Easy answers to bitter lessons:

- Unauthorized trades in your account.
- Consistently suggesting unsuitable recommendations.
- Excessive use of margin, a sign of hunger for more trades in many cases.
- Account activity (your commissions should add up to 1% to 2% of your portfolio value in a year's time; if the total is much higher than that, a heart-to-heart meeting with your broker is called for).
- "He never calls, he never writes. . . ." Sometimes a broker will outgrow you (i.e., your account doesn't warrant his or her increasingly valuable time). You become ignored and are never contacted. Some people are fine with this. If you're not, ask to be referred to another broker who will commit the necessary time to addressing your concerns and investment objectives.

You're Ultimately Responsible for Everything
The client-investor owes it to himself or herself to learn the basics of investing, even if the advising broker is doing a superb job. Why? Because circumstances change, and one day you may just find yourself adrift, looking for a new broker. If a person insists on staying ignorant of the basic mechanics of the market, the burden of responsibility should be placed squarely on the client's shoulders. At the very least, as with attorneys, the best time to find a broker is when you don't need one. Have a contingency plan, just in case. This book is designed to give you the necessary tools so eventually you'll be able to direct your own account.

Discount Brokers

Discount brokers offer access to the markets without all the advice a client would get from a full-service firm. Many experienced investors choose to do their own research, trusting themselves more than anyone else, and as a result pay less than a person doing business at a full-service firm. The discount broker is directed by the customer's orders. The vast majority of the time they will defer offering specific opinions on a stock, a bond, or the markets. Many times this is due to a policy the firm may impose, wishing to avoid liability. They provide real-time quotes, often have computers you may use to check market conditions while in their offices, can assist you with the necessary documents for opening an IRA (individual retirement account) or transferring a 401(k) plan, and can facilitate the purchase of no-load mutual funds.

They charge less because they *do* less. The broker at a discount firm typically won't create an investment strategy, but will suggest ideas when you describe what you're after. They provide accurate, real-time price quotes, have access to the bond market, and even make mutual funds (both load and no-load) available to their clients. (*Note:* Some discount firms charge transaction fees for no-load mutual funds.)

Deep Discount Brokers

Deep discount brokers offer extremely discounted rates on the buying and selling of investment securities. The reduced trading commissions are available to individual investors and are sometimes more than 50% less than traditional full-service brokerage firms. An example of a deep-discount commission is $14.95 per trade for orders less than 5,000 shares. Trading costs will vary from one deep-discount broker to another. In addition, the commissions will vary based on the type of order. For example, some brokerage firms allow investors to place a "market" order for free, or a minimal cost, but charge standard rates for "limit" orders.

Many online brokerage firms are deep-discount brokers. The automated systems associated with web trading have reduced the broker's cost of executing trades and that, in turn, has led to a proliferation of deep-discount brokers on the Internet. One important element that distinguishes web-based and traditional full service firms is the amount of advice available to investors. Online investors receive little to no investment advice. As a result, online deep discount brokers have enabled a large number of do-it-yourself investors to trade securities independently of financial advisers and stockbrokers.

The deep discount broker has emerged as a force to be reckoned with on the Net, as technological advances such as ECNs and the Small Order Execution System (SOES), and new and better access to research information have come together to empower the retail investor.

No longer does the "little guy" require guidance from the full-service brokers, nor does the self-motivated investor need to step into the local office of a national firm to get his or her research information. They simply log onto the Net and, after downloading any number of research reports, or listening to live conference calls with analysts and market gurus, they can decide when to buy and sell, and do so at costs once thought to be unrealistically low.

Deep discount brokerage firms reduce their costs by relying on someone else to provide research. Most times this information is free, but not always. They make their money the same way a bank does: They charge you interest when you borrow (on margin), they collect fees when they "lend" your stock to someone else so they may short sell it. And there's the usual transaction fees, the nickel and dime costs that can infuriate you.

Commissions are around $9.95 a trade, (for a market order), but do go up if you need to speak with a broker or place a limit order. Some cater to the options trader, (Wall Street Access, www.wsaccess.com), Preferred Trade (www.preferredtrade.com), Datek Online, (www.datek.com); Ameritrade (www.ameritrade.com); E-Trade (www.etrade.com/cgi-bin/gx.cgi/applogic+Home); SureTrade (www.suretrade.com), and T.D. Waterhouse (www.tdwaterhouse.com/index.asp), National Discount Brokers (www.ndb.com), Mr. Stock (www.mrstock.com) are just some of the firms competing for your investment dollars. As always, read the fine print. Option trades are NOT the same price as stock trades. They usually involve a flat fee plus a charge per contract.

The list of DDBs (deep discount brokers) is extensive. A few web sites keep up to date listings, and even review them. TheStreet.com has a section that does this (www.thestreet.com/funds/personalfinance/908807.html).

Online Brokers

Both discount and full-service brokers have taken to the Internet the way a duck takes to water, and why shouldn't they? The Internet has provided the ideal platform to transact business, and investors have followed them right into the pond. As of this writing there are currently more than one hundred online brokerage firms to choose from. The waters get very murky here for they are all vying for your business, and to get it, some have spent considerable sums for marketing and the building of extremely high-tech infrastructures. These costs are no doubt recouped from the increased assets under their control and burgeoning commissions. Familiar names such as Charles Schwab have been able to grow considerably, due in large part to the sharp increase in the quality and quantity of research brought about by the Net and the huge surge in computer usage. No longer do the wire houses have an edge in the research department, or even the inside track to the trading floor.

Choosing an online broker comes with a variety of unique questions and issues. Not only do you have to make sure that your broker provides excellent order executions, but you need to investigate its track record when it comes to server breakdowns, and how successful its contingency plans have been during a loss of online service. Currently, battle lines have been drawn in the online arena as full-service brokers go toe-to-toe with discounters. Although the resources of the Internet level the playing field a bit, it's very important to know just what you should be looking for when you go surfing for an online broker.

Today just about every brokerage firm offers online trading, but not all of them offer the same services. Choose carefully—commissions vary widely as well.

RESEARCH

As indicated before, full-service firms lead the way in offering research, and lots of it. Some firms have great research, while others seem lacking. Generally speaking, if you are a client of these firms you receive their research material gratis, either electronically or by snail mail. The nature of being online means the client is able to receive up-to-the-minute research without waiting for the mail, can access daily market commentary, and recently has gained the ability to participate in "chats" with analysts and company executives.

Discount brokers have utilized the incredible power of the Internet to deliver research to you as well—the cost of which varies. Most firms offer freebies such as links to news sites, plus *real-time* or *delayed quotes* (delaying quotes is more a function of the stock exchange than the broker). As usual, performance equals cost, so 20-minute delays are the norm unless, of course, you're willing to pay. There are some firms, however, that offer real-time quotes as part of their service, which is nice but not absolutely necessary in most cases. Of all online investors, not everyone requires real-time quotes. Active traders certainly need it, but many times they'll be subscribing to quote services that cater directly to traders.

Delayed quotes: Quotes that are delayed up to 20 minutes from the actual price changes at the exchanges. Delaying the quotes is more a function of the stock exchange than the broker; as usual, performance equals cost, so 20-minute delays are the norm unless, of course, you're willing to pay.

Real-time quotes: Streaming quotes that are received as the prices change at the exchanges.

As mentioned earlier, research on stocks is updated and disseminated almost immediately these days. There is an abundance of research sites that offer tremendous

amounts of information. Balance sheets, pertinent financial information, and brokerage estimates are all assembled for you to review, most at no cost. Even the companies you're interested in have begun providing profiles online, which can be
extremely helpful to novice and expert alike. However, it's very easy to get information overload or analysis paralysis, as I like to call it. Knowing what kind of information you need prior to searching is a prerequisite. Market analysts and
prognosticators of the market in general are especially prone to sending out conflicting signals, and can make you hesitate, unsure of whom to believe. Spend a little time beforehand evaluating your own needs and wants. The person that seeks his
(or her) own counsel will require more information than the person with a mutual
fund or two looking to check the NAV (net asset value) once a week.

To be sure, the major brokerage firms will allow a prospect to get a taste of their research as an enticement. Quality information, however, either low-cost or free, is easy
to come by on the Internet, so the weighting of research in the decision as to which
brokerage firm to sign with is lessened. I prefer to concentrate on how easy the information is to get and apply, and how easy (or difficult) it is actually to place a trade.

COSTS

It's difficult to make it through a day without hearing about "eight-dollar trades" or
"lower margin rates." The competition is keen to capture the active investor as well
as gather assets. The gathering of assets is critical because in-house assets provide a
greater potential for income to the brokerage firm just as they do for a bank. But beware whenever you hear of low-cost transactions, because the fine print may indicate otherwise in many cases.

Low-cost transactions most often apply to the easiest orders to execute—*market
orders*—because they do not require much effort from the broker. More complicated
orders often require a higher, nonadvertised commission price. The low advertised
price gets you in the door, but read the fine print before placing a trade! Here's a list
of items that can help you get a clear and concise picture of any brokerage firm.

> **Market order:** Buying or selling securities at the price given at the time the order
> reaches the market. A market order is to be executed immediately at the best
> available price, and is the only order that guarantees execution.

What Services Does the Brokerage Firm Offer and at What Cost?

- Does the firm offer stock charts? Are they easy to use? What information do
  they provide?

- What is the interest charged to use margin? (This term refers to borrowing
  money from the broker, using your stock as collateral. You may either buy
  stock or actually take cash from the account.)

- Does the broker offer real-time quotes? Can you track your portfolio online?

- Check on reliability. If the site goes down, how easy it to place an order? Long phone waits can be very frustrating! If possible, call the order desk during market hours, just to see how easy it is to get through.

- Many brokerage firms have a two-tiered commission system. You receive the low advertised rate if you execute a trade 100% electronically, using the firm's web site. Commissions often increase dramatically when your trade directly involves a broker.

- Can you access your money market account using a check-writing feature? Consider the ease with which you can access idle cash at the brokerage firm. Does it have to be mailed out? Or can the firm wire the funds, and, if so, at what cost? If you ever need cash in a hurry or over a holiday, this can be a source of frustration if you haven't learned the system.

- Is the online trading site a web site or is it software-based? A software-driven site is generally faster than a web site-based system. Waiting for a web site to load before you can hit the "buy" or "sell" key can seem to take hours, especially if you trade actively or you want to change some aspect of your order, such as the price. Generally, the easier it is to change information on an order, the less frustration you'll experience. Some online brokerage sites have blazing speed, making it easy to execute changes and trades. Some even permit you to do "paper trades" (no money is involved) just to demonstrate the ease of their system.

- How much do you plan to trade? If you're planning on doing only a few trades a year, the previous points are not nearly as critical as if you want to trade daily. If you're an active trader or want to be, performance counts. It might be worthwhile to pay extra for features that will enhance your execution speed, information quality, and reliability.

- Many people are surprised after they've been with a brokerage firm for a while and experience firsthand the sting of a hidden charge. Here's a list of potential fees: postage and handling charges, funds transfer (in and out), insurance, and even administrative costs. As always, it pays to read the fine print.

- If you get into a less-than-desirable firm and want to transfer, cash transfers are much faster than securities. The firm losing the account has little motivation to surrender assets; it has lost your account already, so why should the staff worry if you're ticked? Stay on them. Speak with the branch manager if your account isn't getting moved.

- Transaction fees are almost certain to be higher when doing an option trade. Find out the price charged per contract, and the minimum charge per trade.

Online brokers suffer from technological snafus just like any other Web-based business. Finding out how often the site crashes or becomes unavailable is critical information. If the site goes down and you're unable to execute a trade, it will cause frustration, and could literally cost you money.

A WORD ABOUT COMPLAINTS

It's an unfortunate part of this business, but there are times when you'll be less than happy with your broker, for any number of reasons. If the source of your unhappiness persists, stronger measures are called for. A written complaint to a broker-dealer really shakes things up. Letters are serious, regardless of the tone or intention behind them. If you're not getting the results you expected from a broker or brokerage firm, a letter to the branch manager and/or broker usually clarifies or rectifies any misunderstandings fairly fast. If this doesn't remedy your dissatisfaction, contacting the NASD (National Association of Securities Dealers), the governing body that oversees the brokerage community, is the next step. No broker wants a call from these people for any reason.

If your account has had unauthorized trades (trades executed without your consent), overtrading (affectionately known as churning), or some other nuance that you don't fully understand, don't be shy. Confront your broker. Face-to-face meetings are best, but don't let anyone bully you. It's *your* money!

Strict and specific rules and regulations govern the broker's activities and recommendations, and are there to protect you!

The Background Check

It's been said that an ounce of prevention is worth a pound of cure. The NASD monitors complaints about every broker and brokerage firm. A call to NASD (800-289-9999) may provide interesting information—good or bad—that will lay bare a broker's history. Plus, it's confidential.

THE FINANCIAL PROFESSIONAL

Outside of the most visible arena of the brokerage community is another genre of financial professionals. They sometimes offer *total financial planning* or promise long-term planning on an ongoing basis. Just like brokers, their range is substantial. Some offer monthly investment options as a way to save. Others provide options, annuities, and tax-deferred strategies involving insurance products. It can be confusing, especially if you start getting conflicting advice from different investment professionals.

Registered Investment Advisers (RIAs)

These individuals have passed a test that permits them to declare that they are Registered Investment Advisers or RIAs. The test is not difficult, but the application of its knowledge is serious business, for it generally implies something more than where to place your *IRA (individual retirement account)* this year. The RIA typically is associated with a less visible brokerage firm, one that caters to one- or two-person shops. These broker-dealers "clear" transactions for their advisers—the ones they sold you.

> **IRA (individual retirement account):** A popular investment tool for currently employed individuals that permits a contribution up to a maximum of $2,000 per year. Some (or all) of the contribution may be free from taxation, depending on the individual's adjusted gross income and coverage by employer-sponsored qualified retirement plans.

However, some advisory firms are very sophisticated and extremely valuable for the person or company that wants to know more about where they are headed and why. The bigger outfits can educate an employer as to how to set up a retirement plan for his or her company. Although brokerage firms can do this as well, the smaller RIA outfits are in many ways well suited to address the needs of small businesses. In many cases, small businesses have vastly different needs than those of individual investors. The RIAs can offer fee-based asset management, which means they are associated with a money manager (or are money managers themselves), and they are compensated on a percentage basis of the assets under management. This method removes the danger of overtrading, as RIAs need a large amount of money under management to make a living. They want to do exactly what you want or need in order to continue being paid.

Money Managers

People calling themselves "money managers" usually have a strong reason to believe they are highly skilled in the art of investing. They typically work on a fee-based system (a percentage of assets under management). Did you ever wonder where the wealthy put their money? Professionals who are too busy making money to spend the time it takes to wisely invest it are the kind of individuals who utilize the services of a money manager. There are plenty of money managers, too. To find a good one, meticulously check their performance records. Unlike a stock picker at a major brokerage firm, money managers cannot conceal their track records.

Here are a few simple questions to ask when evaluating money managers:

- What's your track record (performance history versus the S&P 500)?
- How long have you been in business, and what's your background?
- Do you offer different levels of risk and strategies?
- How much do you currently have under management?
- What references can you provide?

> *Money managers, just like professional investors who direct pension funds and mutual funds, are all measured against the Standard & Poor's 500, a group of stocks that represent a cross section of the U.S. economy. They either "beat the S&P" or they didn't.*

Most importantly, ask for a complete breakdown of the fee structure, although they'll most likely disclose their compensation scale upfront. The percentage they charge is on a sliding scale: The more they manage, the lower the percentage charged. The fee is typically broken into four quarterly charges, paid at the beginning of each quarter.

Certified Financial Planners (CFPs)

The financial professional who has the initials "CFP" after his or her name has completed a rigorous series of courses that encompass the entire spectrum of the investment world. For the record, it is typically done on an at-home basis, although the curriculum is increasingly available through universities. Make no mistake, it takes an honest effort to complete and attain this status. The CFP can help with *asset allocation*, insurance coverage, financial planning, and more. The CFP's compensation varies from a flat charge to evaluate your current situation to fee-based management. Find the one you like the same way you find a broker: Ask around. Interview candidates carefully before disclosing your financial picture to them. Anyone granted access to your financial inner sanctum should pass every sniff test you have and then some. Avoid anyone who claims to be a CFP and doesn't have it printed on stationery or business cards—it would be like printing "M.D." on your card when you're a hairdresser; it's called fraud.

Asset allocation: When you divide your money among various types of investments, such as stocks, bonds, and short-term investments, you are allocating your assets. The way in which your money is divided is called your asset allocation.

Insurance Professionals

The nature of life insurance policies and their place in the universe of financial planning and investing brings to light another type of professional. This person is primarily interested, at least initially, in determining the level of insurance protection you and your family or business may need.

Insurance companies have played a vital role in America's financial picture for a long time. They offer such a wide array of financial products I will not even attempt to evaluate them all here. But the industry hosts a variety of professional designations that can assist you in piecing together your current needs and future goals. These people offer financial products that may be similar to those offered by brokerage firms or mutual funds—many of them *proprietary*. Evaluate an insurance professional as you would any other person attempting to help you invest wisely.

Proprietary investment: Investments offered exclusively to the clients of a specific insurance company, investment firm, or brokerage.

Most of these people are licensed to offer mutual funds only. They cannot and should not be offering advice on individual stocks, other than proffering an opinion. Evaluate their recommendations carefully, especially their proprietary funds. Many times their fund fees are higher than rates you could get elsewhere.

TECHNOLOGY AND THE DAY TRADER

To many the term "day trader" conjures up visions of crowded areas where people yell and make funny hand signals. Not so. A day trader is a person who buys and sells stocks or options intraday, looking more for quick profits than long-term capital appreciation. Some will "scalp" for a quarter point or a half, while others may be in a position for several days. Again, advances in technology and a change in the law have given rise to a new type of player: Welcome the day trader!

Shortly after the 1987 stock market crash, the Nasdaq needed to offer faster executions during periods of heavy trading. The Small Order Execution System (SOES) was developed to allow the faster execution of buys and sells for the retail investor (the term "retail" applies to any orders up to 1,000 shares). In essence, any orders placed over the SOES system are executed very quickly.

TRUSTING YOUR BROKER

The world of brokers is in many ways similar to that of physicians or attorneys: there are specialists and generalists. The more experienced you become as an investor, the more you'll naturally seek out the specialist or more sophisticated brokerage firm. Never, *ever* just plunk your hard-earned money down to the first broker you meet without first evaluating the broker's experience and competency.

Finding a good broker is a lot like buying a used car:
Caveat emptor . . . let the buyer beware!

---

1. Assess your needs and financial goals. What kind of broker is best for you? The person with $100 a month to invest will need a much different broker than the couple who have saved for 40 years and now want to put their millions to work. Perhaps you fall somewhere in between these two extremes. How much are you going to start with, and how long will you commit it to the market?

2. Ask around. Who are your friends and associates at work using? Are their goals and current conditions similar to yours? Informal surveys can help you find a good broker as well as avoid an unscrupulous one. It pays to do a little research.

3. Look for a philosophical match. When you're considering a broker, find out what his (or her) philosophy is regarding stocks and bonds. Is he/she a buy-and-hold fan or does he/she espouse taking a profit if conditions warrant? Are your goals in sync with this style and temperament?

4. If you're going to make all the investment decisions yourself, first determine the quality of a firm's research. You'll probably need outside research sources as well, but you can easily overdo it. Make sure you know what the firm offers, and what it doesn't. Then scout around for the gaps in your information.

5. Verify accessibility. How accessible does your broker need to be for you? If the broker you choose is with an online brokerage, how easy is it to get to speak to him or her? Are you comfortable speaking to any broker who might happen to pick up the phone? The investor who needs one's hand held a lot should determine just exactly how the brokerage system works prior to funding an account.

6. Pay attention. This may be hard to believe, but there are a few bad apples in this business, and you need to be able to determine if you're being sold a bill of goods in order to generate commissions.

7. Learn all you can as you invest. Your broker may not stay with you forever, and the responsibility for financial success is ultimately yours.

8. Set limits. When do you decide that this just isn't working? How do you decide when your relationship with a broker is over? Unauthorized trades, poor investment selections, churning of your account to generate trades, recommendations that aren't suitable for your risk profile and financial goals— if you feel you're consistently being taken advantage of, run (don't walk) to a broker that better fills your needs.

9. Written complaints get attention. If ever you find yourself in the unfortunate position of gross dissatisfaction, a written complaint to the brokerage firm's branch manager and/or the broker is taken very seriously. This generally clears things up. If you still do not receive satisfaction, a written complaint to the National Association of Securities Dealers (NASD) will definitely bring resolution to any misunderstandings or genuine wrongdoing. Be sure this course is taken only as a last resort.

10. Review all statements for accuracy. Check the firm's statements for clarity before you open the account, and accuracy afterward. Brokers are human beings and they make mistakes—and seldom in your favor!

11. Be on the lookout for hidden fees and charges. The fine print on the back of the account application details charges and other restrictions that may affect you later, after you've opened the account. If it's an online firm, is there a higher charge for limit orders? Does it cost more to speak with a live human being? Is there a charge to distribute funds, send and/or receive wire transfers, or a monthly fee to have an "open" account?

12. Know your allies. A broker is not a Certified Financial Planner unless it says so on his or her card. While most brokers can structure a long-term strategy for that portion of your investable funds, they generally are not very expert in overall financial planning. This limitation holds true for a CFP as well; they typically aren't too proficient at picking stocks.

Finding the right broker can be an arduous process. Perhaps the most important part of the relationship can be summed up in one word: trust. Whoever you end up choosing, you are trusting them with your money and inherently the future financial security of both you and your family. Be choosy. Keep searching until you find a brokerage firm that offers you the services you need at a price you can live with. Regardless of how convenient online brokerages have become, I must admit a certain fondness for actual human contact when it comes to putting my money where my mouth is.

ROADMAP TO SUCCESS

What is your level of competence? Check one classification that *best* describes your level of expertise:

_____   **Beginner:** Possessing little or no knowledge of the stock market, or very limited at best.

_____   **Intermediate Level:** An investor that has been in the market for at least one year. Obviously this can vary. If you've been trading six or more times a month for the past six months it would be safe to assume you've escaped novice status, but still have a long way to go.

_____   **Advanced:** If you're in this category, you more than likely:
* Have been through a minimum of one bear market.
* Have been trading two or more years, or have made 100 trades
* Read a financial daily, like *Investor's Business Daily* or the *Wall Street Journal*, more than casually.
* Have a nodding acquaintance with options and how they work.
* Have more than one brokerage account.

_____   **Expert/Professional:** You know who you are. You know the best places for information, the best brokerage firms to trade with, and the best newsletters that fit your style. You've evolved into a trader who is working on the finer points of trading, sharpening your edge.

After determining the one best category that describes your experience and comfort level, look at the following chart to find your category.

Objective	*Course of Action*
	The Beginning Investor
Let the Search Begin!	Call various brokerage firms in your area, or ask someone you know (and trust) who they use, and why. Do not call during market hours (9:30–4:00 EST).
	• Let the broker know your level of experience (none to darn little).
	• Be prepared to disclose how much you plan to invest (will it be one lump sum deposit or do you want to make regular deposits into an account and have him/her invest it as you go along?)
	After identifying two to three prospective brokers (do not fall in love with the first one you meet!), and having set an appointment with each, have your questions ready.

Determine the experience of the prospective broker.	How long has he (or she) been a broker? What size are his or her accounts? Ask questions, but respect brokers' time, so they don't become reluctant to take your calls!
Mutual Understanding	Does the prospective broker have the patience to teach as well as recommend? • Did he or she ask a lot of questions to better understand your risk profile and financial goals? • Did he or she answer your questions to your satisfaction?
Follow-Up	After your meeting(s), a course of action was (hopefully) discussed. • Did the broker follow through in a timely manner? (This one alone will weed them out.) • Did you understand and feel comfortable with "the next step"? • Note! Unless your circumstances warrant extensive tax planning and/or estate issues, taking this to your accountant or attorney is a waste of their time and yours.
Full Service	When starting out, you want to be able to read research reports, as much as time allows. It's *your* money and you are ultimately responsible!
Easy-to-Read Statements	Not a big requirement, but it eases the frustration level. If you don't understand them, call your broker and ask for a detailed description.
Full Disclosure	Find out any and all costs, including but not limited to: • Trade costs • Market versus limit orders • Options and spreads • Online versus speaking with a real person • Wire transfer fees (incoming and outgoing)
Now you have the broker and it's time to open the account!	• Fill out "new account" form. This is simple. Either it's a qualified or a nonqualified account. (An IRA, a 401(k), or Keogh plan is a qualified plan. Your broker will tell you if you're not sure.) • Write a check, or wire transfer funds to your new account. This is very similar to opening a bank account. Like a bank, it's insured (*SIPC*, or Security Insurance Protection Corporation in most cases). SIPC does not guarantee against investment losses, but they do protect you if the brokerage firm goes belly-up. • As soon as the funds are in the account, you're ready to trade!
When you have opened the account and have funds invested:	• Does your broker follow the game plan initially discussed? • If you're unhappy or have concerns, will the broker take the time to meet with you, either in person or at a prearranged time so that you're not interrupted?
Make sure that you:	• Don't call your broker incessantly, unless you're interested in making a trade. Calling for quotes is acceptable (during market hours), but don't chitchat. The broker works on straight commission (usually); so try not to waste his or her time.

- Don't get offended if you speak with his or her assistant more often than the broker. (This is just the broker protecting his or her time for the more critical tasks.)
- If you want to make a trade, say so when you call. You'll be put through faster.

Fee-Based Asset Management	You may be a candidate for this type of asset management. Fee-based asset management (or wrap accounts) has grown in popularity over the years. (One well-known firm has even offered flat fee investing, where you pay X amount of money for unlimited trades for one year.) It's called fee-based because the broker or money manager is compensated on a percentage of the account's value, usually paid out quarterly. The more money that is in the account, the less the percentage. I like it because it takes away the need for the broker having to call you with every trade idea that comes down the path. Then, on some sort of regular basis, you evaluate the progress and see if that broker/manager gets to keep the account. Most people with substantial accounts go this route because it's safer. Watch CNBC or Bloomberg, and you'll see a parade of managers being interviewed. You can evaluate past performance figures first, then decide if you want to hire that person or firm. These people can either be affiliated with a brokerage firm or be independent entities who place their trades through a discount broker.
Brokers are often called Registered Investment Advisers.	A broker may or may not have this title, because there's a separate test that's required. Just because they have this title doesn't mean their judgment is flawless. The same cautionary flags exist. Ask around. For this type of account, it isn't unusual to go beyond the city limits to get the company or person you want.
Margin trading comes with *risk*.	When you're learning, you're doing so with your money—not the broker's! Therefore, avoid buying on margin, no matter how safe the trade is described as being. The broker that insists on trading with margin is a broker you should fire on the spot. Remember, you can always fire your broker, and your broker can fire you as well!

The Intermediate Investor

If you already have a broker, and you're relatively happy, whip out the scorecard and see how his (or her) ideas are treating your portfolio!	- Commissions: Do commission totals exceed 1% to 2% of the size of your account, annualized? If so, are your returns commensurate with the increased transaction costs? (If your account is up net 20% and your commissions are 6%, hey, you're on the right track!)
- Where are the trade ideas coming from?—the broker's personal research or the firm's analysts?
- Are your calls being returned in a timely manner?

- Are there trades occurring without your consent and prior knowledge? Unauthorized trades are a serious transgression.
- How are you doing with your broker? Here's how you measure:

Take your account balance on the date you first deposited it. (Let's say it was $10,000.)

What is it worth today, net of all transaction costs? (Let's say it's worth $12,000.)

Subtract the smaller number from the bigger number:

$$\begin{array}{r} \$12{,}000 \\ -\underline{\$10{,}000} \\ \$\ 2{,}000 \end{array}$$

Divide your answer by the original amount: $2,000/$10,000 = 20%.

Measure that number against the S&P 500 (known as the broad market, the benchmark against which all are judged.

If you're beating it, congratulations. If not, and it's a wide disparity, recheck your strategy.

If your returns stink, or for some reason you're dissatisfied, take your statement to another broker for evaluation.

Match those confirmations with the statements!	Do you really believe that brokerage firms are infallible? • Be sure to check that the price, number of shares, and the stock, bond, or option are correct, and the commission is what you expected. • File your statement separately from your confirmations.
Finding a Broker by Word of Mouth	• A good broker takes time to find, so never stop asking who other people use. • Chances are good that another broker will have taken the initiative to contact you via a cold call or civic affiliations like Kiwanis or the Lions' Club. Build a relationship before you need your broker. Besides, having another person's input isn't a bad idea.

The Advanced Investor

Constantly monitor your trades by keeping accurate records of:	• Length of time in the trade. • Gain or loss average. Keep your losses low, and let those winners run. • Portfolio asset allocation—cash, stocks, bonds; in stocks, what percentage is in aggressive growth to conservative, blue-chip companies. • Costs (commissions) as a percentage of your overall account. • If you're trading your own account, just how hard are you working (and at what cost) to beat the market? If you're not beating it, it's time to rethink your strategy. • Keep your trade ledger or journal either next to your computer or where you open your business mail.

How much of your research comes from one brokerage firm?	If you're relying on one firm to keep you abreast of market conditions, that's no different from listening to one radio station to keep abreast of the music world. At the very least be able to define the current hot sectors you need to be in, and the ones to stay away from. I'm not talking about day trading or even week trading. If you fit most of these descriptions, you're taking an active role in the management of your finances, and that's good (most of the time).
Do you keep a close eye on the trades in your account?	Being advanced means you've likely built a solid relationship with a broker (or two), and there's an understanding that if something needs to be done (on the sell side), just do it. Sometimes you want the broker to catch a good idea (if it's really good) without your authorization. That's okay, but be very clear as to the parameters of discretionary trading. Brokerage firms have limited power of attorney documents that need to be executed prior to this type of arrangement. This is not an area for the naive, especially if the use of margin is involved. Listen, people change when money's on the line, and if catching good trades, means more commissions to the catcher, watch out! This kind of stuff can get out of hand, and fast.
How is your portfolio performing?	• Are you beating the S&P 500? If so, how much risk are you taking to beat it? • How are the expenses (commissions) doing in order to outperform the market? if they're higher than 1% to 2%, you better be bringing in pretty good numbers! • Have you varied from your original objective?
Discount Brokers	• Be sure to look closely at fees! (Transaction costs vary widely from the low-low advertised price.) It pays big time to read the fine print for detailed disclosures of all costs. • Check their statements too for clarity. Some are as clear as Sanskrit. • Opening an account with this kind of firm is no different than with a full-service broker. Have the firm send you an application or, if possible, stop into a local office.
Research Basics	Increasingly you'll want and need to widen your investment knowledge, and research is a major part of this. • The *Wall Street Journal*, *Barron's*, and *Investor's Business Daily* are the places to start. Pick one and go. (I like *Investor's Business Daily*—just a personal preference.) • Magazines—*Forbes*, *Fortune*, *Money*, *SmartMoney*, and a host of others—will go in depth more than the daily papers do.
Online Brokers	As with the discount firms and the full-service companies, online brokers have a lot to offer, but you have to research their services very carefully before venturing into this arena. • Is there ease of use and accessibility to a live broker? • System failures and long hold times when phoning directly are just a few of the potential pitfalls that await you.

Things to Consider When Going Online	• Surf the financial sites and online brokers before you begin. Get familiar with the Internet prior to putting money at risk. • Setting up an online account is no different than with a bricks-and-mortar firm. Fill out the application and send in the money.
Online Research	• Find one or two newsletters you like and that come recommended by other investors. • Take as many free trial offers as possible, and soon you'll be a walking encyclopedia of what's good and what's junk. • Focus on a small market niche; start small, then branch out after you're comfortable. • Keep a notebook for your research.

The Expert/Professional Investor

For you the name of the game is education and fine-tuning. If you're making most or all of the decisions in your portfolio, the information you're receiving must be spot-on accurate.

Service and Commissions	Evaluate what you are paying for versus what you're getting. • Higher commissions should mean greater service, as well as a very good broker. • How easy is it to get through to your broker?
Online Accessibility	• Is your brokerage firm's web site down more than up? • Is it reliable, fast, and easy to navigate? • Can you reach the broker on the phone without being put on hold forever?
Stay Competitive!	What are you reading to stay competitive and on a level playing field with other traders? Here is a list of web sites and publications I visit or read regularly: • *Investor's Business Daily:* "Don't read it, use it." I do. • **Optionetics.com** (www.optionetics.com): A wealth of useful information and articles. • **Quote.com** (www.quote.com): Excellent articles, news, and charts. I use it constantly. • **BigCharts.com** (www.bigcharts.com): One of the best charting sites on the Net. • **The Street.com** (www.thestreet.com): Top-notch market commentary. • **Bloomberg.com** (www.bloomberg.com/markets/index.html): Not as flashy as CNBC, but I like this one a lot. • **CNBC** (www.cnbc.com): The online business news giant.

3

The World of Stocks

Current, up-to-the-minute information on stocks just wasn't available to the individual investor in the pre-Internet age. It seemed the brokerage community and others on the inside knew things well ahead of the public at large. Information flowed through a number of hands before reaching the populace, thus assuring a dependency on the brokerage firms for accurate investment information. Times have changed, thanks to the Internet. These days, you can receive scads of information—investment newsletters, stock-split alerts, index analyses, market watches, news alerts, and portfolio summaries—via e-mail or by just surfing the more than 10,000 financial web sites. But easy access to information and the emergence of more than 100 online brokerages has increased, rather than decreased, the complexity of the investment selection process. The overwhelming task of becoming a savvy online investor is generating a tougher learning curve than ever before.

This chapter introduces the basic parameters of individual stocks. To make money in the stock market, you have to know what you're looking for and what to do with this knowledge once you find it. So just how do you filter out the unimportant stuff? You start by gaining a strong understanding of stock basics.

Learning to trade is a cumulative experience. Successful traders
never stop being actively involved in the learning process.

WHAT IS A COMPANY?

Webster's Dictionary defines a company as "a number of persons united for the same purpose; either in private partnership or a business concern." I like this definition because it cuts to the chase: A company is unified by a central purpose. Determining this purpose is an excellent way to get the general picture of a company's motiva-tion for doing business. If this purpose tangibly relates to the present and future needs of the consumer, then the company's stock has a good chance of surviving. It is important to remember that researching a company is more than just gathering a bunch of small details. Successful investors strive to combine these details with the big picture to create a whole vision of the company in question from the top down and the bottom up.

Determining how a company's business relates to long-term business trends worldwide is akin to recognizing its growth potential. Long-term growth is the key to a company's success.

In their most basic form, there are two kinds of companies: *private* and *public*. The main difference between the two is that stock in a private company is not traded on an organized stock exchange. Hence, it is quite difficult to assess a private com-pany's value. If a small private company is growing by leaps and bounds, it requires an influx of capital to keep up with rising demands. To generate this money, a com-pany may decide to become a public company.

Private company: A company that may or may not issue private stock and is nevertheless not publicly traded.

Public company: A company that issues stock to be traded on the public market.

WHAT IS A STOCK?

Stock is another name for the shares, or partial ownership, of a corporation. If you wish to buy a stock, you do so by purchasing fractional units of ownership called shares. A share's value is the result of a multitude of factors. Discerning whether the price of a share is moving—either up or down—is the crux of the investing game. There are two kinds of shares: *common* and *preferred*. The differences between the two are outlined in Figure 3.1.

Ultimately, the choice between common and preferred shares comes down to risk. If you want a more limited risk-reward situation, then preferred shares are the way to go. But the majority of investors buy stock for the growth opportunities they provide, and are therefore willing to assume the inherent risks that accompany them.

Perhaps the most defining aspect of common stock is determined by its place in the time line of company development. In many ways, a company is a living entity. From birth to old age, it passes through a number of stages that control its daily movements. To become acquainted with a company, it is vital to know which growth phase the company is in. The stages of growth are fivefold and are akin to the stages of human development. Figure 3.2 details the characteristics a company shows in each stage of development.

Common Shares	*Preferred Shares*

• Common shares offer larger potential rewards than preferred shares; shareholders share the rise in stock price more quickly than preferred shares.
• If a common stock declines in price, shareholders share these losses, and the value of their shares may drop dramatically.
• Although shareholders of common stock are eligible to receive dividends, companies are not obligated to distribute a portion of the profits back to the common shareholders (i.e., they do not offer investors guaranteed performance results).
	• Preferred shares are a hybrid between bonds and common stock. Because of their hybrid nature, their prices act like neither the firm's bonds nor the common stock prices. The more bondlike it is, the more it will mirror the bond pricing; the more like common stock it is, the more closely it follows the price changes of the common stock.
	• The particular features of any one preferred stock are spelled out in the legalese of the issuance, as determined by management and approved by the common stockholders.
	• Features of preferred shares may or may not include such criteria as:
	  – Guaranteed dividends at regular intervals—cumulative or noncumulative.
	  – Limited dividend amount, which does not rise in relation to a company's profits.
	  – Voting inferiority (or superiority) to common stock depending on the specific agreement.
	  – Possible convertibility into common stock or bonds.

Figure 3.1   Common versus Preferred Shares

There is actually another stage, often referred to as the "skateboard effect," which takes place when the mature company reinvents itself. My favorite example of this phenomenon is Arm & Hammer (CHD). This old-line company had been selling baking soda to America's families for years, relying on population growth and increased interest in cooking to spur growth and earnings. However, by the late 1950s/early 1960s, prepared and packaged foods were coming into vogue and Arm & Hammer's sales were dwindling. When the odor-absorbing attributes of baking soda were pointed out to the marketing department, a clever ad campaign was developed to convince Americans to buy the yellow box, open it, leave it in the refrigerator for a month or so, and then simply throw it away. Of course, the ads never pointed out that the odor-absorbing capabilities were directly related to the exposed surface area, and that it would do just as much good to sprinkle a little on a flat plate and after a few weeks just throw that small amount away. Probably 90% to 95% of good product was being thrown out each time. The marketing campaign was so clever that the company's sales bounced back. Today, Arm & Hammer has branched out into a multitude of baking soda–based products including toothpaste, carpet cleaners, and detergent. An old-line company that was rapidly losing sales is now back on the upside, and its growth curve looks like a skateboard jump—hence the skateboard effect.

Company Development Cycles and Examples	Human Correlation	Stock Characteristics
Private company	**Birth**	• Fundamentals are not easily discerned due to private nature of vital statistics. • Stock has limited availability, privately placed. • Risk is generally quite high due to requirements for operating capital, lack of revenue.
Initial public offering (new stock that's never been traded) biz.yahoo.com/ipo	**Childhood**	• Stock performance characteristics are not available (no technical analysis available). • Initial excitement (hype) can artificially boost stock price. • An IPO is subject to acceptance by the investment community and integration of its technology into marketplace (when applicable). • Profitability may be years in coming for start-ups. • Long-established companies, privately held for years, represent favorable situation due to strengthened balance sheet and existing name recognition.
Early-stage growth company Amazon.com (AMZN) Verity (VRTY) Red Back (RBAK)	**Adolescence**	• Companies in this stage usually reinvest all of their profits back into the company to promote successful growth. • These companies rarely (if ever) pay dividends to their shareholders. • Stocks in this stage are considered aggressive investments, but have the potential for major gains (and substantial losses). • This is an absolutely critical "make it or break it" time for the development of a company.
Successful growth company Microsoft (MSFT) Sony (SNE) Micron (MU)	**Adulthood**	• Once a company evolves to the point where it can start paying out a percentage of its profits to shareholders in the form of dividends, it moves into its adulthood. • Although it still needs to reinvest most of its profits back into the company, it has paid its dues to create a successful infrastructure fostering consistent growth.
Mature company General Electric (GE) Ford (F) Procter & Gamble (PG)	**Old age**	• Once a company hits full maturity, a larger percentage of its profit is consistently paid out as dividends to shareholders. • It's hard to teach an old dog new tricks—mature companies have to fight just as hard to stay in the game.

Figure 3.2 Stages of Development

WHAT IS A STOCK CERTIFICATE?

A stock certificate is a legal document and can be used to transfer ownership of stock shares. Once you have purchased shares of stock, the company issues you a stock certificate (see Figure 3.3). The certificate includes important information pertaining to stock ownership: the stock's issuer, the shareholder's name, the corporate seal, and the number of shares it represents. Each certificate is identified by a registration number assigned by the Securities and Exchange Commission, which makes it harder to sell stolen certificates.

Another number you'll find is assigned by the Committee on Uniform Securities Identification Procedures, called the CUSIP number. Par value is still another number that can be found on the stock certificate. It represents a dollar amount assigned to a security when first issued. For stocks, par (also known as face value or principal) is usually a small dollar amount that bears no relationship to the security's market price. In other words, it's not that much! Par value does not represent the price you paid for the shares.

Originally, the par value was an estimate of what the company should be worth. That number was used as a guideline for pricing the shares of stock. Even today, when a new corporation is formed, state law generally requires the first shares of stock to be sold at, or above, par value. After the first sale, market pricing takes over and the next sale can be at any price, even below par value. In addition, states charge corporations a franchise tax each year based on the value of the company.

Figure 3.3 Stock Certificate (*Source:* Coca-Cola Co.)

This value is often determined by the par value times the number of authorized shares. Thus, the lower the par value, the lower the tax. As this valuation, and hence tax, can be substantial, you often see par values as fractions of a cent.

> *Most investors have their brokerage firms hold the certificates in "street name," meaning that you still own the stock, but it is held for safekeeping, which is a nice convenience. But the choice is yours to make; you may request to physically retain the certificate if you wish.*

TYPES OF STOCKS

The question every investor faces before putting one cent in the market is: What should I invest in? Although there are no official lists that divide stocks into separate categories, stocks are unofficially classified by size, as well as by the nature of their business, or *sector*. These unofficial classifications help investors to get a sense of a stock's parameters and the nature of the business. The advantages and disadvantages of each kind of stock depend on your investment goals and risk tolerance.

> **Sector:** An unofficial group composed of companies involved in the same industry, such as technology, energy, or biotechnology.

The size of a stock is primarily dependent on its *market capitalization*. Capitalization is easily calculated by multiplying the number of outstanding shares by the current market price per share. For example, if Microsoft (MSFT) currently has approximately 5.3 billion shares outstanding, and is trading at approximately $70 per share, the software giant has a total market capitalization of approximately $371 billion ($70 \times 5.3$ billion = $371 billion).

> **Market capitalization:** The value of a company calculated by multiplying the number of outstanding shares by the current market price per share.

Using market capitalization as a guide, stocks can be broken down into four size categories: large-cap, mid-cap, small-cap, and micro-cap (see Figure 3.4). Large-cap stocks represent companies with a capitalization of more than $5 billion. Also commonly referred to as blue-chip stocks, large-caps are generally mature companies with tremendous assets all over the world. The term "blue-chip" is derived from the game of poker in which blue chips have the highest value. Blue-chip stocks are regarded as safe investments because they do not run the risk of going belly-up. They are traded on the major exchanges and provide regular dividends to shareholders—perhaps their most appealing advantage. Unfortunately, large-caps rarely experience the fast growth that smaller stocks can create. But slower growth is offset by reliable dividends and the reduced risk of loss. Examples of large-caps

Stock Description	Valuation Range	Examples
Large-cap stocks (blue-chip stocks)	More than $5 Billion	GE, MSFT, F, PG Dow Industrials ($INDU)
Mid-cap stocks	$500 million to $5 billion	Minimed (MNMD) Power One (PWER) S&P 400 MidCap ($MID) (www.spglobal.com/ssindexmain400.html)
Small-cap stocks	$150 million to $500 million	Onyx Pharmaceuticals (ONXX) Labor Ready (LRW) Russell 2000 Index ($RUT) S&P SmallCap 600 ($SML) (www.spglobal.com/ssindexmain600.html)
Micro-cap stocks	Less than $150 million	"Penny stocks" and Stocks priced under $2 (www.pinksheets.com)

Figure 3.4   Market Cap Examples and Web Sites

are easily found all over your home. These companies manufactured your appliances, probably designed and built your car, and represent the newly merged, megamedia conglomerates of our time. Blue-chip coompanies are dedicated to maximizing profits for their shareholders. The Dow Jones Industrial Average is primarily comprised of blue-chip stocks.

Mid-cap stocks have a market capitalization of between $500 million and $5 billion. Mid-caps typically experience slower growth than small-caps and faster growth than large-caps. In addition, mid-cap stocks are not difficult to buy and sell since they are actively traded, making mid-cap positions easy to enter and exit. Mid-caps often bestow dividends on their shareholders, but not as regularly as large-cap stocks.

Small-caps have a market capitalization of between $150 million and $500 million. They offer traders the opportunity for fast growth and are usually much cheaper than mid-caps or blue-chip stocks. Lower starting prices give them the ability to generate dramatic price gains. Unfortunately, they also have a greater capacity for failure. Small-cap stocks rarely (if ever) issue dividends because of their need for capital to fuel further growth. They are often undervalued because institutional coverage (by analysts) has not begun or analysts are in the initial stages of research, and therefore their stories haven't been disseminated very well. Institutional investors often can't buy into them because the smaller companies don't meet fiscal requirements that govern the investments of many money managers and pension funds. They may be overvalued because investor sentiment has exceeded even optimistic valuations, removing fear from buying (and selling) decisions, thus driving up the price. The sudden and sometimes extreme pullbacks these stocks experience are sobering events. In spite of that, small-caps are attractive investments because they offer investors the chance to get in on the ground floor of the next Dell Computer.

> *There's a web site—www.smallcapstocks.net.com—that specializes in helping investors find undervalued and overlooked small-cap stocks.*

Micro-cap stocks have a market capitalization of less than $150 million. They can be extremely risky investments because a significant percentage of companies fail early in the development cycle for a variety of reasons: poor management, failure of a marketing strategy, customer rejection of goods or services offered, and so on. If you decide to venture into the realm of micro-caps, make sure you do your homework first. I'm not saying that you can't or won't make a profit (or even a fortune); just be very careful.

> *For more information on micro-caps, check out the Stockpage (www.thestockpage.com) or the Pink Sheets (www.pinksheets.com).*

Another way to classify a stock is by the nature of its objectives. These useful categories include income, cyclical, growth, turnaround, and green stocks. Figure 3.5 shows a breakdown of their characteristics.

I mention these unofficial categories to help you to focus on the kind of stock that fits your investment parameters. If you're in the position to invest aggressively, then growth and turnaround stocks may hold your interest. Long-term investors may prefer to invest in large-cap income and established growth stocks because they provide a safer investment approach. Regardless of which kind of stocks you choose to focus on, it's still absolutely imperative to know how to research them before putting your money on the line.

THE MECHANICS OF STOCK INVESTING

When you get right down to the heart of the issue, the mechanics of stock trading involve either buying or selling shares of stock. Both techniques come with their own sets of advantages and disadvantages depending on market circumstances. When evaluating any trading strategy it is important to assess the risk and reward possibilities and probabilities. This information helps a trader to decide whether a trade is worth the money invested in it.

Buying Stock

The objective of buying shares of stock (or *going long*) is to make money in a rising or *bull market*. Buying stock is pretty self-explanatory. You buy stock in a company for a specific price. If the stock rises in price, you can sell the shares for that higher price and pocket the difference. Buying stock, or going long the market, is easily the most popular method for novice traders to begin with. It starts getting complicated only if you decide to buy the shares on margin.

Type of Stock	Characteristics	Examples
Income stocks— Conservative	• Solid companies that offer slow but steady growth. • Regularly pay out dividends to their shareholders. • Do not offer dramatic returns.	Exxon Mobil (XOM) 3M (MMM) Bank of America (BAC) Duke Energy (DUK)
Cyclical stocks— Conservative	• Fluctuate in relation to the economy, seasons, or events. • An excellent gauge for the strength of the economy.	PPG Industries (PPG) Weyerhaeuser (WY) Alcoa Inc. (AA)
Growth stocks— Aggressive	• Rarely pay out dividends to their shareholders because they prefer to reinvest their profits for future growth. • Two kinds of growth stocks: established-growth and emerging-growth. Established-growth stocks have seen several years of successful expansion. In contrast, emerging-growth stocks are the up-and-comers that are currently experiencing dramatic expansion, yet have limited previous growth experience. Both offer investors the potential to make dramatic gains or heavy losses depending on market performance.	Cisco (CSCO) Dell Computer (DELL) Home Depot (HD) Charles Schwab (SCH)
Turnaround stocks— Agressive	• Stocks that have suffered severe losses that are due for a turnaround—investors have to know when a stock has reached rock bottom and just what can make it rebound. • Offer explosive growth opportunities. • No guarantees and high risk. • Warren Buffett's favorite stock-picking method.	Blockbuster (BBI) Peapod (PPOD) Dr. Koop.com (KOOP) Rite Aid Corp. (RAD)
Green stocks— Varies	• Environmentally friendly and socially conscious stocks. • Spawned the concepts of conscious investing and corporate accountability. • If saving the rain forests is high on your priority list of things to do, green stocks are definitely worth checking out at www.greenmoney.com or www.goodmoney.com.	Enron (ENR) The Williams Co. (WMB) Ben & Jerry's (BJICA) Adolph Coors (RKY) US West (USW)

Figure 3.5   Breakdown of Stock Categories by Objective

Going long: To buy stock, options, or futures in order to profit from a rise in the market price.

Bull market: A rising stock market over a prolonged period of time, usually caused by a strong economy and subsequent increased corporate profits.

There are two ways to place a long stock position: from a cash account or a margin account. If you use a cash account you are simply buying the stock straight out by incurring a debit in your trading account for the total amount ("cash and carry"). With a margin account, you have (but are not obligated to use) borrowing power for purchasing securities. Your brokerage agrees to put up half the cash for the trade, thereby increasing your leveraging power 2 to 1. Each firm will, however, charge you interest on the money lent. Although this sounds good on paper, there are additional risks associated with buying stocks on margin. Specifically, if the stock drops, your brokerage will more than likely require you to post additional money to secure the position. If you don't have enough money to cover the margin call, your position will be automatically closed, incurring a loss on the position.

Cash account: An account in which the customer is required to pay in full for all purchased securities.

Margin account: A customer account in which a brokerage firm lends the customer part of the purchase price of a trade.

Margin: A required deposit contributed by a customer as a percentage of the current market value of the securities held in a margin account. This amount changes as the investment price changes.

In either case, a long stock position is completely at the mercy of market direction to make a profit (see Figure 3.6). Going long demands an uptrend in the market for the trade to be successful. In today's volatile markets, many traders prefer to hedge their positions using a variety of alternative trading instruments (like options and/or bonds).

Bottom line: If you go long without hedging your position, you are depending on market direction to make a profit.

Short Selling Stock

If a market is trending down there's a technique known as *shorting the market* that can be used to take advantage of a drop in prices. Let's say you're watching a stock and you anticipate a price decline. You can borrow the shares from your brokerage firm in order to sell them at a higher price (selling them short) and at a later date buy them back at the lower price to replenish your brokerage's supply. When you short

Long Stock

Entry Strategy = Buy shares of stock.

Exit Strategy = Sell shares previously purchased at a higher price, pocketing the difference.

Market Opportunity = Look for a bullish market where a rise in the price of the stock is anticipated.

Maximum Risk = Limited to the price of the stock as it approaches zero.

Maximum Profit = Unlimited as the price of the stock rises above the initial purchase price.

Breakeven = Price of the stock at trade initiation.

Figure 3.6   Long Stock Strategy Review

the market, you receive a credit in your trading account reflecting the proceeds of the sale. That's right. As long as you have enough money to cover the margin requirements of the sale (usually 150% of the total credit received from the sale), your broker will lend you shares of stock to sell. Sounds inviting, but unfortunately, sooner or later you have to *cover the short* by giving the shares back to the brokerage—hopefully by purchasing them back at a lower price on the open market. This settles the account with the broker, and you get to keep the change. Therefore, your profit on a short position is equal to the amount the stock has moved down between the time you sold short the shares to open the position and the time you bought shares to close the position (minus the commissions).

Shorting the market: The sale of shares that a seller does not currently own. The seller borrows them (usually from a broker) and sells them with the intent to replace what he or she has sold through later repurchase in the market at a lower price.

Cover the short: To buy shares of stock to replenish those borrowed from your brokerage to place a short sale.

Let's look at a specific example of the mathematics of shorting. EMC is currently trading at $85\frac{1}{2}$ per share. If you want to go short 100 shares, you'll receive $8,550 in your account for shorting the shares. To place the trade, most brokerages will require you to post a margin deposit of 150% or in this case $12,825 ($8,550 × 1.5). Let's say the stock drops to 75 and you decide to close the position, or cover your short. You then cover the short by buying the 100 shares at the lower price of $7,500. You get to keep the profit of $1,050—the difference between what you originally sold them at and what you bought the shares for times the number of shares in the transaction [100 shares × (85.5 − 75) = $1,050].

At first, it may be hard to grasp the concept of making money by selling something you don't own; but short selling, although risky, is actually one of the basic methods used by successful traders in the trading game.

Shorting borrowed stock is a more aggressive approach to trading. It is a high-risk strategy, because if the market turns bullish a trader will eventually have to buy the shares back at the higher price to cover the short. For example, as mentioned, to go short 100 shares of EMC at 85½ per share, you'd need to post an additional $12,825 margin requirement (150% of the total credit from the sale) in your trading account. However, you'd also have to have enough money in your account to meet an increased margin requirement for the position in case the market price increases. The amount of money or margin depends on your brokerage's terms, but you can bet it's a lot of money to have tied up in one trade if you're just starting out. However, shorting the market is a very common technique in trading and definitely part of the bigger picture for most experienced traders (see Figure 3.7).

If you are interested in shorting a stock as a means of investing, consider these important points before jumping in headfirst:

1. Margin requirements can be high. Brokerage firms require hefty margins be-cause they are taking a risk. The stock you borrowed may rise (instead of fall) in value. You will then be obligated to buy it back at the higher price to cover your short.

2. If the stock were to pay a dividend, the short seller would be responsible for the payment.

3. Holding a short position in the stock for over one year does not constitute a long-term capital gain.

4. Capital gain tax shelters are for long stockholders, not short sellers.

Short Stock

Entry Strategy = Sell shares of stock you don't own by borrowing them from your brokerage firm.

Exit Strategy = Buy back shares at a lower price, pocket the difference, and return shares to the lender.

Market Opportunity = Look for a bearish market where a fall in the price of the stock is anticipated.

Maximum Risk = Unlimited to the upside.

Maximum Profit = Limited to the full price of the stock shares as they fall to zero.

Breakeven = Price of the stock at initiation.

Figure 3.7 Short Stock Strategy Review

One of the big differences to take into account about buying and short selling stock comes in the form of risk. Short selling stock equals *unlimited risk*, and buying stock equals *limited risk*. But exactly what is the difference? If you jump in front of a bus, you run the risk of dying. That's unlimited risk. If you only ran the risk of breaking your arm, this would be limited risk. Which one would you prefer? Although throwing caution to the wind (whether in a short or a long position) may seem like a courageous act of wild abandon, limited risk is a more sustainable approach to everyday trading. You have to go wherever the least risk and best possible reward is presented in everything you do.

Unlimited risk: The maximum amount of money that can be lost in a trade is infinite. For example, short selling comes with unlimited risk because there is no limit to how high the stock price can rise above the amount for which it was sold.

Limited risk: The maximum amount of money that can be lost in a trade is a finite and known amount. For example, buying stock comes with limited risk because the stock can fall only to zero, which means you risk only the amount you paid for the stock.

As you can see, short selling has its pros and cons. Although the seller receives the money in advance, there is the threat of unlimited risk and high margin requirements to deal with. I prefer to use short selling as a means of hedging risk by employing a combination of stocks and options to create nondirectional trades that make money regardless of whether the stock goes up *or* down! This is the only way I would ever short the market, because I'm protected in the event the stock rises before I can replace the shares I borrowed.

CASH AND MARGIN TRADING

Determining how much money you need in order to make your first trade can be very tricky. The exact amount depends on a number of factors, including your market selection, the size of the transaction (number of shares), and the risk on the trade. It also depends on whether you want to do your trade using a margin or a cash account. Cash trades require you to put up 100% of the money in cash. All costs of the trade need to be in the account before the trade is placed. For example, if you wanted to buy 100 shares of EMC at 85$\frac{1}{2}$, you would have to pay $8,550 plus commissions up front. If EMC were to rise to 90$\frac{1}{2}$, the account would show an open position profit of $500, or a 5.8% *return on investment (ROI)*, not including commissions.

Return: The income profit made on an investment.

Return on investment (ROI): The reward on a trade divided by the trade's risk.

In contrast, margin trades allow you to put up a percentage of the total cost of the trade amount in cash and the rest is "on account." The term "margin" refers to the amount of money an investor must pay to enter a trade, with the remainder of the cash being borrowed from the brokerage firm. The shares you have purchased secure the loan. Most traders prefer a margin account because it allows them to leverage assets in order to produce higher returns. In addition, a margin account is usually required for short positions and options trading.

Brokerages are usually willing to lend you 50% of a trade's cost, but often require a certain amount of money be left untouched in your account to secure the loan. This money is referred to as a margin requirement. Now here's the rub. If the stock you buy on margin goes down, you may receive a *margin call* from your brokerage requiring a larger deposit in your account or you will be automatically exited from the position. That's why margin trading can prove fatal to novice traders who overextend themselves through the use of margin.

Based on the rules of the Securities and Exchange Commission and clearing firms, if you want to purchase stock, margin equals 50% of the amount of the trade. At this rate, margin accounts give traders 2 for 1 buying leverage. If the price of the stock rises, then everyone wins. If the price of the stock falls below 75% of the total value of the initial investment, the trader receives a margin call from the broker requesting additional funds to be placed in the margin account. Brokerages may set their own margin requirements, but they are never less than 75%—the amount required by the Fed.

Margin call: A call from a broker signaling the need for a trader to deposit additional money into a margin account to maintain a trade.

Of course, brokers don't lend money for free. They charge interest on the loan amount over and above the commissions on the trade. The interest and commissions are paid regardless of what happens to the price of the stock. The margin's interest rate is usually broker call rate plus the firm's add-on points. This rate is cheaper than most loans, as it is a secure loan—the broker has your stock, and in most cases will get its cash back before you get your stock back.

Margin on short selling is extremely expensive. In general, you have to be able to cover the entire cost of the stock plus 50% more. However, this value changes as the market price fluctuates. Selling short only works if a drop in the market price occurs. But if the stock price rises, you will eventually have to buy back the stock to cover your position for more than you received for selling it. If a stock has been heavily shorted and the price starts to rise, a buying flurry among short sellers occurs, and this activity can drive the price even higher. If the price rises, you will receive a margin call from your broker requesting more money to cover the increase in the price of the stock. If you don't have enough money to cover the difference, you will lose your position.

Ultimately, there are no absolutes when it comes to margin. Each brokerage sets its own requirements according to company policy. Combining the buying and selling of options and stocks may create a more complex margin calculation. However, these strategies usually have reduced margin requirements in comparison to just buying or shorting stocks alone. Since every trade is unique, margin will depend on the strategy you employ and your broker's requirements.

Margin calls are a reality that traders have to deal with every day. Unless you have a crystal ball that forecasts the future, there are no sure bets. Obviously, the larger your capital base becomes, the less you have to worry about margin. But it's always a good idea to keep margin in mind and do not let yourself get overextended, no matter how enticing that "just-one-more" trade looks.

If you're worried about the margin at the initiation of the trade, you probably shouldn't place the trade. This guideline can keep you from putting on positions that are larger than you can really handle.

GETTING THE LOWDOWN ON QUOTES

The Internet has made the process of reviewing stock prices (or *quotes*) extremely easy. There are hundreds of sites that provide quote services. Some provide real-time quotes, but many more are delayed by at least 15 to 20 minutes. If you want to receive streaming real-time data on a portfolio of stocks and options, you must be willing to pay for it (check out eSignal at www.dbc.com). You can also visit the exchanges directly or simply use your brokerage's online quoting service.

One of my earliest remembrances of the stock market is looking in the newspaper and being overwhelmed by the sheer volume of tiny little numbers in the business section. It's hard to look at those numbers and not be psyched out by the obvious complexity of the markets. Although the Internet has done a lot to temper this situation, understanding the meaning behind the numbers still takes time. It's easy to get a detailed quote at the click of a mouse (see Figure 3.8), but understanding what those numbers mean and why are they important is another story.

When you look up a stock's price, each quote is followed by several categories

Qualcomm Inc (QCOM)

Delayed Quote as of NOV 20, 2000 11:54:12 AM (E.T.)

Last	85.250	Change	↓ -3.563
Open	86.625	% Change	↓ -4.01%
High	87.500	Low	84.250
Bid	85.250	Ask	85.375
52 Week High	200.000	52 Week Low	51.500
Earnings Per Share	0.85	Volume	4.56M
Shares Outstanding	747.65M	Market Cap	63.74B
P/E Ratio	104.49	Exchange	NASDAQ

Figure 3.8   Snapshot Quote for Qualcomm (QCOM) (Courtesy of Optionetics.com)

that describe various price values and additional data. These tiny numbers convey enough information to give you a general feel for a stock. Do not confuse this first impression for knowledge. If you want to get to know a stock, you have to look a lot deeper than a snapshot quote. Even though you can't judge a stock by its cover, you can use these basic numbers to get the lay of the land.

The most immediate number is known as the last and represents the *last* known price for the stock. Obviously this price varies depending on whether you are receiving a delayed or real-time price. The next thing to keep in mind is the bid-ask spread. As previously explained, as an off-floor trader you buy at the *ask* price and sell at the *bid* price. The last price is usually somewhere between the two. The *open* price tells you at what price the stock started out at the beginning of the day, and the *high* price lets you know the highest price the stock has sold for that day. All of these prices give you a feel for how the stock has been trading that day. Figure 3.9 provides a review of the most popular terms used in everyday quotes.

A snapshot quote is just the beginning of the research process. True researching of a stock takes a variety of forms, and the selection process you choose has to fit your objectives. But you can be sure that it will combine elements of the three basic analytical approaches: *fundamental, technical, and sentiment analysis.* Each of these important methodologies has its own set of tools that are used to assess where a stock has been and where it's headed. Entire books have been written about each of these analysis approaches. But since this book is dedicated to helping you develop the ability to filter out too much information, I will restrict my discussion of these subjects to the contents of a few chapters (Chapters 7 through 10).

Fundamental analysis: An approach to trading research that uses economic and production data to determine a company's fair value and to forecast future stock price movements based on balance sheets and income statements, past records of earnings, sales, assets, management, products, and services.

Technical analysis: Built on the theory that market prices display repetitive patterns that can be tracked and used to forecast future stock price movement, technical analysis is a method of evaluating securities and commodities by analyzing chart patterns and statistics generated by market activity, such as past prices, volume, momentum, and stochastics.

Sentiment analysis: An attempt to gauge investor sentiment by analyzing the subconscious of the marketplace through the use of specific psychological market criteria. The interpretation of these criteria is not cut-and-dried; hence, the utilization of psychological market indicators depends on a trader's unique interpretation of the facts (as do fundamental and technical analysis as well).

TYPES OF ORDERS

To do any job well, you have to use the right tool for the right job. So as a trader, you have to find a good trade and use the right order technique that will enhance the trade's success. In short, you have to decide how you want to place it. There are a

Data	Definition
Last	The last price that the option traded for at the exchange. For delayed quotes, this price may not reflect the actual price of the option at the time you view the quote.
Open	The price of the first transaction of the current trading day.
Change	The amount the last sale differs from the previous trading day's closing price.
% Change	The percentage the price has changed since the previous day's closing price.
High	Highest price for the current trading day.
Low	The lowest price for the current trading day.
Bid	The highest price a prospective buyer (floor trader) is prepared to pay for a specified time for a trading unit of a specified security. If there is a high demand for the underlying asset, the prices are bid up to a higher level. Off-floor traders buy at the ask price.
Ask	The lowest price acceptable to a prospective seller (floor trader) of the same security. A low demand for a stock translates to the market being "offered down" to the lowest price at which a person is willing to sell. Off-floor traders sell at the bid price. Together, the bid and ask prices constitute a quotation or quote, and the difference between the two prices is the bid-ask spread. The bid and ask dynamic is common to all stocks and options.
52-Week High	The highest price the stock traded at in the past 52-week period.
52-Week Low	The lowest price the stock traded at in the past 52-week period.
Earnings per Share	The bottom line (net pre-tax profit) divided by the number of shares outstanding.
Volume	The total number of shares traded that day.
Shares Outstanding	The total number of shares the company has issued.
Market Cap	Shares outstanding multiplied by the closing stock price.
P/E Ratio	Stock price divided by the earnings per share; P = Price/E = Earnings per share.
Exchange	This indicates where a company lists, or registers, its shares (e.g., New York Stock Exchange).

Figure 3.9 Quote Term Definitions

wide variety of order techniques you can apply to help your trade work out. Figure 3.10 provides a brief review of various ordering types.

There are two extremely popular ordering techniques: the market order and the limit order. The difference between a market and a limit order is simple. Entering a *market* order means you're willing to pay the lowest asking price at the time your order hits the trader selling it. That price may or may not be the price quoted! Markets move quickly with the new technology that exists, and someone may have entered a huge buy order two seconds before yours hit, nudging the "best ask" price up a quarter point just before your order arrives on the floor. It sometimes works to your favor, too. The final execution price is called a fill. Good fills, bad fills—it's the risk you take when you enter a market order. But one thing's clear: If you enter a market order, you're going to get filled very quickly more times than not.

A *limit* order indicates that you are willing to pay the price you say or less, period. If you say, "I'd like to buy 100 shares of EMC at 85," then you have entered a limit order that requires your broker to purchase 100 shares of EMC only if he (or she) can get the order filled at $85 per share or less. A limit order does not guarantee execution, but it does guarantee that you'll get the price that works for your strategy.

GETTING STARTED

In Chapter 1, we figured out how much money you can and should invest. In Chapter 2, you learned how to open an account at the right kind of brokerage for you. Next, you need to determine the length of time the money will be in the market. If you're a recent college graduate your risk parameters will be very different from those of a person set to retire in 18 months. Time should be considered along with risk because when you will need to have the money will indicate to a great extent how you should invest.

Before they invest a penny, most people want to know: Can I lose money in stocks? Can I lose everything? Yes, you can lose money; and if you set your mind to it, you could lose it all. Companies begin and end all the time, so it's critical to find the right companies to invest in. Even then it's critical to determine how long it will be before you need your investment capital back. Stocks sometimes experience periods where they go up for an extended time, and then consolidate, even drop in price. When they go up, it's called a *bull market*; when they drop it's considered to be a *bear market*. A rising market is referred to as a bull market because bulls buck up with their horns. Declines are called bear markets because bears swat down with their paws.

Bull market: A rising stock market over a prolonged period of time, usually caused by a strong economy and subsequent increased corporate profits.

Bear market: A declining stock market over a prolonged period of time, usually caused by a weak economy and subsequent decreased corporate profits.

If you absolutely need your money by a given date, and it's a bear market, you run the risk of selling when prices are less than when you bought initially. The

Type of Order	Description
At-even orders	Should be placed without a debit or a credit to the account. That means that you may have to wait until the market gets to the right prices for your trade to be placed.
At-the-opening orders	Should be executed at the opening of the market or should be canceled.
Day orders	Remain good only for the duration of the trading day when entered, and are canceled at the end of the trading day if not executed.
Good till canceled orders	Remain in effect until executed or explicitly canceled, or the contract expires.
Immediate or cancel orders	Must be executed immediately in whole or part as soon as entered. Any part not executed is automatically canceled.
Fill-or-kill orders	Must be executed immediately or by a specific date as a whole order. If not, the order is canceled.
Limit orders	Specify a maximum buying price or a minimum selling price.
Limit buy orders	Must be executed below the current market price.
Limit sell orders	Must be executed above the current market price.
Market-on-open orders	Must be executed during the opening of trading.
Market-on-close orders	Must be executed during the closing of trading.
Market orders	The most common type of order—buying or selling securities at the price given at the time the order reaches the market. This can be different from the price on your broker's screen. A market order must be executed at the best price the market has to offer. It is the only order that guarantees execution.
Market-if-touched orders	Combined market and limit orders, whereby the order becomes a market order when the options or stocks reach a specified price.
Market-if-touched buy orders	Become buy market orders when the options or stocks fall below the current market price.
Market-if-touched sell orders	Become sell market orders when the options or stocks rise above the current market price.
Stop orders	Used to limit risk, they become market orders when the options or stocks reach a certain price.
Buy stop orders	Become market buy orders upon a trade at or above the specified price.
Sell stop orders	Become market sell orders upon a trade at or below the specified price.
Stop limit orders	An extension of stop orders, where the activated order becomes a limit order instead of a market order.

Figure 3.10 Types of Orders

avoidance of this situation is obviously very important. The person with a 20-year time horizon can afford to let an investment go through these inevitable cycles, whereas the person set to retire in five years and needs the funds to supplement his or her pension must be more cautious.

So, can you lose money? If you own stock in a good company and sell when conditions are rotten, you bet. So the trick is to invest according to your personal time frame, so you're not creating a market risk. (The major risk is not dependent on the company staying afloat, but rather that you may be forced to sell at an inopportune time—a down cycle in the market.)

As mentioned earlier, there is a wide array of stocks that range from aggressive to conservative investments. Time plays a factor here, but so does personal tolerance for risk. Most of us have had to work very hard to save the money that goes into the stock market. While the market does fluctuate in value, it has outperformed any other kind of investment vehicle over the long run. Even with that knowledge, some people cannot tolerate the thought that the dollar they invested may be worth less than that a few months later. They fret and stew and read the paper daily to see if they're back to even yet, as nightmares of living under a bridge (or worse) haunt them. The stocks they choose to invest in will most likely be much more conservative than the ones bought by a dot-com bachelor who has a much higher risk tolerance, is comfortable with the market's ups and downs, and never loses any sleep over losses.

Stress is not an enhancement to the trading process; it's a liability. Buy stocks and choose strategies that allow you to sleep at night!

That's the key: Buy stocks you can live with, avoiding stocks that make you crazy with worry. Figure 3.11 shows the different categories of stocks. Create a portfolio of these stocks that best suit your particular needs, time horizon, and risk tolerance, otherwise known as your *investment profile*.

Experienced investors know to spread their risk out over a variety of stocks, from conservative to aggressive. This is also known as asset allocation. Asset allocation is the percentage of your portfolio that's invested in stocks, bonds, and cash. More aggressive portfolios will be more weighted in stocks, less in cash. The opposite is true for conservative investors; they'll have a greater percentage of funds in cash and less in stocks. How your portfolio is structured is where a good financial planner or top-notch broker can help tremendously. Your portfolio should be a blend of different types of stocks, from conservative to aggressive; the percentage or *weighting* of each category should meet your own investment profile. In other words, if you're more interested in preservation of capital, you shouldn't have a lot

Income	Growth and Income	Growth	Aggressive Growth	Speculative
Utility stocks	Blue-chip stocks with a dividend	Mid-sized to large-cap stocks	Small to mid-cap stocks	Start-ups, turnaround situations

Figure 3.11 Quick Reference Guide

of aggressive growth stocks (if any) in your portfolio. The opposite is also true. If you're a 28-year-old with no family and making a good living, conservative growth stocks should have the least weighting in your portfolio. It's all about your risk profile. Take your time in the creation of your own profile. Don't worry—you can and probably should change it as time goes on.

Weighting: The percentage breakdown of stocks, bonds, and cash in an investment portfolio, as well as the types of stocks that comprise the stock portion of the portfolio (i.e., aggressive, growth, green, cyclical, and income stocks).

Investment profile: Refers to the risk tolerance of an investor, the suitability of the type of investments based on the person's age, financial condition, and psychological ability to tolerate risk.

If you've ever opened up the financial pages of a newspaper, you've probably been astounded by all the tiny little numbers that detail the previous day's market performance. To a novice's eyes, these pages might as well be written in Greek. But there's no reason to panic. It doesn't take a degree in rocket science to understand the markets—just the patience and determination to monitor the few stocks you choose to specialize in. As you get to know a few stocks, you should be able to learn certain lessons through them that are applicable to other stocks.

Luckily, there are certain steps you can take before investing in the stock market. First, consider that a stock is really a unit of ownership. As such, you want to be the owner of a high-quality company. I feel that the greatest potential lies in identifying growth companies with mid to large capitalization. Second, make an assessment as to what areas of the market are likely to attract money. Personally, I think the flow of capital is likely to favor the U.S. market because of this country's dominance of corporate (especially technology-oriented) enterprises and the sustained growth in our overall economy.

I am a big believer in the future prospects of high-tech stocks. The unparalleled volatility of this sector has provided me with countless opportunities to increase my net worth. These stocks run the gamut from rising Internet standouts to computer-oriented stars. If you want to learn to trade, you absolutely have to get to know the stocks in these sectors.

A good place to start is the "tech section" of CNNfn
(cnnfn.cnn.com/news/technology/techstocks). Another great site is
Whatis.com (www.whatis.com). Bring your lunch, as
there's a ton of useful information about all things technical.

In order to help you learn how to monitor stock performance (and inspire you to specialize), I recommend tracking the following five stocks. These stocks represent five promising investments that should teach you a lot. Since each stock has tremendous influence, tracking them can help you understand various analysis techniques and how news and economics impact stock prices. Start by using Figure 3.12 as a

Company:	Entry Date:
Industry Sector:	Capitalization:
Present Price:	52-Week High:
Target Exit Price:	52-Week Low:

Quarterly Figures

Quarter	Earnings per Share	Sales
Latest Quarter		
Previous Year Quarter		
% Change (Latest Quarter—Previous Year Quarter)		

Five-Year Price-Earnings Figures

Year	Price		Earnings per Share	P/E Ratio			
	52-Week High	52-Week Low		High	EPS	Low	EPS
Total							
Average							
Is the current 52-Week High or Low higher or lower than the average?			Is the current P/E ratio higher or lower than the average P/E ratio?				

Growth Rate

Current EPS		Next Year's Projected EPS		Growth Rate = Projected EPS Current EPS	
Current EPS		Projected EPS Two Years from Now		Growth Rate = Projected EPS Current EPS	

Five-Year Sales/Expenses Performance

Year	Annual Sales	Annual Expenses	Net Profit
% Change (Last Year—Two Years Ago)			

Price to Sales Ratio
(Every $1 of sales = "X" amount of investing value)

Year	Market Capitalization (# Outstanding Shares × Price per Share)	Annual Sales	Price to Sales Ratio (Capitalization—Sales)
% Change (Last Year—Two Years Ago)			

Figure 3.12 Stock Analysis Template

base form for your study and research. From there, please take advantage of the many web sites that offer *portfolio-tracking services*. These sites will send you daily quotes and news on the stocks of your choice directly to your computer via e-mail. There is no substitute for hands-on learning.

1. *America Online (AOL):* Regardless of whether you love it or hate it, you have to admit that AOL is the name to be reckoned with in the Internet access and e-commerce arenas. Since AOL is also one of the few Internet companies to make money, it is a strong long-term investment prospect.

2. *JDS-Uniphase (JDSU):* JDS-Uniphase is a high-technology company that designs, develops, manufactures, and distributes products for the growing fiber-optic communications market. It has been on an acquisition binge, and this is expected to continue. Some refer to JDSU as the Intel of fiber-optics.

3. *EMC Corporation (EMC):* EMC is a worldwide leader in the area of storage devices. As the need for storage continues its incredible growth of the past few years, EMC should also show dramatic growth in years to come.

4. *Qualcomm (QCOM):* Qualcomm was the biggest gainer in the S&P 500 in 1999. It is the world leader in what is expected to be the top technology for wireless technology, CDMA technology. QCOM has worldwide royalties that can propel the stock much higher.

5. *Yahoo! (YHOO):* Yahoo! is one of the most popular Internet companies on the Web. Recently added to the S&P 500, Yahoo! has many advantages over its competitors, including worldwide name recognition. Yahoo! has lots of room to grow over the next year and beyond.

Portfolio tracking service: A portfolio tracker is an online service provided by a financial web site or an online brokerage that enables an investor to keep track of the daily price movement, breaking news, and investor sentiment of a chosen list of stocks, indexes, and options.

ROADMAP TO SUCCESS

Objective	Course of Action
Company Stock	**Definition** • A company is defined by Webster as "a number of persons united for the same purpose; either in private partnership or a business concern." **Privately Held** • Difficult/impossible for outsider to purchase. • Valuations unclear—generally do not have audited financial statements. • Illiquid—no ready market.

Publicly Held
- Relatively simple to buy/sell.
- All financials easily obtained.
- Valuations determined by market forces.
- Generally easily liquidated.

Development Stages	**Birth** • Privately held. • Possible angel/venture capital involvement. • High-risk and illiquid. **Adolescence** • Initial public offering (IPO). • Possible high-risk situation. • Liquidity event for early-stage investors. • Price volatility is usually high. • Technical analysis virtually impossible due to lack of track record. **Childhood** • Early-stage growth company. • No dividends. • Still considered aggressive growth (risk still very much a factor). • Major investment returns still possible. **Adulthood** • Sustainable growth achieved. • Consistently profitable. • Possibility of dividend payouts. • Widely followed by brokerage community. **Mature Company** • Pays dividends. • Usually large market cap. • Long history. **Skateboard Effect** • Reinvention of a mature company after it has gone into decline. • Diversification of product line. • Innovative new marketing that generates major sales revenues.
Stocks	**Preferred** • Usually pays a fixed dividend. • Possible conversion feature. • Possible cumulative dividend (if company misses dividend, must pay missed dividends before any dividends can be paid to common stockholders). • If company is liquidated, preferred shareholders paid before common. • Often stockholders do not have voting rights. **Common** • Straight common has no conversion features. • More volatile than preferred. • Risk/reward ratio higher than preferred.

- No set dividend unless declared by company.
- Public stockholders have voting rights.

Proof of Ownership	**Stock Certificates** • Physical delivery of certificate. • "Denomination" (number of shares) displayed. • Not easily transferred from one person to another—certificate must be physically sent back to the company (or delivered to the brokerage firm) for issuance of a new certificate. **Street Name** • Held by brokerage. • No threat of loss, damage. • Monthly valuation updates. • Dividends, splits, and so on are automatically accounted for and added to the account.
Varieties	**Large-Cap** • Blue-chip stocks. • Long history of profitability. • Low risk. **Mid-Cap** • Mid to high market cap. • More growth oriented. • Slightly higher risk. **Small-Cap** • Much more aggressive growth potential. • $150 million to $500 million market cap. • Under-owned by institutional investors. • Higher risk, greater volatility. **Micro-Cap** • Small market cap, start-up stage. • High risk. • Possible illiquid market (tough to sell). • Wild price swings caused by rumors, and so forth. • Enormous returns possible, as well as similar losses.

Quotes	**Display of Previous and/or Current Trading Day's Information**
	• **Newspapers**
	    Open
	    High/low
	    Closing price
	    Volume (shares traded that day)
	    P/E ratio
	    52-week high/low
	• **Computers/Online**
	    Real-time or delayed
	    Bid/ask
	    High/low for day
	    Volume
	    % change from previous day's close

Types of Orders	**Market Order**

- Order is matched with another; price is flexible, which could mean unfavorable price execution.
- Usually fastest execution, if you want in or out, period.
- Lower commission charged at many brokerage firms.
- At-the-open orders—Executed at the market upon the market's opening. Poor execution prices highly likely.
- Market-if-touched—Combine market and limit orders, whereby order becomes market order when options or stock reach a specified price.
- Market-if-touched buy orders.
- Market-if-touched sell orders.

Limit Order—A limit order specifies a price that must be met (or better). No assurance order will be filled.

- At-even—No debit or credit to account. Delay possible while waiting for correct market to execute.
- Day orders—Good for that trading day only, cancels at the close if not executed.
- Good till canceled or GTC—Order stays open until canceled or executed.
- Immediate or cancel crder—Must be executed, in whole or partially, immediately, or order is canceled.
- Fill-or-kill—Fill the entire order immediately at specified price or cancel.

Stop Order—Used to limit risk, a stop order becomes a market order when option or stock reaches a specified level.

- Buy stop orders—Must be executed when the specified price is above the current market price.
- Sell stop orders—Must be executed when the specified price falls below the current market price.
- Stop limit orders—An extension of stop orders where the activated order becomes a limit order instead of a market order.

Determining a Stock Transaction	**Bull Market**

- Going long a stock in anticipation of an uptrend.
- Fundamental, technical, sentiment analysis show bullish signs.
- Limited risk (can only go to zero).

Bear Market

- Going short a stock in anticipation of a downtrend.
- Margin requirements are high.
- Is stock available to short?
- Unlimited risk. (How high can it go? You're on margin!)
- Fundamental, technical, sentiment analysis show bearish signs.

Payment Options: Cash and margin.

The Use of Margin	**When to Use It**

- Bull market.
- Certain options strategies.
- Short sales.

Margin Requirements
- Brokerage will lend you (usually) 50% of a straight stock purchase (if stock is marginable).
- Requirements vary for shorts, option trades.
- Interest is charged.

How to Use It
- Specify when placing order.
- Broker will tell you margin requirements beforehand.

Margin Calls
- Regulation T issued when account equity drops below certain level.
- Cash deposit required immediately.
- Cannot sell to meet Reg. T in some cases.
- Forced liquidation, usually at the worst times.

Useful Web Sites	**Biofind** (www.biofind.com): Guide to biotech stocks and new findings. **Direct Stock Market** (www.dsm.com): Provides info on public and private offerings. **Good Money** (www.goodmoney.com): Socially and environmentally friendly investment guide. **Moody's Investment Services** (www.moodys.com): Leading provider of credit ratings, research, and financial information of the markets. **Quote.com** (www.quote.com): Comprehensive site for all your stock research needs. **Signal Online** (www.dbc.com): This site is actually hosted by DBC Online and is *the* dynamic state-of-the-art, real-time quoting service. **Standard & Poor's Equity Investor Service** (www.stockinfo.standardpoor.com): Not just a renowned index anymore, this site offers great insight into S&P stocks and more. **Stockpage** (www.thestockpage.com): Specializing in small and micro-cap stocks. **Silicon Investor** (siliconinvestor.com): Comprehensive guide to high-tech stocks. **Yahoo! Finance** (finance.yahoo.com or www.yahoo.com/business.com): One of the best sites on the Web to become familiar with the world of stocks and options.

4

Critical Trading Approaches

For the past decade, the stock market has become more than America's favorite pastime. It has become the lifeblood and driving force behind the U.S. economy. People from all backgrounds have become mesmerized by the incredible wealth generated by the market in such a short period of time. The potential for significant wealth creation is a prime catalyst that will undoubtedly continue to lure more people into the market. Whether you're 25 or 55, if you're serious about the market insofar as it helps you achieve a nest egg of suitable size to provide a measure of support in your golden years, the best place to start is sometimes the least palatable: an unblinking and rigorous self-assessment.

Before you know what you need to become a successful trader, it's necessary to figure out what you already have.

This exercise is in no way meant to replace any planning already done with a Certified Financial Planner or some other financial professional. Hopefully it will help support their advice. But for the rest of the crowd that is wondering what asset allocation is all about, this is the first step.

BRASS TACKS

In Chapter 1, I outlined a system for determining your financial bearings. In order to get where you want to go in the investment arena, you have to take into consideration:

- *How much* you have to get started with.
- *How long* you have until you need the money.
- *How much time and effort* you want to put into the investment process.

If you haven't taken the time to fill out the handy forms in Appendix A, now's the time! Look at it this way: If you're afraid to face the music now, what'll it be like in 5 or 10 years? It doesn't get any easier. Here are a couple of tips for those of you who just don't know how to get started.

- **Savings:** How long could you live off your savings if tomorrow your income suddenly stopped? If it isn't at least three months, start saving. Don't get fancy trying to play catch-up. Put it into the bank and leave it. When you get to three months of rent money, groceries, and utilities, begin stashing away money for your trading account.

Pay yourself first! If you haven't done this before, and your savings aren't what you'd like them to be, do something different! They say that doing the same thing over and over again and expecting different results is a form of insanity. So take 5 to 10% off the top of your next paycheck and put it away.

- **Contributions:** Contribute as much as you possibly can into your company 401(k), IRA, anything. This will lower your annual tax bite and allow your money to grow tax-deferred. This is a big deal, and if you're not doing this, start. If you do have money in a *qualified account*, get a handle on recent performance. Contact information is on the monthly statements. Call the fund. Pay attention!

Qualified account: An account that allows you to deduct your contributions from your gross income, and the money is not taxed until you withdraw it.

If you have both savings and consistent contributions to funds already in the works, and have some capital that's not earmarked for a near-term event (like rent), let's move on to finding the best approach that suits your investment profile.

For performance evaluations and in-depth detail about virtually every fund on the market today, you can't beat Morningstar's free site. Plus it has a very useful feature called the IRA calculator. This is a great way to see the tremendous earnings power that a qualified account can deliver. The longer it's in there, the better it will do. Go to: www.morningstar.com. For a complete list of mutual funds, go to: www.investorlinks.com/mfcomp.html.

ASSET ALLOCATION

Asset allocation is a term that describes the diversification of your investment dollars in order to mitigate risk as well as take advantage of market cycles and trends. If it's a bear market, your mix will be substantially different than if the market's red hot (going up a lot!). To give you a sense of how to divide your portfolio up on a risk basis, I've created the grid found in Figure 4.1. Since markets are forever changing and time marches on, you'll need to reevaluate your initial strategy at least once a quarter (four times a year).

Years until Retirement	% Aggressive/ Small-Cap	% Growth/ Large-Cap	% International	% Bonds	% Cash
30+	25%	25%	20%	15%	15%
20+	25%	30%	15%	15%	15%
15+	20%	35%	10%	20%	15%
10+	20%	30%	15%	20%	15%
5+	15%	30%	10%	30%	15%
Retired!	5%	30%	5%	50%	10%

Figure 4.1 Asset Allocation Table

After you've identified your time horizon and the risk tolerances you can live with, it's time to determine what sector or group of stocks is attracting the most investment dollars. Different sectors move in cycles of their own. An increase in use of semiconductors spells a rally for that group while interest rate–sensitive stocks suffer when interest rates increase. Keep in mind the fund managers of the biggest institutions in the world are overachieving MBAs who work tirelessly to seek out these groups before they begin to move. They anticipate changes in the economy and get there (hopefully) before the crowd. Therefore, looking for volume increases in stocks can help you to determine which sectors are on the move.

John Bollinger's EquityTrader.com is a fun and informative web site that provides an abundance of information to help you research various sectors (www.equitytrader.com). Zacks Investment Research is another great site to screen for finding promising stocks (my.zacks.com/index.php3). Zacks provides snapshot profiles of companies, ranks within the industry group, and a very useful area called "The Whole Enchilada." I use it to look for stocks of all sizes with the strongest broker upgrades (and downgrades) as well as a host of other goodies.

You may want to start by simply looking in the back of *Investor's Business Daily* where 197 sectors are ranked in order of strength. Once you've found the sectors that are the strongest, look for stocks within those groups that meet your personal criteria. Figure 4.2 shows a few examples of stocks that fit into these categories.

THE SIMPLE METHOD (FOR THOSE TOO BUSY TO BE BOTHERED)

If you feel like you just don't have a taste for this sort of thing (i.e., studying charts, sectors, the economy, etc.), you're not alone. Asset allocation in investing is a mighty task. If you're already saving but want things laid out for you and monitored, there are funds available that take the hassle out of it. They're called *life-cycle funds* and they take into account your age and risk tolerance. Life-cycle funds invest your money, either as a lump sum or monthly savings, into strategic portfolios that take into account interest rates, bull markets, bear markets, big- and small-cap stocks, bonds and cash, everything.

Aggressive Growth		Growth		Growth and Income		
Large-Cap	Mid-Cap	Large-Cap	Mid-Cap	Large-Cap	Mid-Cap	Mid-Cap/Income
America Online (AOL)	Smith International (SII)	Hewlett-Packard (HP)	Forest Labs (FRX)	Duke Energy (DUK)	National Fuel Gas (NFG)	Duke Weeks (DRE)
EBay (EBAY)	Silicon Storage Tech. (SSTI)	International Business Machines (IBM)	Seagate Technology (SEG)	Enron Corp. (ENE)	Equitable Resources (EQT)	Boston Properties (BXP)
Immunex (IMNX)	Cree Inc. (CREE)	Cisco (CSCO)	TriQuint Semiconductor (TQNT)	Boeing (BA)	MCN Energy (MCN)	Spieker Properties (SPK)
Juniper Networks (JNPR)	Finisar Digital (FNSR)	Ericsson Telephone (ERICY)	Brocade Comm. (BRCD)	Southern Co. (SO)	American Water Works (AWK)	Equity Office Properties (EOP)
ONI Systems (ONIS)	Avanex (AVNX)	General Electric (GE)	Inverness Med. (IMA)	Reliant Energy (REI)	Raymond James Financial (RJF)	Rite Aid (RAD)

Figure 4.2 Stock Evaluation Chart

The biggest problem with this approach is the fact that many life-cycle funds are too diversified to be effective. Not putting all your eggs in one basket makes sense—to a point. Too much diversification virtually assures you you'll be in a good sector and a bad one at the same time, the two performances canceling one another out. Here's what I recommend doing if you just want someone to take this "problem" off your hands (you still have to do something!).

Age = Under 30

Investment Position = Lump Sum to Invest
Get aggressive and invest in America's future. Put a minimum of 60% in an aggressive growth fund, 30% in a moderate or big-cap growth fund, and keep the rest in cash.

Investment Position = No Funds Available
Save on a monthly deposit plan with an aggressive growth fund. Since you're investing once a month, you'll automatically utilize dollar-cost averaging. When the market is high, you'll buy fewer shares; when it's low, you'll buy more of them (since the dollar amount you invest is constant). The trick to making big money is not so much the rate of return you achieve, it's the number of shares you own! Think about it. If you own 100 shares of a $10 stock and it goes to $20, you make $1,000. However, if you own a thousand shares you'd make ten grand! So the trick with these funds is to accumulate shares. Every uptick means more cash. Downturns in the market should be viewed as buying opportunities. Just don't stop saving.

Age = 35 to 45

Investment Position = Lump Sum to Invest
Keep 10% in cash, and split the remaining 90% into two growth funds, preferably in two different fund families. Different managers have different strategies that work better in some markets than others. Two funds/two families spreads the risk just enough to cover yourself and keep the performance moving full speed ahead.

Investment Position = No Funds Available
If you're starting from scratch, get aggressive, but not stupid. Invest until you've reached $10,000 in one fund (aggressive growth), and then put that same amount into a less aggressive growth fund. When you've done that, keep splitting your deposits between the two for as long as you can, or until you're within five years of retiring.

Over 45

Investment Position = Lump Sum to Invest
Invest 60% in growth, put 35% into a reputable bond fund (reinvest those dividends!), and keep the rest in cash. Keep saving!

Investment Position = No Funds Available
Roll up your sleeves, because you're going to need a killer offense and an even better defense. Put each month's deposit in an aggressive growth fund, and save a minimum of 20% of your gross income. Time is critical, but there's still time enough to let it work in your favor. Benjamin Franklin called compound interest one of the greatest inventions ever: Let the money that earns interest earn more interest. For example, suppose you had a choice between being given a lump sum of $500,000 or a salary of one cent a day that doubles every day for a month. Figure it out. Which one would you choose? (Use 31 days in a month.)

Never chase a stock. If you have your eye on a stock and it begins to move without you, and you sit back and wait for the pullback that never comes, forget about it. Buying after a good run up in price is a good way to lose money.

IDENTIFYING OVERALL TRENDS IN THE MARKET

Identifying the general trend in the market is an important factor every investor needs to determine before committing any capital to an investment. It's not enough just to review the prices of some stocks you're interested in. You have to take a look at the big picture and determine the bullish or bearish nature of the market as a whole.

Market trends have life spans marked by a beginning, midlife, and an end. A person can read the business section in the paper for a week and get a good idea of whether the market is in a bullish trend or a bearish one. But determining where it is along this continuum is even more critical. Committing fresh capital into a lofty market (the kind we saw in the first few months of 2000) could spell trouble. Likewise, entering into a late-stage bear market (buying too early) could be frustrating as stocks keep trying to hit bottom.

Being correct in trend identification can overcome incorrect decisions concerning purchases of inferior stocks. Why? Two of my favorite trading sayings speak to this issue: "Don't confuse a bull market for brains" and "A rising tide lifts all boats." These two sayings are a good way of explaining that, when the bull is running overall in individual sectors, most stocks do well and it's relatively easy to pick a winning stock.

So how do you spot a trend? Start by watching the *market averages*, also known as stock indexes. CNNfn front page lists these in an easy-to-read format (cnnfn.cnn.com/markets/us_markets.html). Some of the most important ones to watch are listed in the market spreadsheet in Figure 4.3.

The best-known indicator of market direction is the Dow Jones Industrial Average. Its daily fluctuations are covered, albeit briefly, on virtually every news channel and financial web site. But in reality it represents only 30 companies—a narrow slice of the broad market. However, since it has been used to gauge market performance for so long, it still carries a lot of weight.

The term *broad market* is a nebulous term that addresses all stocks traded on every exchange. The S&P 500 ($SPX) tracks the movement of 500 companies thought to best exemplify the U.S. economy. The Nasdaq Composite ($COMPQ) measures the market value of all the domestic and foreign common stocks listed on the Nasdaq exchange, while the NYSE Composite ($NYA) measures the New York Stock Exchange's performance. Each index supplies vital information as to the nature of each day's trading action. By monitoring them, you can get a feel for the broad market's performance.

NOW WHAT?

The next six chapters go much deeper into the available tools that help you to find your way in the market. I can't tell you what will work best for you, because everyone needs to find a system that works best for their lifestyle. The stock market is so vast that it requires a variety of measurements to gauge its temperament as well as

Direction	Market	Level	Change	Last Update
Up	Dow Jones Industrial Average ($INDU)	10,964.44	97.43	8/8 15:40
Down	Nasdaq Composite ($COMPQ)	3,852.65	–10.34	8/8 15:39
Up	S&P 500 ($SPX)	1,481.84	2.52	8/8 15:39
Up	Russell 2000 ($RUT)	510.16	0.29	8/8 15:40
Up	NYSE Composite ($NYA)	665.44	1.92	8/8 15:40
Down	Dow Transports ($DJT)	2,887.41	–6.80	8/8 15:40
Up	Dow Utilities ($DJU)	356.76	2.72	8/8 15:40
Down	AMEX Composite ($XAX)	913.87	–1.59	8/8 15:40

Figure 4.3   Market Average Spreadsheet (August 8, 2000)

direction. It's important to look at a variety of things to get a sense of or feel for the market. I'd be the first one to admit that I often get confused by what the market is telling me. But one cliché has served me well: "It's better to be out of the market wishing you were in it, than to be in the market, wishing you were out!" To help you get your bearings, the following sections describe some of the indicators I use when looking for profitable situations in the market.

> *In or out, it's wise to keep an eye on the trends. Sometimes I think that the market is governed with clichés, but they're so true much of time. Here's another good one: "The trend is your friend until the trend ends."*

MARKET ACTION

Since three out of four stocks follow the general trend of the market, assessing overall market action on a day-to-day basis is an important piece of the investment puzzle. Bull and bear markets can be determined by doing everything from watching government reports to gauging specific stocks in leading sectors. Technical analysis can also be of enormous help (see Chapter 9) in determining general market trends while sentiment analysis (see Chapter 10) is a good indicator not only of current trends, but of possible turning points as well. (*Investor's Business Daily* is a great place to review current sentiment conditions.) Figure 4.4 reveals the general characteristics of bear and bull markets.

> *Remember that fear and greed become overdone at market extremes, leading to major movement up or down, high volatility, and heavy volume.*

MOVING AVERAGES

One of the most basic methods of determining a stock's performance is to review a price chart. Prices are plotted each day along with volume to create a visual picture of the stock's movement. But price action is just the beginning of the story. A *moving average*—probably the best known, and most versatile, technical indicator—is an important visual tool used to track price changes using various time lengths. To calculate a 50-day moving average (50-DMA), simply take the last 50 days' closing prices on either a stock or an index, add them up, and divide by 50. Then each day the oldest price is dropped and newest price added, which changes the average. Each day's average is then plotted, connecting the dots, to form a line that extends day-to-day.

> **Moving average:** A moving average is a technical analysis tool used for judging a market's current trend. By using a simple mathematical procedure to smooth or eliminate the fluctuations in data, moving averages assist in determining when to buy and sell.

Bull Market	Bear Market
Bar graph of daily prices are above 200-day moving average.	Bar graph of daily prices are below 200-day moving average.
Interest rates are steady or declining.	Interest rates are increasing.
Unemployment numbers are increasing.	Unemployment numbers are dropping.
Inflation is steady or dropping.	Inflation is on the rise.
Earnings reports show increases compared to last year, same quarter.	Earnings are declining when compared to previous year.
Advance/decline line is consistently positive (more winners than losers).	Advance/decline line is negative (more losers than winners).
Market closes at the high for the day.	Market sells off toward the close, or at the lows for the day.
Strong volume on up days, and rallies for several days in a row.	Weak volume on up days; rallies fail due to increased selling pressure into strength. Big volume on down days.
Trend line is clearly positive.	Trend line is clearly negative.
Pessimism is still clearly evident (fear still exists).	Optimism is still clearly evident (greed still exists).

Figure 4.4   Characteristics of Bull and Bear Markets

Technicians (people who employ technical analysis exclusively to monitor the markets) track moving averages carefully. Individual traders, professionals, and institutional investors primarily use the 50- and 200-DMA as a method of timing buys and sells, as well as locating key support levels. A major signal to buy or sell occurs when a shorter average crosses a longer one (see Figure 4.5). When a crossover occurs, it's a strong signal that the trend has shifted. If you have a computer, moving averages are easy to find and track. Quote.com is one of the best web sites that offers this tool (www.quote.com).

Sometimes a stock will "bounce" or rise again when it reaches the 50-DMA. After bouncing off the 50-DMA, the stock climbs quickly as momentum and buy-and-hold investors feel that the crossover confirms the *support* level and once again buy shares of the stock. On the other hand, the stock may also continue to sell off if the 50-DMA drops below the 200-DMA. In this case, a flood of selling drives the stock down sharply in a no-confidence vote. At some point, however, bargain hunters step in; buyers overwhelm the sellers, and this leads to an upward move in the stock's price. At this point, the 50-DMA serves as a *resistance* point instead. These kinds of interpretations help traders determine market trends as they take an initial scan of a stock or index.

> **Support:** Support is a historical price level at which falling prices stop falling and either move sideways or reverse direction.
>
> **Resistance:** Resistance is a historical price level at which rising prices have a hard time breaking through to the upside.

TRADING APPROACHES

There are numerous strategies people can use when investing in the stock market. However, there are three general approaches: *growth, value,* and *momentum.* Let's take a look at each of these approaches so that you can get a feel for the kind of investing that suits your lifestyle and investment goals.

Growth Investing

Throughout the past decade, investing in growth stocks has been one of the most popular styles of investing. A *growth stock* is a company whose earnings and/or revenues

Figure 4.5   Nasdaq Composite Index with 50- and 200-Day Moving Averages (Courtesy of QCharts (www.qcharts.com))

Growth stock: A relatively new stock that continues to show healthy expansion and strong earnings, and invests its profits into the continued growth of the company rather than providing dividends to its shareholders.

are expected to grow more rapidly than the average earnings of the overall stock market. Generally, growth stocks are extremely well managed companies in expanding industries that consistently show strong earnings. Their objective is to continue delivering the performance their investors expect by developing new products and services and bringing them to market in a timely fashion. For example, a growth investor may purchase Cisco Systems (CSCO) stock because of the company's dominant market share and its potential for sustained high earnings growth. Dell Computer (DELL) also grew at an incredibly fast rate in the 1990s as shown in the price chart in Figure 4.6. These types of companies generally do not pay dividends to shareholders because they need all their available cash to fund the rapid growth. As a result of the potential for spectacular earnings growth, these types of stocks are usually priced higher (in terms of P/E ratios, etc.) than a value stock. As long as earnings continue to grow, investors assume the price of the stock will grow as well.

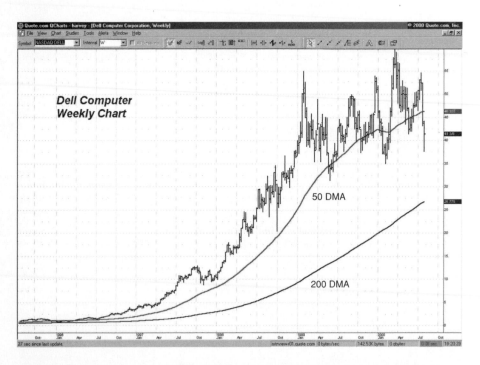

Figure 4.6   Dell Computer Weekly Chart with 50- and 200-Day Moving Averages 1996–2000 (Courtesy of QCharts (www.qcharts.com))

Value Investing

When evaluating a company, the value investor is more interested in a company's tangible assets and not as concerned with the future earnings prospects of the company. A *value stock* signifies a bargain because the stock appears to be priced below its real worth. The great bull market of the past decade has taken the breath out of many value investors because growth stocks have performed superbly and value stocks have underperformed the market. This is because many of the best-performing stocks had no *book value*. They were *cyber* stocks, not brick and mortar. Investors seemed to throw old economy valuations out the window, literally betting these new economy stocks would grow like Dell or Cisco.

Value stocks: Stocks that appear to be bargains because they are priced lower than their calculated worth.

Book value: A fundamental measurement of a common share calculated by subtracting the par value of outstanding preferred shares from the net worth of the company (as shown on the balance sheet), divided by the number of common shares outstanding.

Value investors look to a company's balance sheet (see Chapter 8), subtract liabilities from assets, compare the result to the current market price, and then make a decision as to the attractiveness of the stock. Finding value, especially when investing, does not refer to finding the cheapest stocks out there with respect to prices. Finding value means discovering something others failed to see that provides hidden value to the company and turning that discovery into a profit. Hidden value could be in the form of real estate worth more than it cost as shown on a company's balance sheet. Other types of hidden value can be unlocked by restructuring the company to run more efficiently, improving the operations of the company so that customers buy more products, lowering the cost structure of the company, or introducing a great new product.

The primary objective of a value investor is to use fundamental analysis to buy a company for less than what the investor thinks it is really worth.

Momentum Investing

Momentum investors are more technically oriented than value investors; that is, they look at how a stock is behaving by applying various methods of technical analysis. They are concerned primarily with a stock's price pattern and other technical indicators, rather than the company's earnings, price/earnings (P/E) ratio, or other fundamental criteria. Specifically, they look for indications that a stock is going to continue in the same direction for the time being (see Figure 4.7). Momentum

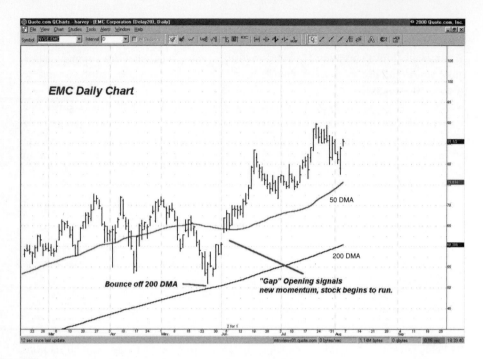

Figure 4.7   Momentum Move in EMC (Courtesy of Quote.com)

investors like to find the primary trend of a stock or index and invest with that momentum in hopes of profiting from it. Once again, as long as earnings expectations are met and on the rise, the price of the stock will follow suit.

> **Momentum:** When a market continues in the same direction for a certain time frame, the market is said to have momentum. A momentum indicator is a technical indicator that utilizes price and volume statistics for predicting the strength or weakness of a current market. Momentum trading exists when a trader invests with (or against) the momentum of the market in hopes of profiting from it.

The momentum style of investing tends to be shorter-term and looks for results immediately. Momentum investors want a quick burst of energy from fast-moving stocks. They employ different tools, like *oscillators*, to help them pinpoint these types of opportunities. Utilizing price and volume statistics, oscillators are used to predict the strength or weakness of a market, determine overbought and oversold conditions, and locate turning points within the market. Momentum charts and *rate of change* (ROC) oscillators can help initiate momentum investing in order to trade with or against the momentum of the market. The trick to momentum investing is being able to anticipate when the primary trend is going to reverse, so that the investor is able to get out of the position profitably and to be in place to take full advantage of a big move in the opposite direction.

Figure 4.8 provides the characteristics of each of these investment approaches (plus the IPO market, discussed in the next section) as well as their advantages and disadvantages.

Oscillators: Technical indicators used to identify stocks and options with overbought or oversold prices that may trigger a trend reversal.

Rate of change: Used to monitor momentum by making direct comparisons between current and past prices on a continual basis. The results can be used to determine the strength of a price trend.

A WORD ABOUT VENTURE CAPITALISTS AND THE IPO

Some new businesses can grow organically: The business owners can buy, lease, or otherwise acquire the necessary resources to grow their business to the point it can generate revenues. But for many businesses, start-up costs are too great for the founders to fund on their own. Costs may include salaries for high-level employees, expenditures for expensive equipment, or funds to develop proprietary technology. Because the business is unproven, a bank is unlikely to lend the new concern money without substantial security. In this case, outside funding becomes necessary.

Many businesses turn to *venture capitalists* (VCs) because new businesses are considered high-risk investments. A venture capital firm is usually comprised of the managing partners and professional staff, who select and manage the investments, and outside investors. Venture capital firms are set up as partnerships, meaning that the investors *are* the partners. Partners do *not* always manage investments. The VC will invest in stages as more capital is needed and certain benchmarks are achieved. Each stage usually brings increasing percentage levels of equity to the VC and its investors.

Venture capitalists: Outside investors that provide financing in the form of equity, secured loans, and unsecured loans to a nonpublic firm, most often in start-up situations. Typically, venture capital financing entails relatively high risk, and consequently venture capitalists look for high potential returns usually from the equity position they take in the firm.

In order to generate a return to their investors, VC firms have to have a way to convert their investments back into cash. This is usually done through some sort of exit strategy, most commonly an initial public offering (IPO) or a merger. This allows the venture capitalists to sell part of their stake in the company for a profit.

The IPO is the first time that shares are made available to the general public. Before the offering occurs, the company has to comply with a wide range of rules and

Approach	Characteristics	Advantages	Disadvantages
Growth	• Growth rate is highly dependent on the rate of compounding. • High return on equity (ROE). • Debt levels vary. • Rarely pay dividends to shareholders—reinvest their profits in R&D, production, and marketing. • Sound balance sheet. • Competitive advantage.	• Proven record of earnings. • Sound management. • Good brokerage research available. • Analysts know the industry and sector well. • Good prospects for long-term wealth creation.	• Sector downturns directly affect them. • Management upheavals can derail growth plans. • Negative earnings surprises can send the stock down for extended periods. • Somewhat dependent on good market conditions to perform.
Value	• Fundamentally sound. • Conservative. • Usually lower beta than market. • In bull market, it's not unusual for this group to lag.	• Assets measurable and marketable. • Low chance for bankruptcy. • Compelling rationale for buyers to buy "$1 for $.50."	• Time required for market to recognize the value may be long. • Experience poor returns when compared to broad market during waiting period.
Momentum	• Technicals are attractive. • Price pattern is consistent, buyers appearing on the dips. • Momentum lasts for varying periods, from days to weeks.	• Quick rewards when you buy correctly. • When they're hot, they stay hot. • Good liquidity.	• Potential high risk from "greater fool" premise. • When they cool off, the losses can be large if you stay in. • Option premiums high.
IPO market	• Frequently large price increases from the offering price to where it opens (begins trading in the open market). • Pent-up demand for those that didn't get shares at offering price. • Price swings wild and unpredictable.	• If you're lucky enough to get shares allocated to you, you're in a good spot. • Rich opportunity for the trader with early entry and a quick exit finger. • Many IPOs turn into good long-term investments.	• Good markets bring increasingly lower-quality IPOs, making it difficult to determine quality. • Poor liquidity when prices fall. • Lots of traders to compete against. • Playing field is not level!

Figure 4.8 Trading Approach Matrix

regulations from the *Securities and Exchange Commission (SEC)*. In brief, the regulations require the company to create a disclosure document that discusses the strengths and weaknesses of the company, the competitive environment, and its plans for the future—in general to protect the new shareholders. The *prospectus*, or document that discloses this information, is then reviewed by the SEC to verify that all statements are true and accurate. The SEC's approval enables potential investors to evaluate the company.

Securities and Exchange Commission (SEC): Commission created by Congress to regulate the securities markets and protect investors. It is composed of five commissioners appointed by the President of the United States and approved by the Senate (www.sec.gov).

Prospectus: A formal written document that describes the plan for a proposed business enterprise, or the facts concerning an existing one, that investors need to make informed decisions.

The IPO is a liquidity event for the initial investors because it is the first time that they are able to resell their equity shares and realize a profit. In an IPO, the company sells a fixed number of shares to the public. Many of the shares sold are shares that were held by the early-stage investors. Many times, the shares held by VCs may have been bought for pennies and can now be sold in the IPO for hundreds (or even thousands) of times their initial investment.

Determining the initial sales price for an IPO stock is both an art and a science. Investment bankers are largely responsible for creating and assessing demand for the IPO. Offering prices fluctuate, sometimes wildly, based on the general atmosphere for IPOs at the time. The investment bankers will try to set an initial price that raises the most money for the company while at the same time making it appealing to a wide number of investors.

It's nearly impossible to tell how reasonable the initial pricing is beforehand. The IPO-oriented investor of the late 1990s has been richly rewarded, with single-day gains of several hundred percent in some cases! A lot of pre-IPO hype creates a huge demand for shares. As the excitement wears off, sometimes the price of the new issue stays higher than the IPO price; other times it sinks, never to recover. Unless you are a founder or one of the early venture investors, you run the risk of buying at the top, and losing big. This is a very aggressive game.

THE SELECTION PROCESS

There are a few ways to select a stock, ranging from the obvious to balance sheet detective work. Peter Lynch, the man credited with making the Fidelity Magellan Fund almost a household word, recommended buying stocks you know about. Stories grew from that wisdom of housewives buying Clorox stock, and there's more than a few rich people in Arkansas who bought into Wal-Mart, early or late, after seeing for themselves the impact and success each new store enjoyed. New fads often translate into skyrocketing charts for companies that catch the attention of investors and then dwindle into oblivion as the fad passes.

There's a multitude of magazines, newsletters, and web sites touting stocks that outperform or somehow enrich the pockets of anyone owning them. A lead to a good investment may be overheard while standing in line to buy groceries, or sitting reading magazines in the doctor's office. But never follow it blindly. Always research it before putting your money on the line. The basics any buyer wants to see before investing in a stock include:

- *What market sector is it in, and what's the competition like?* AT&T tried to sell microcomputers, but failed against the likes of IBM and Compaq. RC Cola versus Coke and Pepsi is a tough hill to climb. A new fast-food chain selling carp sandwiches isn't likely to make it.

- *How strong and entrepreneurial-minded is the management?* Good examples of the importance of solid leadership at the helm can be found at Apple Computer, where Steve Jobs turned a sinking ship into a profitable company with a bright future. Jack Welch of General Electric took a staid and mature company and turned it into a growth vehicle with his vision and leadership. Marc Andreessen, founder of Netscape, brings immediate legitimacy to any company he gets involved with, just like Steve Case of AOL or Wayne Huzienga of Blockbuster.

- *Do you understand what they do?* High-tech companies attracted and burned a ton of investors who were willing to buy anything with a "dot-com" attached to the name. Blind trust and overreliance on the action of the herd, coupled with being clueless about the nature of the business and expected profitability, make a recipe for disaster.

- *Focus on a few sectors.* Trying to learn about the entire market is virtually impossible. Becoming functionally knowledgeable about a few sectors is practical and can be profitable as well. Start with a sector that appeals to you. If you can't stand biotech stocks, don't invest in them. If oil exploration is of interest, you're more likely to enjoy researching it.

- *Find out what the experts think.* Many a web site provides research and offers a compilation of opinions. A brokerage firm's site (or their "hard" research) will keep you abreast of a sector's prospects. Zacks Investment Research gets down and dirty; it's a great place for information and recommendation summaries (my.zacks.com).

DESIGNING YOUR PORTFOLIO

Personal choice is the landmark of a stock portfolio. But to help you get a sense of how to start, I'd like to create a hypothetical portfolio with three stocks: growth and income, growth only (no income), and an aggressive growth company (33% in each category).

Growth and Income Example

Duke Energy Corporation (DUK) is one of North America's leading energy and energy services companies. It is involved in the production, transmission, and sales of energy and the delivery of energy-related services worldwide. This company has the ability to offer physical delivery and management of both electricity and natural gas throughout the United States and abroad. Duke Energy provides these services primarily through four business segments: Electric Operations, Natural Gas Transmission, Energy Services, and Parent and Other Operations, according to Zacks Investment Research company reports.

This corporation operates in the energy sector. Obviously, energy makes the world go around, and Duke Energy possesses the characteristics of a company with an eye toward growth; but it pays a dividend as well, currently $2.20 per share, payable in four quarterly installments.

Utilities tend to appreciate in value as bond yields go down; the stocks go down when bond yields go up. (Think of the two on opposite ends of a teeter-totter.) Figure 4.9 shows how Duke compares to the U.S. 30-year bond (the *long bond* as it's sometimes called). You're not going to hit a home run with Duke, but by reinvesting the dividends to buy more shares, you get the combination of compound interest as well as the potential for price appreciation. Utility stocks are a good start for any conservative portfolio.

Growth Example

EMC Corporation (EMC) is the world's technology and market leader in the rapidly growing market for intelligent enterprise storage systems, software, and services.

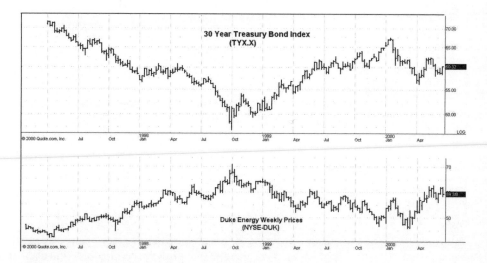

Figure 4.9 Duke Energy versus 30-Year Bond (Courtesy of Quote.com)

The company's products store, retrieve, manage, protect, and share information from all major computing environments, including UNIX, Windows NT, Linux, and mainframe platforms, according to Zacks Investment Research company reports (www.zacksadvisor.com).

Wow! What a chart (see Figure 4.10)! EMC has been a market favorite, and after looking at this chart it's not hard to see why. EMC just keeps plowing ahead, almost unaffected by market conditions. If you really focused in on the day-today fluctuations there would be some worry lines formed as a result, but since you're looking at the long run, tuck this one away and forget about it. This company, like virtually all pure-growth stocks, pays no dividend. You bought it to give your portfolio some high-octane fuel, but it is not considered way out on the risk scale.

Aggressive Growth Example

This category is not quite like Vegas, though some consider it to be. This category consists of newly formed companies with big ideas and bigger dreams. All of the blue-chip companies were once aggressive growth stocks. Stories abound of people who literally made millions. Phil Knight of Nike sold shoes out of the back of his car and stock in his company way back when. Runners got a better shoe than was otherwise available, and a $10,000 investment turned into millions. Microsoft, Dell,

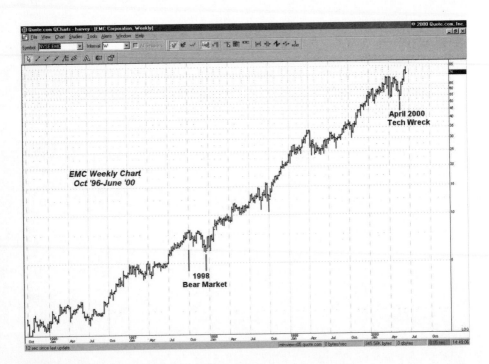

Figure 4.10   EMC Weekly Bar Chart (Courtesy of Quote.com)

and many other success stories convince us that a portion of our portfolio should be looking for these kinds of results.

Check Point Software Technologies Ltd. (CHKP) provides technology that permits the secure transfer of data over the Internet as Web traffic management solutions. As Web traffic increases, the need to provide security for online transactions will soar, as will the need for Web servers to accommodate the ever-increasing demands for server management. Check Point is a leader in these categories. According to Zacks Investment Research, 17 brokerage firms currently follow the company; of the 17, 13 rank CHKP a strong buy, while the others rate it simply a buy. Zacks ranks it a strong buy as well (as of June, 2000). Companies involved in building out the infrastructure of the Internet will do well for the foreseeable future, provided their technology remains at the forefront. Figure 4.11 shows the exploding chart of CHKP.

Portfolio Analysis

Your method for keeping track of your portfolio is a subjective one. Some people examine it daily, others once a month when their statements arrive. Creating a balanced portfolio that adheres to your objectives and risk tolerance is one of the keys to your success. Changes in valuations can skew this balance to a more aggressive weighting than you originally intended. For instance, let's say you want a portfolio

Figure 4.11   Check Point Software Price Chart (Courtesy of QCharts (www.qcharts.com))

consisting of 20% tech stocks and 80% blue-chip stocks. You have one tech stock (Rambus, Inc.—RMBS) and one blue-chip (General Motors—GM) in your portfolio as of December 1, 1999. With RMBS selling at $18 and GM selling at $72, the tech stock weighting is 20%. Three months later, GM is up almost 3% ($74) and RMBS is up 300% ($73). These new prices would give you a tech stock weighting of 50% (see Figure 4.12) if you didn't make any adjustments in that three-month period. This new weighting is far greater than your original 20% goal.

Figure 4.12 shows how a portfolio can remain unchanged stockwise, but the weighting can shift to a more aggressive weighting on its own. The portfolio begins with a technical stock exposure of around 20% and a blue-chip Dow stock makes up the remaining 80%. After the quick run-up, the weighting in the technology stock is approximately 50%, tipping the scales to a more aggressive tone. Now, a 50–50 mix of technology to blue chips is still prudent, provided your time horizon is sufficiently long to ride out any downturns in the tech sector. But if retirement is less than a year or so away, perhaps it's time to reduce your exposure to the techs and shift more toward something a bit more stable.

A word about betas: A stock's volatility is measured against the overall market. If it is more volatile than the Dow, it will have a beta greater than 1.0. If the stock has less price volatility than the Dow, the beta will be less than 1.0. Some web sites will provide you with a beta reading. This helps the investor understand the overall volatility of his or her portfolio.

There's a host of financial web sites with the capability to track the stocks and/or funds you own. I like the Optionetics Portfolio Tracker (www.optionetics.com) for a number of reasons. First, it's free (always a nice feature), but most importantly it allows you to track a wide variety of stocks, funds, options, even money market accounts, so that you're constantly abreast of your portfolio's performance. You can even check in to see the recent news that pertains to your investment, and the site offers the ability to do technical and fundamental analysis on the stocks you own or are thinking about owning.

Besides price, it makes a lot of sense to monitor the sectors your stocks are in. A cool web site that tracks sector performance is *SmartMoney*'s Map of the Market (www.smartmoney.com/marketmap). It's a graphic display that's easy to read and understand. Another good one that's a little trickier to maneuver around in but offers a much more in-depth look at sector performance and how the stock you own ranks within that sector is John Bollinger's Equitytrader.com (www.equitytrader.com). It

Stock	# Shares	Price	Value	% Portfolio	New Price	New Value	New % Portfolio
RMBS	500	$18	$ 9,000	20%	$73	$36,500	50%
GM	500	$72	$36,000	80%	$74	$37,000	50%
Totals			$45,000			$73,500	

Figure 4.12 Sample Portfolio Weighting Changes

takes some time to learn his proprietary system of charting and ranking of stocks and sectors, but it's well worth the effort.

If you're in the correct sector for current conditions, review the fundamentals as best you can. Chances are good the company has its own web site. If you're not yet a denizen of cyberspace, call the company up and ask for annual reports, quarterly reports, anything. Your brokerage firm probably has research that's current, and there's always the library. Many public libraries have the *Value Line Investment Survey*—a publication that's bigger than the New York phone book. The layout comes in easy-to-follow sections with understandable ratings for both the sector and the company. But if you are online, just surf over to Value Line's web site (www.valueline.com). I've read Value Line's stuff for years, and have found it to be a veritable treasure chest of information.

Dealing with Losses

I've been investing and trading for a long time now, and have learned that it doesn't matter who you are or how careful your investment choices are—you're still going to pick a loser now and again. That's just how it goes. A huge danger we all face is our own ego, the part of us that is so certain the market is wrong and we're right as to why our stock pick is certain to rise. So we hang on, and a small loss turns into a major source of pain as the loss keeps increasing or the stock goes dormant well below our entry point.

Cut your losses! *Investor's Business Daily*'s William O'Neil recommends selling a stock once you've incurred a 7% to 8% decline from your purchase price. Sometimes I just know in my heart I made an unwise buy or that the market isn't acting right, so I get out. There's no law that says you can't repurchase that stock later, when conditions improve.

On the other hand, what if you sell too soon in a rising market? Seller's remorse, or the fear of it, keeps many people in a stock or trade, because they're afraid the stock may continue moving up, seemingly forever. No matter who you are, the market will humble you. You'll sell too soon, and the stock will continue on to make a monster-sized move. Or you'll buy at the top, and take an embarrassing (and painful) loss. Or you won't buy, trying to outsmart the market, and it'll leave the station without you. If you invest long enough, all of these circumstances will beset you.

You've probably heard the saying "Cut your losses early." Preservation of capital is the most important thing you can master. Another great idea is just around the corner, so take your lumps and follow Mr. O'Neil's advice (and that of every other trader who has been around awhile): Control your losses. Here are some guidelines that can help:

- If you own a stock that has lost value from the time you purchased it, how has the overall market performed during the same time frame? If the market has done better than your stock, do not double down! (To double down is to buy more to lower your price basis.) If a stock is down 7% or 8%, dump it.

- Know before buying a stock what your parameters are: If it drops this much, I'm selling. Write down your purchase price and the date you bought it in a ledger, then subtract the maximum pain you're willing to endure if it moves against you. Don't ever try to make a decision while the market is open and you're feeling emotional.

- Study Chapter 9 on technical analysis. A stock's charts can often tell you the prudent entry points.

Chasing the Hot Stock

Somewhere along the way, perhaps when tech stocks began creating millionaires on a daily basis, many traders began to seek immediate financial gratification. They began chasing stocks that had already attracted the attention of institutional buyers to such a degree that their trendlines went vertical. Greed overcame good sense, and the *greater fool theory* worked until the fat lady started singing. Value investors buy a dollar for 50 cents; the hot stock chaser is usually buying something that's worth $1 for $1.25 in hopes of reselling it for $1.50. Chasing a train that's left the station is not practical because the odds are high that the person who bought it 20 points lower than you're buying it now is probably selling it to you. Wait for these rocket-stocks to cool off before getting into the game. And if a stock goes to heights heretofore unknown, so what? For every one you missed by not chasing it, there are dozens that fell back to earth. Stick with being a chooser, not a chaser.

Harboring the Fallen Stock

No matter how good at investing you get, there's going to be a loser in your account. As I mentioned before, if a stock falls off 7% from your purchase price, get ready to dump it. If it's down 10%, sell, period. Don't become a *religious* investor—someone who prays for his or her stock to come back up. Don't ever let a small loss turn into a big one. If it turns around after you sell it, you can always buy it back. Just don't argue with the tape, because you'll lose that fight every time. The market is the Great Humbler. Just when you get to thinking you're smarter than everyone, you'll get whacked. Stick to your stop-loss levels. If you take a loss, take it, and then get over it.

RULES OF THE TRADE

I don't mean to be harsh, but it seems with so much information around today, people believe their own malarkey. Nasdaq support, Dow trends, and on they go, fooling no one but themselves. If you're a novice, these rules may help you to stay in the game long enough to get good at it.

1. ***Stay away from chat board recommendations.*** The Net has brought us a lot of wonderful things, and some destructive things, too. Chat rooms that offer hot tips are not one of the wonderful things. If this is where you're getting your education and investment strategies, *stop!* Tips are the single most

destructive thing going, especially when they involve micro-cap stocks. Stranger or best friend, steer clear, or you'll end up learning the hard way.

2. *Avoid stock tips from magazines.* Don't get me wrong; I'm not saying don't buy financial magazines. They offer good information and certainly help educate people. It's just that if you pick up a magazine and it gives you the "10 Best Stocks to Own Today," what happens next month when a new list comes out? Then another? There's no strategy involved, at least not a consistent one that I can see. Plus the articles are written in advance, detracting somewhat from their freshness. Read for big picture topics and strategy insights, but do your own stock picking.

3. *Use education not magazines.* Take the time to investigate stock sectors and their cycles, and if you read only one thing a week about the market, read *Barron's*. The publication riles some people due to its viewpoints on things like technology, but it's current and pertinent, and offers useful information.

4. *Be selective in the counsel you seek.* Once you have a plan (or think you have a plan), use one or two people to bounce your ideas off (besides your spouse). Money discussions and financial decisions as they pertain to investing are serious matters, and too many people offering opinions can be a dangerous game. Find an old hand in the market, preferably someone you already know. You are the one who will live with your decisions, not the adviser. Right before you conduct any transaction, discuss it with your spouse if possible. There may be something you overlooked, some nuance that might affect the outcome. Look before you leap.

5. *Prepare your plan of action the night before you expect to trade.* Don't alter your plans during market hours and/or if you have an open position. If it isn't working like you thought it might when you made your plans without any stress, why on earth would you dream of altering your plans in the heat of battle?

6. *Know your competition.* Remember that you're playing against legions of highly skilled and well-funded professionals, overachievers with talent and experience. They're trying to beat you, period.

7. *Predetermine your exit point prior to opening a trade.* That means predetermining the maximum loss, and sticking to it.

8. *Use caution when you average down.* Pouring good money into a bad trade may succeed every now and then, but it's not worth it in the long run.

9. *Be a gracious loser and take your losses easily.* Never try to justify a bad trade by trying to convince yourself it will probably turn into a winner at some point. A losing trade is to be viewed as overhead in your trading business. There's no way around the occasional loss, other than quitting trading altogether.

10. *Don't fight the trend.* You may win occasionally, but don't get sucked into believing you're smarter than the market. It's arrogant and costly to make this mistake.

11. *Missed opportunities exist only in your mind.* A market opportunity is like a city bus: Another one will be along any minute. If you chase a trade you had mapped out the night before, you've compromised yourself already. Learn from it without learning the hard way.

12. ***The human side of every person is the worst enemy to successful trading.*** The successful trader has to fight two powerful instincts: Fear and greed cannot be avoided, but they can be minimized by planning your trade, and trading your plan.

13. *Never risk more than you can afford to lose.* This is the heart of low-risk trading.

14. *Become a proficient computer geek.* As investors wade through the financial markets, it is imperative that they harness the power of the personal computer and the software that is currently available. The competition that you will be facing is using this technology to its fullest potential, and in order to be successful, you will need to do the same thing.

ROADMAP TO SUCCESS

Objective	Course of Action

Personal Evaluation: What Kind of Investor Are You?	**How you invest will determine your approach:** **What is the time frame you're dealing with?**
	• Before you invest, think about how long it will be realistically before you begin using the money.
	  –Retirement: supplementing your pension, Social Security, and other income.
	  –A major purchase or expense: college; travel, a new home.
	How much risk can you tolerate?
	• Risk is another word for volatility.
	• Can you stand to watch your investment fluctuate? A little or a lot?
	• What is the most risk you can take and still be able to sleep at night?
	  –You may surprise yourself!
	  –You may be more or less risk-tolerant after you begin investing.
	Sites for assisting with your risk profile:
	• **Mutual Fund Investor Center** (www.mfea.com): There's a lot of information here, and a risk profile questionnaire from a leading mutual fund company.
	• **Investor Financial Corporation** (www.investfinancial.com/ais1.asp): A site that includes a questionnaire that can help.

- **Investor Guide.com** (www.investorguide.com): Check out this site's risk profile guide.
- **Investor Home** (www.investorhome.com/asset.htm): A wealth of links designed to assist you in your investment planning and assessment.

Selecting the Tools You'll Need to Begin	**Factors to consider before you begin:** • What system do you currently use? • Will it be able to track a new type of investment? –Where are your assets currently? –Do you track their performance? **Get started on the right foot!** • Put a system in place that can grow with you. • **Quicken** (www.quicken.com/myfinances): This site offers a very easy-to-use online system. • **Kiplinger.com** (www.kiplinger.com/magazine) This site also has some useful tools you can use—free! **Know Where to Look for Information!** • Find out what you don't know. Here are some places to get you pointed in the right direction: –**Financial Engines** (www.financialengines.com): "Your Personal Online Investment Advisor." Very informative, and free! –**CyberInvest** (www.cyberinvest.com): This site offers a tremendous amount of information in an easy-to-use format. Definitely check it out! –**Invest Smart** (library.thinkquest.org/10326/index.html): This is a terrific site. Try Market Simulator and play with $100,000 of play money to see how the market actually works. Lots of good basic information, too. –**Armchair Millionaire** (www.armchairmillionaire.com): This site offers a lot of help for just getting everything together; saving, debt reduction, and so on.
Determining Trends: The Economy	• **Determine interest rate direction; up, down, steady.** • **Briefing.com** does a good job of explaining economic events (www.briefing.com/intro/i_markcal.htm). • **Treasury Corner.com** is also a great place to research bonds, the economy, and a whole lot more (www.treasurycorner.com). • **CNBC's** Kathleen Hayes does a tremendous job of explaining the mysteries of the bond market, and how the economy influences it (www.cnbc.com/bond/bond_main.asp).
Determining Trends: The Market	**Determining the direction of the market is half the battle with investing.** Here are some sites I look at to get a better idea of how things are going: • **Optionetics.com** (www.optionetics.com): Daily commentary and other useful information, daily commentary and articles, plus a huge library of past articles. • *Investor's Business Daily* (www.investors.com): I look at sentiment indicators, read *IBD*'s thoughts on the latest in market levels and volume interpretations. Bookmark it.

- **Signal Watch Light** (www.signalwatch.com): Ed Downs is a market technician who offers a free daily service that can be helpful. Sometimes he's spot-on accurate; other times he misses badly. Still good to read to get a better understanding of technical analysis.
- **The Street.com** (www.thestreet.com): Jim Cramer is a well-known trader on Wall Street. He and his staff offer some intriguing insights and commentaries worth reading.

Determining Trends: Sector Watch	Being in the right sector is a very important ingredient to making money in the market. Find out what sectors are doing well.

- Look for sectors with the most new highs.
- It's a very good idea to read the *Wall Street Journal* and/or *Investor's Business Daily* to become familiar with what the current buzz is all about.
- *Barron's* is often opinionated, but very good to read. It comes out weekly, on a Saturday.

Various sectors/industry groups have free online newsletters that can be a bit too technical, but still worth reviewing. Here are two I like for tech stocks:

- **The Internet Analyst** (www.theinternetanalyst.com/default.asp).
- **TheStandard.com** (www.thestandard.net): At last count TheStandard offered 18 different newsletters on different sectors under the "technology" heading. Free!

HOLDRS are being used to buy the strongest stocks in a sector, and more are coming out all the time. Merrill Lynch has developed them, and they trade on the AMEX. For a current list of what sectors are represented in HOLDRS and the stocks they cover, go to: www.holdrs.com/holdrs/main/index.asp.

Determining Trends: Stock Research	Once you narrow down the sector or sectors you want to be in, become a specialist in those sectors. Know what stocks they consist of and their relative rank within the group. There are some sites I've already mentioned but are worth listing again:

- *Investor's Business Daily* (www.investors.com): Online or in print, a great place to find stock information and sector rankings.
- **Market Guide** (www.marketguide.com/mgi/home.asp): A good site with lots of good insights and research, too.
- **Zacks Investment Research** (www.zacks.com): If you want to know everything about a company and how it ranks within a sector, bookmark this site.
- **John Bollinger's Equitytrader.com** (www.equitytrader.com): No commentary here, just hard technical data that interprets volume and price information.

Building a Portfolio	**How are you going to do it?**

- Lump sum.
- Monthly deposits.
- A mixture of the two.

Lump sum
- Don't invest it all at once!
- Be patient when evaluating entry points.
- Find support and resistance levels (see Chapter 9 on technical analysis).
- Look for breakouts—stocks moving up and out of a trading range. (*Investor's Business Daily* has a good list every day of stocks and sectors with the most new highs.)

Monthly deposits
- Go for a mutual fund to begin with.
- Check the track record.
- Fund description (does it meet your risk profile?) Do your research at these sites:

  –**Zacks** (my.zacks.com/funds/index.php3)

  –**Morningstar** (www.morningstar.com)

  –**Money.com** (www.money.com/money/fundcenter)—A mixture of both.

Write down your asset allocation mix.
- Funds may overlap in terms of their portfolios. Look for their 10–20 top holdings, and use Zacks to determine their risk characteristics.
- Don't get too concerned with the minutiae. Set an allocation of cash, stocks, and bonds

  –**Aggressive:** 80% stocks, 15% bonds, 5% cash

  –**Moderate:** 65% stocks, 25% bonds, 10% cash

  –**Conservative:** 50% blue chips, 35% bonds, and 15% cash

- **Silicon Investor** has a pretty decent stock screen feature you can use to help screen for stocks that will match your portfolio's objective (big caps, small caps, etc.), plus a good newsletter. Free! (www.siliconinvestor.com)

Check fund families for monthly deposit features.
- Do an MSN search for "mutual funds."
- **CyberInvest** (www.cyberinvest.com/guides/sharebuilder.html) offers a feature called "Share Builder." Click on site to review details.
- For further help with building a portfolio, go to: **Investor Home.com** (asset allocation—www.investorhome.com/asset.htm.)
- Read William O'Neil's *How to Make Money in Stocks.* The founder of *Investor's Business Daily* offers sound advice when looking for winners.

The Three Approaches to Evaluating a Stock	**Growth Investing**: A growth stock is a company whose earnings and/or revenues are expected to grow more rapidly than the average earnings of the overall stock market.

- Look at five-year earnings record.
- Look at rank within its industry. How did it fare comparatively? (Zacks has a good tool for this, as does *Investor's Business Daily.*)

- Look at annual and quarterly earnings. Any surprises, good or bad?
- Do you understand the industry group enough to be comfortable?

Momentum Investing: Momentum investors like to find the primary trend of a market and invest with that momentum in hopes of profiting from it.

- Technical analysis is a requisite for this type of investing.
- Look for breakouts into a higher trading range.
- Look for price increases or decreases of 20%+ in the past 60 days.
- For shorter-term ideas, look for price increases or decreases of more than 30% since yesterday.
  - –Is momentum strengthening or weakening?
  - –Check for strong volume.
  - –Is it optionable? (May be able to take advantage of short moves with less money.)

Value Investing: The primary objective of a value investor is to use fundamental analysis to buy a company for less than the investor thinks it is really worth.

- Market may take time to discover this.
- Buy-and-hold strategy is required.
- Patience is a virtue, because the market will move and this type of stock won't.
- Warren Buffett is the best-known value investor.
- **CyberInvest** has a great site for this (www.cyberinvest.com/buffett.html).

Tracking Your Portfolio	**Once your portfolio is in place, don't micromanage it! However, check it regularly.**
	
	- Keep a journal of all transactions. Make it convenient, safe, and organized.
	- Record the name of the security, the date you bought or sold it, the price paid (including any commissions), and your exit price.
	- There are software programs and web sites that enable you to track performance:
	  –**Optionetics.com** (www.optionetics.com)
	  –**Zacks Investment Research** (my.zacks.com/index.php3)
	  –**Quicken** (www.quicken.com/myfinances)
	
	Rank your portfolio.
	- Who's doing best, worst?
	- What is the annual return? To calculate your annual return, take the amount of all securities at the end of the year (or quarter, if you so choose), subtract the beginning balance, then divide the answer into the beginning balance.
	
	Revisit your original plan.
	- Are you still comfortable with it?
	- Is it meeting your expectations?

Rebalance the portfolio.

- Look at the weighting of your holdings.
- Is the portfolio still within your original parameters?
- If not, are you more or less comfortable with the new risk?
- Are you overexposed to one sector?
  - –Overexposure can lead to painful drops in account value.
  - –Rebalance quarterly!

The Initial Public Offering

First time a private company offers its stock to the public.

- Often it's a liquidity *event* for the original investors.
- Lots of hype surrounding it initially.
- Quiet period causes hype to die down.
- Stock can move sharply in the beginning, only to fall off after the quiet period begins.
- Shares are offered through *Offering Syndicate*. The only place to purchase them is through a brokerage firm that's involved in the syndicate.
- Pre-IPO prospectus is called a *red herring* due to the red print on the cover. Final prospectus issued on date of offering.
  - –Prospectus offers full disclosure of all pertinent financials, management profiles, business objectives, and risks involved.
  - –Offering made only by the prospectus. If you intend to buy the stock, a prospectus must be in your hands prior to or on the day of the offering.

For a listing of upcoming IPOs, go to:

- –**CyberInvest** (www.cyberinvest.com/guides/ipodpo.html)
- –**Alert!-IPO** (www.ostman.com/alert-ipo/ai.exe? cobrand=ostman)
- –**IPO.com** (www.ipo.com)
- Many insiders own restricted stock; they cannot sell it until a lock-up period ends. This often involves employees, directors, management, and venture capitalists. The end of a lock-up period can have a negative influence on the price of a stock. For a list of all companies with lock-up periods and the dates they come out, go to: www.ipolockup.com/may00.htm).

Dealing with Losses

What do you do when you've made a mistake? Either you bought too early or the stock has changed somehow, fundamentally.

- Before entering the trade, accept the fact everyone takes a loss on occasion.
- Calculate the maximum loss you'll accept—usually it's as little as 5%, or as high as 7% to 8% less than your purchase price.
- Keep your losses small! A small loss is less painful, maintains your confidence, and keeps you in the market so you can find another winner.

- If you hold onto a loser, it will distract you from finding another winner. It's too consuming and demoralizing.
- Never *double-down*. You made a mistake, so don't argue with the tape.
- If you're making regular monthly deposits into a mutual fund, the market will rise and fall. When it's down below your purchase price, determine if there's been a change in fund managers. If not, keep putting money in. The lower NAV will enable you to purchase more shares. Not every investment manager's style will work in every market.

Don't Chase a Stock!	**If a stock has moved up and you were thinking about buying it, don't wait until it's moved up for a week before getting in.** - Check its trading range. If it's breaking out, what was the breakout price? - If it's more than just a few points above that level, forget about it. - When you sell a winner, don't buy it back if it keeps going up. Seller's remorse could quickly turn into buyer's remorse. - New opportunities come along daily; if you miss one, another one will come your way soon enough.
Other Good Web Sites	**Quote.com** (www.quote.com/quotecom): Undoubtedly, one of the best web sites on the Net. Great charting and quotes as well as commentary and analysis tools. **Russell Investments** (www.russell.com/us/home/default.asp): A longtime institutional Investment firm; value-oriented. **Whisper Number** (lycos.whispernumber.com/index.cfm): This site is looked at for what the true earnings number will be for publicly traded companies. If a company meets the estimates but misses the whisper number, it can really make the stock sell off. **Equis "Free Stuff"** (www.equis.com/free): A good glossary for technical analysis explanations. From trend lines to retracements, this is a great site. **Open Fund** (www.metamarkets.com): The world's first (and only) interactive mutual fund. These guys post their trades as they make them. You get to look over the shoulders of institutional traders buying and selling. Very cool. **ClearStation** (clearstation.com): Nice site for observing what others are thinking. Also spotlights stocks with notable developments in their technicals.

5

The Versatility of Options

The last decade of the twentieth century fostered an explosive bull market. Everyone wanted to jump aboard and participate in the meteoric rise in U.S. stocks. As volatility rates soared and overnight high-tech sensations became the mainstay of this so-called new age of investing, online trading and investment-oriented Internet sites further changed the nature of the game once and for all. But for all the hype, newly created channels of information, and advancements in trading technology, making money in the market still proved to be an exercise of skill.

A divergence between the new economy tech stocks and old economy Dow stocks rang in the new millennium, and volatility soared. Investors who had only known bull markets and temporary pullbacks received some tough lessons as first the Dow rolled over, dropping over 17%, followed by the Nasdaq, once believed to be immune to such carnage. Good buying opportunities got better, and by May 24, 2000, the Nasdaq had dropped a whopping 40%. A drop in the market of that magnitude served as a grim reminder that successful trading requires a comprehensive understanding of all the trading tools and instruments available. Hence, those traders with the foresight to use options and hedge their positions had the last laugh after all.

If in the old days, finding a broker who could spot winners was essential to increasing your capital, these days survival can be found through the use of an increasingly popular trading instrument: the *option*. An option gives you the right to do something. One of its uses is as a hedging instrument, to protect against sudden or prolonged downturns in the market. But options are much more than a hedge; they are often used in creative ways to reduce risk while enhancing a trade's profit potential.

Options are a contract between two parties—a buyer and a seller—conveying the right (but not the obligation) to buy (call) or sell (put) a specified underlying security at a fixed price within a predefined time period for a specific premium. Let's break this statement down.

117

> **Option:** A trading instrument that represents the right to buy or sell a specified amount of an underlying stock at a predetermined price within a specified time. The option purchaser has the right, but not the obligation, to exercise the specifics of the contract. The option seller assumes a legal obligation to fulfill the specifics of the contract if the option is assigned to him or her.

"An option serves as a contract between two parties—a buyer and a seller—conveying the right (but not the obligation) to . . .

1. *"buy or sell . . ."* There are two types of options: a *call*, which gives the owner the right to buy the underlying security, and a *put*, which gives the owner the right to sell the underlying security.

2. *"a specified underlying security . . ."* Although options are available on stocks, indexes, bonds, currencies, and futures contracts, we are going to concentrate on the dynamics of stock options. Each stock is unique—some have options, while others do not. If options are available, they can be bought and sold at a fraction of the cost of the underlying stock. But remember, you are not buying or selling actual stock, just the right to buy or sell the stock at a specific price within a specific period of time.

3. *"at a fixed price . . ."* This fixed price is called the *strike price*, or the price at which the stock underlying an option can be purchased (call) or sold (put). Options are available in several strike prices at $2^1/_2$- or 5-point intervals, depending on the current price of the underlying stock.

4. *"within a predefined time period . . ."* Unlike stocks, options come with a deadline. An option must be exercised or sold to another option buyer before its expiration date or it will expire worthless and you will not recoup the premium paid for it. The existence of an expiration date is probably the most important distinction between options and stocks.

5. *"for a specific premium."* Getting this right to buy or sell at a strike price is not free. But, because you always have the option not to exercise a call or put, the premium is the extent of your potential risk.

In the past, options have received a bad rap. But learning to use them is a lot easier than it appears. If people lose money with options, it's because most don't really understand how they work. If you want to learn how to use them, you can start by understanding that options suffer from a phenomenon known as *time decay*. That is, options lose value with time, and lose it the fastest as they near expiration. But an option also provides a trader with flexibility and strategic choices. For example, you get to decide in advance the exact price you are willing to buy (or sell) a stock for at a certain future date, then speculate on whether your option will increase in value during that time. For this privilege you pay a price (if you are a buyer) or receive a credit (if you are a seller) for the cost of the option. Without a doubt, options are versatile instruments and, for the student of the stock market, worthy of study.

> **Time decay:** Part of the premium paid for an option known as time value. This amount is nothing more than a payment to the seller of the option to tie up the obligation on the stock for the requisite time period—the longer until expiration, the higher the premium. Time value will decay, or disappear, as the option approaches the expiration date.

To summarize, options have a wide variety of uses including the following applications:

- Options offer protection from a decline in the market price of a long underlying stock or an increase in the market price of a short underlying stock.

- Call options enable you to buy a stock at a lower price by exercising an in-the-money call option.

- Put options enable you to sell a stock at a higher price by exercising an in-the-money put option.

- Options create additional income against a long or short stock position.

- Options can be combined to create options strategies that offer limited risk approaches to taking advantage of bullish, bearish, and sideways markets.

- Specific option strategies can profit from a move in the price of the underlying asset regardless of market direction.

A HISTORY LESSON

Options have traded *over the counter* throughout the twentieth century. In the early days, option dealers would advertise open option positions in newspapers—an inefficient process at best. In April of 1973, the Chicago Board Options Exchange (CBOE) altered the nature of trading by formally listing options. Each stock option contract was standardized to represent 100 shares of stock, and expiration dates were set at specific intervals.

> **Chicago Board Options Exchange (CBOE):** The CBOE is the largest options exchange in the United States. The CBOE's web site offers new option listings, information on equities, options and leaps (long-term equity anticipation securites), and tutorials. Specialization includes calls and puts on NYSE stocks, the S&P 500, U.S. Treasury bonds, and other indexes (www.cboe.com).

Options have since experienced explosive growth, most recently driven by the advent of online trading. Currently the CBOE lists options on 680 stocks with more than 700,000 option contracts traded daily—approximately 51% of all options traded domestically. The CBOE uses an *auction market system*, employing floor brokers and market makers to execute customers' orders and inspire competition in the markets.

There are several option trading exchanges that you can visit on the Web:

- *Chicago Board Options Exchange (CBOE): www.cboe.com*
- *American Stock Exchange (AMEX): www.amex.com*
- *Philadelphia Exchange (PHLX): www.phlx.com/index.stm*
- *Pacific Exchange of San Francisco (PCX): www.pacificex.com*

On May 26, 2000, a new all-electronic exchange was launched—the *International Securities Exchange (ISE)*. It is the first new U.S.-based exchange to open for trading in over 27 years. There are three main reasons why the launch of the ISE is significant:

International Securities Exchange (ISE): A fully electronic exchange for trading stock options. Unlike the other option exchanges, it does not have a trading floor, but instead offers members screen-based trading.

First, unlike other exchanges offering options trading—CBOE, AMEX, PHLX, and PCX—there is no trading floor, which reflects the trend toward increased electronic trading evident throughout the world.

Second, ISE is proving instrumental in developing linkages among the various exchanges. Prior to August 1999, each specific option was listed on only one exchange. For example, options on Dell Computer were available only on the CBOE. Since that time, exchanges have been moving toward multiple listings. Given that ISE anticipates trading options on over 600 stocks and ensuring that customers are getting the best price offered on any of the exchanges, ISE is making the market more efficient and interdependent.

Third, it is interesting to note that the last two exchanges to open in the United States are both designed for option investing. Since 1973, option trading has emerged as a legitimate and popular method of achieving and protecting wealth. Shortly after the launch of the CBOE in 1974, the total number of options traded annually was 5.7 million contracts. By 1999, that figure had mushroomed to 444 million. There is ample evidence to suggest that this trend will continue and perhaps one of the most telling indications is the creation of the ISE.

WHY TRADE OPTIONS?

Why has options trading grown so popular? For one thing, the amazing versatility that an option offers in today's highly volatile markets is a welcome relief from the limited directional profitability and uncertainties of traditional investing. Options can be used in a variety of ways to profit from a rise or fall in the market. Most of my favorite trading strategies employ options as insurance policies in a wide variety of trading scenarios. You probably have insurance on your car or house because it is the responsible and safe thing to do. Options provide the same kind of safety net for trades and investments. They also increase your leverage by enabling you to control the shares of a specific stock without tying up a large amount of capital in your trading account.

Furthermore, options enable traders to capitalize on the bullish or bearish moves of an underlying market—usually with much less initial investment capital. Buying an option offers limited risk and unlimited profit potential. In contrast, selling an option (also known as writing an option) comes with an obligation to complete the trade if the party who buys it chooses to exercise the option. Selling an option, therefore, presents the writer with limited profit potential and significant risk unless the position is hedged in some manner.

It is vital to remember that an option has a limited shelf life. Every option contract is good up to a certain month and year. If you buy one call option on a stock, you can exercise your right to buy 100 shares of the underlying stock at any time until market close on the third Friday of the option's expiration month. If you do not exercise an option or sell it to another option buyer before its deadline, the option expires worthless and you will not recoup the premium paid for it—game over.

The most important difference is that unlike stocks, options come with a deadline. When you buy options, you pay money and time is not on your side. When you sell options, you receive a credit and time decay is on your side.

DEFINING AN OPTION'S CHARACTERISTICS

Options have five main standardized terms by which they are defined:

1. Type of option (call or put)
2. Underlying asset
3. Strike price
4. Expiration date
5. Option premium

These five variables distinguish each individual option from every other available option. Each time you enter a trade using options, these five terms define the parameters of your trade. It is essential to understand how these factors affect the nature of each trade in order maximize your chances of success.

Type of Option

There are two kinds of options—calls and puts—that can be bought (go long) or sold (go short):

- A *call option* gives the buyer the right, but not the obligation, to buy a fixed number of shares of an underlying stock at a specified price until the option's expiration date.

- A *put option* gives the buyer the right, but not the obligation, to sell a fixed number of shares of an underlying stock at a specified price until the option's expiration date.

Call option: An option contract that gives the holder the right, but not the obligation, to buy a specified amount of an underlying security at a specified price within a specified time in exchange for a premium. The call option buyer hopes the price of the underlying stock will rise by the call's expiration, while the call option seller (or writer) hopes that the price of the underlying stock will decline or remain stable.

Put option: An option contract giving the owner the right, but not the obligation, to sell a specified amount of an underlying security at a specified price within a specified time in exchange for a premium. The put option buyer hopes the price of the underlying stock will drop by a specific date, while the put option seller (or writer) hopes that the price of the underlying stock will rise or remain stable.

Put and call options are absolutely separate transactions. They are not opposite sides of the same transaction. If you buy a call, you cannot get out of it by selling a put. You must exit the trade by selling the call or simply allow it to expire worthless. Here's a basic summary of the process for closing out an option trade:

1. If you bought a call, you have to sell a call.
2. If you sold a call, you have to buy a call.
3. If you bought a put, you have to sell a put.
4. If you sold a put, you have to buy a put.

Underlying Asset

Each option provides the right to buy or sell a specific stock also called the *underlying asset*. Not all stocks have options. If options are available, they can be bought and sold at a fraction of the cost of the underlying stock. Thus, options provide a high-leverage approach that in many instances can reap large rewards from minimum-risk trades in comparison to traditional buy-and-hold stock investing.

Strike Price

The *strike price* is the fixed price at which the stock underlying an option can be purchased (call) or sold (put). Options are available in several strike prices at $2^{1}/_{2}$-point intervals for stocks priced $25 and less, or 5-point intervals for stocks over $25.

Strike price: All options have strike prices. They represent the price at which the underlying stock can be purchased (call) or sold (put) at any time prior to the option's expiration date if the option is exercised.

For example, if IBM is currently trading at 121, you may choose to buy a call option at 110, 115, 120, 125, or 130. You then have the right (but not the obligation) to buy IBM at the strike price of your choice until close of business on the third Friday of the expiration month—regardless of how high or low the price of IBM rises or falls. If the price of IBM rises and you have the ability to buy it at a lower price, the value of your option increases. If the price of IBM falls and you have the right to buy it at a higher price, your option will probably expire worthless and you will not recoup the money spent buying the option.

Exercising a call is accomplished as follows: Assuming you have purchased the 115 call option, you would call your broker on or before the third Friday of the expiration month and say you want to exercise the 115 call option on IBM. Then with the surrender of your option and the debit of $11,500 ($115 per share times 100 shares per option contract) from your account, you will own 100 shares of IBM regardless of the current price.

Expiration Date

An option's *expiration date* designates the last day on which an option may be exercised. American-style stock options officially expire on the third Saturday of the expiration month and must be traded by close of business on the last trading day prior to expiration. Since American options can be exercised at any time, they tend to have a slightly higher value than their European counterparts. After an option expires, you lose the right to buy or sell the underlying instrument at the specified price.

Expiration date: The last day on which an option may be exercised. American-style options can be exercised at any time *before* the expiration date. European-style options can be exercised only *on* the expiration date.

In order to decide which expiration months to use, you have to know which months are available. All stocks with options have available expiration months for the current month and the next month. When the front month options expire, the following month options become the front month and the next month options become available, and so on. In addition to the front and following months, each stock is assigned to one of three quarterly cycles: Cycle 1, Cycle 2, and Cycle 3 or alternatively January, February, and March.

- Cycle 1 stocks have quarterly options representing the first month of the quarter (January, April, July, and October).

- Cycle 2 starts with the second month (February, May, August, and November expirations).

- Cycle 3 starts with the third month (March, June, September, and December expirations).

Always confirm available expiration dates by asking your broker, reading the literature from the exchanges, or visiting an exchange's web site.

There are also longer-term option contracts called *LEAPS* (long-term equity anticipation securities) with expiration dates up to three years in the future. LEAPS always expire in the month of January and are also classified in one of the three cycles previously mentioned. They offer a terrific alternative to buying stocks and come with the advantage of an expiration that is many months or years away.

LEAPS: Long-term equity anticipation securities are long-term stock or index options with up to three years until expiration.

Option Premium

An option's *premium* denotes the actual price a trader pays to buy an option or receives from selling an option. The potential loss on a long option is limited to the premium paid for the contract, regardless of the underlying stock's price movement. That's why the purchase of an option enables traders to control the amount of risk assumed. In contrast, the potential profit on a short option is limited to the premium received, regardless of the underlying stock's performance.

Premium: The amount of cash that an option buyer pays to an option seller, or that an option seller receives from the sale of an option.

UNDERSTANDING OPTION QUOTES

The Internet has made the process of reviewing option prices extremely easy. There are dozens of sites that provide quote services. Some of these services provide real-time quotes, but many more are delayed by at least 15 to 20 minutes. If you want to receive streaming real-time data on a portfolio of stocks and options, you must be willing to pay for it (check out eSignal at www.dbc.com). You can also visit the Chicago Board Options Exchange (www.cboe.com) for a detailed list of delayed stock option quotes. Figure 5.1 shows a basic options quote for IBM.

When you look up an option's price, each quote is followed by several categories that describe various values of an option's price. Understanding these tiny numbers is essential to your success. Let's review a few of the most popular quote terms.

- *Last sale:* The last price that the option traded for at the exchange. For delayed quotes, this price may not reflect the actual price of the option at the time you view the quote. It could even be from a day or two prior for options that do not trade that frequently.

- *Net:* The amount that the option changed in price since the last price was quoted.

IBM (NYSE)   107 5/16 -35/8

May 31,2000 @ 19:55 ET (Data 20 Minutes Delayed)   Bid N/A   Ask N/A   Size N/AxN/A   Vol 3732500

Calls	Last Sale	Net	Bid	Ask	Vol.	Open Int	Puts	Last Sale	Net	Bid	Ask	Vo	Open Int
00 Jun 80 (IBM FP-E)	28 1/4	pc	27 3/8	28 1/8	0	2	00 Jun 80(IBM RP-E)	1/8	pc	0	1/8	0	62
00 Jun 85 (IBM FQ-E)	28 1/8	pc	22 3/8	23	1/8	0	10 00 Jun 85 (IBM RQ-E)	1/8	pc	0	3/16	0	128
00 Jun 90 (IBM FR-E)	17 7/8	+1	7 5/8	18 1/8	5	49	00 Jun 90 (IBM RR-E)	3/16	pc	3/16	5/16	0	960
00 Jun 95 (IBM FS-E)	15 1/2	pc	12 3/4	13 1/4	0	232	00 Jun 95 (IBM RS-E)	5/16	–	1/4	3/8	20	1508
00 Jun 100 (IBM FT-E)	8 3/8	-2 1/2	8 3/8	8 3/4	55	691	00 Jun 100 (IBM RT-E)	3/4	+1/8	3/4	15/16	70	4748
00 Jun 105 (IBM FA-E)	5 7/8	-1 3/8	4 5/8	4 7/8	102	1927	00 Jun 105 (IBM RA-E)	2 1/16	13/16	2	2 1/4	530	4345
00 Jun 110 (IBM FB-E)	2 1/4	-1 1/2	2 1/8	2 3/8	853	7616	00 Jun 110 (IBM RB-E)	4 1/2	+1 5/8	4 1/2	4 3/4	688	5357
00 Jun 115 (IBM FC-E)	11/16	-1 1/16	11/16	13/16	726	12203	00 Jun 115 (IBM RC-E)	7 1/4	+5/8	8	8 3/8	70	1400

Figure 5.1   Closing Quote for IBM Options (Courtesy of cboe.com)

- **Bid:** The bid is the highest price a prospective buyer is prepared to pay for a specified time for a trading unit of a specified security. If there is a high demand for the underlying asset, the prices are bid up to a higher level. Off-floor traders buy at the ask price.

- **Ask:** The ask is the lowest price acceptable to a prospective seller of the same security. A low demand for a stock translates to the market being offered down to the lowest price at which a person is willing to sell. Off-floor traders sell at the bid price. Together, the bid and ask prices constitute a quotation or quote and the difference between the two prices is the bid-ask spread. The bid and ask dynamic is common to all stocks and options.

- **Volume:** Option volume is the total number of contracts traded in the previous day.

- **Open interest:** Open interest is the total number of outstanding contracts. It also defines an option's liquidity—the higher the number, the easier it is to move in and out of a trade.

OPTION SYMBOLS

To understand quotes, you must be able to decipher option symbols. Option symbols vary depending on their source. However, all option orders are composed of the following components:

IBM FB-E = IBM June 2001 110 Call
Root symbol = IBM
Expiration month and type of option = F= June call
Strike price = B = 110
Exchange = E = CBOE

- *Root symbol:* The symbol used to identify the underlying stock, future, index, or security instrument on which an option is based.

- *Expiration month and type of option:* The month in which the option contract expires and type (call or put) are represented by a letter of the alphabet. (See Appendix E for a comprehensive chart.) In futures markets, a C represents calls and P represents puts.

- *Strike price:* The specific price at which the option holder has the right to buy or sell the underlying financial instrument. In futures, strike prices are usually numeric. In stocks, a letter of the alphabet represents strike prices. (See Appendix F for a list of *strike price codes.*)

- *Exchange:* Some options are traded on more than one exchange. Each exchange has its own unique prices and information. Some brokerages let you pick the exchange and others just place your order at the exchange with the best prices.

Strike price codes: A system of alphabetical symbols that represent option strike prices, used to describe an option when actually placing an order through an exchange.

OPTION PRICING PROCESS

Option pricing is a complex process. There are seven major components that affect the premium of an option:

1. The current price of the underlying stock.

2. The type of option (put or call).

3. The strike price of an option in comparison to the current market price of the underlying stock (its intrinsic value).

4. The amount of time remaining until expiration (the option's time value).

5. The current risk-free interest rate.

6. The volatility of the underlying financial instrument.

7. The dividend rate, if any, of the underlying stock.

Each of these factors plays a unique part in the determination of an option's premium. The first four variables are relatively self-explanatory. The last three are often overlooked, although each variable is important. For example, higher interest rates will increase call option premiums and decrease put option premiums—and vice versa for lower interest rates. Dividends act in a similar way, increasing and decreasing an option premium as they increase or decrease the price of the underlying asset.

Intrinsic Value and Time Value

Intrinsic value and time value (also called extrinsic value) are the two determinants of an option's price. The formula is very simple:

Option premium = Intrinsic value + Time value

Intrinsic value measures the amount by which the strike price of an option is *in-the-money (ITM)* in relation to the current price of the underlying stock. An *out-of-the-money (OTM)* or *at-the-money (ATM)* call or put has an intrinsic value of zero because it has no real value. Hence, the option premium is made up entirely of time value. The intrinsic value does not vary with time. Any intrinsic value remains constant regardless of any changes in the option environment except for the price of the underlying stock. If the underlying stock price doesn't change, the intrinsic value doesn't change, all the way through expiration.

Intrinsic value: The amount by which an option is in-the-money. Out-of-the-money and at-the-money options have no intrinsic value. Calls = underlying security minus strike price. Puts = strike price minus underlying security.

In-the-money (ITM): If you were to exercise an option and it would generate a profit at the time, it is known to be in-the-money. A call option is in-the-money if the strike price is less than the market price of the underlying security. A put option is in-the-money if the strike price is greater than the market price of the underlying security.

Out-of-the-money (OTM): An option whose exercise price has no intrinsic value. A call option is out-of-the-money if its exercise or strike price is above the current market price of the underlying security. A put option is out-of-the-money if its exercise or strike price is below the current market price of the underlying security.

At-the-money (ATM): When the strike price of an option is the same as the current price of the underlying instrument.

If an option is ITM (i.e., the stock price is above a call option's strike price or below a put option's strike price), then the time value is simply the option value less the intrinsic value. This extrinsic value is known as *time value* because as the option approaches expiration (loses time), the extrinsic value goes to zero. At expiration the only value in an option, if any, is intrinsic value.

Time value (extrinsic value): The amount that the current market price of a right, warrant, or option exceeds its intrinsic value. Time value = Option premium − Intrinsic value.

The time value portion of the option premium actually consists of a number of factors. Included in the time value is the number of days until expiration, the volatility of the underlying asset, the risk-free interest rate, and an adjustment for any dividends payable by the firm, and the psychological bias of the investor. At any point in time, the extrinsic value would be affected by each of its components as shown in Figure 5.2.

The following equations will allow you to calculate the intrinsic value of call and put options:

- **Call options:** Intrinsic value = Underlying security's current price – Call strike price.

- **Put options:** Intrinsic value = Put strike price – Underlying security's current price.

If the calculation results in a negative number, then the intrinsic value is zero by definition. Since time value is the amount by which the price of an option exceeds its intrinsic value, time value is calculated by subtracting the intrinsic value from the option premium. For example, if a call option costs $5 and its intrinsic value is $1, the time value would be $4 ($5 – $1 = $4). Let's calculate the intrinsic value and time value of a few call options with XYZ trading at $68 per share.

1. **Strike Price = 60   Option Premium = 8³/₄**

   Intrinsic value = 68 – 60 = **8** (Intrinsic value = Underlying security's price – Strike price)

   Time Value = 8³/₄ – 8 = ³/₄ (Time value = Call premium – Intrinsic value)

2. **Strike Price = 65   Option Premium = 6⁵/₈**

   Intrinsic value = 68 – 65 = **3**

   Time value = 6⁵/₈ – 3 = **3⁵/₈**

Component of Time Value	Calls	Puts
Time until expiration	Premium decreases as time expires.	Premium decreases as time expires.
Volatility of underlying asset	Premium increases as volatility increases.	Premium increases as volatility increases.
Risk-free interest	Premium increases as interest rates increase.	Premium decreases as interest rates increase.
Dividends payable	Premium decreases if there are one or more dividends payable before expiration.	Premium increases if there are one or more dividends payable before expiration.
Psychological bias	Premium increases if investors are suddenly bullish on the underlying stock.	Premium increases if investors are suddenly bearish on the underlying stock.

Figure 5.2   The Influence of Various Factors on the Time Value Portion of an Option Premium

3. **Strike Price = 70   Option Premium = 5$^1/_2$**

Intrinsic value = 68 − 70 = **− 2** = Zero intrinsic value

Time value = 5$^1/_2$ − 0 = **5$^1/_2$** = All time value

An option's intrinsic value is also called the minimum value because it tells you the minimum amount the option should be selling for. This means that the cheaper the option, the less real value you are buying. It is important to note that the intrinsic value of an option is the same regardless of how much time is left until expiration. Since theoretically an option with three months until expiration has a better chance of ending up in-the-money than an option expiring in the present month, options with more time until expiration are usually priced higher.

The prices of OTM options are cheap, and they get even cheaper as you get further out-of-the-money. That's because an OTM option consists of nothing but time value, and the more out-of-the-money an option is, the less chance it has of moving in-the-money. To many traders, OTM options appear to be a great deal because of their inexpensive prices. However, the probability that an extremely OTM option will turn profitable is really quite slim.

Time value has a snowball effect. If you have ever bought options, you might have noticed that at a certain point close to expiration, the price of the option stops moving completely. That's because option prices are exponential—the closer an option gets to expiration, the more money is lost if the market doesn't move in a direction that puts the option in-the-money. On the expiration day, all an option is worth is its intrinsic value. It's either in-the-money or it isn't. The deeper in-the-money a call or put is, the less time value and more intrinsic value the option has. Since you are paying less for time, an in-the-money option's premium moves more like the price of the underlying asset. This is also referred to as the *delta* of an option. The delta of an option is the key to creating *delta neutral* strategies and is the foundation for many of my favorite options strategies.

Delta: The amount by which the price of an option changes for every dollar move in the underlying instrument.

Delta neutral: A position arranged by selecting a calculated ratio of short and long positions that balance out to an overall position delta of zero.

Volatility

Volatility is not only a primary determinant of an option's price, but it also helps to define which strategy can best be used to make money in a specific market. Specifically, volatility is a percentage that measures the amount by which an underlying stock or market is expected to change in a given period of time. This sounds quite imposing, so I prefer to think of it as the speed of change in a market. For example, if a stock is trading at 100 and has a volatility of 25%, in one year the stock should be trading between 75 and 125. It is important to note that volatility does not have a directional bias—a high-volatility stock has the propensity to move quickly in either direction, while a stable market moves more slowly.

Volatility: The amount by which an underlying instrument is expected to fluctuate in a given period of time. Options often increase in price when there is a rise in volatility even if the price of the underlying security doesn't move anywhere.

A stock's volatility has a significant effect on the price of its options. A highly volatile stock has a better chance of making a substantial move than a low-volatility stock. In other words, a more volatile asset offers larger swings upward or downward in price in shorter time spans than less volatile assets. Large movements, in turn, are attractive to option traders, who are always looking for big directional swings to make their contracts more profitable. Therefore, the options of a high-volatility stock generally command a higher premium because they have a greater chance of making a big move and being in-the-money by expiration.

There are many reasons and events that trigger high volatility. For example, on the third Friday of each month, the government releases the *Employment Report*, which often triggers a fluctuation of prices in the bond market. This often produces a simultaneous volatility increase in the stock markets. If a stock's volatility was sitting just below 10, it may increase to 12.5 as a result of the report's release. You can equate that 2.5 rise to an approximate 8% increase in the price of an option. Options often increase in price when there is a rise in volatility even if the price of the underlying asset doesn't move at all. As a general rule of thumb, traders buy options in low volatility and sell them during periods of high volatility.

There are two basic kinds of volatility: historical and implied. In basic terms, historical volatility gauges stock price movement in terms of past performance, and implied volatility approximates how much the marketplace thinks option prices will move.

Historical volatility (also known as statistical volatility) measures a stock's propensity for movement based on the stock's past price action during a specific time period. Historical volatility can be calculated by using the standard deviation of a stock's price changes from close to close of trading going back 21 to 23 days. Since statistical volatility measures a stock's propensity for movement, it is an important variable that helps to determine an option's worth. High or low historical volatility also gives traders a clue as to the type of strategy that can best be implemented to optimize profits in a specific market.

Historic volatility: A measurement of how much a stock's price has fluctuated over a period of time in the past; usually calculated by taking a standard deviation of price changes over a specific time period.

Implied volatility is a computed value that measures an option's volatility, rather than the underlying asset. The fair value of an option is calculated by entering the historical volatility of the underlying asset into an option pricing model (Black-

Scholes for stocks). The computed fair value may differ from the actual market price of the option. Implied volatility is the volatility needed to achieve the option's actual market price.

Implied volatility: Volatility computed using the actual market price of an option and a pricing model (Black-Scholes). For example, if the market price of an option rises without a change in the price of the underlying stock or future, implied volatility will have risen.

The best thing about implied volatility is that it is very cyclical; that is, it tends to fluctuate within a given range. The key to utilizing implied volatility is in knowing that when it actually changes direction it often moves quickly in the new direction. Buying options when the implied volatility drops can cause some trades to actually end up losing money even when the price of the underlying asset moves in your direction. However, you can take advantage of this situation by selling options, instead of buying them.

Volatility not only contributes to the option's price, it also helps define which strategy can be best utilized to take advantage of specific market movement. High-volatility stocks usually have higher-priced options. Low-volatility stocks have lower-priced options; the extrinsic value is lower. There are different strategies that can take advantage of either of these conditions. You can also use volatility levels to look for skews, or differences, in volatility between higher-strike and lower-strike options of the same underlying stock (or between different expiration months).

Volatility skews measure and account for the limitation found in most option pricing models and can be used to give traders an edge in estimating an option's real worth. Volatility increases the price of a trading instrument. A volatility skew exists when higher-strike options are overpriced in comparison to the lower-strike options or vice versa. A forward volatility skew is found in markets where higher-strike options have high implied volatility and are therefore overpriced, and lower-strike options have low implied volatility and are often underpriced. A reverse volatility skew is found in markets in which lower-strike options have high implied volatility and are therefore overpriced, and higher-strike options have low implied volatility and are often underpriced. There are specific option strategies that take advantage of these kinds of volatility skew scenarios. Skews can also occur between different months.

Determining the current volatility level is critical. A basic rule of thumb is to buy low volatility and sell high volatility. If you see that the volatility is high, that means there's a lot of extrinsic value that somehow has been assigned the option. A good example of how this happens is when a company makes an announcement on a subject such as earnings. Whether they're good or bad is immaterial; the news attracts activity, which makes the stock move up or down more than usual, and this movement attracts the options trader. More trading activity (demand) will naturally push the volatility up. So even if the stock doesn't move, the options may move up. Eventually the buying slows down, and the volatility drops to normal levels again.

Two web sites I know of that track and report volatility levels are: Optionetics.com (www.optionetics.com) and Option Club (www.optionclub.com/cgi-bin/longvol.htm). For more information about volatility, Yahoo! Finance has a glossary worth bookmarking (biz.yahoo.com/f/g/bfglosv.html).

OPTION GREEKS

The option Greeks represent a set of measurements that explore the risk exposures of a specific trade. Options and other trading instruments have a variety of risk exposures that can vary dramatically over time or as markets move. Often, it is not enough to know the total risk associated with an options position. To create a delta neutral trade, you need to select a calculated ratio of short and long positions that together create an overall position delta of zero. To recognize the probabilities of the trade making money, it is essential to be able to determine a variety of risk exposure measurements. Changes in the price of the underlying instrument trigger changes in the delta, which triggers changes in the rest of the Greeks.

Each risk measurement is named after a different letter in the Greek alphabet including delta, gamma, theta, and vega (vega is not actually a Greek letter, but is used in this context anyway). In the beginning, comprehending the definition of each of the Greeks will give you the tools to decipher option pricing. Each of the terms defined has a specific use in day-to-day trading.

- *Delta:* The change in the price of an option relative to the change of the underlying security. Delta helps you to understand how an option's premium will rise or fall in comparison to the price of the underlying asset.

- *Gamma:* Change in the delta of an option with respect to the change in price of its underlying security. Gamma helps you to gauge the change in an option's delta when the underlying asset moves.

- *Theta:* Change in the price of an option with respect to a change in its time until expiration. Theta measures the amount an option will lose with the passage of one day.

- *Vega:* Change in the price of an option with respect to its change in volatility. Vega measures the amount an option will gain or lose with a 1 percentage point change in the implied volatility of the option.

The Greeks help us to break option price movement into bite-size pieces that can be more easily swallowed and digested. Learning to use them will enhance your ability to decide which strategy has the best chance of making money in a certain market. This information can be easily found by visiting the Platinum area of the Optionetics.com web site. This site is dedicated to empowering investors by providing access to a host of additional data and information, as well as a number of advanced screening techniques.

CALL OPTION BASICS

Call options offer an attractive alternative to buying stock by providing the buyer the right, but not the obligation, to buy an underlying stock at the call's strike price. Since each option represents 100 shares of the underlying stock, a call option listed as an IBM Aug 2001 115 Call @ 7³/₄ would give the purchaser the right to buy 100 shares of IBM (the underlying asset) at the strike price of $115 per share until the expiration date of the close of business on the third Friday in August 2001. To acquire this right, an investor would pay a premium of $775 (7³/₄ × 100 shares = $775) for each call option.

Call buyers have unlimited potential to profit from a rise in the price of an underlying stock; but unlike long stock positions, risk is limited to the premium paid for the option.

Since calls can be purchased at a fraction of the price of buying stock, it is an economical way to leverage trading capital in order to participate in market movement without the need for margin. Call options are wasting assets, though, and their value declines as they approach expiration. As they get closer to their expiration date, the time decay accelerates (see Figure 5.3). This is one of the main reasons people lose money on options: they buy them too close to the expiration date, thinking they are cheap and end up getting clobbered.

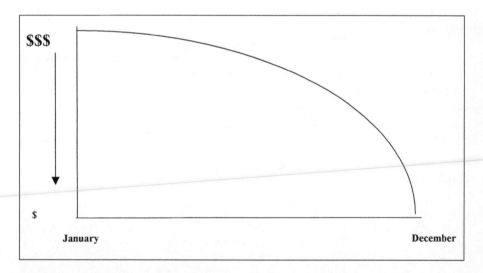

Figure 5.3 Option Time Decay

---

*Options lose the majority of their time value
in the last 30 days before expiration.*

Depending on the mood of the market, you may choose to buy (go long) or sell (go short) a call option. The premium of the long call option will show up as a debit in your trading account and is the maximum loss you risk by purchasing the call. In contrast, the maximum profit of a long call option is unlimited depending on how high the underlying instrument rises in price (the upside) above the strike price. As the underlying stock rises, the long call increases in value because it gives the option holder the right to buy the underlying stock at its lower strike price. That's why you want to go long a call option on a stock or an index during a rising or bull market.

---

*If you choose to buy a call option, you are purchasing the right
to buy the underlying instrument at a specified strike
price until the third Friday of the expiration month.*

If you choose to sell or go short a call option, you are selling the right to buy the underlying stock at a specific strike price until the third Friday of the expiration month. This is called *writing* an option. The short call strategy should be applied in bearish markets. The call's premium is the maximum profit available on the position and shows up as a credit in your trading account. The maximum loss, however, is unlimited depending on how high the price of the underlying stock rises to the upside beyond the call's strike price.

If the underlying stock rises above a call's strike price, the call buyer then has the right to exercise the option. If this happens, the call seller is obligated to deliver 100 shares of the underlying stock at the call's strike price to the option buyer. The option seller still gets to keep the premium received from the short call, which can then be used to hedge the loss on having to buy the underlying stock at a higher price to fulfill this obligation. This can be quite expensive, which is why I never recommend selling unprotected or *naked options*. However, experienced traders who choose to short call options do so in a stable or bear market, because theoretically the call has little chance of being exercised unless a dramatic reversal occurs. Theoretically, the call buyer could exercise the call even if the stock price is below the strike price, but that doesn't make any economic sense and is therefore extremely unlikely.

Long Call Example

There are many ways to take advantage of a bullish (rising) market. The simplest strategy is to buy shares of stock and sell them when the price rises, pocketing the difference. But even if you buy the shares using a margin account, buying stock may require a substantial amount of money. Based on the rules of the Securities and Exchange Commission (SEC), if you want to purchase stock, margin equals 50% of the amount of the trade. For example, if 100 shares of IBM cost a total of $10,000, then you are required to have a minimum of $5,000 on deposit in your margin account. At this rate, margin accounts give traders 2 for 1 buying leverage. If the price of the stock rises, then everyone wins. If the price of the stock falls below 75% of the total value of the investment, the trader receives a margin call from the broker requesting additional funds to be placed in the margin account.

Instead of buying stock, you may want to consider buying a call option in order to participate in the bullish movement of a stock with limited downside risk. A long call strategy has many advantages over buying stock. First of all, the premium of an option is significantly lower than the amount required to purchase a stock. Since the maximum risk on a long call strategy is equal to the premium paid for the option, buying a call is a limited risk strategy—you know exactly how much money you could potentially lose before entering the trade. Less initial investment also means that you can leverage your money a great deal more than the 2 for 1 leverage buying stock on margin offers. Perhaps the only drawback is that options have a limited time until they expire. But even this disadvantage can be seen as an advantage if you consider the opportunity cost of waiting months and sometimes years for a stock that has taken a bearish turn to reverse its direction. A long call is a low-risk strategy that takes advantage of a bullish-performing stock without risking a lot of money.

To illustrate the dynamics of a long call trade versus a long stock position, let's create an example using a fictitious stock with a symbol of XYX. On August 1, XYX is trading at $68 per share. Buying 100 shares would therefore cost a total of $6,800 from a cash account or $3,400 using a margin account. Now, let's see what kind of positions we can find using call options. All long call positions offer an unlimited profit potential, and the maximum risk is limited to the price of the premium. In addition, it is very important to calculate the price the underlying stock must reach for the option position to break even. Figure 5.4 shows various call option premiums for XYX at different strike prices and expirations.

For a long call position, the more time an option has until expiration, the better chance the position has of becoming profitable. Therefore, let's eliminate the August and September calls from consideration and concentrate on the October and January calls. The calls with strike prices less than 68 are in-the-money and there-

Call Strike Prices and Premiums for XYX @ 68

Call Strike Price	August	September	October	January
55	13¾	14½	15⅜	17¾
60	8¾	10	11½	14¾
65	5¾	6⅝	8⅛	12⅛
70	2	4	5½	9½
75	⅞	2⅛	3⅝	7½

Figure 5.4   Call Options and Premiums

fore come with a higher premium. Since we are hoping to profit from a rise in the price of XYX, it is important to keep the upside breakeven as low as possible.

Let's take a look at a couple of examples using October and January 65 and 70 calls. Figure 5.5 shows the maximum risk and breakevens for these four long calls. Each option offers its own unique advantages and disadvantages. The October 65 call has the lowest breakeven, but you can lose $812.50 if XYX doesn't rise above $73\frac{1}{8}$ by the third Friday of October. The October 70 call offers a slightly higher breakeven, but with a lower risk. The January options cost more and have higher breakevens, but they provide more time for the option to ripen. Any of these options could conceivably harvest a healthy profit in the event that XYX makes a move to the upside. Since limiting risk is the name of the game, let's track the October 70 Call @ $5\frac{1}{2}$.

A month later, let's say XYX rises $10\frac{1}{2}$ points to $78\frac{1}{2}$. There are two ways to take advantage of a rise in the price of XYX: exercise or offset. By exercising the October 70 call, you will become the owner of 100 shares of XYX at the lower price of $70 per share. You can then sell the shares for the current price of $78 per share and pocket the difference of $800. But since you paid $550 for the option, this process reaps only a $250 profit ($800 − $550 = $250). The more profitable technique is to sell the October 70 call for the new premium of $14\frac{3}{4}$, an increase of $9\frac{1}{4}$ points. By selling the October 70 call, you can make a profit of $925 ($1,475 − $550 = $925).

Conversely, if you had bought 100 shares of XYX at $68 per share, you would have made a profit of $1,050 (not including commissions) when the stock reached $78\frac{1}{2}$ per share—an increase of $10\frac{1}{2}$ points. The profit on the long stock position is slightly higher than the profit on the long call—a big $125. However, the return on investment is much higher for the long call position because the initial investment was significantly lower than the initial capital needed to buy the stock shares (see Figure 5.6). Both trades offered profit-making opportunities, but the long call position offered a significantly lower limited risk and the ability to use the rest of the available trading capital in other trades. For an initial investment of $3,300, you could have purchased six call options and made a total profit of $5,550—now, that's a healthy return.

The ability of a call option to be in-the-money by expiration is determined by the movement of the underlying stock. It is therefore essential to know how to analyze stock markets and accurately forecast future price action in order to pick the call with the best chance of making a profit. Understanding market movement is not an easy task.

Call Option	Maximum Risk	Breakeven
October 65	$812.50	$73\frac{1}{8}$ ($65 + 8\frac{1}{8}$)
October 70	$550.00	$75\frac{1}{2}$ ($70 + 5\frac{1}{2}$)
January 65	$1,212.50	$77\frac{1}{8}$ ($65 + 12\frac{1}{8}$)
January 70	$950.00	$79\frac{1}{2}$ ($70 + 9\frac{1}{2}$)

Figure 5.5   Long Call Calculations

	100 Shares of XYX	Oct XYX 70 Call
XYX @ 68 at Trade Initiation		
Price per share	$68	5½
Maximum risk	$6,800	$550
Breakeven price	$68	75½
1 Month Later XYX @ 78½		
Price per share	$78½	14¾
Profit	$1,050	$925
Return on risk	15%	168%

Figure 5.6   Comparison of Long Stock to Long Call Trade

RISK PROFILES

Another way to view the difference between a long stock position and buying a call is to take a look at the risk profiles they present. A risk profile is a graphic representation of the profit/loss of a position in relation to price changes in the underlying asset. The horizontal numbers at the bottom of the graph read from left to right showing the underlying stock's price. The vertical numbers from top to bottom show profit and loss. The sloping graph line indicates the theoretical profit and loss of the position at expiration as it corresponds to the price of the underlying stock. By looking at any given market price, you can determine a trade's corresponding profit or loss. Risk profiles enable a trader to get a visual feel for the trade's probability for making a profit. Figures 5.7 and 5.8 provide risk graphs for the long stock and long call examples just discussed. They can help you to visually understand how the risk differs between a long stock and a long call positions.

Short Call Example

Shorting a call option, or *writing* an option, can be an extremely risky business. By writing a call option, a trader grants someone else the right, but not the obligation, to purchase 100 shares of underlying stock at the option strike price. In exchange, the option writer receives a credit in the amount of the option's premium. The premium received is the maximum amount of profit that can be made on the short call position. The risk, however, is unlimited as the price of the underlying stock rises above the position's breakeven.

Selling a call enables traders to profit from a decrease in the underlying market. If the underlying stock stays below the strike price of the short call until the option's expiration, the option expires worthless and the trader gets to keep the credit received. But if the price of the underlying stock rises above the strike price of the short call before expiration, the call seller's option has a very good chance of being assigned to a call buyer. A call buyer (as discussed in the previous section on long

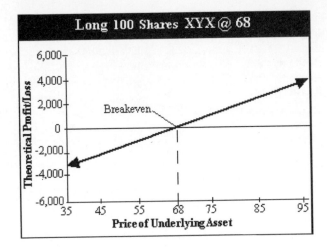

Figure 5.7   Long Stock Risk Graph

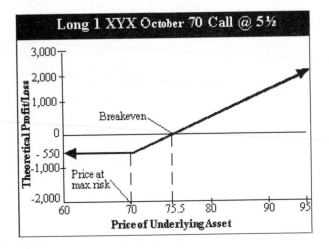

Figure 5.8   Long Call Risk Graph

calls) has the right to buy the underlying asset at the call strike price at any time before expiration by exercising the call. If the call buyer exercises the option, the call is assigned to an option writer who sold an option with the same strike price and expiration date. The option seller then receives notification of *assignment* and is obligated to deliver 100 shares of the underlying stock to the option buyer at the call option's strike price. This entails buying the underlying stock at the higher price and delivering it to the option buyer at the lower price. The difference between these two prices constitutes the seller's loss and the buyer's open position profit.

Selling naked calls is not allowed by many brokerages. Others require you to have at least $50,000 as a margin deposit. This speaks volumes about just how risky this strategy can be. However, since a short call is very useful in hedging and combination options strategies, it is important to understand its basic properties.

To illustrate the dynamics of a short call option, let's see what is involved in the sale of 1 September XYX 70 Call @ 4. The key to profiting on a short call is for the underlying stock to stay below the call strike price so that the option can avoid assignment and expire worthless. Hence, it is best to choose options with less than 45 days till expiration. An option that expires relatively soon has less time until expiration, and that gives the underlying stock less time to rise above the option's strike price.

Assignment: The decision by an option holder to exercise an option results in an assignment to an option seller. In the case of the assignment of a call, the option seller must deliver the underlying stock to the option holder at the short call option's strike price regardless of the current price of the underlying asset. In the case of assignment of a put, the option seller must buy the underlying stock at the short put's option strike price regardless of how low the underlying asset is priced at that time.

Naked option: An option written (sold) without an underlying hedge position.

In this example, the maximum profit is limited to the option's premium, or $400, which is deposited electronically into your trading account. The breakeven on a short call position is calculated by adding the premium to the strike price. In this example, the position breaks even when the underlying market rises beyond 74 (70 + 4 = 74). Even if the call is assigned, as long as XYX remains below 74, a small profit can be achieved.

Let's take a look at the difference between shorting a call and short selling shares of stock outright (see Figure 5.9). In a short stock trade, you are borrowing the shares from your brokerage house and selling them at the current price in the hope that the price will decline (bearish market). You will receive a credit in your account for the sales price (minus the commission).

The best stock for a short stock trade must be steadily decreasing in price and show enough liquidity to allow a trader to exit the position when necessary. Selling stock comes with unlimited risk as the price of the underlying stock rises above the initial cost of the shares—there is no limit to how much you can lose. In addition, a short stock position requires at least $1\frac{1}{2}$ times the total cost of the shares as margin in your account to execute the trade. If the price of the stock starts to rise, you will be required to post additional margin funds.

The main differences between short stock and short call positions are the profit potentials, and breakevens. The profit on a short stock is limited to the price of the stock as it falls all the way to zero. The profit on a short call is limited to the premium received when the trade is placed. However, the breakeven on a short call is offset by the premium of the option and is therefore higher than that of a short stock—the price of the position at trade entry. This relationship can also be exploited by a well-used strategy known as a covered call.

Short Stock versus Short Call

Price of XYX at Expiration	XYX @ 65	XYX @ 70	XYX @ 72	XYX @ 74	XYX @ 80
Profit/Loss of 100 Short Shares of XYX @ 68					
Procedure	Buy shares back for a profit	Buy shares back for a loss	Buy shares back for a loss	Buy shares back for a loss	Buy shares back for a loss
Profit/loss of 100 shares of XYX @ 68	$300 [(68 – 65) × 100 = $300]	–$200 [(68 – 70) × 100 = – $200]	–$400 [(68 – 72) × 100 = – $400]	–$600 [(68 – 74) × 100 = – $600]	–$1,200 [(68 – 80) × 100 = – $1,200]
Profit/Loss of 1 Short September XYX 70 Call @ 4					
Procedure	Call expires worthless	Call expires worthless	Call is assigned, seller must buy 100 shares @ 72 and deliver to buyer @ 70	Call is assigned, seller must buy 100 shares @ 74 and deliver to buyer @ 70	Call is assigned, seller must buy 100 shares @ 80 and deliver to buyer @ 70
Profit/loss of 70 call option	$400	$400	$200 [4 – (72 – 70) × 100 = $200]	0 [4 – (74 – 70) × 100 = 0]	–$600 [4 – (80 – 70) × 100 = – $600]

Figure 5.9   Short Stock versus Short Call Comparison

> **Covered call:** A short call position sold as a hedge against a long stock position.

Figure 5.10 shows the risk profile of the short stock position. The risk curve falls from the upper left-hand corner to the lower right-hand corner—when the stock price falls, you make money; when it rises, you lose money. Figure 5.11 shows the risk profile of the short call position. Notice how the line slants upward from right to left providing insight as to its bearish nature. When the underlying

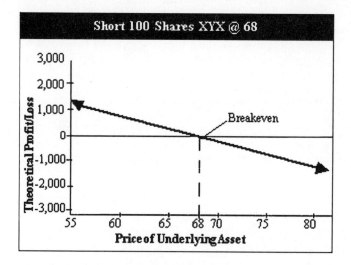

Figure 5.10 Short Stock Risk Graph

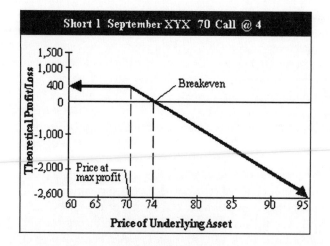

Figure 5.11 Short Call Risk Graph

stock reaches a price of 70, the position's profit hits a maximum profit of $400. The call's potential loss continues to increase as the price of the underlying asset rises above the breakeven.

PUT OPTION BASICS

A put option gives the buyer the right, but not the obligation, to sell 100 shares of an underlying stock at a fixed price until the option's expiration date. Just like call options, put options come in various strike prices with a variety of expiration dates. However, unlike call options, if you are bearish (expect market prices to fall), you might consider going long a put option. If you were bullish (expect the market to rise), you might (theoretically) consider shorting a put option.

Buying a put option is a welcome alternative to short selling stock. Although both strategies offer traders the chance to profit from a decrease in a market, only put buying does so with limited risk.

If you choose to buy or go long a put option, you are purchasing the right to sell the underlying instrument at a specific strike price of your choice until the date of the expiration of your choice. The premium of the long put option will show up as a debit in your trading account. The cost of the premium is the maximum loss at risk from purchasing a put option. The maximum profit occurs if the stock drops to zero (although this is unlikely to happen). As the underlying stock falls, the long put becomes more valuable because it gives you the right to sell the underlying stock at the put option's higher strike price. So instead of incurring a much higher risk by shorting a stock, you reduce your exposure by buying a put.

If you choose to sell or go short a put option, you are selling the right to sell the underlying instrument at a specific strike price from the time the position is established until the expiration date. However, shorting a put option also comes with an obligation to buy 100 shares of the underlying stock if an assigned option holder exercises the option. No matter what, you get to keep the premium paid for the short put; the premium of the short put will show up as a credit in your trading account. The cost of the premium is the maximum credit you receive by selling a put option. However, the maximum loss is virtually unlimited; it depends, naturally, on how low the price of the underlying stock falls. In most cases, you are anticipating that the short put option will simply expire before the expiration date, enabling you to keep the premium received. However, if your put option is assigned and exercised, you are obligated to purchase 100 shares of the underlying stock from the buyer of your put at the option's strike price. Experienced traders who choose to go short put options do so in a stable or bull market because the put will not be exercised unless the market falls.

Long Put Example

In a long put trade, you are purchasing the right, but not the obligation, to sell the underlying stock at the put strike price until the option expires. A long put strategy should be used when you anticipate a fall in the price of the underlying market. This strategy provides unlimited profit potential with limited risk. The most you can lose is the price of the option, regardless of how high the underlying stock rises. Profit occurs as the price of the underlying stock falls below the breakeven.

Buying a put is a limited risk bearish strategy that can be used instead of shorting stock.

Let's create an example of a long put strategy with XYX trading at $69^3/_8$ using the premiums in Figure 5.12. Time is one of the more important contributing variables in an option's premium. Therefore, the further away the expiration date, the higher the premium. But the cost that time contributes to a put's premium must be balanced out by the need for sufficient time until expiration. Profit on a long put position depends on the underlying stock moving below the put breakeven. The breakeven on a long put is derived by subtracting the put premium from the option strike price. Hence, the higher the premium, the lower the breakeven, and this means the underlying stock has to move lower for the long put position to make a profit.

Looking at the values in Figure 5.12, which option seems to have the best balance between maximum risk and breakeven? As with most trading decisions, the question is subjective at best. It depends on a variety of factors from when the earnings report will be released to interest rates. If you anticipate a big move in the near future, you may want to buy a September 70 Put @ $4^7/_8$. The maximum risk on this position is $487.50 and the breakeven is $65^7/_8$ (see Figure 5.13). If you think you need more time, you could buy an October XYX 75 call @ $9^1/_8$ for a maximum risk $912.50 and a breakeven of $65^7/_8$. In this case, a decrease of $3^1/_2$ points will start to initiate a profit and you have more than 60 days for XYX to move.

Choosing an exit strategy depends on the movement of the underlying stock. If the market falls, you can either sell a put option with the same strike price and

Put Option Premiums for XYX @ $69^3/_8$

Put Strike Prices	August	September	October	January
55	$^3/_{16}$	$^9/_{16}$	$1^3/_{16}$	3
60	$^3/_8$	$1^1/_4$	$2^3/_8$	$4^5/_8$
65	$1^1/_8$	2	$3^7/_8$	$6^5/_8$
70	3	$4^7/_8$	$6^1/_4$	9
75	$6^5/_8$	8	$9^1/_8$	$12^1/_4$
80	$11^1/_8$	12	$12^3/_4$	$15^5/_8$

Figure 5.12 Put Premiums for XYX @ $69^3/_8$

Long Put Calculation	Long 1 Sep XYX 70 Put @ $4^7/_8$	Long 1 Oct XYX 75 Call @ $9^1/_8$
Maximum risk = Put premium	$4^7/_8 \times 100 = \$478.50$	$9^1/_8 \times 100 = \$912.50$
Maximum reward = Unlimited	Unlimited below breakeven	Unlimited below breakeven
Breakeven = Strike price – Put premium	$70 - 4^7/_8 = 65^1/_8$	$75 - 9^1/_8 = 65^7/_8$

Figure 5.13   Long Put Results

expiration at an acceptable profit, or exercise the put option and be short the underlying market. You can hold this position or cover the short by buying them back at the current lower price thereby garnering a profit. If the market rises, you may prefer to sell your option to minimize the loss or wait for a reversal if you have enough time until expiration.

In this example, let's say the price of XYX falls to $62^3/_4$. This results in a rise in the premium of the October 75 put to $18^3/_4$. You now have a decision to make. To exit a long put, you can offset it, exercise it, or let it expire (see Figure 5.14). To offset this position, you can sell the October 75 put and reap a profit of $962.50 [($18^3/_4$ – $9^1/_8$) × 100 = \$962.50]. If you choose to exercise the position, you will end up with a short position of 100 shares of XYX @ 75. This would bring in an additional credit of \$7,500 (minus commissions). However, you would then be obligated to cover the short some time in the future by purchasing 100 shares of XYX at the current price. If you covered the short with the shares priced at $62^3/_4$, you would make a profit of \$1,225. Although you have the opportunity to make a slightly higher profit by exercising the long put, you would need enough money in your trading account to post a deposit of at least \$11,250 (\$7,500 × $1^1/_2$ = \$11,250; the actual amount would be determined by your broker).

The profit/loss line for a long put strategy slopes upward from right to left. This signifies that the profit increases as the market price of the underlying stock falls. The risk profile for this example is shown in Figure 5.15.

A long put strategy, just like shorting a stock, makes a profit when the underlying asset decreases in price. However, these two bearish strategies differ greatly when it comes to profit potentials, risk, margin requirements, and breakevens. The profit on

Long 1 October XYX 75 Put @ $9^1/_8$

Exit Method	Procedure	Profit	Margin
Offset	Sell 1 Oct 75 Put @ $18^3/_4$	\$ 962.50	\$ 0
Exercise	Exercise put, hold a short stock position, buy 100 shares of XYX @ $62^3/_4$	\$1,225.00	\$11,250

Figure 5.14   Exit Strategy of Long Put Position

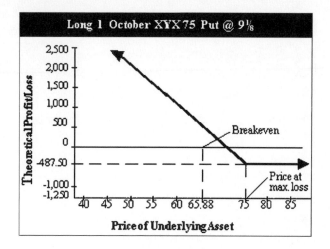

Figure 5.15   Long Put Risk Graph

a long put position is unlimited as the price of the stock falls below the breakeven. The profit on a short stock position is unlimited as the stock price falls below the initial price where the stock was sold. The risk, however, is significantly different, which leads to different returns on investment (ROIs).

In the case of a long put, the risk is limited to the premium paid to purchase the option. In contrast, the risk of the short stock position is unlimited as the price of the underlying asset rises. Thus, the ROI for the long put will be much greater than for the short stock. This risk differential shows up dramatically in the margin requirements for the two positions. The long put requires the payment of the premium, but no additional margin. The maximum potential loss is limited to the premium paid. The short stock position will result in an initial credit to your trading account in the amount of the sale, but will also require a margin availability of $1^{1}/_{2}$ times that amount or more upon entering the position (much more with a highly volatile tech stock). Also, if the price goes against you and moves up, you would be subject to increasing margin requirements.

The one positive benefit of the short stock over the long put is the breakeven point. With the short stock, the breakeven point is the price at which the stock was initially sold. As the stock moves below that price, the trade becomes profitable. With the long put, the price of the stock must move below the strike price of the put minus the premium paid for the trade to become profitable.

Shorting a stock comes with unlimited risk as you can see by reviewing the risk profile of the short stock strategy in Figure 5.16. An increase in the price of the stock above the breakeven triggers a loss of $1 per point per share. In contrast, the purchase of a long put is a managed risk strategy that takes advantage of bearish movement with minimal investment capital.

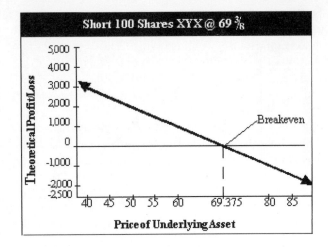

Figure 5.16 Short Stock Risk Graph

Short Put Example

The sale of a put option garners a credit into your trading account in the amount of the option's premium. The premium received is the maximum reward for a short put position. In most cases, you are anticipating that the short put will expire worthless by expiration. If the price of the underlying stock remains higher than the strike price of the put, you will not be in danger of having the put assigned by an option buyer. There is no reason for an option buyer to exercise the put option when the person can sell the underlying stock at a higher current price. If the price of the underlying stock falls below the strike price, a corresponding put buyer may choose to exercise it and your put may be assigned.

> *A short put strategy offers limited profit potential and unlimited risk.*
> *It is best placed in a bullish market when you anticipate a rise in*
> *the price of the underlying market beyond the breakeven.*

By shorting a put option, you are selling the right to sell the underlying instrument at the strike price until the expiration date. That means that if you are assigned, you have an obligation to buy the underlying stock from the assigned option buyer at the strike price of the short put. This results in a long stock position at a higher price. However, you still get to keep the premium paid for the short call to offset any losses you take. The maximum loss has limited downside risk as the underlying asset falls to zero.

Let's create an example using the put premium values in Figure 5.12. Since the way to make money on a short put is to let the put expire worthless, it is important to sell an option with less than 45 days until expiration. Although an option with more time until expiration will bring in a higher initial credit and a lower breakeven, more than 45 days will leave the underlying stock too much time to fall beneath the put's strike price. Therefore, let's track the scenario of one short September XYX 70 Put @ $4^7/_8$.

Upon initiation of the trade, the option writer receives a credit of $487.50, which is the maximum profit available on this trade (see Figure 5.17). The breakeven is calculated by subtracting the put premium from the strike price. In this example, the breakeven is $65^1/_8$—as long as XYX remains above $65.13 per share, you will not lose money on this position.

A short put strategy offers three distinct exit scenarios. Each scenario depends on the movement of the underlying stock. The best exit strategy occurs if the underlying stock rises above the put strike price and the put expires worthless. If this occurs, you get to keep the premium, which is the maximum profit on a short put position. However, if the underlying stock reverses and starts to fall, you may want to offset the position by purchasing a put option with the same strike price and expiration to exit the trade. If the underlying asset falls below the put strike price, the put may be assigned to a put holder. If your put is assigned, you will be obligated to buy 100 shares of XYX at $70 per share. This gives you a long stock position that you can either sell at a loss or wait for a reversal. The maximum loss occurs if the price of XYX falls to zero. The short put writer then loses $7,000 (100 shares × 70 = $7,000) less the $487.50 credit received from the premium or a total of $6,512.50 ($7,000 − $487.50 = $6,512.50).

The short put strategy, like a long stock position, makes a profit in a bullish market. There are many differences between these two strategies including profit potentials, margin requirements, and breakevens. The profit on a long stock position is unlimited as the price of the stock rises above the initial price, while the profit on a short put is limited to the premium received when the trade is placed. The breakeven of a long stock position is the price of the stock at initiation. The breakeven of the short put is usually lower than that of a long stock because the breakeven of a short put is offset by the credit received from the put premium. This relationship is exploited by a strategy known as a covered put.

Covered put: A short put option position hedged against a short stock position.

The margin on a short put can be as high as $50,000, depending on the brokerage. The margin on a long stock position rarely exceeds 50% of the total cost of the shares. Since a short put comes with high margin rates, limited profit potential, and high risk, we do not recommend selling a naked put option. But it is important to understand how a short put works, for it is used in many low-risk, combination options strategies.

Short 1 September XYX 70 Put @ $4^7/_8$

Maximum risk = Unlimited as stock falls to zero	Reaches maximum if the stock reaches zero
Maximum reward = Net credit	$4^7/_8 \times 100 = \$478.50$
Breakeven = Short strike price − Put premium	$65^1/_8 \ (70 − 4^7/_8 = 65^1/_8)$

Figure 5.17 Short Put Results

A long stock risk profile slants down from right to left (see Figure 5.18). A short put strategy also creates a risk profile that slants down from right to left (see Figure 5.19) but has a horizontal line that represents the limited credit available from the sale. Notice that as the price of the asset falls, the loss of your short put position increases until the price of the underlying stock hits zero. This signifies that the profit increases as the market price of the underlying stock rises.

COVERED WRITES

Options are effective tools that make an invaluable contribution to your trading arsenal. They provide high-leverage opportunities that can really make a difference to your trading approach. The secret to making a profit on them, however, lies in your ability to understand how they work and the best ways in which they can be applied.

One conservative income strategy quite popular among traditional buy-and-hold investors uses options as protection on long and short stock positions. A covered write is designed to secure additional cash from stock positions and provide limited protection against decreases in the price of a long underlying stock position (covered call) or increases in the price of a short underlying stock position (covered put). The key word to remember here is *limited*. Unfortunately, investors who are not well versed in options often employ covered write strategies without a concrete understanding of the risks involved. Bottom line: If a market makes a big move, losses can occur. However, covered writes do provide traders with more protection than traditional uncovered stock positions.

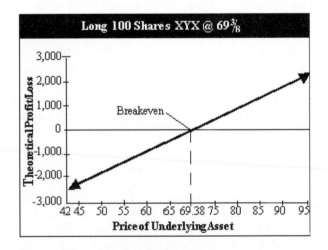

Figure 5.18   Long Stock Risk Graph

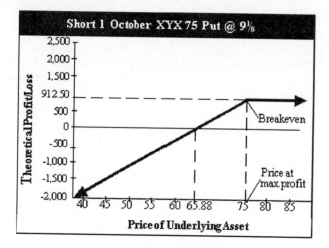

Short 1 October XYX 75 Put @ 9⅛

Figure 5.19   Short Put Risk Graph

Since writing an option involves the sale of an option, a profit is made on the time decay of the short option. Your success with this strategy lies in your ability to skillfully discern the nature of a market's directional trend.

There are two kinds of covered writes: covered calls and covered puts. A covered call is composed of the purchase of stock shares and the sale of call options. A covered put consists of the sale of stock shares and the sale of put options. Profit on the options is derived from the credit received from the options premiums at the initiation of the trade. Investors receive a credit for the amount of the option premium and get to keep that credit if and when the option expires worthless.

It is important to note that writing (selling) options comes with an obligation to deliver (call) or purchase (put) the underlying stock at the option's strike price if the option is exercised. This obligation increases the risk of a covered write. A limited profit, however, can still be made even if the option is assigned and exercised if the move stays within the trade's profit range. Therefore, it is best to place covered writes in stable or sideways markets. A sideways or range-trading market exhibits price action between two specified points: resistance and support. Resistance is the point at which prices stop rising and tend to drop. Support is the point at which prices tend to stop dropping and start to rise. When a range-trading stock rises, it hits a certain price where the sellers rush in, soon outnumbering the buyers. At this point, prices start to fall off. The support level is the price where buyers start to outnumber the sellers and the price begins to rise again. Stocks exhibiting these characteristics can be excellent candidates for covered writing. However, you should also note that range-bound stocks can begin trending at any time—there are no guarantees. Let the seller beware!

Covered Calls

A covered call trade combines a long stock position with the sale of call options against it. This strategy is best implemented in a bullish to neutral market where a slow rise in the market price of the underlying stock is anticipated. This strategy allows traders to handle moderate price declines because the call premium reduces the position's breakeven. The success of a covered call relies on the short option expiring worthless. Hence, try to sell options with 45 days or less until expiration. However, since the profit on a covered call is limited to the premium received plus any stock appreciation up to the strike price of the short option, the premium needs to be high enough to balance out the trade's risk. Figure 5.20 illustrates the advantages a covered call offers in comparison to simply purchasing stock.

Let's create a hypothetical example using XYX currently trading at 71½. Unlike *vertical spreads*, there are a limited number of options that can be used successfully with covered calls. As previously mentioned, the key to a successful covered call lies in finding a stable market with slightly OTM options with less than 45 days till expiration with enough premium to make the trade worthwhile. Using the values in Figure 5.21, there are a few winning options that fit the criteria previously mentioned. Although the October 75 option brings in a larger premium than the 80 call,

---

Vertical spreads: Combined options strategies that offer limited potential profits as well as limited risks by combining long and short options with different strike prices and like expiration dates. The juxtaposition of long and short options has a directional bias and results in a net debit or net credit.

Covered Call Strategy versus Long Stock Strategy

Market Scenario	Covered Call	Long Stock
Stock price increases: Call is assigned to an option buyer and the underlying stock shares must be sold at the call's strike price.	Profits are limited to the premium received on the short call plus the profit made from the difference between the stock's price at initiation and the call strike price.	Profits may be garnered if the stock is sold at the higher price.
Stock price remains stable: Call expires worthless and the trader still owns the stock shares.	Profits are limited to the premium received on the short call.	No profit is made.
Stock price decreases: Call expires worthless and the trader still owns the stock shares.	The breakeven on the stock is lowered by the premium received on the short call.	Losses accumulate as the stock price declines.

Figure 5.20   Covered Call versus Long Stock Strategy Comparison

Price of XYX = 71$\frac{1}{2}$

Call Strike Price	September	October
65	11$\frac{3}{4}$	12$\frac{3}{4}$
70	7	8$\frac{7}{8}$
75	3$\frac{1}{4}$	6
80	1$\frac{15}{16}$	4$\frac{1}{4}$
85	$\frac{3}{4}$	2$\frac{1}{2}$

Figure 5.21   XYX Call Option Premiums

it only allows the underlying stock to move 3$\frac{1}{2}$ points before assignment. The September options do not offer high enough premiums to make them worthwhile positions. Instead, let's create a covered call by selling 1 October XYX 80 Call @ 4$\frac{1}{4}$ against 100 shares of XYX stock purchased at 71$\frac{1}{2}$.

The maximum profit for this trade is the premium received for the short call option plus the profit to be gained on the long stock. The maximum reward on the option side of this position is $425. The maximum reward on the stock side of this position is $850. The maximum profit on this example of a covered call strategy is $1,275 (see Figure 5.22). The maximum risk is limited to the downside as XYX falls below the breakeven to zero. The option side of this trade should not require a heavy margin deposit to place because the short call option is covered by the long stock.

The breakeven on a covered call is calculated by subtracting the call premium from the price of the underlying stock at initiation. In this example, the breakeven is 67$\frac{1}{4}$. XYX must drop below 67$\frac{1}{4}$ for the trade to begin to take a loss. If the stock rises to or above 80, the call will be assigned. You can then use the original XYX shares purchased at 71$\frac{1}{2}$ to fulfill your obligation to deliver 100 XYX shares to the option holder at 80, thereby garnering the maximum profit of $1,275.

Covered Call: Long 100 Shares XYX@ 71$\frac{1}{2}$, Short 1 October XYX80 Call @ 4$\frac{1}{4}$

Maximum risk = Limited to the price of the underlying stock at initiation – short call premium	$(71\frac{1}{2} - 4\frac{1}{4}) \times 100 = \$6,725$
Maximum reward = [Short call premium + (short call strike price – price of long underlying asset)] × value per point	$[4\frac{1}{4} + (80 - 71\frac{1}{2})] \times 100 = \$1,275$
Breakeven = Price of the underlying asset at initiation – short call premium	$71\frac{1}{2} - 4\frac{1}{4} = 67\frac{1}{4}$

Figure 5.22   Covered Call Results

The risk graph for this trade is shown in Figure 5.23. The profit line on this trade slopes up from left to right, conveying the trader's desire for the market price of the stock to rise slightly. It also shows the trade's limited protection. As XYX declines beyond the breakeven (67¼), the value of the position plummets as the stock falls to zero.

Since a covered call only protects a stock within a specific range, it is vital to monitor the daily price movement of the underlying stock. Let's investigate optimal exit strategies in the following four scenarios:

1. ***XYX rises above the short strike (80):*** The short call is assigned. You can use the 100 shares from the original long stock position to satisfy your obligation to deliver 100 shares of XYZ to the option holder at $80 a share. This scenario allows you to take in the maximum profit of $1,275.

2. ***XYX falls below the short strike (80), but above initial stock price (71½):*** The short call expires worthless and you get to keep the premium received. No losses have occurred on the long stock position, and you are ready to place another covered call to offset the risk on the long stock position if you wish.

3. ***XYX falls below the initial stock price (71½),*** but stays above the breakeven (67¼): The long stock position starts to lose money, but this loss is offset by the credit received from the short call. If XYX stays above 67¼, the position will break even or make a small profit.

4. ***XYX falls below the breakeven (67¼):*** Let the short option expire worthless and use the credit received to partially hedge the loss on the long stock position.

Covered calls are the most popular option strategy used in today's markets. If you want to gain additional income on a long stock position, you can sell a slightly OTM call every month. The risk lies in the strategy's limited ability to protect the

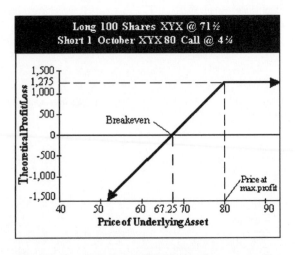

Figure 5.23   Covered Call Risk Graph

underlying stock from major moves down and the potential loss of future profits on the stock above the strike price. Covered calls can also be combined with a number of bearish options strategies to create additional downside protection.

Covered Puts

In a covered put strategy, you are shorting the underlying stock and selling a put option against it. This strategy is best implemented in a bearish to neutral market where a slow fall in the market price of the underlying stock is anticipated. This strategy's profit-making ability depends on the short option's ability to expire worthless at expiration. Therefore, although an option with more time yields a higher premium, never sell puts in a covered put strategy with more than 45 days until expiration. Too much time increases the chance of the market price moving into a range where the short option is no longer effective at mitigating the loss on the short stock position. However, if the short put is assigned, you can use the 100 shares of the underlying stock you were obligated to buy at the put's strike price from the option holder to cover the short stock position and make the maximum profit. This strategy requires a large margin deposit to place.

Let's create an example of a covered put strategy using the values in Figure 5.24 with XYX trading at 71½. Looking at the prices, the October 65 put is probably the best trade available. To make the maximum profit, XYX needs to fall below $65. If the put option is assigned, you can then use the shares you are obligated to buy from the assigned option holder to cover the short stock position. You get to keep the premium received from the short put plus receive the money accrued from the difference between the initial stock price (71½) and the put strike price (65). The maximum reward on the option side of this position is $400. The maximum reward on the stock side of this position is $650. This creates a maximum total profit of $1,050 (see Figure 5.25).

The breakeven is calculated by adding the price of the underlying asset at initiation to the short put premium. In this example, the breakeven is 75½. The maximum risk is unlimited to the upside beyond the breakeven. This is a very important point to remember. A covered put only offers limited protection on a short stock position.

The risk graph of a covered put (see Figure 5.26) shows the profit/loss line slanting upward from right to left to a maximum profit of $1,050. As the underlying stock rises above the breakeven, the loss on the position is unlimited.

Price of XYX = 71½

Put Strike Price	September	October
60	$7/8$	$1^9/_{16}$
65	$1½$	4
70	$2^3/_8$	$6¼$
75	$5¼$	$8^{11}/_{16}$
80	$9^7/_{16}$	$10½$

Figure 5.24 Put Option Premiums

Short 100 Shares XYX @ 71½, Short 1 October XYX 65 Put @ 4

Maximum risk = Unlimited above the breakeven	Unlimited above 75½
Maximum reward = [Short put premium + (price of long underlying asset at initiation – short put strike price)] × value per point	[4 + (71½ – 65)] × 100 = $1,050
Breakeven = Price of the underlying asset at initiation + short put premium	71½ + 4 = 75½

Figure 5.25   Covered Put Results

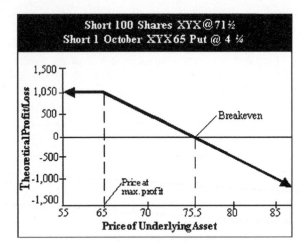

Figure 5.26   Covered Put Risk Graph

To make a profit on a covered put position, it is important to monitor the underlying stock to watch for breakouts above the breakeven. Let's take a look at the exit strategies in the following four scenarios:

1. *XYX falls below the short strike (65):* The short put is assigned. You can use the 100 shares you are obligated to buy at the short put strike price to cover the original short stock position. This scenario allows you to take in the maximum profit of $1,050.

2. *XYX rises above the short strike (65), but below the initial stock price (71½):* The short put expires worthless and you get to keep the premium received. No losses have occurred on the short stock position and you are ready to place another covered put to bring in additional profit on the position if you wish.

3. *XYX rises above the initial stock price (71½) but stays below the breakeven (75½):* The short stock position starts to lose money, but this loss is offset by the credit received from the short put. As long as the stock stays below the breakeven, the position will break even or make a small profit.

4. *XYX rises above the breakeven (75½):* Let the short put expire worthless and use the credit received to partially hedge the loss on the short stock position.

Covered puts enable traders to bring in some extra premium on short positions. Once again, you can keep selling a put against the short shares every month to increase your profit. However, shorting stock is a risky trade no matter how you look at it because there is no limit to how much you can lose if the price of the stock rises above the breakeven. There are many other ways to take advantage of a stock's bearish movement using options to limit the trade's risk and maximize the leveraging ability of your trading account.

Options are effective trading tools. In the beginning, options trading will most likely be a little confusing. But, hopefully, the terms discussed in this introductory chapter will help you locate and understand specific information that can be used to find profitable trades. Options are the mainstay of my trading approach, and I have spent the past decade of my life perfecting their implementation. They have become an indispensable part of my hedge trading operation. I highly encourage you to learn more about them. I am positive that they will enable you to maximize your returns if you take the time to learn how to use them correctly.

ROADMAP TO SUCCESS

Objective	Course of Action
Understand call option basics.	• Call options give traders the right to buy the underlying stock at the strike price until market close on the third Friday of the expiration month. • A call option is in-the-money (ITM) if its strike price is below the current price of the underlying stock. • A call option is out-of-the-money (OTM) if its strike price is above the current price of the underlying stock. • A call option is at-the-money (ATM) if its strike price is the same as (or close to) the current price of the underlying stock.
Understand the process of buying calls.	• If bullish—believe the market will rise—buy (go long) calls. • Buyers have rights. A call buyer has the right, but not the obligation, to buy the underlying stock at the strike price until the expiration date. • If you buy a call option, your maximum risk is the money paid for the option, the debit. • The maximum profit is unlimited depending on the rise in the price of the underlying asset. • To offset a long call, you have to sell a call with the same strike price and identical expiration date to close out the position. • By exercising a long call, you are choosing to purchase 100 shares of the underlying stock at the strike price of the call option.
Understand the process of selling naked calls.	• If bearish—believe the market will fall—sell (go short) calls. • Sellers have obligations. If a call is assigned, the call seller has the obligation to buy 100 shares of the underlying stock at the strike price from the person to whom the option was sold.

- If you sell a call option, your risk is unlimited to the upside.
- The profit is limited to the credit received from the sale of the call.
- When selling calls, make sure to choose options with little time left until expiration. Call sellers want the call to expire worthless so that they can keep the whole premium.
- To offset a short call, you have to buy a call with the same strike price to close out the position.
- Selling naked calls is an extremely risky strategy that comes with unlimited risk.

Understand put option basics.	• Put options give traders the right, but not the obligation, to sell the underlying stock at the strike price until market close on the third Friday of the expiration month. • A put option is in-the-money (ITM) if its strike price is above the current price of the underlying stock. • A put option is out-of-the-money (OTM) if its strike price is below the current price of the underlying stock. • A put option is at-the-money (ATM) if its strike price is the same as (or close to) the current price of the underlying stock.
Understand the process of buying puts.	• If bearish—believe the market will fall—buy (go long) puts. • Buyers have rights. A put buyer has the right, but not the obligation, to sell the underlying stock at the strike price until the expiration date. • If you buy a put option, your risk is the money paid for the option, the debit. • The profit is unlimited depending on the fall in the price of the underlying asset. • To offset a long put, you have to sell a put with the same strike price and identical expiration date to close out the position. • By exercising your long put, you are choosing to go short the underlying stock at the strike price of the put option.
Understand the process of selling naked puts.	• If bullish—believe the market will rise—sell (go short) puts. • Sellers have obligations. A put seller has the obligation to buy 100 shares (per option) of the underlying stock at the put strike price from the option holder if the put is assigned. • If you sell a put option, your risk is unlimited as the underlying stock falls to zero. • The profit is limited to the credit received from the sale of the put. • When selling puts, make sure to choose options with little time left until expiration. Put sellers want a put to expire worthless so that they can keep the whole premium. • To offset a short put, you have to buy a put with the same strike price and expiration to close out the position. • Selling naked puts is an extremely risky strategy that comes with unlimited risk as the underlying stock falls to zero.

Understand how to create a covered call trade.	• Choose a higher-strike call no more than two months out to sell against long shares of the underlying stock. • The maximum potential profit is the credit received from the short call option, plus the difference between the strike price and the price of the underlying stock at initiation. • The maximum potential risk is unlimited to the downside and requires margin to place. • Calculate the breakeven by subtracting the short call premium from the price of the underlying stock at initiation. • Choose an exit strategy before placing the trade. • Watch the market closely as it fluctuates. The profit on this strategy is limited—an unlimited loss occurs if and when the underlying stock falls below the breakeven point.
Understand how to create a covered put trade.	• Choose a lower-strike put no more than two months out to sell against short shares of the underlying stock. • The maximum potential profit is the credit received from the short put option, plus the difference between the strike price of the put and the price of the underlying stock at the inception of the trade. • The maximum potential risk is unlimited to the upside and requires margin to place. • Calculate the breakeven by adding the short put premium to the price of the underlying stock at initiation. • Choose an exit strategy before placing the trade. • Watch the market closely as it fluctuates. The profit on this strategy is limited—an unlimited loss occurs if and when the underlying stock rises above the breakeven point.
Option-Specific Web Sites	**CoveredCall.com** (www.coveredcall.com): Strategy advice on covered calls, credit spreads, LEAPS, and stock splits. **Financial Web** (www.strikeprice.com): Offers fundamental data and historical prices of options and stocks. **INO** (www.ino.com): This well-organized site features futures and options. **Optionetics.com** (www.optionetics.com): Check out the link to an in-house section called Platinum, a comprehensive options analysis software. **OptionsInvestor.com** (optioninvestor.com): One of the fastest-growing options advisory sites on the Net. **Options Industry Association** (www.optionscentral.com): The Options Industry Council (OIC) is the educational arm of several exchanges. **OptionSource.com** (www.options-iri.com): Bernie Schaeffer's excellent options web site. **Stricknet.com** (www.stricknet.com/index.htm): Options and covered call picks, pure plays, and naked puts.

6

Broad Market Analysis

Since three out of four stocks move in tandem with the general trend of the market, determining the general direction of the marketplace is vital to your success. To assess the general movement of the market—up, down or sideways—you need to know how to use the tools that provide clues to the nature of general market performance. Broad market analysis offers traders the tools to assess the marketplace as a whole, monitor specific exchanges and industrial sectors, and examine an individual stock's performance in comparison to its competitors.

> **Broad market analysis:** Analysis techniques that accurately identify market trends by reviewing the flow of money, analyzing index performance, keeping tabs on industry group leadership, scanning changes in the advance-decline line (A/D line), and monitoring the release of government reports.

If you want to become involved in the stock market, you're literally betting your financial well-being on market performance. In order to meet this challenge, I strongly urge you to begin watching it and not just the sound bite on the evening news. Actively monitoring everything from seasonal changes to scheduled and unscheduled news that affects the markets will help you to keep up with what's going on in the business world. You even need to monitor domestic and global economies to gauge future market direction.

But studying the markets is just part of the picture. You also have to take into account that the market will change course when it suspects the economy is heating up or slowing down. This chapter is designed to help you get a handle on how the economy works and how certain events influence market performance.

If you study the U.S. economy, you'll find it expands (grows) and contracts (shrinks). In the old days, this inevitable cycle would mean terrific boom times followed by recessions, even depressions. These days the cycle has been evened out to a great extent; but it still cycles. If the economy grows too quickly, inflation results. If it shrinks too dramatically, productivity drops, and we have layoffs, bankruptcies, and widespread unemployment.

Stock movement tends to precede these cycles because investors are always looking forward, anticipating the direction of a company. Anything that puts a strain on a company's ability to maintain their profit ratio can send a stock south. Likewise, any factor that increases a stock's ability to make a profit can make a stock advance. This is because we invest in things that grow, and we close out our investment when we anticipate growth is ebbing.

Without a crystal ball, investors practically have to grow antennae when it comes to forecasting market performance. Luckily, there are a variety of reports, indicators, and general tools that enable investors and traders to keep their fingers on the pulse of the stock market. The Internet has made this information easily available, further enabling the investor to track and interpret data as it's released. These tools come in the form of monetary policy (such as interest rates and the value of the dollar), scheduled government reports, index analysis, sector comparisons, market indicators, seasonal factors, and changes in the political climate. Some of these factors have an immediate or short-term effect on stock market activity while others come to fruition over the long term.

You don't have to become an expert in economics to gauge market performance; but you do need to know what you're looking for and how to use the information that's out there. Part of a trader's learning curve depends on his or her ability to integrate an understanding of the big picture with the multitude of details that trading individual stocks requires. Since money is the lifeblood of the stock market, understanding how it moves and where it moves is a major key to financial success. Events not only move the markets, but also the international flow of money as investors seek the highest possible rate of return. The thought of international money flow may be incomprehensible to many of us; but it is an important part of the big picture. So put on your high waders—the water's just fine.

INFLATION, INTEREST RATES, AND THE FED

If preservation of capital is at the heart of the investment battle, inflation is the first line drawn in the sand. Even though the media would like to be able to classify inflation using a glib number pulled from the teeth of some influential government report, the rate of inflation is an ever-changing presence. It's at the gas pump and the 7-Eleven. It's waiting for you online. Inflation is always nipping at our heels in one way or another. Staying ahead of it is the task at hand—a cause taken up by many a baby-booming investor.

When we speak about *inflation*, we are specifically talking about the increase in the annual cost of living. As long as the rate runs at about 3% to 4%, inflation is said to be held in check. But looking back over the past 20 years, we've seen rates of inflation top 15%. The outcome is grim: Inflation means less profits, and less profits mean lower stock valuations. Why? High inflation triggers a rise in interest rates. An increase in interest rates slows the economy down by putting the reins on lending and business expansion, increasing home mortgage rates, and scaling back consumer spending. Low inflation and low interest rates keep money flowing into the stock market.

Figure 6.1 shows the rate of inflation since 1994. Between 1994 and 1999, the inflation rate has risen 2.5%. This may not seem like much, but every increase in inflation eats away at the strength of a dollar's purchasing power. In fact, the threat of inflation alone can move the market. The market likes inflation reports to show that inflation is under control. If the economy shows signs of continued future growth, company management will be more confident that consumers will be able to buy new cars, finance them at reasonable interest rates, and retain a positive consumer attitude that encourages heavy spending.

If inflationary pressures become increasingly worrisome, look out! Enter the Fed, or the Federal Reserve Board to be exact. The Fed is a conglomerate of 12 separate district banks governed by a seven-member Board of Governors that works more like a government agency than a corporation. The Federal Reserve System is charged with fostering national growth without generating inflation. It accomplishes this feat by holding a Federal Open Market Committee (FOMC) meeting every six weeks (eight times a year) to balance the amount of money in circulation and keep the economy prosperous without creating inflation. If the members decide that the economy needs a boost, they tell the Federal Reserve Bank of New York to speed up the creation of dollars to keep the economy running smoothly. If they think inflation is on the rise, they may decide to use their secret weapon: interest rates.

Money supply is the key to keeping the economy expanding or contracting.

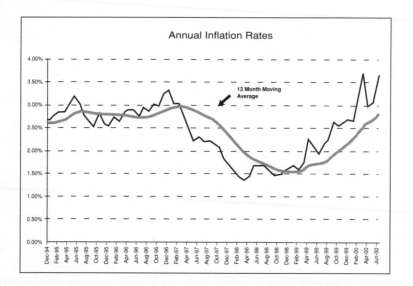

Figure 6.1   Annual Inflation Rates (1999–2000) (Courtesy of Economagic.com)

When the economy shows signs of faltering, money is pumped into the economy, done so by the easing of interest rates and the redemption of government paper (Treasury notes, bills, and bonds). Money that was formerly out of circulation reenters the economy. Money becomes cheaper (because there's more of it), meaning businesses will borrow more to expand, which creates new jobs and higher wages; and if left unchecked, inflationary pressures begin to build. This is when the Federal Reserve says "Enough!" and begins to restrict the availability of money. The Fed auctions more paper and raises interest rates, both of which work in unison to reduce the monetary supply. When you see the *M1*, *M2*, and *M3* reports, they are measurements of money in the system.

M1: Money that can be spent immediately. Includes cash, checking accounts, and NOW accounts.

M2: M1 plus assets invested for the short term. These assets include money market accounts and money market mutual funds.

M3: M2 plus big deposits. Big deposits include institutional money market funds and agreements among banks.

You don't really need to fully understand every last little detail, but you need to know how these indicators work and if they are likely to prompt the Fed to raise or lower interest rates. The amount of reserves a bank has to hold changes as its deposits and transactions change. When a bank needs additional reserves on a short-term basis, it can borrow them from other banks that happen to have more reserves than they need. These loans take place in a private financial market called the federal funds market. The interest rate on the overnight borrowing of reserves is called the federal funds rate or simply the funds rate. It adjusts to balance the supply of and demand for reserves. For example, an increase in the amount of reserves supplied to the federal funds market causes the funds rate to fall, while a decrease in the supply of reserves raises that rate.

Federal funds rate: Set daily by the market, this rate is the most sensitive indicator of the direction of interest rates. It is the interest rate at which banks lend and borrow federal funds among themselves.

Figures 6.2 and 6.3 point to the strong influence interest rates hold over stock prices. The first graph shows interest rate levels as measured by the fed funds rate, and the second shows how the market performed, as measured by the S&P 500 over the same period. In the first half of 1998, rates were running between 5.4% and 5.6%. When the Fed began lowering interest rates—partially to allay fears created by the financial crises in South America and Russia—the market began a rally that surprised many. Even in 1999, when rates began rising again, the market seemed to shrug off the hikes, but still staggered a bit when the rate hikes were enacted.

Federal Funds Rate

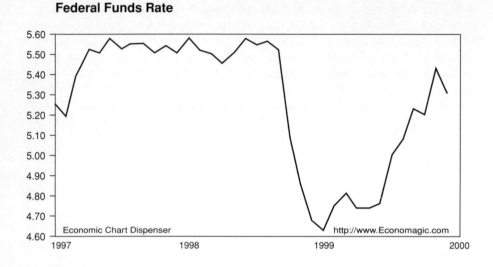

Figure 6.2 Federal Funds Rate 1997–1999 (Courtesy of Economagic.com)

S&P 500 Total Return; Monthly Dividend Reinvest '97–'99

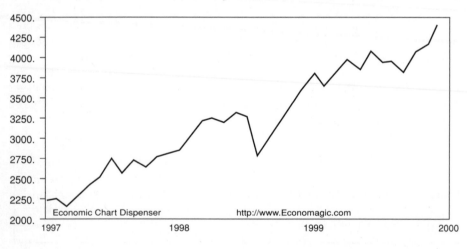

Figure 6.3 S&P 500 1997–1999 (Courtesy of Economagic.com)

The Federal Reserve Board controls interest rates by moving the *discount rate* up or down. Banks key off the discount rate to set interest rates they charge to customers for loans, because the discount rate is the cost of funds to a bank. Banks borrow money from the Fed, and then lend it out as loans at a slightly higher rate. This is one of the ways they earn profits. Interest rates are the *cost of money* that businesses and consumers alike must pay. When this cost goes up, the economy and corporate profits go down. This is why the stock market abhors rising interest rates and loves falling rates. Figures 6.2 and 6.3 show this inverse relationship. In 1998, the Fed began lowering interest rates in the middle of the year. The stock market, as reflected in the S&P 500, began to rally almost immediately, a clear example of the strong influence interest rates have over the stocks.

Discount rate: The interest rate charged by the 12 Federal Reserve banks for short-term loans made to member banks.

We are in an environment where a great deal of attention is focused on monetary policy changes, especially those contemplated by Alan Greenspan, the current chairman of the Federal Open Market Committee. He and the other Fed governors are in charge of setting interest rates in order to curb inflation, while maintaining a sustainable level of growth in our nation's economy. Twice a year, the Federal Reserve chairman officially speaks to Congress at the Humphrey-Hawkins Testimony (www.bog.frb.fed.us/boarddocs/hh), and stocks rally or descend in anticipation of what he'll say. In the wake of his testimony, the bearing of the economy may be adjusted with an increase or decrease of interest rates. This kind of information has a powerful effect on the markets, which is why whenever Alan Greenspan speaks, the stock market hums with volatility. However, if the market expects the Fed to raise interest rates, as long as the hike is in line with expectations the market will not experience too much of a correction, and may in fact rally—called a *relief rally*.

Interest rate decisions have far-reaching effects on companies as they make decisions about raising capital to build plants or purchase equipment. Additionally, companies have to monitor their own respective customers' financial condition, need for their products and services, and future growth. For example, Boeing (BA) is a large aerospace firm in Seattle that does very well when the economy is expanding. A healthy economy means new orders for planes, which leads to the hiring of additional employees; but when the economy slows down, the number of jets being ordered drops, and the company is forced to lay people off. People, in turn, buy Boeing stock when the outlook is good, and sell it when the new orders slow down. In good times, people spend more because they're more confident. This leads to a rise in spending, so companies that benefit directly from this spending increase become attractive investments.

Even the least market-savvy person in your office is probably aware that the market is watching interest rate policy carefully. Interest rates are the price of money and have an inverse relationship with the stock market. An increase in interest rates has a negative effect on stock prices, while an interest rate decline is good for stock prices.

Interest Rates	Dollar	Bonds	Stocks
Up	Up	Down	Down
Down	Down	Up	Up
Sideways	Sideways	Sideways	Up

Figure 6.4 Typical Relationships of Interest Rates versus Dollar, Bonds, and Stocks

Figure 6.4 illustrates the typical relationship a change in interest rates has to bonds, the stock market, and the value of the dollar (i.e., the normal expected action given the theory behind the economics). But keep in mind the word *typical*, because there are times when a divergence from this chart happens.

It is interesting to note that a rise in interest rates can lead to an increase in the value of the dollar. If the Fed wants the value of the dollar to go up, it accomplishes this by raising interest rates so that investors will put money in dollars. It is the natural law of financial physics that money always flows to the highest return on capital (i.e., you always want to get the highest return on your money relative to risk). For example, if a foreign government wants a safe place to invest cash, it'll look to buy the bonds with the highest interest rates. Therefore, one of the ways to firm up the U.S. dollar is to raise interest rates.

An inverse relationship exists between bond prices and interest rates. If interest rates go up, bond prices go down; and if interest rates go down, bond prices go up. Why? An increase in interest rates discourages loans and slows the economy down, while a decrease encourages loans in order to jump-start the economy. Let's say you decide to lend me $1,000 for a five-year period of time. I agree to pay you 8% interest charges ($80 per year interest). If interest rates suddenly jump to 10%, you could have lent the same $1,000 and received $100 per year interest. Therefore the value of the first loan went down with the rise in interest rates.

Since interest rates have an inverse relationship to the stock market, the correlation can be made that bond prices and the stock market move in tandem. This relationship is easy to explain. Let's say your company has to buy $10,000 worth of equipment and you don't want to pay cash for the equipment. If you want to finance the purchase, you have to pay interest. Let's say you have to pay 8% interest or $800 per year on $10,000. Interest is an expense that gets subtracted from earnings. Therefore, if you earn $20,000 before interest expenses, you will have earned $19,200 after interest is paid. Now what if interest rates are at 10%? The same $10,000 loan now requires you to pay $1,000 per year in interest decreasing earnings to $19,000 ($20,000 − $1,000 = $19,000). These examples show that an inverse relationship exists between interest rates and earnings—the higher your interest rate, the less money flows to your earnings. A decline in earnings can have a significant (negative) effect on a stock's price. Therefore, if interest rates go up, bond prices fall and stock prices decrease.

This inverse relationship does not always hold. There are periods when a divergence will occur—a company's earnings will increase even though interest rates go up. However, these divergences are generally short-term in nature. You can usually count on the market coming back, reacting to the change in interest rates.

There are a multitude of web sites that offer sound economic information, including:

- **Briefing.com** *(www.briefing.com): Offers a number of graphs that can tell you in an instant which direction rates are going.*
- **Cleveland Federal Reserve** *(www.clev.frb.org): Helps to explain everything about economics.*
- **Economic Indicators.com** *(www.economic-indicators.com/Economic News.html): Provides a tremendous number of links that will assist you in understanding how the economy is performing.*
- **Financial Trends.com** *(www.fintrend.com/ftf): Offers useful information about inflation.*

THE FLOW OF CAPITAL

Like a stream transforming and mutating, money controls the economies of nations and the quality of life for individuals all over the world. Electronically controlled and extremely sensitive, its worth depends on the agreement of all participants. Since the success of a company's stock depends on money, it is essential to have a broad understanding of this unique raw material.

Flow of money sometimes becomes flight of capital. What drives capital to take flight? As previously stated, it is the nature of investors to constantly seek the highest reward for the least risk. If interest rates in one country are lower than risk-adjusted rates in other countries, capital flows out of that country in search of higher rates abroad. This causes the foreign exchange rate of the low-interest country to fall. On the other hand, if interest rates in one country are higher than other countries, capital will then flow into the country with the higher rates. This would cause the foreign exchange rate of the higher-interest country to rise.

This is one reason money moves rapidly between countries; between investment categories such as bonds, equities, and commodities; and between individual stocks, commodities, and bonds. It is helpful to understand that a flight of capital from a particular investment (more sellers than buyers) results in falling prices, while capital flowing to an investment (more buyers than sellers) results in rising prices.

The mere fact that money has moved and prices have changed results in a shift in the risk/reward ratio of any investment. Fluctuations in the perceived risk/reward ratio can trigger the flight of capital from one investment opportunity to the next. Countries with high inflation seek financial stability for their money. If the investing public believes that the best reward for the risk lies in the U.S. equity markets, capital will flow from all over the world, and from bonds and commodities, into the U.S. stock markets. Conversely, if the general sentiment of the worldwide investing public is that there is about to be a significant degradation of the U.S. equity market (major tax increases, profit warnings, interest rate hikes, adverse political/judicial climate, etc.), capital will flee from the U.S. stocks into any and all other types of investments—bonds, commodities, foreign stocks, and so on. This capital flight will result in a reduction of individual U.S. stock prices and a subsequent increase in price of other assets. These kinds of trends usually continue until investors believe that the potential reward of stocks is higher than other assets.

It is the general tendency of all stocks to follow the market. In fact, various studies attribute as much as 70% of a stock's performance to the movement of the market as a whole. In other words, if money is flowing into the market, most stocks within the market will increase. After all, the market is made up of the sum of all the stocks. In order for the market to increase, most of these stocks will have to increase. Conversely, if the market is declining, then any particular stock is likely to decrease in value as well. While this sounds self-evident, many investors fight the trend by taking a *contrarian* stance.

Contrarian: A contrarian fades the trend by going against the majority view of the marketplace.

What tends to happen in the stock market is a mini-version of the flow of global capital. Just as money will flow from country to country and from commodities to hard assets to stocks, so too does money flow within the stock market as a whole, always searching for the best reward-to-risk ratio. In fact, money tends to seek out the hottest sectors or groups of related stocks. This is why, regardless of overall market direction, not all sectors go up or down at the same time.

ECONOMIC TURNING POINTS AND GOVERNMENT REPORTS

Since capital flow is based, at least partially, on interest rates, what does the Fed look at to measure our economy? The Fed collects data from a number of sources, uses this data to judge whether the economy is expanding or contracting, and most importantly the pace at which it is doing so. Investors also key off this rate of change, for they understand that unusually high or low readings will have a direct effect on interest rates and thus the flow of capital. There are a number of government reports that enable the Fed and investors to keep tabs on the nuts and bolts of our economy. Keeping abreast of these reports is a big priority for investors—they know the market's direction ultimately depends on the severity of inflation.

Employment Report

Closely followed by the investment community, the Employment Report provides a monthly picture of the nation's economic health. It hosts several important components detailing the unemployment rate, nonfarm job growth, weekly hours, and hourly earnings. Figure 6.5 shows a brief rundown of market reaction to these components. Many profitable trading strategies take their cue from the release of this telltale report the first Friday of every month. There has always been a drive to lower employment rates, but when employment rates drop too low, employers have to raise wages to compete for

Figure 6.5   U.S. Unemployment Rate 1990–1999 (Courtesy of Economagic.com)

the best available employees in a shrinking workforce. Wages are often the largest percentage of a company's expenditures. Reduced unemployment has helped give rise to inflation as companies raise prices to cover increased labor costs. Less money for employment leads to lower production costs and the tempering of inflation.

Employment Cost Index (ECI)

The Employment Cost Index (ECI) data are based on a survey of employer payrolls at the end of each quarter. It measures changes in labor costs of money wages and salaries and noncash fringe benefits in nonfarm private industry and state and local government for workers at all levels of responsibility. Analysts specifically look for acceleration or deceleration.

Consumer Price Index (CPI)

The Consumer Price Index (CPI) measures the value of a basket of goods in the current year to the value of that same basket of goods in an earlier year. It measures the average level of prices of the goods and services typically consumed by an urban American family. Widely regarded as the most important inflation report, the CPI gauges retail sales by measuring consumer goods and services. Publishing information about the last month late in the next month, the CPI releases two rates: the overall rate and the core rate (excluding the food and energy sectors).

A year-to-year CPI report can give a clear picture of the rate of inflation. The core rate is perceived as an important inflation indicator. A rise in the CPI rate (increase in inflation) has a negative impact while a decline (a tempering of inflation)

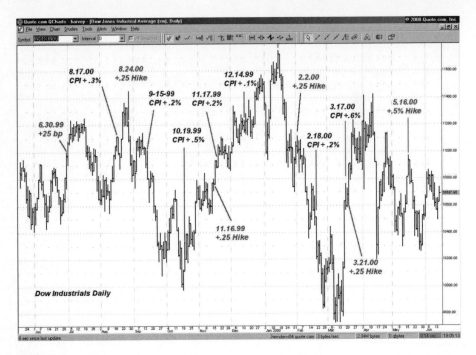

Figure 6.6 1999 Dow Industrials and a Time Line for Interest Rate Hikes (Courtesy of QCharts (www.qcharts.com))

is a positive sign for the stock market. The Fed keeps a close eye on the correlation between the CPI and the Producer Price Index (PPI—the costs of production), as a gauge for inflation divergences. The CPI announcement can often have a volatile effect on the markets, as shown in Figure 6.6. Figure 6.7 shows what a basket of goods would cost during successive time periods.

Inflation has a subtle effect, one you don't really notice, unless it's at the gas pump. To calculate the effects of inflation for any given period of time, go to: Woodrow The Federal Reserve Bank of Minneapolis (woodrow.mpls.frb.fed.us/economy/calc/cpihome.html). You'll find a calculator there that's easy to use, and that graphically illustrates the effects inflation has actually had.

Producer Price Index (PPI)

The PPI is released each month about a week before the release of the CPI and has a strong influence on the Fed's reaction to wholesale pricing inflation and is therefore closely studied by investors and traders. Considered the first inflation report of the month, this important index gauges the prices of commodities at

Year	Jan	Feb	Mar	Apr	May	Jun
1990	127.40	128.00	128.70	128.90	129.20	129.90
1991	134.60	134.80	135.00	135.20	135.60	136.00
1992	138.10	138.60	139.30	139.50	139.70	140.20
1993	142.60	143.10	143.60	144.00	144.20	144.40
1994	146.20	146.70	147.20	147.40	147.50	148.00
1995	150.30	150.90	151.40	151.90	152.20	152.50
1996	154.40	154.90	155.70	156.30	156.60	156.70
1997	159.10	159.60	160.00	160.20	160.10	160.30
1998	161.60	161.90	162.20	162.50	162.80	163.00
1999	164.30	164.50	165.00	166.20	166.20	166.20
2000	168.80	169.80	171.20	171.30	171.50	172.40

Year	Jul	Aug	Sep	Oct	Nov	Dec
1990	130.40	131.60	132.70	133.50	133.80	133.80
1991	136.20	136.60	137.20	137.40	137.80	137.90
1992	140.50	140.90	141.30	141.80	142.00	141.90
1993	144.40	144.80	145.10	145.70	145.80	145.80
1994	148.40	149.00	149.40	149.50	149.70	149.70
1995	152.50	152.90	153.20	153.70	153.60	153.50
1996	157.00	157.30	157.80	158.30	158.60	158.60
1997	160.50	160.80	161.20	161.60	161.50	161.30
1998	163.20	163.40	163.60	164.00	164.00	163.90
1999	166.70	167.10	167.80	168.20	168.30	168.30
2000	172.80	172.80	173.70	174.00		

Figure 6.7   CPI Increases by Month 1990–2000—Shows what a basket of goods would cost during successive time periods. (All Items, All Urban Consumers (CPI-U), 1982–1984 = 100, as revised)

three levels of production: raw materials, intermediate goods, and finished products. In addition, the PPI tallies the overall rate and the core rate of production (excludes food and energy sectors). Of the two, the core rate is more important to investors who look for an annualized PPI rate to stay below 3%. If it rises above this point, inflation is perceived to be on the increase, which has a negative effect on the stock market.

The Price Producer Index has it own web site at stats.bls.gov/ppihome.htm.

National Association of Purchasing Management Index (NAPM Index)

Another indicator of economic growth, the *NAPM Index* presents a wide-ranging view of the manufacturing sectors' ups and downs. This growth or decline reflects in the general economy; as the NAPM rises it will usually bring the stock market up along with it, while forcing bonds down. The NAPM is broken down into specific components of supplier deliveries, order backlog, new orders, production, employment, inventories, import orders, new export orders, and prices paid. Each component reflects the activity of each specific sector. For instance, statistics for order backlogs and new orders reflect the vendor performance index and can become a factor in the Fed's decision to raise interest rates.

The NAPM Index web site can be accessed at www.napm.org.

Retail Sales

Reported monthly by the Commerce Department, the retail sales component is one of the most closely watched economic indicators. Since consumer spending makes up approximately two-thirds of the national economy, bonds decline and stocks rise with reports of increased retail sales. This report reviews monthly sales for auto manufacturers, major retailers, and chain store sales. A rising retail sales component is good for retailers and gives an up-to-date indication of the consumer-spending mood.

Current retail sales data is available online at
www.census.gov/mtis/www/current.html.

Gross Domestic Product (GDP)

Gross Domestic Product is a measurement of the total production and consumption of goods and services in the United States, and is therefore an excellent

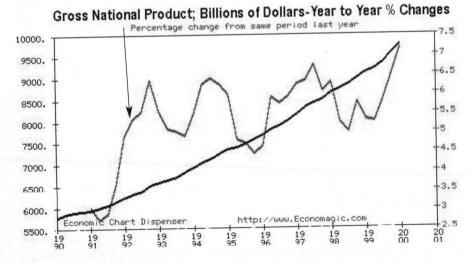

Figure 6.8 Gross Domestic Product (GDP) 1990–2000 (Courtesy of Economagic.com)

gauge of economic growth. It's released quarterly and obviously isn't as timely as the monthly data. The GDP provides probably the single most comprehensive picture of the economy. A GDP that advances at a healthy rate indicates a potential for a vigorous business atmosphere and ever-increasing profits. These reports rarely include major surprises and only impact the stock market when the GDP figures are significantly above or below the latest advance economic estimations. Figure 6.8 shows the year-to-year percentage changes of the GDP from 1990 to the year 2000.

Housing Starts and Sales of New and Existing Homes

Housing starts are the best indication of current residential construction activity. Permits are a good indication of residential construction activity in the next few months. The housing indicators show the first signs of any new direction in the economy. These changes are usually set off by any changes in home mortgage rates, which are of course affected by high inflation and rising interest rates. The housing starts and building permits indicator is watched by the stock market because high starts indicate a healthy economy. The report also gauges building permits, as they can give an indication of the housing starts of the future; but it doesn't delineate the types of homes being built. Reported monthly, it's very timely in its data. Another important way to judge future growth is to look at sales of new and existing homes. This gives analysts ideas about the future sales of things that go along with a new house, such as new appliances, furniture, and other durable goods.

Construction Spending

Construction spending is an indicator of not only residential construction as in housing starts, but also nonresidential and public construction projects. A strong number here represents a high degree of confidence in the private sector about the economy. It is considered to be a lagging indicator because the numbers are not reported until the structures are completed. Mortgage rates have a direct impact on all types of construction as well as national levels of construction spending. Though issued monthly by the Commerce Department, this report is usually taken into account by analysts only every three months, because these figures can be highly volatile month to month. The number of building permits is a better leading indicator of current economic activity, available from the Census Bureau. Check out the state-by-state breakdown at www.economagic.com/cenc40.htm.

Industrial Production Index

The Industrial Production Index gauges the aggregate output of all of the country's utilities, factories, and mines. This is another indicator that can directly affect the stock market. Analysts generally see a slackening in this sector as a signal of an impending reduction in the nation's economy.

Capacity Utilization

The capacity utilization component measures at what rate the manufacturing capacity of the nation is being utilized. A capacity utilization of 80% or lower can cause concerns of underutilization, and excess capacity and can affect the economy with less demand for capital equipment and new plants and factories. A high (but not too high) capacity utilization brings up stocks and drives down bonds. A capacity rate of 85% can indicate the point at which inflationary stress begins. It's considered that as long as capacity rises at a more rapid rate than production, inflation will remain stable. Figure 6.9 shows the capacity utilization from 1990 to 2000.

Personal Income and Consumption Expenditures

Personal income and consumption expenditures help measure and gauge the prospect of future consumer spending. The personal income component tracks increases in personal incomes—as incomes rise, so does the stock market. Consumption expenditures represent how much has been spent by individuals on all market goods and services for the past month and is another important way to measure overall economic activity. Figure 6.10 details personal income from 1998 to 2000.

Factory Orders—Durable Goods and Nondurable Goods

The factory orders report is released each month by the Commerce Department and is made up of different accounts of each component of factory production. This report

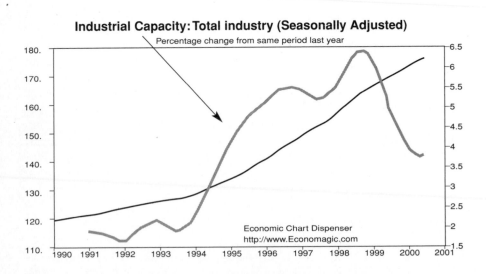

Figure 6.9   Capacity Utilization 1990–2000 (Courtesy of Economagic.com)

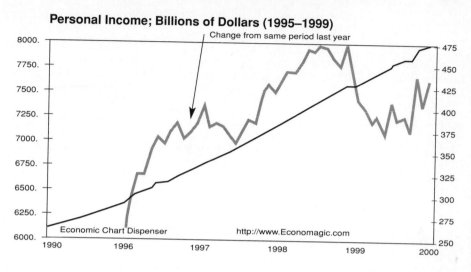

Figure 6.10 Personal Income 1998–2000 (Courtesy of Economagic.com)

looks at factory shipments that are measures of current demands, new factory orders for durable and nondurable goods, inventories, and unfilled orders that are a measure of backlogs and built-up demand. Tracking orders for big-ticket items such as cars and refrigerators that are expected to last more than three years can help market analysts, investors, and traders calculate and determine changes in national productivity.

Figure 6.11 provides a review of these important government reports and what their numbers mean to investors.

The following web sites can help you keep up-to-date on the release of government reports:

- **Economagic.com** (www.economagic.com): A free, easily available site filled with more than 100,000 data files, charts, and Excel files useful for economic research.

- **Briefing.com** (www.briefing.com): This site posts a handy calendar of upcoming announcements.

- **Economic Indicators.com** (www.economic-indicators.com/Economic News.html): A slightly more in-depth web site—just click over to the Calendar section.

- **The Dismal Scientist** (www.dismal.com/economy/releases/calendar.asp): An easy-to-use site that provides a guide to report announcements.

- **Infobeat.com** (www.infobeat.com): This site will e-mail you directly providing timely announcements of government report releases.

Component	Release Date	Advancing Numbers	Declining Numbers
Unemployment Rate	First Friday of the month	A rise in unemployment rate is a positive sign for the bond market.	A decrease in unemployment numbers is a positive sign for the equity markets.
Nonfarm Jobs Growth	First week of the month	Job creation is a good thing. It is a sign that companies are expanding and prospects are good for future growth. However, job creation must be looked at in conjunction with unemployment and productivity figures—if the number of new jobs is growing significantly faster than they can be absorbed by the workforce, then the elements are in place for inflationary wage pressures.	Declining jobs indicate a contraction of the economy and portend problems for the stock market in general.
Wholesale Trade (Very accurate indicator, even though the lag is two months.)	Second week each month	*Wholesale trade inventories*—If this number rises, consumption is slowing *Inventory-to-sales ratio*—Rising numbers again reflect a slowdown in the economy.	*Wholesale trade inventories*—If inventories are falling, consumption is on the rise. *Inventory-to-sales ratio*—If this number begins to fall, consumer spending increased, indicating more confidence.
Import and Export Prices	Around midmonth	Imports constitute 15% of U.S. consumption and directly affect the profitability of U.S. companies. Higher prices from imports translate to higher prices of domestic goods. Good news for businesses; bad for the consumer.	If import prices fall, U.S. companies must lower prices to compete. Bad for businesses, good for the consumer.

Figure 6.11   Government Reports Matrix

Component	Release Date	Advancing Numbers	Declining Numbers
Employment Situation (The single most closely watched economic statistic. Offers timeliness and accuracy, and is an important indicator of economic activity.)	First week of the month	Gives good indication of emerging wage pressures in average hourly earnings component. This is a good proxy for GDP growth; rising numbers mean economy expanding. May or may not be greeted as good news by the market.	Declining numbers indicate that wages and jobs are on the decline. May be interpreted either way by the market, depending on desired interest rate change.
Employment Cost Index (ECI)	Once a quarter, toward end of month, for preceding quarter	Analyzes wages and fringe benefits. Rising wages alone have less meaning, but are used in conjunction with other reports, like housing starts.	Lower wages mean a slowing economy, and are used in conjunction with other economic measurements to gauge the economy's strength.
Consumer Price Index (CPI)	Around the 15th of each month, 8:30 A.M. EST	Since the CPI describes price changes of a basket of consumer goods, a rising number means inflationary pressures at work. Bad for the market because inflation is held in check with rising interest rates.	A drop in prices is generally considered a good sign for consumers and good for the market.
Producer Price Index (PPI)	Second full week of month	Increases may or may not be good news: If interest rates are declining then a rising PPI number means economy is reacting to the rate cuts. If rates are increasing, this is bad because further rate hikes may be required.	Decreases mean the economy is slowing. Best to look at trends. Prolonged slowing may lead to recession. However, if rates have been increasing, decreasing numbers would mean no further hikes are necessary. Good news for the market usually.
National Association of Purchasing Management Index (NAPM)	First of month	Increase accelerates the economy.	Decrease slows the economy.

(Continued)

Figure 6.11   Continued

Component	Release Date	Advancing Numbers	Declining Numbers
Retail Sales	Midmonth	If people are spending more and confidence is high, it's a good sign for the market.	If people spend less and confidence shrinks, it's a bad sign for the market, especially retail stocks.
Gross Domestic Product (GDP)	One month after end of quarter	Takes into account consumer demand, trade balance, and so on. Economy expanding is good news, but not too fast—the Fed raises rates when that happens.	Decrease means economy slowing. If it continues Fed will (possibly) lower rates; good for market.
Housing Starts and Sales of New and Existing Homes	Third week of month	Increasing starts indicate confidence—a good sign for the market.	Decrease means economy slowing. Red flag for Fed to be on lookout for downturn in economy. Market reaction is anybody's guess.
Construction Spending	First of month	Lagging indicator. Reports come in only after building is finished. An increase in numbers is a good sign.	Since it's a lagging indicator, may serve to confirm the economy is slowing and rates need to be lowered. Good for the market.
Industrial Production Index	Midmonth, 9:15 A.M. EST	Increases indicate the slack is being taken out of the economy; we're maxing out.	Decrease means factories are slowing down. Might be considered bad for the market, is considered bad for the economy.
Personal Income and Consumption Expenditures	Third or fourth week after the month it reports on	Not much impact. It reports after other key data (employment and retail sales).	Prolonged decrease in consumer demand is definitely bad for consumer stocks.
Factory Orders— Durable Goods and Nondurable Goods	Four weeks from end of reporting month (8:30 A.M. EST); however, everyone keys off of the advance release one-week earlier	Leading indicator of industrial demand. Numbers going up are generally a positive for the markets.	Slowing demand means a slowing economy, if it stays in a declining mode for several months. Might adversely affect markets, but if it prompts interest rate reductions it could be good for markets.

Figure 6.11 Continued

SEASONAL FACTORS

Seasonal factors have an impact on the performance of the markets year round. Although some stocks can be affected by the weather changes (e.g., oil in wintertime, utilities in summertime), seasonal factors are much broader than climate issues. Investors can't plan all their trades around seasonal factors; but it would be unwise to ignore them completely. For instance, it's good to know that from 1950 to 1998, during the November through May period the average monthly gain in the markets was 0.98% higher than the average monthly gain from June through October. Some of the quirkier seasonal factors have to do with the oddly coincidental behavior of the market during election years—they have been historically high-performing years. Contrarily, for some reason, there is almost always a market drop in the first year of every reelected president's second term. In all, it's a good idea to prepare to make stock acquisitions near the beginning of a favorable seasonal period and try to delay sales until the end of the favorable period.

A popular publication called The Stock Trader's Almanac, *by Yale Hirsch, identifies many of these quirky statistics. History tends to repeat itself, and this book is a good tool for identifying seasonal tendencies (hirschorganization.com/almanac/almframe.htm).*

January Effect

The January effect describes a pattern in which smaller-cap stocks outperform their blue-chip brethren in January. Many have analyzed this effect, and there has even been a book written about it: *The Incredible January Effect* by Robert Haugen and Josef Lakonichok (Irwin Professional Publishing). Statistically the pattern has been evident since the introduction of income tax! However, in the past four years (1996–1999), the January effect has failed to materialize.

October Jinx

The great crash of 1929 and its spooky repetition in 1987, as well as the minus-554-point day in 1997, have made the October jinx seem to be more than just a superstitious legend. In the history of the Dow, 6 of the 12 largest daily drops have occurred in October. Yet October signaled the end of the line for nine bear markets (1946, 1957, 1960, 1962, 1966, 1974, 1987, 1990, and 1998). Many good runs have begun in November. According to some market prognosticators, November is often a good time to be a buyer.

Quarter-End Fluctuations

The end of each quarter is of special significance to portfolio managers. The SEC requires mutual funds to post performances and holdings for shareholder review. If there are some real clunkers in the portfolio, these are often jettisoned in favor of a stock or stocks that are the current favorite among the institutional crowd and traders in general. This so-called window dressing creates some wild times on the last trading days of March, June, September, and December.

Monthly Options Expirations

The third Friday of every month means options expire on the close (technically they don't expire until the next day, but Friday is the last day you can trade them). The final hour or two of trading can bring some wild price gyrations to stocks that have a lot of options with open interest. Money managers and traders will often create sophisticated hedge positions that must be unwound before the close. Sometimes this means buying the stock and selling the option, and sometimes it's the opposite— selling the stock and buying the options back (buying to close). If you like to trade, this is perhaps the wildest time to do it because price swings can be dramatic. More than likely, it'll be back to business as usual by Monday.

Max Pain is a web site that theorizes a very interesting concept: On the day an option's front month contracts expire, an optionable stock will close at a price that will lose the most people the most money. Let's say there's a stock trading in the upper $60 range. There's large open interest at $65 for both puts and calls, and another block of open contracts at the $70 strike. Max Pain predicts the stock will close around the midpoint between these strikes, in the $67–$68 range. Go to the site and see for yourself how it works (www.ez-pnf.com/ezpopt_1.htm).

SUPPLY AND DEMAND

At any time, it can be stated that the total number (supply) of shares is fixed. Demand for the fixed supply of shares will vary continuously depending on the investment community's interpretation of all the data available on the company, its industrial sector, and prevailing economic trends. If the consensus is bullish, more investors will want to purchase shares; if the consensus is bearish, more investors will want to sell shares. In many ways, a stock exchange is like an auction. If there are more buyers than sellers, prices will rise. If there are more sellers than buyers, prices will fall. Thus, the dynamic flow of supply and demand for shares has a solid impact on the price of the shares.

A firm can increase or decrease its total number of shares, but it is a rather lengthy and involved process involving the board of directors, amendments to the articles of incorporation, and general stockholders meetings.

INTERNATIONAL AND POLITICAL FACTORS

Although a laissez-faire approach to business tends to bolster the markets and keep investors happy, politics doesn't always reinforce business interests. In fact,

sometimes a tug-of-war develops between business interests and and political ma-
neuverings that call for laws that restrict business by imposing environmental
standards and protective labor laws. These laws are often viewed as a threat to
economic prosperity by the business community and vigilantly fought against
through the use of lobbyists and political action committees.

These days it's not enough to understand domestic economics.
A general understanding of world developments is critical,
especially when a balance of trade issue or a currency exchange
rate exerts an effect on a company you happen to own stock in.

In recent years, worldwide economic dependency has indeed moved to the forefront, especially now that we're digitally linked, with fewer trade barriers than ever
before. In 1998, Brazil and Russia were experiencing terrible financial woes that
threatened to do serious harm to the U.S. economy. That was due to U.S.-based
banks having huge loan exposure, especially in South America. Had Brazil gone
under or defaulted on its debt and let hyperinflation consume its economy, it would
have caused a very serious liquidity crisis here. The ripple effect would have gone
through our economy like a hot knife through butter, with interest rates dropping in
order to provide liquidity. The Fed, in turn, would have been holding its collective
breath, hoping in vain that inflation wouldn't rear its ugly head. The mere threat of
this scenario sent the Dow into a nasty bear market. When the crisis had apparently
passed, the Dow rallied strongly, and the Nasdaq really began to move as global demand for technology increased exponentially.

With the opening of China's borders, the single biggest untapped market on Earth
has created a stampede by U.S. corporations to establish business connections there. In
addition, Hong Kong's reversion back to Chinese rule after Great Britain had allowed
it to grow into an economic supercity has investors everywhere watching anxiously.

Elsewhere, countless manufacturers are using the cheaper labor available in
third-world countries to cut costs and increase profits. The North American Free
Trade Agreement (NAFTA) has made border cities in Mexico (like Juarez, Tijuana,
and Nuevo Laredo) swell in size, dwarfing their U.S. counterparts. Many U.S. corporations have set up factories in Mexico and warehouses in the United States. In-
terstate 35 runs from the upper Midwest to Laredo, the highway changing names
only as it continues on into Mexico City. It truly is the NAFTA Highway.

North America is now one market as it competes with the European Union. Africa
has even been the target for new economic development. U.S.-based technology companies are attracting brilliant minds from all over the world as they come here to train
in American universities, and then stay to develop new Internet-related businesses.

As worldwide participation in our economy increases, it is absolutely vital to
keep as aware as possible regarding global business practices. Tensions around the
country and the world are heating up as questions concerning human rights viola-
tions and environmental negligence supported by the World Trade Organization
(WTO) are brought into public view. In the years to come, it will be interesting to
see how the politics of profits versus people affect all of our lives.

Countless websites offer investors clues to politics, trade negotiations, and economic corollaries, including:

- **U.S. Census Bureau** *(www.census.gov/ftp/pub/foreign-trade/www): Maintains a site devoted to international trade with a lot of good information.*

- **World Trade Organization** *(www.wto.org/index.htm): The official site of the World Trade Organization details its take on trade negotiations and globalization.*

- **WTO Watch** *(www.wtowatch.org): Advocating "a human face for globalization," this site provides press-related resources and information on the WTO, global trade policy, and sustainable development from the activist point of view.*

- **Corporate Watch** *(www.corpwatch.org/trac): Known as the "Watchdog of the Web," this site actively pursues corporate and political wrongdoings.*

STRATEGIC MARKET ASSESSMENT USING INDEXES

Investors who own a portfolio of stocks may notice a tendency for the stock prices of individual companies to move together, up and down in price. There are events that have an impact on entire industries, sectors, or at times, the market as a whole. Take America Online and Yahoo! Both companies are leaders in the Internet. As a result, news events pertaining to developments within the Internet sector—say information related to the rise or fall in the cost of Web-based advertising—is reflected in the bottom line of each individual company and ultimately impacts the share prices of companies in the entire sector. The degree to which stocks move together in a similar manner is referred to as *comovement*, or *covariance*. Since most of the companies I consider to be worthwhile investments are engaged in various areas of the technology world, the individual stocks within my portfolio tend to have a significant amount of comovement.

Instead of thinking in terms of each individual stock, it is often useful to think of the aggregate or composite performance of stocks. Indexes serve such a purpose. An index, as mentioned in Chapter 1, is a list of stocks that represents a cross section of an economy or market sector. Its value is calculated by various methods so that it can display the relative price movement or strength of that grouping. On the one hand, indexes help investors see stocks as a whole. On the other, understanding indexes offers an effective way of subdividing the stock market into groups or sectors.

Various financial firms and publications have developed indexes to monitor the overall performance of the stock market. Instead of using the *price-weighted* method, many have turned to a market- or *capitalization-weighted* system; that is, the larger the company's market value (common shares trading times stock price), the more the company will weigh in the index. The total market values of all companies are added together. Then, as with a price-weighted index, a divisor is used to determine the index value and to achieve continuity throughout time. Once indexes are created, they are continually modified to reflect changes in the economy and events within the stock market.

Price-weighted: An index that is constructed by adding up all of the stock prices of the components of the index and then dividing by a divisor. The Dow Jones Industrial Average is the most familiar. In computing the Dow Jones Industrial Average, the stock prices of all 30 stocks are added together and divided by a divisor (current divisor = 17.67761842) to arrive at an index value.

Capitalization-weighted: Computed by adding up the total market capitalization (common shares traded times market price) of all of the components of the index and then dividing by the divisor. The S&P 500 is an example of a capitalization- or market-weighted index. The market caps of all 500 stocks are added together and then a divisor is used to arrive at a value for the index.

THE DOW

The fact that stock prices tend to move up and down together, or exhibit comovement, is not a new insight. Back in 1884, Charles Dow published the average closing prices of 11 U.S. companies in the *Customer's Afternoon Letter*, the forerunner to today's *Wall Street Journal*. In computing the average, Dow simply added the closing price of each stock and divided by 11. This method of creating a price-weighted average, although it has been slightly modified, is still used today. Until 1896, the average was printed sporadically, but after that, two new averages were published daily. The first was the average closing price of 20 railroad stocks; the second consisted of 12 industrial stocks. They became known as the *Dow Jones Railroad Average* and *Dow Jones Industrial Average*. In effect, Dow simplified the cumbersome activity of monitoring a large number of stocks individually by compiling and publishing the average performance of a list of popular stocks.

Although Charles Dow is known as the father of stock market indexes, he is also a predominant figure in stock market history for a number of other reasons. First and foremost, he was the original editor of the *Wall Street Journal*. In addition, he used market averages, not as a means of studying the daily price changes in the stock market, but as a way of gauging trends within the U.S. economy. Dow emphasized the fact that the daily price changes in the stock market reflect the views of thousands of investors, including those gifted with the greatest foresight and information. The stock market was therefore, a reliable measure of business conditions. In the words of Charles Dow:

> The market is not like a balloon plunging hither and thither in the wind. As a whole, it represents a serious, well-considered effort on the part of far-sighted well-informed men to adjust prices to such values as exist or which are expected to exist in the not too remote future . . . . The man who as a woolen merchant sees the demand for his goods suddenly disappear, or who as an iron dealer finds prices uncertain and bills receivable becoming somewhat doubtful in quality, will not be quickened thereby to trade on the long side (buy) of stock. He is much more likely to sell stocks.

Charles Dow also put forth the idea of market trends. Likening them to tides, waves, and ripples in the sea, he considered a trend to have three parts: primary, secondary, and minor. The *primary trend* is the tide; the *secondary trend* (sometimes called the intermediate trend) is the wave, and the *minor trends* are the ripples. The primary trend is the long period of rising or falling stock prices. The secondary trend generally lasts three weeks to three months, and moves against the primary trend. These secondary trends will retrace, or correct, anywhere from one-third to two-thirds of the prior trend's movement, with the most frequent correction being about 50%.

Dow believed the third or minor trend represented fluctuations in the secondary trend and would last around three weeks. For example, during a period of two or more years of rising stock prices, the primary trend is up. When the primary trend is up, it is referred to as a bull market. During a long period of rising stock prices, the primary trend takes stock prices higher; but occasionally the secondary trend will move counter to the main market movement. Therefore, the secondary movement in a bull market is generally a period of three weeks to three months in which stock prices fall. In contrast, when the primary trend is down, stock prices are said to be in a bear market. In this case, the secondary trends will move counter to the market and take stock prices higher. The minor trend occurs within the secondary trend and represents fluctuations in the secondary trend—generally considered unimportant.

In addition to market averages and the idea of market trends, Charles Dow developed a number of other interesting insights with respect to stock market activity. After his death in 1902, his successor at the *Wall Street Journal*, William P. Hamilton, refined Dow's early ideas. Over the course of 27 years, Hamilton developed the *Dow Theory*, which has several basic tenets:

1. ***The averages discount everything.*** The market is the world's most efficient processor of information. Anything that happens, including an act of God (!), is automatically priced into the market.

2. ***The market has three trends.*** (As discussed earlier.)

3. ***Major trends have three phases.*** The accumulation phase (informed buying by those closest to the company), the public participation phase, and a distribution phase.

4. ***The averages must confirm each other.*** Originally Mr. Dow was speaking of the railroads and the industrials, the only averages at that time. Although they both needed to be in the same primary trend, they didn't have to begin at the exact time. This relationship confirms the trend.

5. ***Volume must confirm the trend.*** Mr. Dow was a big believer in volume; it should increase in the direction of the primary trend.

6. ***A trend is assumed to be in effect until it gives a definite signal it has reversed.*** Talk about a visionary! This last tenet is one of the basic rules of modern-day technical analysis (which will be discussed in Chapter 9).

The Dow Jones Industrial Average and Dow's early insights have withstood the test of time. The DJIA is still the quintessential barometer of stock market performance and is quoted daily on the evening news. While the DJIA has evolved through the years, the information derived from it is essentially the same. It gauges the stock prices of 30 U.S. companies and reflects developments within the U.S. economy. In addition, the publishers at Dow Jones & Co. take special care to ensure the index evolves as the nature of the economy changes. For example, in 1999 software maker Microsoft and semiconductor company Intel were added to the index to reflect the growing importance of high technology in the U.S. stock market.

The Dow is still a price-weighted index in that the average prices of all 30 components are added together and one final average is computed. Due to stock splits and changes within the index, however, a simple average created discontinuity in the performance of the index. For example, if a company within the index has a high stock price and is replaced with a company with a lower stock price, the average value will drop. To ensure continuity, then, the sum of all the stock prices is divided using a divisor that is continually adjusted to reflect stock splits and changes within the index.

To learn more about the Dow, its components and history, go the Dow Jones Indexes home web site at averages.dowjones.com/home.html.

INDEXES

In the late 1800s, bonds were highly regarded as the investment instrument of choice primarily because they offered investors a guaranteed interest rate. In contrast, the stock market was unknown territory. Information on stocks was hard to come by and even more difficult to understand. Most of the available information was the product of precarious tips and disreputable rumors.

An index is made up of a select group of stocks. A trader can use an index to measure and report value changes to the whole group by tracking its high and low prices, today's performance in relation to yesterday's close (or the past year), trading volume, and volatility. Each measurement signals a possible trend in whichever sector the index represents. Monitoring index performance is another key to understanding the general mood of the marketplace.

There are a variety of indexes tailored to reflect the performance of many different sectors of the marketplace. Some indexes are referred to as the major or senior averages in that, like the DJIA, they measure the performance of the largest and most widely followed companies trading on the U.S. exchanges. Major averages include the following:

- **The Dow Jones Industrial Average ($INDU)**: Sometimes referred to as the Dow 30, because it consists of 30 stocks, the Dow Jones Industrial Average is the oldest market average in the world.
- **The Standard & Poor's 500 ($SPX)**: The S&P 500 is capitalization-weighted and widely followed by institutional investors. The index consists of 500

stocks: 376 industrials, 39 utilities, 75 financials, and 10 transportation companies (as of Nov. 15, 2000).

- **The New York Stock Exchange Index ($NYA)**: The NYSE index measures the aggregate performance of all stocks trading on the New York Stock Exchange.

- **The Nasdaq Composite Index ($COMPQ):** The Nasdaq Composite is a capitalization-weighted index and measures the performance of all stocks trading on the Nasdaq.

- **The Wilshire 5000 ($TMW):** One of the broadest measures of U.S. stocks, the Wilshire 5000 was created in 1974. Since that time, the number of stocks within the index has increased from 5,000 to 7,000.

- **U.S. Total Market Index:** In February 2000, Dow Jones & Co. launched this new index designed to represent a fixed percentage (95%) of all U.S. stocks.

Another popular way of categorizing stocks is by market capitalization or market cap. Recall from the discussion in Chapter 3 that market capitalization refers to the value of all a company's shares. Indexes that have been created to gauge the performance of stocks based on market capitalization (also known as asset class) include the following:

- **The Russell 2000 Small Cap Index ($RUT)**: Often referred to as the Russell, the Russell 2000 is one of many indexes created by the Frank Russell Group in Tacoma, Washington. It is a measure of the 3,000 most actively trading stocks on the New York Stock Exchange, the Nasdaq, and the American Stock Exchange, with the 1,000 largest companies removed. It is the most widely followed gauge of small-cap stock performance.

- **The S&P Midcap 400 Index ($MID)**: The Standard & Poor's Midcap index consists of 400 (mostly industrial) companies. Selection is based on market size and popularity (measured by liquidity or trading volume) and is a widely followed barometer for the performance of mid-cap stocks.

- **The Wilshire 4500 Index**: This index includes all of the companies of the Wilshire 5000 with the components of the S&P 500 removed. Therefore, it provides a measure of both small and mid-cap stocks.

So, while the Dow Jones Industrial Average, the S&P 500, and the other senior averages measure the performance of America's largest companies, there are a number of indexes designed to track the activity of other asset classes (i.e., small- and mid-cap stocks). As an investor, understanding the difference between the performance of small-cap, mid-cap, and large-cap stocks can help in your investment decisions. There will be times when small-cap stocks perform better than large-cap stocks; and other times when the opposite occurs. Understanding how your particular portfolio is weighted in terms of asset classes can help you to interpret the relative performance of each individual issue. For example, if you find that your portfolio consisting primarily of small-capitalization stocks is not performing well, and at the same time the Russell 2000 Small Cap Index is lagging behind the large-cap or senior averages, you may want to consider decreasing your exposure to small-cap stocks and adding some larger companies to your portfolio.

Just as there are ways to separate the stock market into small-, mid-, and large-cap stocks, indexes allow you to view the performance of the stock market in terms of specific economic sectors. Standard & Poor's, for example, separates the stock market into 11 economic sectors: utilities, basic materials, cyclicals, consumer staples, energy, transportation, financials, technology, capital goods, health care, and communication services. The performance of most economic sectors can thus be measured using the following indexes:

- **The NASDAQ 100 ($NDX):** The Nasdaq 100, or NDX, is a measure of the 100 largest nonfinancial companies trading on the Nasdaq (see Figure 6.12). Given that most are technology companies, the index offers an accurate gauge of the technology sector.

- **The Dow Jones Utility Average ($DJU):** The Dow Jones Utility Average was developed in 1929 when all utility stocks were removed from the Dow Jones Industrial Average and a separate index of only utility stocks was created (see Figure 6.13).

- **The Dow Jones Transportation Average ($DJT):** Originally known as the Dow Jones Railroad Average, the Dow Jones Transportation Average offers a reliable means of studying the transportation sector (see Figure 6.14).

Nasdaq 100 Index Daily
July '99 - July '00

Figure 6.12 Annual Price Graph of the NDX Index (Courtesy of QCharts (www.qcharts.com))

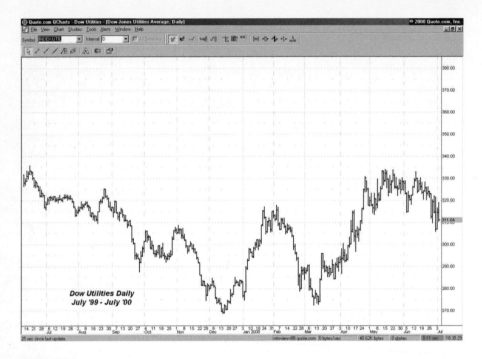

Figure 6.13   Annual Price Graph of the Dow Utility Index (Courtesy of QCharts (www.qcharts.com))

- **The AMEX Oil Index ($XOI):** A number of indexes track the performance of the energy sector (see Figure 6.15). For a comprehensive list, go to Stockscape.com (www.stockscape.com/stockscape_com/energy.cfm)

A large number of indexes are designed to track the performance of economic sectors and industry groups. Most sectors have at least one representative index. Some, such as the technology sector, have several. Going further, an economic sector can be divided into industry groups, and there are also indexes designed to gauge the performance of those specific groups. For example, there are a number of industry-specific indexes within the technology sector, including:

- **The PHLX Semiconductor Index ($SOX):** The PHLX Semiconductor Index, or SOX, is a price-weighted index of 16 U.S. companies engaged in the manufacture and distribution of semiconductors and semiconductor capital equipment (www.phlx.com/products/sox.html).

- **The PHLX Box-Maker Index ($BMX):** The PHLX Box-Maker Index is a price-weighted index consisting of nine companies involved in various aspects

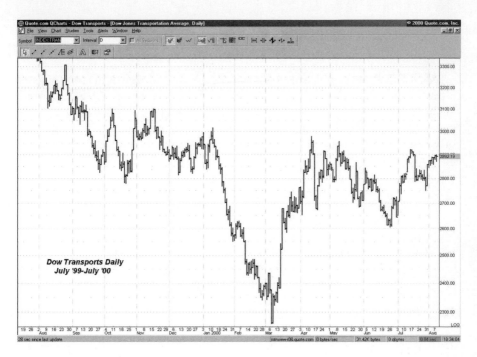

Figure 6.14 Annual Price Graph of the Dow Transportation Index (Courtesy of QCharts (www.qcharts.com))

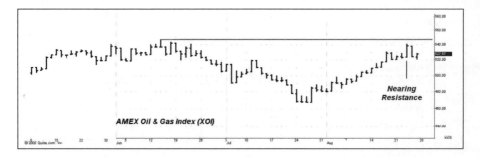

Figure 6.15 Annual Price Graph of the AMEX Oil Index (Courtesy of QCharts (www.qcharts.com))

of the manufacture, distribution, and sales of desktop and notebook personal computers (www.phlx.com/products/bmx.html).

- *The Street.com Internet Index ($DOT):* The Street.com Internet Index consists of 20 companies engaged in the Internet commerce, software, and service sector (www.thestreet.com).

- *Labpuppy.com:* Don't laugh; it's a real site. Go here to see what to me is the handiest, most convenient way to view virtually every major index and their performance charts, all on one web site (www.labpuppy.com).

Today's investors use indexes to dissect the market and view it in terms of asset classes, economic sectors, industry groups, and sector rotation. Given the overwhelming size of today's market, the primary trend within one group or sector may be up while another is down. By developing and following your own list of indexes, you can gain insight as to sector dynamics within the overall market, which should help you to make better trading decisions.

Some places to turn to for performance data on various indexes are the Wall Street Journal, Barron's, Investor's Business Daily, *and the* Financial Times. *For specific information on how indexes are constructed and the components of each index, investors can go online and visit the Chicago Board of Options Exchange (www.cboe.com), the American Stock Exchange (www.amex.com), or the Philadelphia Stock Exchange (www.phlx.com).*

HOLDRS

Merrill Lynch has been developing *HOLDRS*, sector-specific depositary receipts that trade like stocks, but actually are made up of a group of stocks. This enables the trader to easily and conveniently buy a basket of stocks within a sector.

HOLDRS: Holding company depositary receipts represent ownership in stock of a group of companies engaged in a specific industry. For example, there are biotechnology, semiconductor, pharmaceutical, and other industry-specific HOLDRS. Unlike index funds or index shares, they are not designed to track a specific index. Rather, they represent ownership in a group of stocks engaged in one particular industry.

One study I'm aware of discovered that being in the right sector outperformed being in the market at the right time by a margin of 4:1! Sector selection is critical, and HOLDRS are a good way to take advantage of a sector's price action (www.holdrs.com/holdrs/main/index.asp).

Index Shares (iShares)

Exchange-traded funds (or index shares) are funds that are designed to match the performance of an index. That is, the funds buy the same stocks that are in the index. The shares of the funds are traded on an exchange like a stock. The first index share—the S&P Depositary Receipt (SPDR, also known as Spiders)—was launched by the American Stock Exchange (AMEX) in 1993. It is designed to track the performance of the S&P 500 index. Later, the AMEX launched index shares on the Dow Jones Industrial Average (Diamonds) and the Nasdaq 100 (QQQ).

The AMEX has also begun listing sector-specific index shares or *iShares*. They represent ownership in either funds or unit investment trusts that hold portfolios that generally correspond to the price action of broad-market, sector-specific, or international securities. They are traded and quoted on the AMEX as a common stock would be.

> **iShares:** A new series of exchange-traded funds (ETFs) created by Barclays Global Investors. The family of iShares includes more than 50 different index funds with shares that trade on the American Stock Exchange like stocks.

USING INDUSTRY SECTORS AS FORECASTING TOOLS

As alluded to previously, the economy has an array of sectors that can be doing well as another is doing poorly. There's usually a direct translation to that sector in the market for why it is performing poorly. Obviously, it's important to know which sectors are performing well at all times. If you are researching a particular stock, definitely take the time to study the company's respective industry sector. Many investors believe that almost half of a stock's price performance can be attributed to its respective industrial sector.

Keeping tabs on industry group leadership is another important key to analyzing the marketplace. To compare the price performance of each industry, simply use the Internet to access lists that detail the 10 best- and worst-performing industries. These lists confirm which industries have been experiencing the highest and lowest percentage of profits. From there, you can look at the 10 best and worst specific companies, the top 100 dollar-volume issues, or the greatest price percentage gainers and losers of the day. Some sites even let you key in a specific stock's symbol to compare its performance to the overall industry's or that of an index. Each list and chart provides a piece of the puzzle. Once you have gathered enough tidbits of information, you start to get a feel for the big picture. Figure 6.16 features a partial list of sector indexes and their respective symbols.

Obviously, some sectors outperform other sectors at different times. It stands to reason we want to own stocks in sectors that are doing well. This information can be found in various places, including the *Wall Street Journal* and *Investor's Business Daily*.

Recently we have seen money flowing into and out of various sectors (sometimes called *sector rotation*). For example, money might flow from semiconductors to Internet portals to dot-coms to biotechnology. As money flows into a sector, all the stocks in that sector tend to benefit with increasing prices, sometimes with meteoric increases. Just as quickly, as the capital flows out of that sector and into

Sector	Ticker Symbol	Exchange
Auto Parts	AUX	
Banks	BIX	S&P
Chemicals	CEX	S&P
Computers	IXCO—U.S. Computer Index	Nasdaq
	HWI—Computer Hardware Index	AMEX
Financial	IXF	Nasdaq
Insurance	INSR	Nasdaq
	IUX	S&P
Internet	INX	CBOE
	IIX	AMEX
	ECM	Dow Jones Internet Commerce Index
Medical/Health care	HCX	S&P
Oil and Gas Drilling	OSX	PHLX
Oil and Gas Producers/ Pipeline	XOI	AMEX
Retail	RLX	AMEX
Software	CWX	CBOE
Telecomm	XTC	AMEX
Transportation	$TRAN	Dow Jones Transports
Utilities	$UTIL	Dow Jones Utility Index

Figure 6.16   Sector Breakdown

another, the price increases deflate (often leaving them languishing below the prices they enjoyed before the capital flowed into that sector).

One prominent source of daily information on sector performance is *Investor's Business Daily*. The paper has divided the market into 197 different sectors. Each day they publish and rank the relative price performance of each group for the prior six months in a section titled "*Investor's Business Daily* Industry Prices." By searching out the best-performing sectors, one can quickly develop a list of the firms most likely to increase their share prices and then can apply appropriate strategies with a bullish bias. Conversely, if one chooses to be bearish, then search out the worst-performing sectors and look at the firms in those sectors ready to tumble.

Another useful method to determine what sector is hot is to watch the number of new issues or IPOs being brought to market. More IPOs means conditions are good; investors are receptive to the prospects in this part of the economy.

Go to IPO Maven for a very extensive list of sectors and the companies that are scheduled to go public or that already have (ipomaven.123jump.com/index.php3).

MARKET INDICATORS

In addition to indexes and sectors, there are a number of tools called indicators that provide insight into the broad market analysis within the stock market. Specifically, let's take a brief look at the following four indicators: the advance/decline line, up and down volume, TRIN, and new highs/new lows. Additional indicators will be explored in the technical analysis and sentiment analysis chapters still to come (see Chapters 9 and 10).

Market Breadth

The *advance/decline line (A/D line)*, also known as market breadth, is simply a measure of the number of stocks advancing versus the number that are declining. For example, if 2,400 stocks advanced and 1,200 declined during a trading session, market breadth is said to be two-to-one positive (2,400/1,200 = 2/1). If the opposite occurs, breadth is said to be two-to-one negative. The A/D line is a graphic representation of the advance-decline ratio over a period of time. It is cumulative. That is, each day declining stocks are subtracted from advancing stocks, and the total, whether positive or negative, is added to the previous running total. Therefore, during a trading session when advances outpace declines, market breadth will be up (after subtracting declining from advancing issues, the result will be positive), and the A/D line will improve or move higher.

Advance/decline line (A/D line): A technical analysis tool representing the total differences between advances and declines of security prices. The advance/decline line is considered the best indicator of market movement as a whole.

The advance/decline line is best used in conjunction with the senior averages. For example, it is generally considered a good sign when the Dow Jones Industrial Average and the New York Stock Exchange A/D line are rising together. However, when the Dow Jones Industrial Average is setting new highs but the A/D line is moving lower, it is considered an unhealthy sign; in a nutshell, more stocks are falling than advancing. In that case, breadth is said to be lagging or poor. Figure 6.17 shows the advance/decline line of the NYSE from January 1996 through December 1998. In the period from September 1997 through December 1998, the NYSE Composite index showed higher moves, while the advance-decline line, after some gyrations, ended up considerably below where it started. Since more stocks were declining than advancing, many market strategists considered it an unhealthy sign.

Volume

Volume is the level of activity associated with a specific market or security. Up volume and down volume are helpful market indicators. Each day, the New York Stock

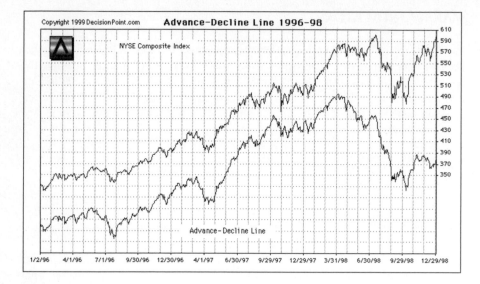

Figure 6.17 New York Stock Exchange Advance-Decline Line (Courtesy of DecisionPoint.com)

Exchange reports the level of trading activity—the total number of shares traded. The *Wall Street Journal* reports this daily in both print and online publications. For example, the table in Figure 6.18 shows that the total volume on the New York Stock Exchange on Friday, April 7, 2000, was 888,387,000 shares. The market strategist, however, will look beyond the total volume and to the advancing versus declining volume (the two rows just above it). In this case, there was more declining than advancing volume. This is generally interpreted as a negative sign because it shows a greater number of sellers than buyers. An important factor to consider was the performance of the senior averages in conjunction with up and down volume. When the market rises and advancing volume outpaces declining volume, it is interpreted as a positive or bullish sign. In this case, the market moved modestly lower, but down volume exceeded up volume—a convincingly bearish sign.

TRIN

The closing Arms Index, or TRIN, is a volume indicator derived by using the advance/decline ratio and up and down volume. Again, the *Wall Street Journal* reports TRIN daily. The formula to compute TRIN is pretty straightforward:

$$\text{TRIN} = \frac{\text{Volume declining / Number declining}}{\text{Volume advancing / Number advancing}}$$

NYSE MARKET DIARY	FRI	THU	WEEK 4/7
Issues traded	3,424	3,443	3,606
Advances	1,451	1,816	1,795
Declines	1,438	1,173	1,589
Unchanged	535	454	222
New highs	53	45	151
New lows	35	31	160
zAdv vol (000)	391,917	625,186	2,702,621
zDecl vol (000)	428,922	290,105	2,439,575
zTotal vol (000)	888,387	999,371	5,527,060
Closing tick1	–64	–91	
Closing Arms2 (trin)	1.1	0.72	
zBlock trades	18,153	20,416	118,751

Figure 6.18   Stock Market Diary (April 7, 2000)

Using Figure 6.18 yields:

$$\text{TRIN} = \frac{428,922 \, / \, 1,438}{391,917 \, / \, 1,451} = 1.1$$

Market analysts use TRIN to focus on the volume of trading. Specifically, if a drop in the senior averages is accompanied by heavier trading volume, it is considered to be a bearish sign. A ratio above 1.0 is considered to be a market negative because the falling stocks have greater average volume than advancing stocks. When TRIN is below 1.0 it is interpreted as a market positive since there is a greater percentage of volume associated with advancing rather than declining issues.

New Highs and Lows

As a final indicator, market analysts focus on the ratio of new highs to new lows. New highs refer to stocks that are setting new one-year highs during the trading session. New lows are stocks that are setting new one-year lows. The new highs/new lows indicator is simply the number of new highs minus the number of new lows. This type of data offers the most insight when used in conjunction with the senior averages. When the Dow Jones Industrial Average is rising to new highs and the primary trend is bullish, if the New York Stock Exchange new highs/new lows ratio is also moving higher, it is interpreted as a bullish sign because there is strength in the overall market. On the other hand, if the senior averages are recording new highs, but the new highs/new lows ratio is moving lower, it is considered bearish because more stocks are moving lower than higher.

In addition to the statistics on New York Stock Exchange trading, the *Wall*

Street Journal and *Investor's Business Daily* both report similar data with respect to Nasdaq and American Stock Exchange trading. It is sometimes insightful to compare the data between the Nasdaq and the New York Stock Exchange. Occasionally, trading activity and market data on one exchange will differ substantially from another. For example, on March 1, 2000, there were 31 fewer stocks setting new highs than stocks setting new lows on the New York Stock Exchange, but 364 more stocks were setting new highs than new lows on the Nasdaq. The wide disparity served as evidence that overall market strength favored the stocks on the Nasdaq.

THE BIG PICTURE

A variety of important factors impact the performance of stock prices as a whole, and there are an equal number of tools for monitoring their performance. Charles Dow understood that stock prices exhibited a degree of comovement when he developed the first index in 1884. Since then, however, the market has grown in size and complexity, and investors now have a number of other tools available for studying the happenings within the stock market. While the Dow Jones Industrial Average is one means of gauging trends within the market, a number of other sector and industry indexes now exist. Using them allows you to compartmentalize the market to get a better feel for which groups are in bull versus bear markets. Indicators such as the advance/decline line, TRIN, and new highs/new lows provide additional information into the composite performance of stocks. In sum, by understanding which factors influence stocks as a whole and the tools for monitoring the activity of the market, you will be better equipped to evaluate the performance of your stock portfolio and make changes as events warrant.

ROADMAP TO SUCCESS

Objective	Course of Action
Assessing the Economy	The economy is cyclical in nature: • Expands and contracts. • If it expands too quickly inflation is the result. • If it contracts too much we have a recession. • Inflation is a general increase in the price of goods and services. • Inflation erodes purchasing power, and is always present.

- Economic reports issued by various government agencies indicate where the U.S. economy is in its economic cycle—growing or slowing.

Regular measurements indicate where the United States is in the economic cycle.	How do you measure inflation?
	- Benchmark measurements—a specific point in time is used as a starting point.
	- Inflation is calculated from an arbitrary starting point. Example: Base year is 1975. How has inflation grown from January 1, 1975, to present?
	- Economy is too large and complex to rely on one measurement.
	- A number of indexes track the growth of inflation.
	    –Month to month.
	    –Quarter to quarter.
	- Leading and lagging indicators.
	    –Leading indicators: forecast.
	    –Lagging indicators: diagnose the data retrieved.
	For the most popular charts (most requested), go to Economagic (www.economagic.com).

Who is in charge of overseeing the economy?	The Federal Reserve Board (the Fed): - Founded in 1913 - Primary purpose is to provide the nation with a safer, more flexible, and more stable monetary and financial system. - Influence money and credit conditions in the pursuit of full employment and stable prices. - Supervise and regulate the banking system. - Maintain stability in the financial system and containing risk that may arise in the financial markets. - Provide certain financial services to the U.S. government and the public.

Federal Reserve System Structure	Board of Governors: Alan Greenspan is the Fed Chairman.
	- There are 12 regional Federal Reserve banks.
	- Federal Open Market Committee (FOMC), made up of:
	    –Board of Governors.
	    –President of Federal Reserve Bank of New York.
	    –Four other regional presidents on a rotating basis.
	- FOMC oversees open market operations, which is the main tool used by the Federal Reserve to influence growth of money and credit.

Tools Used by FOMC to Influence the Economy	FOMC uses three major tools: - Open market operations; the buying and selling of government securities to influence the liquidity in the depository system.

- Set reserve requirements for banks; how much money they need to keep on hand.
- The discount rate—the interest rate charged commercial banks when they borrow money from a regional reserve bank.

To learn more about the FOMC, go to www.federalreserve.gov/fomc.

Setting interest rates is the most influential thing the Fed can do to modulate the economy.	Interest: the price paid for borrowing money. - Interest is the cost of money. - Businesses of all sizes use borrowed money to grow their companies. - If money is cheap (low interest rates), more is borrowed. Low interest also stimulates growth in all sectors of the economy. - If money is expensive (high interest rates) businesses put off expansion; things slow down; people defer major purchases. The economy begins to contract. - Banks set their interest rates according to the amount they have to borrow from the Fed. (They don't use their own money all the time.) - If the Fed hikes rates to the banks, the banks hike rates to you. Go to Economagic, and under its "Most Popular Charts" section, click on Discount Rate to see history of interest rate changes (www.economagic.com/popular.htm).
Interest rates are the primary tool the Fed uses.	To understand interest rates as a tool for heating or cooling the economy, think of a teeter-totter. - Envision rates on one side of the teeter-totter, the economy on the other. - The trick is to keep the economy growing without causing inflation. - If the economy side of the teeter-totter gets too high, the Fed raises rates to bring it down. - If the economy side gets too low, the Fed lowers rates to bring the economy up.
Stock Market and Interest Rates	Take the teeter-totter example, only this time use "stock market" instead of "economy." - The stock market goes up if rates go down. - The stock market goes down when rates go up. - The economy (ultimately) makes rates go up. - The stock market anticipates the direction of rates before they actually move!
Bond prices indicate the direction (up or down) most interest rate professionals think rates are headed.	Bonds are debt instruments. Their prices fluctuate like stocks, to a certain extent. - The bond market as referred to by stock traders is the price of the 30-year U.S. Treasury bond. - This bond has the greatest price swings because it has the longest maturity of any bond traded. - This indicator will tell you, at a glance, how traders who rely on forecasting interest rates interpret economic reports.

- The Chicago Mercantile Exchange has a site to track daily developments in bond prices. Bookmark it (www.barchart.com/cme/cmeft.htm).

What moves the bond market and interest rates and then affects the stock market?	Economic reports released by various government agencies. • Some are monthly and others quarterly. • Each one provides a piece to the puzzle which the Fed studies to determine if the economy is expanding or contracting. • If interest rates are already low, and an economic report indicates a robust economy, this is bad news for the stock market. It means the Fed will be inclined to raise interest rates. This would send the bond market down (yields would rise in anticipation of higher interest rates). • If interest rates are high (relatively speaking), and economic reports indicate a slowing economy, this is good news for the stock market, because rates will probably be lowered to avoid a recession. This would send the bond market up (yields would drop) in anticipation of the Fed lowering rates. For bond market basics, and an overall good place to study bonds, head to BondsOnline (www.bondsonline.com). For easy-to-understand charts and insights for the bond market (and all markets) head to BarCharts.com (www.barchart.com).
Fitting All This Together	Some economic data is worth studying because: • It moves the market. • Policy makers (the people who set interest rates) study it closely. • Some reports are very accurate in forecasting economic trends. • Which ones to follow and why? • Economic data needs to be watched for indications to assess the state of the economy. Is it expanding or contracting? Are interest rates likely to rise of fall within the foreseeable future?
Construction Spending Report	*What it is:* The value of all construction, public and private. Reported after it's completed. *Issued:* Monthly. *By:* Census Bureau. *Importance:* Low.
Consumer Price Index (CPI)	*What it is:* Indexed off of 1982–1984 time period; a basket of goods used to measure inflation. *Issued:* Monthly, around the 15th, 8:30 A.M. *By:* Labor Department. *Importance:* High. Considered a timely indicator. Has the ability to move markets because it's one of the first and most reliable signs of inflation.
Employment Cost Index (ECI)	*What it is:* An index based on 1989 prices (= 100) that measures the change in wages and salaries as well as employer costs for employee benefits.

Issued: Quarterly, last business day of January, April, July, and
October at 8:30 A.M. for prior quarter.
By: Labor Department.
Importance: High. Usually moves market, accurate leading
indicator of inflation.

Employment Report	*What it is:* Measures net new jobs created and unemployment rate, average hourly earnings, and average workweek length. *Issued:* Monthly, first Friday of each month at 8:30 A.M. *By:* Labor Department. *Importance:* High. Usually moves markets due to timeliness; considered the best measure of economy's health.
Factory Orders—Durable Goods and Nondurable Goods	*What it is:* Preliminary report on manufacturers' shipments, inventories, and orders. *Issued:* Monthly, first week of month at 8:30 A.M. *By:* Census Bureau. *Importance:* Low.
Gross Domestic Product (GDP)	*What it is:* A measure of the economy's total output, goods and services, and structures. *Issued:* Quarterly, last business day of January, April, July, and October. Covers prior quarter. *By:* Commerce Department. *Importance:* High. This is an actual measurement of the pace at which economy is expanding or contracting. Includes an index called the Price Index that measures everything consumers buy, including imports.
Housing Starts and Sales of New and Existing Homes	*What it is:* A measure of housing starts and building permits. *Issued:* Monthly, around the 18th at 8:30 A.M. for prior month. *By:* Census Bureau. *Importance:* Varies. It's a good leading indicator of home sales. Housing starts are used to forecast residential portion of GDP. It moves markets on occasion.
Industrial Production Index	*What it is:* Measures the change in total production of country's factories, mines, and utilities. Also indicates the percent of total capacity (capacity utilization). *Issued:* Monthly, around the 15th at 9:15 A.M. for prior month. *By:* The Federal Reserve. *Importance:* High. Usually moves the market due to timeliness—accurate gauge of inflation.
National Association of Purchasing Management Index (NAPM)	*What it is:* A national manufacturing index based on a survey of purchasing managers. Indicates expansion when the reading is +50; contraction when it's below 50. *Issued:* Monthly, first business day of month at 10:00 A.M. *By:* National Association of Purchasing Management. *Importance:* High. Count on it to move markets due to timeliness, accuracy of depicting factory sector.

Personal Income and Consumption Expenditures	*What it is:* Measures personal income and spending. *Issued:* Monthly, first business day of month at 8:30 A.M. Data covers two months prior. *By:* Commerce Department. *Importance:* So-so. Data already a part of previously released reports (e.g., retail sales report). Includes data on personal savings rate as well.
Producer Price Index (PPI)	*What it is:* Index using 1982 as a base, measures the change in prices received by domestic producers of commodities. *Issued:* Monthly, around the 13th at 8:30 A.M., covers prior month. *By:* Labor Department. *Importance:* High. The core PPI will be mentioned as well, as it excludes food and energy prices, which are more volatile. If it's an inflation indicator, it will probably influence the market.
Philadelphia Fed Index	*What it is:* Regional manufacturing index covering part of the Northeast that's a measurement of factory expansion and contraction. *Issued:* Monthly, around the 18th a 10:00 A.M. *By:* Federal Reserve Bank of Philadelphia. *Importance:* Some. Occasionally has an impact on market due to the insight it provides for the National Association of Purchasing Managers Index.
Retail Sales	*What it is:* Sales at retail stores. *Issued:* Monthly, around the 12th at 8:30 A.M. Data covers prior month. *By:* Census Bureau. *Importance:* High. Nearly always moves markets because it's timely (two weeks after the end of the reporting period). Reveals a strong insight into GDP and offers a preview of personal consumption expenditures, which reports around the first of the next month.

Indexes	An index, as it relates to the market, is a grouping of stocks designed to reflect the price changes in the group it represents.
	• Some indexes are broad-based, showing a wide variety of stocks from different sectors in an attempt to show what the broad market is doing, or the U.S. economy in general.
	  –Dow Industrials ($DJIA)
	  –S&P 500 (SPX) or S&P 100 ($OEX)
	  –Russell 2000 ($RTX)
	• Some indexes are sector-specific, reflecting the market action of a single industry group. These are very narrow in scope, and can be used by the investor to determine the strength of a specific part of the economy.
	  –AMEX Oil Index ($XOI)
	  –Morgan Stanley High Tech 35 ($MSH)

–Philadelphia Semiconductor Index ($SOX)

–Dow Jones Utilities ($UTIL)

For a comprehensive list, SmartMoney.com has a good one—easy to read and understand (www.smartmoney.com/si/sectors/).

Sector selection is critical to success.	Studies indicate that being in the right sector (the one that's moving up the strongest) will return more than just being in the market at correct times by a 4:1 margin! • Finding the right sector. • Pay attention to economic reports; what are they saying? 　–Inflation fears on the rise or fall? 　–Interest rate direction? 　–Factory orders increasing? • Study the financial papers and periodicals. • *Barron's* is a good place for sector overviews. • *Investor's Business Daily.* • *Wall Street Journal.* • *Business Week, Forbes, Fortune.* • Investment newsletters.
HOLDRS and iShares	Focused investment vehicles that make it very easy to participate in a sector. What they are: • A basket of stocks. • Industry (sector) specific. • Trade like a single stock (can buy and sell them just like a stock). • Contained in a depositary receipt or unit trust. The AMEX trades them. For a current list, go to: www.amex.com/structuredeq/sp_holdrs.stm. Review a list of iShares available and download a prospectus at the Nasdaq-AMEX market site: www.nasdaq-amex.com/asp/prospectus.asp.
So, how do I know when to buy?	Basic studies that can indicate good buying (and selling) opportunities. Relative strength—How is the stock/sector performing as compared to another, broader index (like the S&P 500)? • Go to chart service (www.optionetics.com) and click on Markets. • Enter ticker symbol of stock in blank quote box and hit Go. • Click scroll-down menu Detailed Quote/News, select Chart option. Click Get Info. • Under Indicator heading, check Relative Strength choice. • Under Display, go to scroll-down menu next to Comparison Index, then select S&P 500. • A chart will be drawn depicting how the stock of your choice has performed against the S&P 500 (in this example).

- Go to **Bar Charts.com** for an extensive explanation of technical indicators when you get a quote (www.barchart.com).
- **Wall Street City** also has a wonderfully simple method for finding and ranking the sectors (www.wallstreetcity.com).

Other Methods for Identifying Sectors	Insider buying is the greatest vote of confidence any investor could hope to see in a company and the more the better. • Look for companies that have large amounts of insider buying. LabPuppy.com has good links to this information (www.labpuppy.com/insider.htm). • Watch for unusual volume trends—*Investor's Business Daily* once again (www.investors.com).
Just how "hot" is the market, anyway? Use indicators to determine overall market strength, direction, and momentum.	Indicators provide a deeper look at what the market is really doing. Just knowing what the Dow, Nasdaq, or S&P 500 did on any given day doesn't provide the investor with market internals. • Indicators provide new ways to determine market strength/weakness. • Indicators track: market activity, investor activity, economic data. • Indicators used to confirm trends or signal possible changes. Two types of indicators: • Oscillators—Help determine whether the market has reached an extreme condition—overbought or oversold. Examples: momentum, relative strength, and stochastics. • Lagging indicators—Help to determine changes in the trend, but only after the fact. Examples: moving averages, envelopes, bollinger bands.
Market Breadth— The Advance/ Decline Line	The advance/decline line (A/D line): • Gauges the overall market. • If it's moving higher, the majority of stocks are moving up. • If it's declining, the majority of stocks are declining. • Watch for a divergence between the movement of the major indexes and the A/D line. If the Dow and S&P 500 are moving higher and the A/D line is moving lower there is said to be an erosion of support, and a correction is expected. • Daily updates on the A/D and other indicators can be found at www.wallstreetcourier.com or each day in *Investor's Business Daily*.
Market Breadth— Volume	Volume is said to confirm any solid move, up or down. The measure of volume indicates the strength, or demand behind a stock. • Large volume with no price movement indicates stock is being accumulated. • Volume precedes price.

- Look for "biggest volume % changes" in the newspaper or online.
- Volume should move higher with a stock to confirm advance. If volume declines while stock is going up, it's called a *divergence*. Rally is suspect, won't usually last.
- If stock goes down on increasing volume, it is said to be *distributed*. If you're in it, get out.
- If volume dries up on down days, this indicates investors that are not willing to sell.

TRIN: The Arms Index	By calculating advancing volume versus declining volume, investors can use the A/D line and volume together.
	• The TRIN shows an inverse or opposite reading than what you'd think: If it's going up, the market is heading lower; if the TRIN is dropping, the market is strengthening to the upside.
	• Above 1—market (on balance) is declining.
	• Below 1—market (on balance) is climbing.
	• Extreme readings are the most useful for buying or selling.
	  –A reading of 1.5 indicates an unsustainable level of selling. Contrarian move would be to buy.
	  –A low reading of 0.35 would indicate "irrational exuberance." Perhaps it's time to take some profits?
	• The number isn't as important as the direction.

Moving Averages— Easy to See, Easy to Understand	Moving averages are used to help identify the different kinds of trends (short-term, intermediate, medium, etc.). • Length can vary. Shorter moving averages are more volatile. Long ones are slow to signal a reversal in the trend. • Use several together to spot trends (10-day, 50-day, 200-day).
New Highs/New Lows	By measuring new highs and new lows, you can gauge overall optimism or fear. • More new highs mean optimism is growing. Trend likely to continue up. • More lows indicates downtrend is beginning or continuing.
Web Sites for the Market	• **Barchart.com** (www.barchart.com/cme/cmeft.htm) • **BondsOnline** (www.bondsonline.com) • **SmartMoney.com** (www.smartmoney.com/si/sectors) • **Barron's Online** (www.barrons.com) • ***Investor's Business Daily*** (www.investors.com) • **Wall Street Journal Online** (interactive.wsj.com/ushome.html) • **Nasdaq-AMEX market site** (www.nasdaq.com and www.amex.com/default.asp) **HOLDRS** Good explanations by: • **TheStreet.com** (www.thestreet.com/funds/deardagen/ 968391.html) • **AMEX** (www.amex.com/structuredeq/sp_holdrs.stm)

- **Merrill Lynch** (www.ml.com/welcome)

iShares
- **Index Shares**
  (www.amex.com/indexshares/index_shares_over.stm)
- **iShares.com** (www.ishares.com/home.html)
- **Nasdaq Quote Summary** (options.nasdaq-amex.com/
  asp/option_index_trackers.asp): Packed with information—an
  all-around great site.

Market Sectors
- **LabPuppy.com** (www.labpuppy.com)
- **Stock Smart** (www.stocksmart.com): Pay site, seven-day free
  trial
- **Smart Money.com/Market Map**
  (www.smartmoney.com/marketmap)
- **The Telecom Analyst**
  (www.thetelecommanalyst.com/default.asp)
- **Optionetics.com** (www.optionetics.com/default.asp)
- *Investor's Business Daily* (www.investors.com)

Useful Internet Sites for the Economy	• **Economagic** (www.economagic.com): The best for economic charts. • **Federal Reserve** (www.federalreserve.gov/fomc) • **TheStreet.com Economic Indicators** (www.thestreet.com/markets/databank/693853.html) • **Financial Trend Forecaster** (www.fintrend.com/ftf/default.htm) • **Economic Cycle Research Institute** (www.businesscycle.com/index.html) • **Economic Indicators.com** (www.economic-indicators.com) • **The Dismal Scientist** (www.dismal.com/home.htm): Great site! • **Bureau of Labor and Statistics** (stats.bls.gov/blshome.htm) • **Financial Forecast Center** (www.neatideas.com/index.htm)
Other Useful Financial Sites	• **Bloomberg.com** (www.bloomberg.com/welcome.html) • **Equity Analytics** (www.e-analytics.com): Holy Moly! • **First Union Economic Indicators** (www.firstunion.com/library/econews) • **Investor Links** (www.msdw.com) • **Zacks Investment Research** (my.zacks.com/index.php3) • **Tradition-Axone Financial Database** (tradition.axone.ch): Multilingual glossary.

7

Exploring Fundamental Analysis

In the previous chapter, we learned how to examine the market by studying broad market indicators such as sectors. Now it's time to turn our attention to analyzing the individual stock. Exactly what are investors looking for in a stock? Basically, there are times when investing in the market or a specific industry group is more profitable than at others. In order to better understand the day-to-day fluctuations in the stock market and increase the odds of success, the reader has learned how to interpret economic data, study volume and breadth, as well as view the market in terms of different sectors. But that is only half the battle. Successful investing requires not only an understanding of the market, but also the ability to dig deeply into each individual company and determine whether it is a viable investment.

Therefore, just as there are a number of factors to consider when studying the market, there are an equal number to think about when analyzing a specific company. Is it profitable? Does the company have a competitive advantage? Is the management team strong? How efficient is the enterprise?

These types of questions are at the crux of fundamental analysis and the subject of the next two chapters. This chapter defines fundamental analysis and begins its investigation, while the next focuses on company reports and financial statements.

A common misunderstanding in the investment community is the difference between technical analysis and fundamental analysis. The easiest way I can explain it is: *Fundamental analysis* is the study of the company, and *technical analysis* is the study of the stock price. The distinction will be made clearer as the chapter progresses.

Fundamentals: Earnings, dividends, sales, revenues, profit margins, and so on.

Technicals: Charts with graphical representations of price, last trade, change, volume, 52-week highs and lows, and so on.

Also, in this chapter the reader will become familiar with what I consider to be the 15 most important tools of fundamental analysis. The first five are covered in this chapter. In order to prepare for the remaining 10, however, it is necessary to investigate financial statements. The last part of this chapter will show the reader how to go about accessing these statements.

WHAT ARE THE FUNDAMENTALS?

Fundamentals indicate the financial health of a company. Most people are familiar with what I'll call the fundamental snapshot that provides an initial view of a company in terms of stock price, volume, 52-week range, and so on. Snapshots are easily found on a multitude of websites including Optionetics.com. If you punch in a stock symbol (for instance, the stock symbol for EMC Corporation is EMC as in Figure 7.1), and click Go, the image in Figure 7.2 appears.

The data in Figure 7.2 represents a *snapshot* of the current market valuation, the range the stock has traded for the past 52 weeks as well as various other important values. Although it's important not to attach too much importance to any one of these details, looked at together they provide an initial picture of the stock. Last, Open, High, Low, Change, % Change, Bid, and Ask all describe the stock's current price action. The 52-week High and Low provide a historical account of the stock's price performance. Accordingly, with EMC currently trading at 95.75, EMC is only $4^{1}/_{4}$ points from its 52-week high of 100. These are all relevant pieces of information, but not essential ingredients for fundamental analysis.

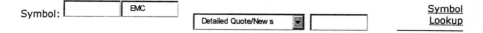

Figure 7.1   Optionetics.com Get Quote and Fundamentals (Courtesy of Optionetics.com)

Emc Corporation (EMC)

			Delayed Quote as of SEP 14, 2000
			2:23:06 PM (E.T.)
Last	**95.750**	Change	1.063
Open	95.938	% Change	1.12%
High	96.938	Low	92.125
Bid	N/A	Ask	N/A
52-Week High	100.000	52-Week Low	30.000
Earnings Per Share	0.57	Volume	3.31M
Shares Outstanding	2.18B	Market Cap	208.77B
P/E Ratio	166.12	Exchange	NYSE

Figure 7.2   Get Quote and Fundamentals of EMC (Courtesy of Optionetics.com)

The purpose of fundamental analysis is to assess the financial history and current conditions of a company's income, expenditure of money, and measure how efficiently they manage their business. I usually start by looking at one of the most commonly used measurements of a company: market capitalization. Market capitalization refers to the overall valuation the market gives to a company. Just to review, market capitalization is equal to the number of shares outstanding times the share price. It tells the company's size and enables a trader to place a stock in the correct size category: large-cap, mid-cap, small-cap, or micro-cap. Knowing a company's size is useful in that it helps traders to compare that company to those of similar size.

More important, however, are two other pieces of data. For the fundamental analyst, *EPS* or the earnings per share describes how profitable a company is, while the *P/E ratio* or price-to-earnings ratio is a measure of the market price of the stock relative to those earnings. Both are commonly used fundamental analysis tools that I will describe in detail in Chapter 8.

EPS: The primary tool that analysts look at to determine a company's profitability: the net income or earnings of the company divided by the number of shares outstanding.

P/E ratio: This ratio is most helpful when compared to industry averages and the overall market. Some will use this ratio as a means to gauge whether a security is overvalued or undervalued. Companies with high P/Es are considered overvalued, and companies with low P/Es are considered undervalued. The price-to-earnings ratio equals the last price divided by the earnings per share. In this case, 95.75 / 0.57 = 166.12.

The objective of this chapter is to introduce the reader to the basic concepts of fundamental analysis and how this discipline is used as a tool for making superior investment decisions. Stocks represent a unit of ownership in a company. In other words, if you buy a stock, you become a fractional owner in the company. Fundamental analysis is a way of studying not the stock, but the company.

The fact is, successful companies have certain defining attributes. A successful company, for instance, will make profits and through the years, the profits will increase. At the same time, a successful company will see its stock price increase in value. As an investor, this is important. The goal is to buy stock in a company and see the stock price increase in value. Through the years, the stocks of successful companies will increase in value. But how do you determine if a company is successful? Fundamental analysis seeks to answer that question.

As a result, fundamental analysis can help you make better investment decisions in two ways. First, studying each company's fundamentals makes it becomes possible to see whether the company has desirable attributes. For instance, are the company's revenues increasing from one year to the next, is the company profitable, and is it generating a positive cash flow? The second goal of fundamental analysis is to determine, given the company's fundamentals, if the stock is a good buy—a value. In other words, if a company has all of the attributes of success (in terms of sales, revenues, profits, etc.) is the current market price for the stock a reasonable one? As we will see, sometimes a company can have exceptional fundamentals but the stock price is too high to buy. In short, it is better to buy a stock when the company's fundamentals are strong and the stock price seems low, or seems to offer a good value. As we progress through the next two chapters, you will learn how to assess whether a stock price is attractive given a company's fundamentals.

THE FIRST FIVE CRITICAL TOOLS OF FUNDAMENTAL ANALYSIS

So what are the attributes that we look for when examining a company from a fundamental perspective? Let's take a look.

1. The Basics

Fundamental analysis starts at the rudimentary level. First, what line of business is the company in? Is it an insurance company, a restaurant chain, a maker of personal computers? The type of business is extremely important to the fundamental analyst. For instance, consider Home Depot (HD), the number one retailer of home building supplies. When would you expect the company's sales to grow the most—during periods when the economy is strong and home building is robust, or in periods of recession? Obviously, when the economy is strong and Americans are doing well, they tend to spend more money on home building and improvements. This can significantly increase the net sales of home improvement companies such as Home Depot. On the other hand, a less than robust economy can be a boost for home-improvement companies as well. People's housing needs change over time. If they do not have the financial resources or their resources are uncertain, rather than purchase a new home or hire a contractor homeowners frequently turn to home-improvement companies for solutions. This demonstrates an important point to remember: When it comes to consumer spending, answers are rarely black or white.

Another goal behind fundamental analysis is to measure the performance of a company. In order to do so, it is important to understand the company and how it earns money. Therefore, the more your investments in stocks reflect your personal areas of knowledge, the greater your odds of success. For example, a farmer will probably have a better understanding of the supply and demand for John Deere products than he or she will for Internet software. An airline pilot will be able to interpret the impact of higher fuel costs on airline corporate profits. A homemaker might see the potential future profits behind the launch of a new laundry detergent that has the neighborhood buzzing. In short, each individual has a specific area of expertise. Since one of the goals behind fundamental analysis is to study the company, the simpler and more understandable the company, the better.

> *As famed investor Warren Buffett once said, "Invest within*
> *your circle of competence. It's not how big the circle is*
> *that counts, it's how well you define the parameters."*

2. Identifying Industry Leaders

Successful companies are often industry leaders. This doesn't necessarily mean that they are the largest in size; but rather that within a certain sector, the company is recognized as a major player. It has captured a significant percentage of the sector's sales and revenues, plus the sector itself is experiencing a healthy rate of growth. Thus, the total revenues of an industry can be seen as a pie: the larger a company's slice or *market share*, the better (see Figure 7.3).

> **Market share:** The percentage of an industry's goods and services controlled by one firm. The larger the market share, the less likely the company's profits will be squeezed by competition.

As new technologies emerge, some companies will set the standard for their particular industry in years to come. If you own a computer, what operating system do you use? Chances are it is a Microsoft product. Are there any new products on the market that are likely to change the way we live? Are your friends and neighbors all buying the same thing—a new and innovative product? If so, who makes it? Are there many competitors likely to step in and take away market share?

Another fundamental question when studying a company is: How does it rank in its particular sector? You want to be in the company with the strongest track record. There are a few services that can help you see how stocks rank within particular industries. One place to look is Zacks Investment Research (my.zacks.com/index.php3)

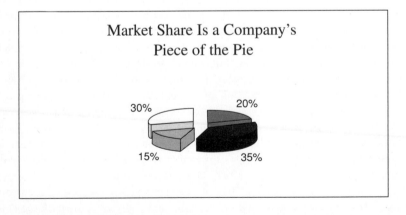

Figure 7.3   Market Share Pie Chart

by checking its "rank within industry." The rankings are designed to isolate companies with the strongest earnings prospects. *Value Line Investment Survey* (with print and electronic products available on a subscription basis, as well as available in most local libraries) offers a ranking system that is useful in sorting out the strongest stocks within industry groups. Standard & Poor's also has a ranking system, and its five-star rating system can be found in its weekly publication, the *Outlook*, and in its *Stock Reports*. *Investor's Business Daily* is also a great place to turn. Five days a week it ranks industry groups (sectors) according to strength (www.investors.com). Finally, Stock Worm.com (www.stockworm.com) has an interesting site for evaluating industry groups and important stocks within each sector.

From a fundamental analyst's perspective, a company's position within an industry is a significant factor to consider before making an investment decision. A sizable market share in a growing industry is highly desirable because it suggests that competition is not likely to eat into the company's profits.

There are a number of web sites that offer information on how stocks rank within their respective industries. Check out: www.investors.com, www.valueline.com, my.zacks.com/index. php3, and www.stockworm.com. Nondigital ways to conduct the initial investigation can be found by consulting: Value Line Investment Survey, Investor's Business Daily, S&P Stock Reports *and the* Outlook.

---

3. Insider Holdings

Knowing if company insiders are buying or selling their company's stock is an indicator that has proven helpful to investors in their decision making. Not surprisingly, insiders know better than anyone else whether a company's earnings are likely to increase or decrease. The Securities and Exchange Commission (SEC) defines corporate insiders as the officers, directors, and major shareholders who own more than 10% of a company's shares. These people are usually the most knowledgeable, and will sometimes buy and sell their stock based on what they believe will happen next. If the president, chairman, and directors are selling significant portions of their positions that could be cause for concern. But if a couple of insiders are selling small percentages of their holdings, then the selling is probably not significant. There are many reasons an insider might decide to sell stock. Perhaps he or she wants to buy a new house or car, or it's time to send the kids to college. Neither of these reasons has any bearings on the firm or its expected fortune—it's just part of human realities. But if insiders start investing additional money into the company by purchasing shares of stock, this is a very good indication that they believe the firm has a bright and prosperous future.

Insider: (1) A person, due to his or her position at a company, who has access to proprietary information not yet available to the general public; and (2) An officer, or director of a firm with a 10% or greater ownership stake in the company's securities.

According to Dow Theory, the accumulation phase of a stock exists when a stock begins to move higher or is in the first leg of an uptrend. During this initial rise, informed and astute investors are buying the stock and pushing it higher. Additionally, if major shareholders are buying large amounts of the stock, then that could be a sign that positive news is going to be released in the near future.

However, it is important not to make an investment decision solely based on this one source of information. This is just one piece of the puzzle that provides additional insight on the company you are investigating. Besides, sometimes investors sour on a stock simply because there has been significant insider activity. This can prove to be a mistake. After all, insiders have bills to pay just like anyone else. Sometimes their living expenses are greater than their salaries and they need to sell stock in order to cover them. In general, there will be much more insider selling than buying in any particular stock.

Insider selling and buying information is easy to access on the Internet. Yahoo! Finance lists all of the insider buy/sell transactions that have been filed with the Securities and Exchange Commission. You can find this information at:

- *finance.yahoo.com/?u*
- *www.zacks.com*
- *www.insidertrading.com*
- *www.insiderscores.com/nindex.asp*

When considering insider buying and selling, it is generally better to invest in companies with more insiders holding shares (i.e., the more insiders of the company who own stock, the better). Why? Who is likely to manage the company more efficiently—an insider with a large stake in the company or someone with no vested interest? In other words, if you are a large owner of a company (because you own many shares) you will be more likely to work diligently to increase shareholder value and increase the stock price. Insider ownership of 15% or more is a healthy sign.

4. Management Interviews

Another means of assessing the performance of your potential investment is to listen to interviews with top management. This will not only give you a feel for management's opinion of the future, but also key you in to what drives the opinions of the professionals. Although you can't sit down with Jeff Bezos of Amazon.com, or Tim Koogle at Yahoo!, the Internet is tearing down some of these barriers and opening up access to company conference calls. The number of companies broadcasting their conference calls in real-time and archiving these calls to be reviewed later is increasing rapidly—so much so that the investment community is beginning to expect it as standard procedure. A great deal can be learned from listening in to these calls and interviews, even if you are not able to ask specific questions yourself.

The management of a public company also has a financial incentive to communicate with the Wall Street analysts. It keeps the doors open to raise capital in the future. They also have incentive to communicate with the media and investors to keep them informed of both positive and negative developments. In this way, they can manage expectations and avoid negative surprises that might be damaging to the stock price.

Most individual investors can satisfy their need for information by monitoring the newswires, the Internet, company conference calls, management communiqués, and annual reports. In a detailed analysis of a company, though, an analyst will raise difficult questions about management, including:

- Who is leaving?
- Who are the key men or women?
- What would the loss of these individuals mean to the company?
- Is the compensation reasonable?
- Are there any capital expenditures that could or should have been avoided?
- What are the future plans for expansion and capital expenditure?
- What is the company's outlook for its industry?
- Who are its chief competitors?
- Are there going to be any significant write-offs or adverse charges that will reduce earnings?
- What kind of guidance can management give about revenue and earnings for the quarter?
- Are there any big contingent liabilities such as unresolved court cases, or problems with unfunded pensions?
- What is the nature of the company's contractual relationships with customers and suppliers? Is it heavily dependent on a single customer?

From the perspective of valuation, the main goal of these interviews is to determine the internal risks to the company and whether those risks have been reflected in the financial analysis you perform.

Another way to stay abreast of company-specific information is to visit the web site of the company you are investigating. You will be able to request an investor information packet online, and additional information regarding the company is available.

Radio@WallStreet (www.radiowallstreet.com) broadcasts many different conference calls with a variety of companies. Top-level management discuss the future prospects of their companies in a timely fashion. This is a great way to confirm or reject ideas that you have developed about a company, and to stay abreast of upcoming events.

---

5. Analyst Coverage

An *analyst* in street parlance is someone who works for an investment bank, broker-age firm, or some other type of financial services company. Analysts study compa-nies, write research reports, and make specific recommendations based on their conclusions. For instance, there are a large number of analysts that issue reports on Intel Corporation. A company with a large number of Wall Street analysts research-ing it is said to have a large following, or *analyst coverage*.

> **Analyst coverage:** The number of analysts issuing specific recommendations on a specific company; also known as a *following*.

After studying the company (mainly using fundamental analysis techniques), the analyst will issue a specific recommendation on the company. For instance, if the analyst expects the stock price of the company to increase, he or she may say it is a strong buy or a buy. Simply put, if an analyst believes that a company is underval-ued, a buy recommendation might be made. If that company is overvalued, the company might be downgraded to a lower recommendation.

Often there may be discrepancies or differing opinions among analysts, and this is what makes a market. For example, Merrill Lynch may believe Cisco Systems (CSCO) is overvalued because of low earnings per share, but at the same time Goldman Sachs may believe Cisco is undervalued due to the great growth prospects that the company has in the future. It is your job as an investor to gather the infor-mation, analyze it, and make your own decision about the prospects of the com-pany. Furthermore, as new information about a company, its industry, or the economy becomes available, you and the analysts will be forced to wrestle with these facts and make new determinations of value.

Fundamental analysis is an ongoing process in which the value of the company is continually being assessed in light of new information. The more analysts that cover the stock, the greater the speed the new information will be incorporated into the stock price.

Whether it is better to invest in stocks with a large following is subject to debate. Specifically, a stock with many analysts covering it will have a good institutional following because large investors (mutual funds, insurance companies, financial ad-visers, etc.) rely heavily on analyst recommendations. After all, if a large investor buys a stock and it turns out to be a loser, he or she doesn't have to accept full re-sponsibility if every brokerage firm on the Street had it as a strong buy. Therefore, a company with many buys and strong buys will often have many large institutions buying the stock and that, of course, is a positive for the stock. Conversely, a com-pany with no analyst coverage whatsoever may turn out to be an uncut gem. Since it hasn't been studied by dozens of Wall Street analysts, it has a greater chance of having strong fundamentals that have so far been overlooked. In short, there appears to be no magic number with respect to analyst coverage.

Here are some of the common terms used when analysts make recommendations concerning a stock.

- **Strong buy:** If an analyst issues a strong buy on a stock, it means that he or she believes that it will be among the best-performing stocks over the course of the next year or two.

- **Buy:** The analyst is confident in the company and expects the stock price to increase. When an analyst issues a buy, he or she is advising the firm's clients to own shares of the company.

- **Attractive:** When an analyst says a stock is attractive, his or her analysis suggests that the stock is a good value and shares can be purchased.

- **Accumulate:** The analyst recommends that investors make periodic purchases over coming months—buy on the dips.

- **Market outperform:** The analyst expects the stock to perform better than the market (S&P 500).

- **Market perform:** The analyst expects the stock to perform similarly to the market.

- **Market underperform:** The stock is expected to perform less well than the market.

- **Hold:** The analyst has no strong feelings toward the stock either way. He or she would not buy new shares, but if they are already in the investor's portfolio, the analyst would not sell them, either. The analyst recommends that the investor hold the stock.

- **Avoid:** When a stock is rated avoid, the analyst is recommending that investors not add any shares to their portfolios.

- **Sell:** The analyst is very negative on the company and expects the share price to fall.

- **Strong sell:** The analyst feels very strongly that there is a fundamental problem with the company and the share price is going to fall in the near future. Avoid any stock with a strong sell rating.

Nevertheless, when dealing with analysts, there are a few guidelines to follow. First, avoid stocks with a majority of sell or hold ratings. It is a sign that there is a serious fundamental problem. Only in rare cases will a Wall Street analyst issue a sell rating. Why? Since most brokerage firms also have investment banks that work to help companies raise capital and go public, issuing a sell might hurt future business and is therefore not a good public relations move by an analyst. A sell or strong sell is often a sign of a serious fundamental problem.

Second, the changes in analyst recommendations can often cause drastic swings in a stock price. For instance, stocks can sometimes get a boost when there is a change in rating from hold to buy. When an analyst downgrades the outlook for a company, it can cause the share price to fall. That was the case in the example in Figure 7.4.

ACCESSING COMPANY INFORMATION

In order to really understand a company's operations, it becomes necessary to open up its books and look at its financial statements. In the next chapter, we will look at 10 more tools of fundamental analysis. But before that, the reader needs to find access to company reports or financial statements. There are three principal reports: the income statement, the balance sheet, and the statement of cash flows. The important elements of all three are covered in the next chapter. First, let's see if you can get your hands on some.

Publicly traded companies are required to file periodic financial statements with the SEC. Specifically, the Securities Exchange Act of 1934 requires all public companies to report quarterly and annual reports—called the 10-Q and 10-K respectively. These reports include the income statement, balance sheet, and statement of cash flows.

There are a number of ways to obtain the 10-K and 10-Q. If you have online access, you can go to the company's web site or surf over to www.10kwizard.com or secedgar.com. The Securities and Exchange Commission also has a web site

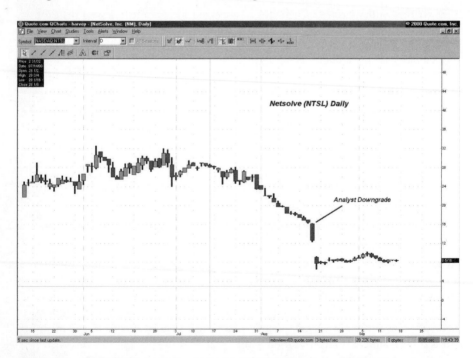

Figure 7.4 Analyst Downgrade—Netsolve (NTSL) (Courtesy of QCharts (www.qcharts.com))

(www.sec.gov) with a database of company financial statements—known as EDGAR—available to the investing public. From www.sec.gov/edgarhp.htm, it is possible to search for 10-Ks and 10-Qs of almost any company. The 10kWizard web site (www.10kwizard.com) also offers access to company financial statements free of charge.

A number of other services provide more polished versions of the financial statements. Investors have used *S&P Stock Reports* for years. Today, the reports are available in print and online. The online reports are available at the S&P Personal Wealthsite (www.personalwealth.com) for a fee and include all of the important elements from the financial statements. For instance, the online reports offer a synopsis of the income statement (see Figure 7.5).

There are several information services that allow investors to search and screen stocks based on fundamental information pulled from the financial statements including *Value Line Investment Survey*, Market Guide, and Zacks. Unlike the 10-Ks and 10-Qs available from EDGAR and 10kWizard, they are not the actual statements, but contain elements taken from the financial statements.

Financial statements can also be found in a company's annual report. Finding the annual report on the company's Internet site is often a matter of going to the home page. For instance, Wal-Mart (WMT) has a site at www.wal-mart.com. Once you plug the URL into your browser and pull up the start page, click on About Wal-Mart. Then, click on Wal-Mart Stores Corporate Information, and voilà—a selection of the financial information can be accessed.

Individual company web sites will vary in the information that they make available. Obviously, not all companies offer financial statements online. Nonetheless,

Income Statement Analysis (Million $)

	1999	1998	1997	1996	1995	1994	1993	1992	1991	1990
Revs.	6,716	3,974	2,938	2,274	1,878	1,377	783	349	232	171
Oper. Inc.	3,138	1,185	798	583	489	383	202	63.9	30.1	16.7
Depr.	447	203	136	86.9	53.6	32.7	21.7	17.4	9.3	7.5
Int. Exp.	33.5	20.2	15.5	12.0	12.9	15.3	6.0	4.8	1.9	1.9
Pretax Inc.	1,357	1,058	718	519	451	355	180	42.3	20.1	12.5
Eff. Tax Rate	26%	25%	25%	26%	28%	30%	29%	32%	35%	29%
Net Inc.	1,011	793	539	386	327	251	127	28.7	13.0	8.9

Figure 7.5   Sample of Income Statement Analysis from S&P Online Report for EMC

many do, and that's why a company's web site is a good place to start looking for financial statements.

If you are really interested in a company and want to see its financial statements but do not have the desire to do an online search, the best course of action is to call a company's headquarters. If you do not have the telephone number, contact the location nearest you and ask for the number for corporate headquarters. *Value Line Investment Survey* (again, available in most local libraries) also has company telephone numbers within their stock reports. If you can get online, go to Excite stock quotes and check a stock's profile. The phone number and address is listed there.

Once you have the telephone number, call the company and ask the receptionist for investor relations. In most cases, an automated system or voice mail will tell you to leave your name and address after the beep if you want financial information or reports. Then the ball's in your court. You have to decide what you want: an annual report (10-K), a quarterly report (10-Q), recent press releases, or some analyst reports. If, by chance, you actually have the chance to speak to a living person, make the same request or simply ask for an investor relations package. In a few days, you should receive the package.

Investor relations: The department within a company that is responsible for handling investor questions, issuing press releases, creating financial documents, and sending out financial information.

CONCLUSION

There are a number of factors to consider when analyzing a company. In this chapter, you have been introduced to the first part of fundamental analysis—the study of the company. Unlike technical analysis, which is really a look at the performance of the stock price (and the subject of Chapter 9), fundamental analysis is concerned with the operations of the company. Is the company efficient? How profitable is it? Are sales and revenues growing?

At this point, you should be busy trying to get your hands on the annual report of your favorite company. Maybe you already have one. If not, annual reports are easily found online. Therefore, try a company's home page. If this fails, try a search using Yahoo! or Lycos (or your favorite search engine) and type in the company's name. This often leads to the home page and then the annual report. Other sites offer financial statements online, and several were noted in this chapter. EDGAR at the SEC site is the most widely used (www.sec.gov).

However you choose to do it, actually having the documents before beginning the next chapter may help you to understand the remaining 10 key elements of fundamental analysis (although it is not essential). The first five were covered in this chapter. They don't require calculators or complex calculations. In fact, the process of fundamental analysis starts at a very basic level—simply finding out what a company does.

Other factors to consider are the number of shares insiders hold, management interviews in the media, the company's position in the industry and market share, and what Wall Street analysts are saying about the stock. The remaining 10 tools are equally important, but require information pulled from the financial statements. So, open that investor relations package, and get ready to start crunching numbers.

ROADMAP TO SUCCESS

Objective	Course of Action
Fundamental Analysis	**Definition:** A form of securities analysis that attempts to gauge a stock's true value based on the business prospects of the company. The focus often centers on the company's future earnings and dividends prospects. **Fundamental:** The study of the company—earnings, sales, profit margins, return on equity, debt, assets, and so on. **Technical:** The study of the stock price—price, last trade, high, low, open, close, volume, and so on. **What is the purpose of fundamental analysis?** • Identify companies with desirable or undesirable attributes: growing profits, increasing sales, positive cash flow, and so on. • Consider the stock price in light of the company's fundamentals. • Identify a misvalued stock. If fundamental analysis suggests that the company is worth more than the stock price, the investor will buy the stock in anticipation that it will increase in value.
Chapter 7 Contents	1. The Basics 2. Identifying Industry Leaders 3. Insider Holdings 4. Management Interviews 5. Analyst Coverage
The Remaining 10 Tools of Fundamental Analysis	6. Revenues or Sales 7. Earnings or EPS 8. Price-to-Earnings (P/E) 9. Price-to-Sales 10. Research and Development 11. Current Ratio 12. Debt/Equity 13. Management Effectiveness Ratios 14. Cash Flow from Operations 15. PEG Ratio
Understanding the Basics	**The basics reveal a lot:** • Understand what the company does. Is it a technology, retailer, or financial services company?

- How does the company make money?
- Is the company's business seasonal, cyclical, or dependent on the weather?
- Do you understand the company?
- Where is your particular area of expertise?
- Fundamental analysis is easier to understand when you investigate a company in which you developed a working understanding of its business sector.

Industry Leaders	**Successful companies are often industry leaders.** • Industry leadership does not necessarily mean the largest in size or revenues. • Successful companies are often trendsetters. For example, Microsoft set the standard for computer operating systems and became one of the largest companies in the world. • In your area of expertise, are there any companies setting the standard for a way of doing business or a product? • Look around—what are your friends and neighbors buying? • Are there any companies that are capitalizing on changes in the industry and increasing market share? • Is competition a threat to future profitability? • Market share is like a piece of pie—the bigger a company's piece of the pie, the better.
What to Look For	• Examine market share—if you can't find the exact percentage or have questions, contact the company's investor relations department. • How does the company rank within the industry? • Check Zacks ranking. • Check Value Line ranking. • Check S&P ranking. • Check the *Investor's Business Daily* industry rankings. • Learn more about the major players in specific industries at www.stockworm.com or www.zacks.com.
Insider Holdings	**Insiders:** Officers, directors, and shareholders who own more than 10% of a company's shares. • Insiders often have access to information that the general public does not. • Watching what insiders are doing is often insightful. Are they buying or selling shares? • Well-informed investors often buy shares before a big move in the stock. • Insiders often sell shares for legitimate reasons such as to pay for a child's college education. In general, there is much more insider selling than buying. • Insider activity is just one source of information and, taken alone, not sufficient for making investment decisions. • A company with a large percentage of insider ownership is a positive.

- 15% or more is a healthy sign.
- Access insider buying and selling on the Internet:
  - –www.insidertrading.com
  - –www.insiderscores.com/nindex.asp
  - –finance.yahoo.com
  - –www.zacks.com
- Check the percentage of insider ownership in the *Value Line Investment Survey* stock reports.

Management Interviews	**Interviews with top management can be insightful.**

- What is management's opinion of the future?
- Can you access a conference call?
- Questions to ask about management:
  - –Who is leaving?
  - –Who are the key members?
  - –Is the compensation reasonable?
  - –What is the company's outlook for the industry?
- Visit www.bloomberg.com.
- Listen to radio@Wallstreet (www.radiowallstreet.com).
- Watch for television interviews—CNBC, CNN, *Wall Street Week* (public television—Friday evenings), *Moneyline* (CNN—nightly), and *Nightly Business Report* (public television—nightly).

Analyst Coverage	

- Wall Street Analysts: Study individual companies, assess their fundamentals, and issue recommendations.
- If an analyst rates a company a strong buy or buy, it suggests that he or she anticipates the share price to move higher in the future.
- Companies with a large number of buy recommendations will have a large institutional following. Meaning, many large investors will have an ownership stake and represent an important source of buying power to keep the stock moving higher.
- A stock with no analyst coverage may prove to be a hidden value not yet discovered by the Street.
- Avoid stocks with sell and strong sell recommendations. They are a sign of fundamental problems companies are experiencing.
- Know what analysts are saying about the stocks you are interested in—visit www.zacks.com to find out.
- Monitor the day-to-day changes in analyst recommendations.
  - –finance.yahoo.com
  - –www.bloomberg.com
  - –www.etrade.com

Accessing Company Information	**A large amount of financial information can be found in a company's financial reports.**

- 10-Q—A company's quarterly financial statements filed with the SEC.

- 10-K—The annual report to the SEC.
- Annual report—A report issued once a year to a company's shareholders. It contains information from the 10-K and management discussions of the company's operations.
- There are three key financial statements investors need for the next chapter:
    - –Income statement
    - –Balance sheet
    - –Statement of cash flows
- Search the EDGAR database at www.sec.gov to obtain financial statements for the companies that interest you; or:
- Visit www.10kwizard.com to obtain the financial statements; or:
- Go to the company's web site and pull up the annual report; or:
- Call the company and ask for an investor relation's package; or:
- Visit your local library's business section and look up a company's annual reports.

8

Analyzing Company Reports

If you were bold enough to call for an investor packet, it is possible that you have already learned something about the company as a potential investment just by going through this process. A primary avenue for learning about a firm is to have personal contact with an employee. During this process you should have observed how well you were treated and how responsive the investor relations department was to your request. Many large companies are inundated with calls for information and simply do not have the time to give attention to each individual request. Smaller companies, however, will often spend considerable time with interested investors and even try to sell them on the company. What was your experience with the investor relations department? Did the company seem efficient? Is it portraying itself well to the investment community? These are all important questions that can be answered simply by being observant while doing your homework on the company.

If you really want to see how the company operates, and it is in your area, ask if you can pick up the investor relations package in person. Sometimes, as a potential investor, you can even get a tour of the facility.

The primary goal at this point, though, is to obtain an investor relations package and, specifically, the annual report. Why the fuss about an annual report? Actually, it is a very important document containing vital information about the company, as well as the sector you're researching. At the same time, beyond the detailed financial information, it is a marketing piece and another vehicle for the company to communicate with potential investors. Keep these questions in mind when perusing the annual report:

- What is the main message conveyed by the company?
- Are objectives addressed squarely, or is the report too vague?

- Does it appear the company is spending its money wisely? How would you grade it in the following categories?

     Research and development: Is R&D increasing or decreasing (or nonexistent)?

     Debt service and reduction: Look at the debt level from past years moving to the present; is debt increasing or decreasing? Have earnings suffered as a result?

     Salaries and bonuses: This is an area that sometimes causes shareholder angst to rise. Is management being overcompensated for mediocre performance?

All these qualitative elements of the company are part of fundamental analysis. In order to be confident in your investment, it is important to be confident that management is efficient and looking to add shareholder value. The investor relations department is responsible for conveying these attributes of their company and if they have done their job properly, then you should feel quite impressed with the organization.

Now that you have the investor relations package in hand—or you've found the company's financial statements on the Internet—you're ready to dig deeper and really take a closer look at the company's finances. In Chapter 7, we covered the first five tools of fundamental analysis:

1. The basics

2. Industry leaders

3. Insider holdings

4. Management interviews

5. Analyst coverage

The remaining 10 steps call for you to inspect the company's books (i.e., its financial statements). At first, the thought of analyzing financial statements might have you moving toward the kitchen to brew up a pot of coffee. Fortunately, I am not going to teach you how to analyze every line on each financial statement. Rather, the focus will center on the most meaningful aspects. A student of the market can spend years trying to figure out how to interpret financial statements. Our goal is to focus on the most relevant aspects and the financial ratios that really matter.

If you want more details on studying financial statements, a good source is The Analysis and Use of Financial Statements (second edition, June 1997) by Gerald I. White, Ashwlnpaul C. Sondhi, Dov Fried—it's only 900 pages long!

As we have already determined, the annual report is an important piece of information. It will include management's discussion of the company, the operations over the past year, and the outlook going forward. It can sometimes be very persuasive, but given that company management writes it, the report is not always objective. In addition, management may try to bend and shape the actual numbers to put the company in a better light than perhaps it deserves. This is why you hear of so-called accounting irregularities from time to time—some accountant got overly creative with the numbers and got caught! Be watchful for accounting irregularities, for they often send the guilty stock into a tailspin.

To study the numbers, there are three key financial statements included in the annual report: the *income statement*, the *balance sheet*, and the *statement of cash flows*. All three of these financial statements reveal unique pieces of information in regard to the success of a company's operations.

Income statement: A financial report of all revenues and expenses pertaining to a specific time period. This report provides the information necessary to calculate the earnings per share, profit margin, P/E (price-to-earnings) ratio, and P/S (price-to-sales) ratio.

Balance sheet: A report that shows the financial status of a business entity at a particular instant in time. It is like a snapshot of a business, and it also contains the financial information to calculate the current ratio, debt/equity ratio, return on equity, and return on assets.

Statement of cash flows: A report that shows the cash receipts and cash payments of an entity during a particular period. The important part of this statement is to see positive cash flow from operations. This implies that the company is actually making money at what it is doing.

THE INCOME STATEMENT

The income statement is a report of all revenues and expenses pertaining to a specific time period. It is a relatively simple, but extremely useful table. When referring to a company's financial results, analysts and reporters often talk of the "top line" and "bottom line." The reason is that on the income statement the top line lists the company's sales or revenues. Therefore, if someone says that a company has had significant top-line growth over the past year, it means that the sales have increased significantly over the past year. The bottom line is the profit, or earnings, of the company. It appears on—you guessed it—the bottom line of the financial statement and is the most widely followed measure of a company's performance. Figure 8.1 shows the quarterly income statement dated June 30, 2000, from EMC Corporation (EMC). Let's break each section down into bite-sized pieces.

Revenues or Sales

The primary objective of all companies is to generate sales and revenues. This is what generates the cash flow in order for the company to meet obligations and to grow. Again, the sales or revenue figure is also referred to as the top line, because these numbers are reported at the top of the income statement. Figure 8.2 takes the first items from the income statement in Figure 8.1.

Statement of Income
(In Millions, Except Per Share Figures)

	December 31, 1999	December 31, 1998	December 31, 1997
Revenues:			
Net sales	$5,983	$4,861	$4,023
Services	733	575	465
Total:	6,716	5,436	4,488
(See Figure 8.2)			
Operating Expenses:			
Cost of Sales	2,751	2,600	2,317
Cost of Service	507	396	295
Research & Development	573	435	332
Selling, General, & Admin.	1,436	1,088	826
Other Charges	208	82	—
Operating Income	1,241	834	717
(See Figure 8.3)			
Investment Income	132	114	83
Interest Income	(33)	(35)	(31)
Other Income/Expense	18	.4	1
Income before Taxes	1,357	914	769
Income Taxes	347	260	182
(See Figure 8.4)			
Net Income	1,011	654	588
Earnings per Share	.98	.64	.59
Shares Outstanding	1,031	1,015	1,011
(See Figure 8.5)			

Figure 8.1   EMC Income Statement (Courtesy of EMC Corporation—www.emc.com)

What to look for: *Increasing year-to-year revenue growth. EMC showed a healthy increase in year over year sales from 1997 through 1999. In 1998, total revenues increased at a 21% clip and the number increased to 23% in 1999.*

The absolute level of sales growth isn't as important as the percentage increase of revenue growth. Is the company's revenue increasing at an adequate rate? Ideally, a company will be increasing revenues at least 20% annually. Remember, however, that corporate financial statements (*10-Qs*) are filed quarterly. As an investor, you should monitor them at least that often.

Growth rates are dependent on many things including the size of the firm, the industry, and so on. For example, a 20% to 50% growth in a large cap stock is spectacular; but the same growth in a micro-cap would be very disappointing. Likewise, the growth rate of a dot-com is usually much higher than a retailer. It all comes down to knowing an industry and the firms in that industry. As a basic rule of thumb, you're looking for firms that are significantly outperforming their fellow competitors.

	1999	*1998*	*1997*
Revenues:			
Net Sales	$5,983	$4,861	$4,023
Services	733	575	465
Total:	6,716	5,436	4,488

Revenues: The company's total income from sales before expenses.

Figure 8.2   The Top Line of the Income Statement

10-Q: The quarterly financial report filed by firms that have securities listed with the SEC. It is less detailed, but filed more frequently than the 10-K found in the annual report. This report will contain the quarterly balance sheet, income statement, and statement of cash flows.

---

*With the right strategy, you can make as much money in a
slow-growth industry as a high-growth one with much less risk.*

In the process of generating revenues, all companies incur costs and expenses. If you own a restaurant, for instance, you have to pay the lease on the building, the costs of the raw ingredients, and the salaries of the staff. On the income statement, the business's expenses or costs of doing business, are subtracted from revenues to arrive at the *operating income* (see Figure 8.3).

Research and Development

One of the key tools of fundamental analysis can be found in the "Operating Expenses" section of the income statement—research and development costs. Many businesses spend significant amounts of money on research and development to

Total Revenues	6,716	5,436	4,488
Operating Expenses:			
Cost of Sales	2,751	2,600	2,317
Cost of Service	507	396	295
Research & Development	573	435	332
Selling, General, & Admin.	1,436	1,088	826
Other Charges	208	82	—
Operating Income	1,241	834	717

Operating Expenses: The costs associated with doing business and developing sales.
Operating Income: The company's income after expenses have been subtracted from total revenues.

Figure 8.3   Operating Expenses and Operating Income

create new products or processes, to improve present products, and to discover new knowledge that may be valuable at some future date. This is especially important in the drug and biotechnology industries because their revenue streams are dependent upon the new drugs that they have in their pipelines for future sales.

It can be helpful to compare the percentage of sales that R&D comprises in a company's expenses to other companies in the same industry. It is an indicator of how dedicated a firm is to remaining or becoming the leader in its respective market sector. As we can see, the dollar figure for R&D is found on the income statement under the category "Operating Expenses."

What to Look For: *Make sure research and development is a company priority. Many companies will reduce the amount of money they allocate toward research and development in order to cut costs and appear more profitable in the present. By doing so, they could be jeopardizing their future. EMC is, again, demonstrating a desirable attribute in this case: It is steadily increasing R&D expenditures.*

After operating expenses like research and development are subtracted from revenues, nonbusiness income and expenses are added or subtracted from operating income. For example, if you own an auto repair shop and took out a loan to buy the tools, you will make periodic payments on that loan. That is known as interest expense. If you have a lot of cash in the bank for your business needs and earn interest on that money, you will report interest income. As you can see from Figure 8.4, EMC is generating more money from its investments than it is paying out in interest income—a favorable sign.

After investment income and expenses are either added or subtracted from operating income, we now have the income for the company. Is that what the company gets to keep? Of course not! It's time to pay Uncle Sam.

Earnings and Earnings per Share

After taxes are considered, the result is net income and represents the company's bottom line. Net income or earnings are perhaps the most widely followed piece of fundamental information monitored by investors. They represent the real profits generated by the company.

Investment Income	132	114	83
Interest Income	(33)	(35)	(31)
Other Income/Expense	18	.4	1
Income before Taxes	1,358	914	771
Income Taxes	347	260	182
Net Income	1,011	654	588

Income before Taxes: *This number tells you how much a company has made before paying its tax obligations.*

Figure 8.4   Income before Taxes

Earnings per share are calculated by dividing a company's total after tax profits by the company's number of common shares outstanding (see Figure 8.5). The annual and quarterly earnings figures are most meaningful when compared to the previous year or the same quarter of the prior year. In this way, you end up comparing apples to apples by taking into account seasonal fluctuations in demand for the product. A large percentage increase in quarterly earnings compared to the same quarter in the prior year would indicate the company is making more money than it was in the past (i.e., it is growing at a profitable pace). It's important to see *earnings acceleration* in the stocks you are considering owning. Earnings should be growing percentage-wise on a quarter-to-quarter basis, as well as simple earnings per share numbers. Quarterly earnings should be increasing by, say, 15% to 30%. Make sure you compare the most recent quarter to the same quarter of the prior year.

Earnings acceleration: The rate at which quarterly earnings per share are increasing. It is important to see your company's earnings increasing 15% to 30% per quarter.

It is also important to study the annual earnings performance of the company. This is a simple process that compares the total earnings of the most recent fiscal year to the total earnings of the prior year. Generally, investors will want to see meaningful growth in a company's annual earnings compared to the prior year. Annual earnings should also be increasing at a 15% to 30% rate. For more aggressive investors, it should be larger.

Earnings data can be found in financial publications, such as the Wall Street Journal *and* Investor's Business Daily, *or by going online to visit one of the many websites that feature this kind of data. Visit Yahoo! Finance, Zacks, or Quicken.com for earnings information on your potential investments.*

Earnings Surprises
One final note regarding earnings: A number of analysts will cover a company and establish a range of *earnings estimates*. Often the range is fairly narrow. That is, if

Net Income	1,011	654	589
Earnings per Share	.98	.64	.58
Shares Outstanding	1,031	1,015	1,011

Net Income: The company's total profits.
Earnings per Share: *The net income or earnings of the company divided by the number of shares outstanding. This is the primary tool that analysts look at to determine a company's profitability.*

Figure 8.5 Earnings per Share (EPS)

an analyst at Merrill Lynch expects EMC to report 25 cents in quarterly earnings per share, estimates at competing brokerage firms will probably be similar—at least within a penny. However, there is another, unofficial estimate that Wall Street speaks of called the *"whisper number."* So, for instance, if the average estimate of analysts is for EMC Corporation to earn 25 cents in the quarter, talk and rumors among investors may be for the company to report 28 cents. The whisper number will almost always be higher by 2 or 3 cents.

A company that beats analysts' estimates and the whisper number is said to post a *positive earnings surprise*. This is a solid sign that management is doing a good job. The opposite is also true, and is called a *negative earnings surprise*. This kind

---

Earnings estimates: This is the anticipated earnings per share figure that analysts expect a company to report on the release date. It is very important that companies beat their earnings estimates; otherwise their stocks run the risk of getting clobbered.

Whisper number: A company's unofficial earnings estimate anticipated by stock market investors. If a company does not meet or beat the whisper number, then there is a possibility that the stock will get thrashed. This number is derived from perceptions, and if the perceptions are not met, then short-term traders do not want to be in the stock.

---

of surprise can cause the price of the stock to get hammered. When viewing earnings histories, it is important to make sure that the potential investment does not have a habit of delivering these negative surprises to the street. Unfortunately, this type of news has a way of repeating itself with companies.

Stocks can also see short-term price moves when analysts change their earnings forecasts for the companies. In the example from Chapter 7, we saw how Netsolve lost considerable ground on the day it was downgraded from buy to attractive and, at the same time, the analyst cut earnings estimates for the stock. The opposite can happen when earnings estimates are upgraded; a stock can gain in price very quickly.

The earnings per share number found on the financial statements is not the only important factor to consider when looking at a company. Fundamental analysis calls for looking at what stock market investors expect the company to report in the future—the whisper number.

Earnings per Share Rank

The earnings per share rank is a rating spearheaded by *Investor's Business Daily*. It measures a company's growth over the last two quarters in comparison to the same quarters in the past year and then factors in the past three- to five-year annual growth rate. The resulting number is then compared to other companies and given a rank of 1 (lowest) to 99 (highest). The EPS rank basically tells a trader how profitable a stock is in comparison to the more than 10,000 stocks available to be traded. I prefer to work with stocks with a ranking of 95 or better when buying, and stocks with an EPS rank of 20 or less when selling. It is a good idea to track the EPS rank of your stocks on at least a weekly basis. This will give you the chance to make changes to your portfolio if there is a dramatic change in the character of your investments. Also, pay attention to a stock's ability to consistently grow by researching the EPS rank at least five years back. If you find a consistent growth pattern, you can bet that investors are willing to pay more for that stock.

Profit Margin

Another profitability ratio is called *profit margin*. This number is calculated by dividing net income of the company by sales and gives the profit per dollar of sales. This ratio is not very helpful if looked at by itself. However, when compared to other companies in the same industry, it can help determine the more efficient organization. Many times, you will hear analysts or guests on CNBC talking about how they expect margins to be improving for a particular company in the next quarter. This profit margin figure is exactly what they are referring to, and it is readily available on several of the Internet-based stock market research services such as Yahoo! Finance, Zacks, and Hoover's.

Profit margin: This number, calculated by dividing net income of the company by sales, gives the profit per dollar of sales. The higher the profit margins, the more money the company is making on each sale that it completes. Analysts pay close attention to this figure, and any signals of profit margins decreasing should be considered a red flag by the investor.

Price-to-Earnings Ratio

The most popular valuation ratios are the price/earnings ratio (P/E) and the price/sales ratio (P/S). P/E ratios are used to easily compare the value that is being paid for a company's earnings. To calculate a stock's P/E ratio, you have to divide the company's market price by its earnings per share (see Figure 8.6). Typically, this is quoted for the most recent 12 months, but can also be quoted using an analyst's estimates for forward periods. For example, if XYZ stock is trading at $20 per share and had earnings last year of $1 per share, its trailing P/E would be 20. If XYZ was expected to earn $1.33 next year, it would have a leading, or forward P/E of 15 (20 / 1.33 = 15). This is especially instructive for a fast-growing company. For instance, let's say XYZ earned only 20 cents per share last year, but was expected to earn $1 per share in the upcoming 12 months. If XYZ was presently selling for $20 per share, it would have a trailing P/E of 100 (20 / .20 = 100) and a leading P/E of 20 (20 / 1 = 20). Since the P/E

Price/Earnings Ratio (P/E)	Current Market Price of Stock	Typically shown as "Last Trade." It is the last price at which a share was purchased or sold.
	Earnings per Share	Also referred to as "Primary Earnings per Share." Net income for the past 12 months divided by the number of common shares outstanding,

Figure 8.6   P/E Ratio Basics

for the Dow Jones Industrial Average ranged from a low of 16 to a high of 28 from 1995 to 2000, the P/E of 100 for XYZ based on trailing earnings is quite high. However, if the firm can meet its estimated earnings, it would be attractively priced. Thus, as an investor, you have to be concerned with not only the quality of the estimates, but the probability of the firm to grow at its estimated rate.

The P/E ratio is also used by money managers to make a quick determination of whether a stock is cheap or expensive relative to its peers in the industry or compared to the broader market, such as the S&P 500. You may have heard an analyst or investor make a statement that they expect a company's P/E multiple to expand. This means typically that this particular stock has a much lower multiple than its peers; and because the analyst feels that the company's fundamental situation is good or improving, the stock should trade at a level that compares favorably with the rest in its industry. If the average for XYZ's industry is a P/E of 40, then this stock may be undervalued. If XYZ is trading at a P/E of 100 ($100 per share) with an industry average of 40, then the stock is probably overvalued. On any sign of weakness, the stock will likely come tumbling down.

How are industry averages established? Brokerage firm analysts establish guidelines for each industry. For example, a slow-growth industry, such as the steel industry, may have a P/E of only 10, while a high-growth industry, such as the Internet businesses, may have a P/E of 40 or higher.

The P/E ratio is used to describe the current state of a stock's price. Because it is related to the market price of the stock, the P/E ratio changes with every trade. It is not generally used to forecast future prices. It simply lets traders know how well the stock is doing right now. In general terms, faster-growing companies have higher P/Es than more mature entities, as investors are willing to "pay up" for the higher earnings growth rate. However, valuing a company by its future earnings is a dangerous game since earnings range significantly.

Price-to-Sales Ratio

The price/sales ratio is very similar to the price/earnings ratio. This single number is arrived at by dividing the market price of the company by the sales of the company, typically for the recent fiscal year. Price/sales is more typically used for companies

> **Price/earnings ratio:** Divides the company's market price by their earnings per share. This ratio is most helpful when compared to industry averages and the overall market. Some will use this ratio as a means to gauge whether a security is overvalued or undervalued. Companies with high P/Es are considered over-valued, and companies with low P/Es are considered undervalued.

or industries without net income, or earnings, particularly when profitability is relatively far out into the future. This means of valuing a company has been very popular recently, especially with young high-technology companies that have the prospects of great success in the future, but lack current earnings. Again, both the P/E ratio and P/S ratios are calculated for you at Yahoo! Finance or Zacks.

THE BALANCE SHEET

The balance sheet shows the financial status of a business entity at a particular instant in time. A good way to think about the balance sheet is that it is a snapshot of the financial health of a company on a specified date. A summary of EMC Corporation's balance sheet is displayed in Figure 8.7. It shows a listing of what the company owns (assets) and what it owes (debt to lenders and equity to shareholders).

There are really two sections to the balance sheet separated by the dark solid line. On the top half, you have *assets*, and on the bottom, *liabilities*. This financial statement gets its name from the fact that the two sections balance themselves out. That is, for every asset there is a liability. Furthermore, both assets and liabilities are subdivided into two categories: current and noncurrent. If an item is current, it means that, in the ordinary course of business, it will be turned into cash over the next 12 months (in the case of a *current asset*) or will be paid in the next 12 months (in the case of *current liabilities*). For example, inventory should be sold and accounts receivable

> **Current assets:** That portion of a company's assets that, in the normal course of business, are or will be turned into cash in the next 12 months. Current assets include cash and cash equivalents (short-term investments), accounts receivable (moneys owed the firm by its customers), inventory, and prepaid expenses (like annual insurance premiums). In most companies, automobiles would be classed as long-term assets because they will last more than one year. However, automobiles held for resale by an automobile manufacturer (Ford, GM, etc.) would be classed as inventory, or a current asset.
>
> **Current liabilities:** Short-term obligations that a company has to its creditors, employees, and so on. This figure tells you how much the company owes in the near future.
>
> **Total assets:** The sum of current and long-term assets.
>
> **Total liabilities:** The sum of current and long-term liabilities.

Balance Sheet (Millions)

	December 31, 1999	December 31, 1998
Current Assets:		
Cash and Cash Equivalents	$1,109	$ 835
Short-term Investments	715	982
Accounts Receivable	1,625	1,293
Inventories	619	620
Deferred Income Taxes	147	50
Other Assets	104	86
Total Current Assets:	4,319	3,866
(See Figure 8.8)		
Long-term Investments	1,350	562
Notes, Receivables	77	35
Property, Plant, and Equipment	1,023	823
Deferred Income Taxes	109	27
Intangible and Other Assets	295	314
Total Assets:	7,173	5,627
(See Figure 8.10)		
Current Liabilities:		
Current Portion of Long-term Debt	9	29
Accounts Payable	370	299
Accrued Expenses	611	457
Income Taxes	249	161
Deferred Revenue	158	94
Total Current Liabilities:	1,397	1,040
Deferred Income Taxes	125	75
Long-term Obligations	686	752
Other Liabilities	12	30
Total Liabilities:	2,220	1,897
Stockholders' Equity:		
Common Stock, par value $.01	10	10
Additional Paid-in Capital	1,706	1,480
Retained Earnings	3,300	2,289
Total Stockholders' Equity	4,952	3,729
Total Liabilities and Stockholders' Equity:	7,173	5,627
(See Figure 8.11)		

Figure 8.7   EMC Balance Sheet

should be collected in the upcoming year. Similarly, accounts payable (bills from suppliers) and the current portion of long-term debt will be paid in the next 12 months.

The most obvious example of a current asset is cash. Figure 8.8 shows the top section of EMC's balance sheet. Notice that the first line is cash or cash equivalents. Cash equivalents are simply short-term investments that can be readily sold or liquidated, but at the same time earn a small amount of interest. At the end of 1999,

	1999	1998
Current Assets:		
Cash and Cash Equivalents	$1,109	$ 835
Short-term Investments	715	982
Accounts Receivable	1,625	1,293
Inventories	619	620
Deferred Income Taxes	147	50
Other Assets	104	86
Total Current Assets:	4,319	3,866

Current Assets: A company's assets that will, in the normal course of business, be turned into cash in the next 12 months.

Figure 8.8   Current Assets from EMC's Balance Sheet

EMC had over a billion dollars in cash, and that is up considerably from 1998. Cash is good. That is, successful operations generate cash. As the cash is stockpiled, it generates interest. Recall from the income statement: EMC is generating significant interest income. However, fundamental analysis is not that simple. Many pieces must be synthesized to come up with an accurate picture of a company. For example, the accumulation of cash may also be an indication of poor financial management unless there is a specific need for it, such as acquisitions or impending major asset purchases.

> **What to Do:** Develop an affinity for a company that increases cash on the balance sheet from one year to the next, and you may find your own profits growing.

Current Ratio

The balance sheet has the information needed to compute important ratios. Specifically, financial strength or solvency ratios help to assess the ability of a firm to meet the financial obligations they will have over the coming year. The ratio that is most widely used in this category is the current ratio. The current ratio is calculated by dividing current assets by current liabilities (see Figure 8.9). It measures the company's abilities to pay its current obligations from its current assets. This number is used primarily to make relative comparisons among firms in a given industry, and is a quick look at the operating strength of the company.

The current ratio helps to determine if a company can pay its obligations on time with the cash that it has available. A general rule of thumb states that the current ratio should be 2 or greater. That does not mean a current ratio of 1 or 1.5 is terrible, but it may raise a red flag. Also, this number is very industry-specific. It is important that companies have the cash available to meet their short-term obligations, and that is why this number is used. For EMC (see Figure 8.10), the current ratio calculation is as follows:

| **Current Ratio** Indicator of short-term debt paying ability. Determined by dividing current assets by current liabilities. The higher the ratio, the more liquid the company. | **Current Assets** | Value of cash, accounts receivable, inventories, marketable securities, and other assets that will, in the normal course of business, be converted to cash in less than one year. |
| | **Current Liabilities** | Amount owed for salaries, interest, accounts payable, and other debts due within one year. |

Figure 8.9   Current Ratio = Current Assets / Current Liabilities

Current Assets	4,319	3,866
Long-term Investments	1,350	562
Notes, Receivables	77	35
Property, Plant, and Equipment	1,023	823
Deferred Income Taxes	109	27
Intangible and Other Assets	295	314
Total Assets:	7,173	5,627

Total Assets: *The sum of current and long-term assets.*

Figure 8.10   EMC Long-Term and Total Assets

$$\text{Current ratio} \; = \; \frac{\text{Current assets}}{\text{Current liabilities}} = \frac{4,319}{1,397} = 3.1$$

EMC's current ratio at 3.1 is quite high, and hence they should have little difficulty meeting its near-term obligations.

In addition to the current items, the balance sheet also lists longer-term assets and liabilities. This includes long-term investments, receivables, property, plant, equipment, patents, and other assets that are not easily liquidated. Together, the long-term and current assets equal the company's total assets. The same is true on the liability side. Longer-term debt (that which is due in 13 months or more) is found below the current liability section of the balance sheet.

Debt/Equity Ratio

Is debt good or bad? Are there certain levels that raise a red flag? I'm glad you asked. The *debt-to-equity* ratio is used similarly to the current ratio and can help answer those questions. The ratio is total liabilities divided by stockholders' equity (see Figure 8.11).

The debt-to-equity ratio reflects to what extent the owners' equity will be able to

Stockholders' Equity:

Common Stock, par value $.01	10	10
Additional Paid-in Capital	1,706	1,480
Retained Earnings	3,300	2,289
Total Stockholders' Equity:	4,952	3,729
Total Liabilities and Stockholders' Equity:	7,173	5,627

Stockholder's Equity: The owners' interest in the assets of the business. It equals the amount invested by the owners in the company plus any profits (or minus losses). This has no relationship to either the stock price or the cash in the business.

Figure 8.11   EMC Stockholders' Equity

Debt-to-Equity Ratio Determined by dividing long-term debt by common stockholders' equity.	**Total Liabilities**	Assets provided by creditors.
Debt to equity = $\dfrac{\text{Total liabilities}}{\text{Shareholders' equity}}$	**Shareholders' Equity**	Assets provided by shareholders.

Figure 8.12   Debt-to-Equity Ratio Basics

cushion or cover the claims of creditors if the company should go to liquidation. A company with more debt, relative to its peers, is regarded as one with more inherent risk as an investment. Again, this number is very industry-specific (the calculation is shown in Figure 8.12), and these are also calculated for you on Yahoo! Finance and Zacks. In the case of EMC, the debt/equity ratio would be calculated as follows:

$$\text{Debt/equity ratio} = \frac{\text{Total long-term debt}}{\text{Total equity}} = \frac{2,854}{4,952} = 0.58$$

Debt/equity helps the analyst determine if a company is overleveraged, and if the company is using the appropriate amount of debt. Generally, there is not just one level of debt that is appropriate. This is a company- and industry-specific issue. But it is helpful to compare the company's debt/equity to its industry and the overall market. If a company's debt/equity ratio continues to increase every year, and the overall trend in the industry is going lower, then that would be a red flag.

However, and this is an important point, the amount of debt, and the debt/equity ratio of a company is a financing decision, not an operating decision. If a company has good operations but a heavy debt load (and the stock's performance is being harmed because of it), this can change literally overnight with the sale of a firm, a new stock issue (equity infusion), or a judicious acquisition. Remember that the business of business ultimately comes down to producing, selling, and delivering goods and services. While financing choices may constrain or enhance such endeavors in the short run, in the long haul it is operations that triumph. For instance, if XYZ had a billion dollars in debt and was acquired by EMC, which used its billion dollars in loose cash to pay off the debt, XYZ would be left with its operations—good or bad.

MANAGEMENT EFFECTIVENESS RATIOS

Management effectiveness ratios help investors determine how efficiently the management of the company has used its assets and how successful the company has been at executing its business strategy. These ratios include *return on equity* (ROE) and *return on assets* (ROA). In general terms, if you want to compare the skill of the management team of one company to another, these ratios are a good place to start. Return on equity is computed by dividing net income by net worth (net worth is also known as shareholders' equity). Shareholders' equity is listed separately near the bottom of a company's balance sheet. Return on assets (ROA) is computed by dividing net income by total assets. However, these ratios are calculated for you on many different Internet web sites, such as Yahoo! Finance, so that you do not have to go through the tedious computations yourself.

Return on equity: Is computed by dividing net income by net worth (net worth is also known as shareholders' equity). This is one of the ratios used to determine the effectiveness of a management team. The higher the ROE, the more efficiently the management team is using their resources.

Return on assets: Is computed by dividing net income by total assets. This is another ratio used to determine how well a management team is using the overall resources they have available to produce returns for their shareholders. This ratio is best analyzed by comparing one company to its industry average and the overall market. The higher the ROA, the more efficiently a company is operating.

These numbers answer the simple question of how efficiently invested capital is being used to earn a return. ROA is the most critical number—it tells how well management is utilizing the resources of the firm. ROE simply adjusts the ROA for the financial leverage management has chosen to utilize. ROA is calculated as follows:

$$\text{ROA} = \frac{\text{Net income}}{\text{Total assets}} = \frac{\$1,011}{\$7,173} = 0.141 \text{ or } 14.1\%$$

This number tells you what kind of a return each dollar invested in the firm (borrowed or equity) is earning. If that number is very low (say, below Treasury bill rates of return), then you can be assured that someone will come along to break up the company, convert the assets to cash, and then reinvest the proceeds in more productive assets. As ROA increases, such a sale redistribution becomes much less likely. Return on equity is calculated as follows:

$$\text{ROE} = \frac{\text{Net income}}{\text{Net equity}} = \frac{\$1,011}{\$4,952} = 0.204 \text{ or } 20.4\%$$

When using the ROE or ROA, company-to-company comparisons have to be made carefully. One company might have an ROE of 25% with very little debt, while another might have the same 25% return on equity but with a much heavier debt load. A familiar example might be the use of margin in a brokerage account. If you made 1,000% on your Qualcomm (QCOM) stock in 1999, buying all the shares you could afford without borrowing any money, and I made 1,000% on Qualcomm shares, but half of the shares were purchased with money I borrowed from the brokerage firm, my return on equity is going to be twice your return. However, if we were around to watch Qualcomm's dramatic decline in early 2000, my risk was much higher than yours and I may have experienced margin calls on the way down.

The same is true with these management effectiveness ratios. Borrowed money can help you to generate more earnings, but at a higher level of risk. As with any field of study, the deeper you get into it, the more important the subtle nuances become. When each of these important relationships is reduced to a single data point or ratio, comparisons can be made quickly and easily. As you begin to work with these ratios, you'll be able to understand the performance of one company relative to others in its industry with relative ease. It is important to note that the normal range of a ratio for one industry may not be similar to that of another industry. The discussion about why you might buy shares in a company with a lower ROE is a portfolio management issue rather than a fundamental analysis question. However, since one industry might be more favorably positioned to benefit at one point in an economic or interest rate cycle than another, even though the companies in that industry have lower performance ratios, they might be more desirable investments. One example would be to buy consumer staples companies like Gillette (G) or Johnson & Johnson (JNJ) over technology companies like EMC Corporation in a rising interest rate or otherwise difficult market environment.

PRACTICAL APPLICATIONS

Figure 8.13 provides a quick snapshot of EMC Corporation's fundamental data and ratios compared to its industry group and the S&P 500.

The most practical use of this information is to compare an individual company to its industry. Market Guide (www.marketguide.com) has many free services available on the Internet that allow an individual investor to quickly access and manipulate fundamental and other market data.

Starting at the top section—profitability ratios—you can quickly see that EMC's profitability exceeds that of its peers with profit margins of approximately 16% versus 15.4% for the industry and less than 13% for the overall S&P 500. EMC is also enjoying faster growth of its earnings per share on both a quarterly basis and an annual basis.

In terms of valuation, EMC's P/E ratio is more than five times that of its industry,

Ratios	EMC Corp.	Industry Average	S&P 500
Profitability			
Five-year earnings % increase	27.40%	27.10%	21.90%
Quarterly earnings % increase	46%	37.8%	20.70%
Profit margins	15.90%	15.40%	12.90%
Valuation			
Price/earnings	143.71	28.1	34.7
Price/sales	23.11	20.90	8.4
Solvency			
Current ratio	3.20	3.20	1.8
Debt/equity	0.0	0.00	0.9
Management Effectiveness			
ROE	24.60%	23.50%	23.10%
ROA	18.38%	17.00%	10.70%

Figure 8.13   EMC Fundamentals versus Industry Group and S&P 500 as of July 20, 2000

and about four times that of the S&P 500. The company's price/sales ratio is more than 23, compared to less than 21 for the industry, which means that in the market, the company is more richly valued than the industry as a whole. In no more than a few minutes, you can get a firm grasp on the company's valuation relative to its industry and to the market in general.

Looking quickly at the financial strength ratios shows that EMC and the companies in the storage industry do not carry much debt, and that they have less than the overall market. Additionally, it is apparent that EMC can meet all of its short-term obligations through the use of its current assets. Looking at the current ratio can help you to easily see this.

If you're not convinced by now that the company is well managed, the management effectiveness numbers (ROA and ROE) will make it clear. In every measure, the company has outperformed its peers and the overall market.

Many times you will hear analysts speak about the dividends that are paid out to shareholders by the company. Some companies pay a dividend and others do not. Just because a company does not pay a dividend, it doesn't mean it wouldn't be a good investment. For example, EMC does not pay a dividend, and this is typical of a company that is growing rapidly. The company management believes that the best use for the income produced is to reinvest it into the growth of the company. In more mature industries, and more mature companies, the growth rate slows; and with diminishing returns on the income reinvested in the company, the management will opt to distribute a certain part of its income to shareholders in the form of a dividend.

LIMITATIONS OF RATIO ANALYSIS

Ratio analysis is a quick and convenient method of getting a financial snapshot of a business enterprise; however, it is important to realize that this is just one of many approaches that an investor should use before making an investment. The ratios are only as good as the data upon which they are based and the information with which they are compared. For example, a company may announce that they are changing their accounting policies for recognizing revenue, and that they are going to restate earnings for the last five years. Any ratio calculated prior to the accounting change will be worthless, since they do not reflect the new policies that are going to be implemented. Lastly, it must be recognized that a substantial amount of important information about a company is not included in its financial statements. Events involving such things as industry changes, management changes, competitors' actions, technological developments, government actions, and union activities are often critical to the successful operation of a company. These types of activities are not reflected in the financials and must be discovered through additional investigation.

Additionally, Wall Street is more concerned about the future growth prospects of a company as opposed to past results. Ratio analysis can help you analyze past results but does not provide information on future performance. Your focus needs to be on future performance. Ratio analysis just gives you a baseline against which estimates of the future actions of the firm can be calculated.

Statement of Cash Flows

The statement of cash flows reports the cash receipts and cash payments of a company during a particular period. Like the income statement, the statement of cash flows looks at income and expenses, but from a different perspective—when and what money is coming in and what is going out. The statement of cash flows has three parts: operating activities, investing activities, and financing activities. Since we are mainly concerned with the operations of the company, "Cash Flows from Operating Activity" is the focus of the first section of the statement. Figure 8.14 shows the most recent annual statement of cash flows for EMC Corporation. Specifically, it is a summation of the "Cash Flows from Operating Activity" section of the statement.

Look for Positive Cash Flows from Operations

In a nutshell, the cash flow from operations is cash that is generated by transactions affecting the sale and the purchase or production of goods and services, including collections from customers, payments to suppliers and employees, and payments for items such as rent, taxes, and interest.

What to Do: It is important that your potential investment has positive operating cash flow. Positive operational cash flow means that income is being generated, and it is not all being consumed to pay the obligations that it has to employees, creditors, and so on.

Statement of Cash Flows (millions)	December 31, 1999	December 31, 1998
Cash Flows from Operating Activity:		
Net Income	$1,010	$654
Adjustments to Reconcile Net Income to Net Cash Provided/Used by Operating Activities:		
Depreciation and Amortization	447	366
Deferred Income Taxes	(123)	(.62)
Net Gain/Loss on Disposal Prop. & Equip.	10	9
Tax Benefit from Stock Options	58	44
Minority Interest	.14	(.5)
Changes in Assets and Liabilities	(31)	(101)
Net Cash Provided by Operating Activity:	1,371	971

Figure 8.14   EMC Statement of Cash Flows

The PEG Ratio

I will leave you with one last fundamental tool that is basically a combination of two others discussed earlier. It is known by different names, but in this book it is called the price-to-earnings-to-growth or PEG ratio. The first ingredient in computing the ratio is the company's price-to-earnings or P/E ratio.

Review: The price-to-earnings (P/E) ratio of a company equals the stock price divided by the company's earnings per share over the past 12 months.

The P/E ratio is relatively easy to find. It is often listed in the quote tables of financial newspapers. The ratio accompanies stock quotes on some of the more popular sites. However, it is always changing. Obviously, the stock price changes every day. Meanwhile, earnings change every quarter, when a company files its 10-Q.

Therefore, P/E ratios vary across time and between companies. Why will the same company sport a very high P/E ratio at certain times and a lower one at others? And how is it that two companies within the same industry can have vastly different price-to-earnings ratios? Often, the P/E ratio will correspond to the market's expectations regarding the company's future growth. That is, a company with an exceptionally strong growth rate will command a higher ratio than a slower-growing company. Why?

Well, as an investor, if you are confronted with a choice between two stocks—both with $1 of earnings over the next 12 months—but one is growing earnings at 5% annually and the other at 35%, which would you prefer? Obviously, the faster-growing company will deliver greater earnings in the near future. Stock market investors consider growth when making investment decisions and price stocks accordingly. Therefore, as an investor, you might have to pay 40 times earnings (or a P/E ratio of 40) for the company growing at 35% annually and only 10 times earnings for the one growing by only 5%.

The PEG ratio is a way to gauge the value of a company by considering both the P/E ratio and the company's growth rate. To compute the company's true growth rate, we take the average annual growth rate over a period of years—for example, the past five years or the past three years plus the next two based on analyst estimates.

One place to turn to for reliable information concerning earnings growth rates is www.bloomberg.com. At the home page, enter the company's name in the Stock Quotes box, click Go, and you will see a stock quote. Then, click on the company's symbol and you will see a stock chart and fundamental data— including earnings estimates. Click on earnings estimates. Both earnings estimates and long-term growth rates are found on this area of the site.

The PEG ratio is then computed as the P/E ratio divided by the growth rate. For instance, if a company has a P/E ratio of 40 and an expected annual growth rate of 20%, the price/earnings-to-growth ratio is 2.00 (40 / 20 = 2).

- *.50 or less:* A price-to-earnings-to-growth ratio of less than .50 is extremely attractive, and the stock definitely merits consideration.

- *Between .50 and 1.0:* The PEG ratio alone is not enough to determine whether the stock is a viable investment. The lower the better, but in this case the future appreciation of the stock will be dependent on the company's ability to deliver earnings growth in line with or above market expectations.

- *Over 1.00:* A PEG ratio over 1.00 indicates that the stock is probably overvalued and not an attractive investment. Until the stock price falls or the company delivers superior earnings growth, it is better to look elsewhere.

One last caveat: The PEG ratio is best used when comparing a stock within the same industry group. For example, it makes little sense to compare the PEG ratio of an automaker with that of a biotechnology firm. Here is a quote from a *Barron's* article to illustrate: "Alpharma also is one of the cheapest generic drug stocks on a price/earnings-to-growth (PEG) basis. Its PEG ratio of 1.3x is lower than its peers' 1.6x average. Some pros have set price targets in the 75 to 77 range" (*Barron's*, August 17, 2000, "Alpharma Is Hardly a Generic Stock").

What to Do: *The PEG ratio will tell you the relative attractiveness of a stock given its current share price and expected growth rate (PEG ratio = P/E ratio / EPS growth rate).*

CONCLUSION

Chapters 7 and 8 have offered what I consider to be the 15 most important tools of fundamental analysis. Some are qualitative in nature and more subjective. For example, "Do you understand the company?" is the basic question that you should ask yourself. But many other tools, like the ones covered in this chapter, are quantitative in nature (financial statements, earnings forecasts, important ratios, etc.).

Through time, these fundamental analysis tools can become an important part of your investment plan. With little more than about 15 minutes of time, you can take a serious look at a company from a fundamental standpoint. The process will either serve to reinforce or cause you to rethink your decision to invest in the company. As you gain familiarity with these numbers and what they mean, you can use them to screen for companies that fit your criteria. For example, you might screen for companies in a favorable industry, with return on equity (ROE) higher than their peers, earnings growth rates higher than their peers, and lower debt-to-equity ratios.

The boom in technology has opened up massive amounts of information to individual investors and at the same time has given them the means to manipulate it easily. The first technology innovation to have a meaningful impact on financial analysis was the personal computer loaded with spreadsheet software. The Internet and its widespread and immediate distribution of financial data promise to eclipse these advances. The result is a more educated investing public, and greater financial accountability to shareholders. The tyranny of technology, though, is that with the easy access to real-time charting, individual investors are tempted to rely only on information that is visual and quick. Technical analysis has become predominant among individual investors and recently contributed to a certain amount of detachment from realistic valuation levels, as seen in the dramatically bullish market action of the late 1990s. As stocks with no earnings or hope of producing any for years into the future were trading at stratospheric levels, momentum investing became the norm. An environment developed where stock prices were *commoditized* (trading like commodities, with price the only concern); and investors gave little thought to what the company produced, to its profitability, or to the company's ability to stay in business for the long term. Just a few months later, many investors saw their unrealistic gains evaporate as economic and fundamental realities forced a repricing of financial assets.

So, the next time you hear an enticing story about a stock in the financial media, or a friend mentions a company to you, or you uncover a potential investment while scanning your stock charts, take a few minutes to incorporate the fundamental data into your decision before you pull the trigger.

1. Go to Yahoo! Finance, Multex.com, or some similar service and pull up the fundamental data for a quick review.

2. Compare the company to its peers. How does its profitability ratios compare to those of other companies in the same industry? Is it growing its sales faster than the industry? Is it carrying more debt than its peers?

3. Compare the company to the market in general. Typically, the S&P 500 is used as a proxy for the broad market.

4. Consider what impact the current economic environment will have on the prospective company. Will rising interest rates affect its customers' ability to

purchase its products? Will tight labor markets make it difficult to staff its manufacturing or engineering facilities? Are its raw materials increasing in price? Will international relations developments such as China's trade status have a positive or negative impact on the company?

5. Consider the company's industry. Is it in favor or out of favor with the analysts?

If you don't have a particular investment in mind and you want to start from a fundamental perspective, there are many screening services available that will allow you to screen, or search from among the universe of companies, to find attractive investments that fit your criteria. You can screen for companies with high growth rates, with high management effectiveness ratios, such as return on equity, or if value is more your style, screen for companies with low price-to-earnings or price-to-book ratios. You're going to need to just roll up your sleeves and learn to use these screening tools. Many of them will generate, as a product of your search, a fundamental data sheet that you can then review in order to make judgments about the fundamental strength or quality of the company, compared to its industry or the market, as we did for the EMC data earlier in this chapter.

Armed with a little bit of knowledge of fundamental analysis and ready access to financial information and news delivered via the Internet, individual investors can easily be grounded in sound investment decisions without having to spend an inordinate amount of time to do it. At the very least, you can have a little more understanding of how an analyst arrives at those earnings estimates we all base our trading and investing decisions on. Understanding the fundamentals will enable you to comprehend the financial terms that are tossed around in the financial media and press, and make you a more informed and successful investor.

ROADMAP TO SUCCESS

Objective	Course of Action
Income Statement	**Definition:** A financial statement that lists revenues, expenses, and profits over a period of time. It is filed quarterly and annually. **What to Look For** • Sales or revenues: Healthy year-over-year and quarter-over-quarter increases. • Research and development: Is it being shortchanged? R&D expenditures, ideally, will be increasing from one year to the next. • Earnings and earnings per share (EPS): The total after-tax profits of the company. • Accelerating earnings growth. Quarterly earnings should be growing 15% to 30%. • Annual earnings should be experiencing at least 15% to 20% growth.

- Earnings surprises: Look for companies that consistently beat Wall Street expectations and the whisper number. Avoid companies that consistently disappoint with poor earnings results. Zacks spells this out clearly (my.zacks.com/index.php3).
- Profit margin: Divide net income by revenues to arrive at profit margin. Net profit margins should be increasing or at least remaining constant from one year to the next.
- Price to earnings (P/E): The most widely followed barometer of a stock price. P/E = Price divided by earnings per share (12 months). Stocks with higher P/E ratios must deliver higher future earnings growth. Avoid stocks with high P/E ratios and lackluster earnings growth.

Balance Sheet

Definition: The financial statement of a company that lists the assets and liabilities at a certain date. Assets are listed as current or noncurrent based on how quickly they are converted to cash. Liabilities are also grouped by their payment status; which indicates how soon they have to be paid.

What to Look For

- Cash: Cash is good. When cash is increasing from one year to the next, it suggests that the company's operations are generating significant cash flows.
- Avoid companies with too much debt. Most companies have some debt in one form or another. Make sure it isn't too much! *See debt-to-equity ratio below.*
- Accounts receivable should be growing along with sales and revenues.
- Compute the current ratio: Current assets/current liabilities. It is an indicator of the company's ability to meet short-term debt obligations. The higher the ratio, the more liquid the company. Ideally, the company will have a current ratio of 2 or greater. Although it is not essential, a number less than that may raise a red flag.
- Examine the debt-to-equity ratio: Total long-term liabilities/stockholder equity.

Management Effectiveness Ratios

Management effectiveness ratios help to determine how efficiently the company has used its assets and how successful the company is in executing their business strategy.

What to Look For

- Return on equity (ROE): Net income/stockholder equity.
- Compare one company's ROE to another within the same sector or industry group.
- Look at the company's overall debt level when considering ROE: Borrowed money can help generate larger return on equity, but more risk is involved. In some ways, it's like buying stock on margin: The returns can be great, but so can the losses. The higher the debt, the greater the leverage.

More debt indicates more cash is spent to service the debt (principal and interest).

- Look at companies with higher ROE than peers, but not as much debt. When you see this situation, it indicates savvy management that is fiscally conservative, which leads to greater profitability. With more profits, the company can afford to attract top talent and invest more in R&D, a process that helps ensure it'll retain their dominant position within their industry.
- Return on assets (ROA): Net income/total assets. A company that's efficient with a high ROA indicates less waste and more productivity, and is a promising situation.
- As with ROE, comparisons between companies using ROA must also consider overall debt levels. How much leverage did it take to achieve its respective ROA? More debt indicates a less stable financial condition, which makes the company more vulnerable when economic slowdowns occur. (And they always do!)
- Look for companies with above average ROA and ROE, but not saddled with large levels of debt. These corporations will do well in good times and can stay afloat in bad times. Fiscal strength is the hallmark of a sound investment.

Statement of Cash Flows	**Definition:** A financial statement that measures a company's income and expenses. There are three sections in the statement of cash flows. • Cash Flows from Operating Activities • Cash Flows from Investment Activities • Cash Flows from Financing Activities **What to Look For** • Positive operating cash flow. (They're taking more in than they're spending.) • Increasing net income from one year to the next. • Examine the sources of cash flow—where is it coming from?

Analyzing Fundamentals	**Things You Can Do**
	• The PEG ratio = P/E ratio divided by earnings per share growth rate.
	    –P/E equals the share price divided by earnings per share.
	    –Earnings per share growth rate can be found by doing a search of a company's fundamentals on www.bloomberg.com, www.zacks.com, and other investment-related sites.
	    –Consider a PEG ratio of a company relative to its peers (i.e., same sector or industry group).
	    –PEG ratio rules of thumb:
	    If the PEG ratio is below .50, the stock definitely meets the criteria; it can be considered a purchase candidate.

–A PEG ratio between .50 and 1.00 does not give enough information to make a decision. Whether to buy or sell the stock will depend on further fundamental analysis.

–A PEG ratio above 1.00 should eliminate the stock from consideration.

–In addition to the PEG ratio, go to www.siliconinvestor.com, Yahoo! Finance (finance.yahoo.com), www.multex.com, www.personal-wealth, or similar services and pull up a fundamental data quick view.

Determine which is fundamental and which is technical information. See Chapter 7 for a recap.

- Compare one company to its peers.
  - –How do the profitability ratios compare?
  - –Is a company growing sales faster than the industry average?
  - –Does it carry more debt than its peers?
  - –EquityTrader.com has an easy-to-use grouping of stocks in a sector, and even uses its own criteria for ranking them according to strength (www.equitytrader.com).
- Compare the company's fundamentals (P/E ratio, dividend, earnings growth rate, etc.) to the market as a whole—for instance, the S&P 500, the Dow Jones Industrial Average, or the S&P 100.

Screening

Screening: The process of scanning and sorting through a universe of stocks based on certain variables. The goal is to search among a universe of companies to find investments that meet your criteria.

- Find a web site that offers stock screening capabilities:
  - –my.zacks.com/index.php3
  - –www.nasdaq-amex.com
  - –www.personalwealth.com
- Zacks has predefined screens that help you see how a screen works. Click on Screen Tab to begin.
- The screen allows you to progressively narrow your search. Since earnings are what you're after, specifically fast earnings growth, begin your search by screening for earnings surprises.
- Then select the sector and industry.
- Select Broker Ratings and Zacks Rating as well.
- This will assemble a list that's a great place to begin deeper investigations.
- Take each stock the screen identifies and go back to the start page; after typing in the ticker symbol, request "The Whole Enchilada." Now you'll be able to delve into the various financials of one company versus another.

- Use EquityTrader.com to find other closely related companies and make a note of them; then return to Zacks to assemble your fundamental comparisons of items we've covered in Chapters 7 and 8.
- Screen for stocks with certain characteristics. Start with something simple. For instance, stocks with P/E ratios under 10 (notice how quickly the list is narrowed down using that screen!).
- Look for companies with high growth rates.
- Screen for stocks with effective management ratios.
- Screen, screen, screen! Be creative and use your own ratios!
- Through time, you'll discover the stocks you consider worthwhile have a specific theme or share a certain attribute. Maybe you prefer high-growth stocks, value (low P/E ratios) companies, or those within a specific sector.
- As a final note, once you have identified the stocks for your portfolio, the work isn't over. An important element in investment success is monitoring them through time. Use the 15 fundamental tools outlined in the last chapter and this one as a guide. If a company begins to stumble, you want to be the first to know and get rid of the stock before other shareholders rush for the exit.

9

Technical Analysis Unveiled

Technical analysis could be described as looking into the rearview mirror to see where you're going next. It sounds silly but in a way, it's true. Technical analysis is built on the theory that market prices display repetitive patterns that can be tracked and used to forecast future price movement. It evaluates price movement by analyzing statistics generated by market activity—such as past prices and volume—to study market performance. Since price is the bottom line, technical analysts primarily look at price movement to determine price patterns. The nature of future price movements is forecasted from these patterns. This is a vast subject of Amazonian proportion. One chapter will only scratch the surface, but hopefully will motivate you to learn more, and tell you what you need to learn more about!

There exist three kinds of analysis techniques: fundamental, sentiment, and technical. To state it succinctly, fundamental analysis looks at financial data; sentiment looks at the mind-set of the market or individual stock; and technical analysis cares not one iota about news, earnings, sentiment, or what you had for breakfast. *Technical analysis* looks at data displayed in chart form, and seeks to determine the recurring patterns in order to elicit a signal to buy or sell. In essence, we are looking backward to see where we're headed. Let's start scratching this surface by learning about charts and chart types.

> **Technical analysis:** The evaluation of price movement through chart analysis and statistics generated by market activity—such as past prices and volume. Market prices often display repetitive patterns that can be tracked and used to forecast optimal trading entries and exits.

248

CHART SMARTS

Charts graphically display time and price action. At a glance, even the most inexperienced investor can see how a stock or index has performed over a given period. The *intervals* or time units indicate what time frame you're looking at. A daily chart looks at how a stock performed each day, generally indicating the price range it experienced in one day's time. The chart will show a sequence of days, going back perhaps as much as a year or more. By viewing this big picture of price action and time, an investor or trader interested in the future price action can get a better feel for what's to come.

The main objective in investing is of course to make money. Simple. Everyone has probably heard the old saying, "Buy low; sell high." Figuring out current prices and their value in relation to past prices is determined by looking at a chart. You have to find out where a stock has been?

The chart in Figure 9.1 displays the Dow Jones Industrial Average on a daily basis from July 1999 to July 2000. Traders and investors will look at this and see a variety of things including support and resistance levels, trends, and channels. Don't worry; we'll discuss these terms later in the chapter.

The chart in Figure 9.1 is called a candlestick chart, one of several charting types. Candlestick charts have grown in popularity recently because of the information a person can easily glean from them at a glance. They are color coded to reveal the

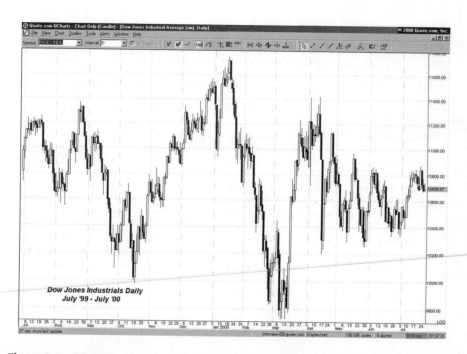

Figure 9.1 DJIA One-Day Interval Candlestick Chart (Courtesy of QCharts (www.qcharts.com))

relationship between a stock's open and close while also revealing a stock's price range. If a stock closed higher than it opened, the body of the candlestick is white indicating a bullish market. If the candlestick is dark, then the stock closed lower than it opened indicating a bearish market. These colored areas are known as the body of the candlestick, while the line above and/or below is the shadow. (see Figure 9.2).

There's a great web site for learning more about candlestick charts. Go to www.wick-ed.com to further your understanding.

A bar chart is another method used to chart prices and is composed of a vertical bar and two small horizontal ticks at 90-degree angles (see Figure 9.3). The vertical line itself represents the stock's price range for the time period (15 minutes, hourly, daily, weekly). The horizontal tick to the left indicates the opening price; the one to

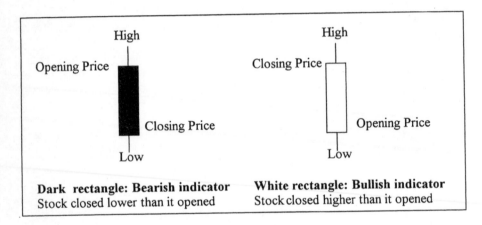

Figure 9.2   Candlestick Basics

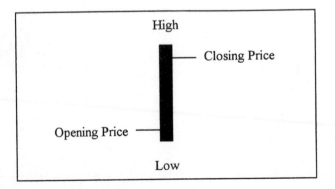

Figure 9.3   Bar Chart Basics

the right, the closing price. Bar charts work well to get a sense of a stock's daily price range and for creating channel lines. They are most commonly used in newspapers and elsewhere, because of their simplicity. Figure 9.4 shows the Dow Jones Industrial Average illustrated using a daily bar chart.

The next style is called a line chart, shown in Figure 9.5. Line charts are the most simple of the three. They show a stock's closing price from tick-to-tick, day-to-day, week-to-week, and month-to-month, like a child's join-the-dots game. Many technicians (those people who use technical analysis as their sole or primary method for determining future price action) cite the closing price as the most important price of the day, and therefore a more valid measure of market activity. Line charts work well when you are adding additional analysis techniques such as moving averages or momentum indicators.

The next style is more esoteric because it must be created—it is not just a graph of price versus time. Point-and-figure (P&F) charts use marks that are a series of Xs and Os, and a column on the left-hand side for price (see Figure 9.6). An X is used to signify an increasing price and an O is used to signify a price decrease. P&F charts are created with alternating columns of Xs and Os that form patterns used to evaluate supply and demand. There is, however, no scale for time or volume, which makes P&F charts primarily sensitive to price movements.

The first step in creating a P&F chart is to choose a scale. The choice is arbitrary, but is selected to signify what the analyst believes is a significant move for the stock. Thus, a volatile stock like SDL, Inc. (SDLI) might have a five-point scale while a more sedate stock like AT&T (T) might have a half-point or one-point scale.

Figure 9.4 DJIA One-Day-Interval Bar Chart (Courtesy of QCharts (www.qcharts.com))

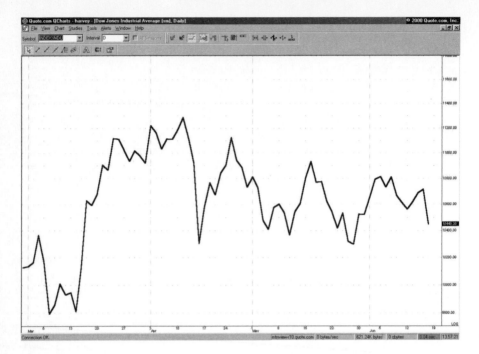

Figure 9.5   DJIA One-Day-Interval Line Chart (Courtesy of QCharts (www.qcharts.com))

Figure 9.6 shows an example of a one-point scale. Starting when the stock price was at $25, an X was placed on the chart. The stock then moved up to $26, and another X was placed above the first one. As the stock continued to move upward, Xs were placed one above another until the price reached $29. Then, before the stock could touch the $30 mark, it dropped back down to $28 (or below) and the chart shifted over a column and a series of Os were inserted in the new column to signify the decline. The stock continued downward until reaching $26 per share, whereupon it reversed and hit $27 and a new column was started and a new series of Xs introduced. The example then ends with the stock at $32 on an upward run. The next mark on the chart would depend on where the stock price moves next. If the price is $33, there will be another X placed above the last one. If it drops back to $31, a new column will be started with an O at the $31 level. Until one of those events takes place, there will be no new additions to the chart—regardless of whether it takes a week or a month. In this case, time simply doesn't matter.

P&F charts were developed years before the advent of computerized charting. They were primarily a method of detailing trends in a format that was easy to track. Modern data suppliers and computer technology provide the means to look at price data across time and with various moving averages, volume data, and so on. This has, for all practical purposes, reduced the use of P&F charts to the ash heap of historical curiosities, as the amount of information a P&F chart conveys is severely

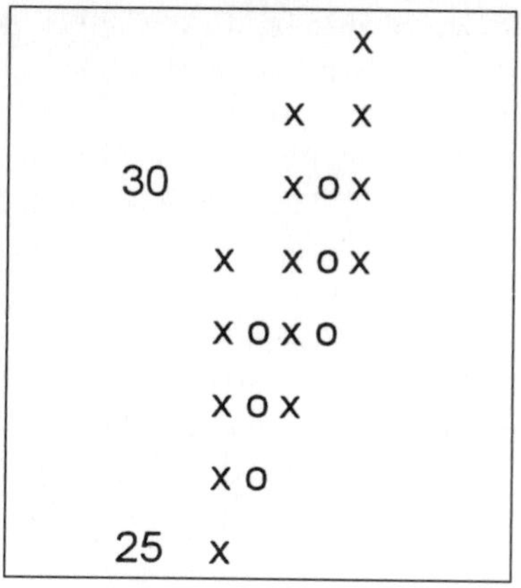

```
                              X

                         X   X

            30           X O X

                   X   X O X

                   X O X O

                   X O X

                   X O

            25   X
```

Figure 9.6   Point-and-Figure Chart

limited. I include it so that when you do run across it, you are not fooled into thinking that it is some sort of complex chart that only a genius can understand.

All the other charting techniques can be constructed to represent specific time perspectives—intraday, daily, weekly, or monthly—that correspond to your trading needs. In most price charts, the vertical axis represents price fluctuation and the horizontal axis denotes time. As a beginner, you may want to start by looking at markets over the longer term. You need to assess a market's movement by reviewing its price movements throughout the past year, paying close attention to the most recent weeks.

Online technical sites are geared to provide you with various charts that show price movement over different time spans. You can easily check out a stock's daily movement or the past year by one stroke on the keyboard. Check out www.quote.com or www.bigcharts.com.

VOLUME

Price action over time is only part of the picture. Volume is the best measure of interest in a stock, and its importance cannot be overstated. Among traders there's a saying: "Volume precedes price." Let's take a look at why volume is so important.

Let's say you're a motion picture executive, and your new movie has just been released to over 500 theaters nationwide. What good is it to know the number of theaters, if you don't know how many tickets have been sold? If no one is watching the show, it won't be in the theaters for long! If everyone is buying a stock, but the price hasn't changed, it probably won't stay unchanged for long. The law of supply and demand is critical to determining the future course of a stock or index.

Institutional money managers—the people making the investment decisions for large mutual funds, state retirement programs, and other pension funds—often catch wind of changing fundamentals in a stock or sector, good or bad. The chart in Figure 9.7 has an added feature along the bottom that indicates volume. You can easily see the big spike in volume on the left side. Shortly thereafter, this stock made a monster move, gaining over 600%! I wish I could say this happens every time, but it doesn't. However, if you're hunting for a stock that has been overlooked and could triple in value, volume certainly bears watching.

Volume patterns are extremely important, as they indicate at what levels and to what degree most activity occurs. Look at the right side of Figure 9.7. After the stock peaked, it went into a very choppy style of price action. One thing is clearly indicated here: There were lots of buyers on each dip. Institutions were stepping up to the plate and buying here consistently, which signals to you and me that this would be a relatively safe entry point if we were looking to own the stock, or put on an option position.

What if the volume dropped off as the stock climbed higher? That would tell me there's no conviction among buyers and that the stock was not strong enough for a major up move. The chances of it returning to earth are pretty good. Figure 9.8 shows clearly that, even though this stock is advancing, the volume is drying up on each successive day. By drawing a trend line to the upside, the subsequent break to the downside is easier to spot.

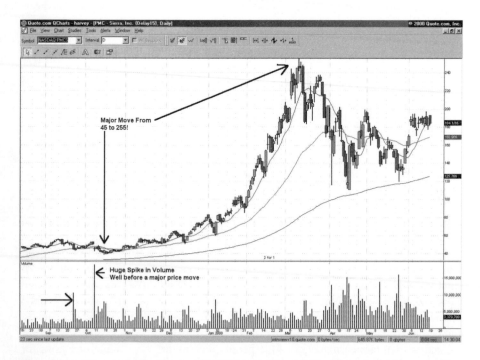

Figure 9.7   Price-Volume Chart of PMCS (Courtesy of QCharts (www.qcharts.com))

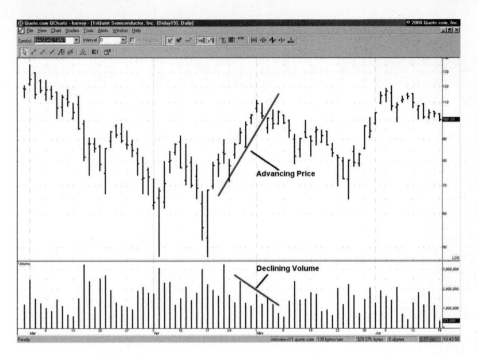

Figure 9.8 Advancing Price and Declining Volume (Courtesy of QCharts (www.qcharts.com))

MOVING AVERAGES

Moving averages are another useful technical tool that help traders to determine when a trend may be changing. It is usually calculated by using the closing prices, adding them together for the desired time period, then dividing by the number of days, as with any average. If you wished to know the five-day moving average, and today is Monday, simply add the closing prices for the previous week (Monday through Friday) and divide by five. Easy. This is a *simple moving average (SMA)*, named because all days are equally weighted.

An *exponential moving average (EMA)* is a method by which the most recent data points are more heavily weighted. The theory behind exponentially smoothed moving averages asserts that the most recent data is the most important. Keep in mind that there any number of ways to weight the front data more heavily. For this example, let's use a five-period moving average where the five most recent data points are averaged together. As a new period is added, the oldest one is dropped off, and a new five-period average is calculated. The percentage weight attributed to each data point (day, week, month, etc.) would be as follows:

| | *Percentage Weight in Calculation* | |
Data Point	*Simple Average*	*Exponential Average*
Most recent data point	20%	33%
One period back	20%	27%
Two periods back	20%	20%
Three periods back	20%	13%
Four periods back	20%	7%

Luckily, there's an abundance of software programs that figure all this stuff out for you, allowing you the leeway of plugging in your own parameters or using the defaults. Don't worry about how to do it; just remember that most technicians seem to favor the simple moving average.

Simple moving average (SMA): An arithmetic mean calculated by taking *n* number of data points, summing the data points, and then dividing the sum by the number of data points. You can plot this single point on a chart, and by adding successive points (created by dropping the oldest data item and including the newest data item in the calculation), the series of points creates a simple moving average line in which all data points have equal value.

Exponential moving average (EMA): A variant of the simple moving average in which more emphasis is placed on the most recent prices than the older ones. The EMA follows the actual price more closely than the SMA.

Traders use moving averages to identify trend shifts as well as the relative value of a stock or index. *Investor's Business Daily* shows the 200-day moving average (DMA) for the Dow, S&P 500, and Nasdaq Composite each day. The relative distance above or below is sometimes noted in newsletters and financial programs to indicate the relative value of the market.

An extremely simple system for using moving averages is to sell when the trend turns down and to buy when the trend turns up. Okay, it's too simple, but that's the basic concept. The shorter the time frame used, the more erratic the average becomes. If you were trading the OEX based on the 5 DMA moving up or down, you'd be making a lot of false-start trades, because a true picture would never be formed. At the same time, if your time frame is too long, a significant portion of a new trend has already occurred by the time you get in (or out).

Many traders use a combination of different averages to generate buy and sell signals. Some use two averages in what is termed a *crossover* method. Let's say the two they use are the 5 and the 20 DMA. When the 5 passes *over* the 20, that's a buy signal; when the 5 passes *under* the 20, a sell signal is generated. Other traders prefer to use three in a similar fashion, such as a 10, 50, and 200 DMA. When the 5 passes above the 10, and then the 10 passes above the 200, that's a buy signal. They use the second crossover as a confirmation the trend has changed. While this is very reliable, it's also a very cautious approach to trading. It really is up to the individual and his or her own personal style. If you're aggressive, shorten up and use two. I like to use them in conjunction with other signals, but seldom by themselves. My favorites are the 50-day and 200-day moving averages that many institutional traders follow. If the 50-day drops below the 200-day, it's a sell signal, and if it moves above, it's a buy signal.

The next two graphs simply illustrate the sell and buy signals that followed the market top in July 1998, the bottom in October, and its subsequent rally. Figure 9.9 shows the timing for a two-averages signal and Figure 9.10 shows the timing for a three-averages signal.

These two methods trigger two different sets of results. In Figure 9.10, the bear trap rally made for a better (higher) exit point, but I suspect the emotional trauma of riding out that late August swoon was tough to endure. The system kept you in the market longer and got you in later than the two-averages method shown in Figure 9.9. Either method would have saved you from the bottom reached on October 8; and both methods certainly provided good entry points after that. As I said, it's a matter of style, not to mention nerves.

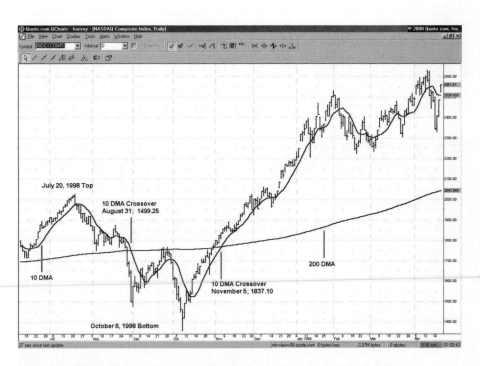

Figure 9.9 Crossover Using 10 and 200 DMA Method (Courtesy of QCharts (www.qcharts.com))

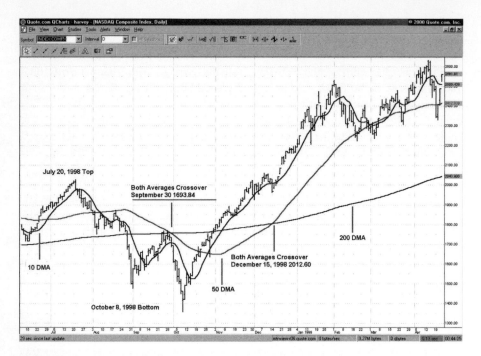

Figure 9.10 Crossover Using 10, 50, and 200 DMA (Courtesy of QCharts (www.qcharts.com))

ON-BALANCE VOLUME

On-balance volume (OBV) is a tool that dissects trading volume into two categories: the amount bought and the amount sold. (Sounds good so far.) This is a computer-generated statistic, as I could not begin to imagine doing this task manually. The purpose of course is to determine whether a stock is under accumulation or not. By tracking OBV in a flat market, a trader can get a sense of future price action; OBV is closely linked to the "volume precedes price" axiom.

> **On-balance volume (OBV):** A technical indicator that signals the buying and selling momentum of a stock by comparing price to volume. OBV works on the theory that when a stock closes up for the day, the volume of shares traded represents buying power; and when a stock closes down for the day, the volume of shares denotes selling power. Since trend changes in OBV often precede trend changes in price, on-balance volume can be used to forecast market reversals.

There are different ways to look at this. If a stock is channeling sideways on average volume, a trader would look at OBV to see if there's a net accumulation occurring. If the stock is under accumulation, the law of supply and demand will eventually begin pushing the price up; to what degree depends on how aggressive the buyers are.

This works both ways. Let's say that there's a large amount of stock being fed into the market. Institutions sell it off piecemeal to prevent killing a stock. OBV is a good way to detect this action. Why would you want to sell if a stock is under serious accumulation? Why would you want to buy if there's an overall trend of distribution underway?

Figure 9.11 features a daily bar chart with on-balance volume (the middle line) and volume (at the bottom). The left side of the OBV indicator is flatter than South Dakota, giving no indication of any sentiment one way or the other. However, something happened of huge significance, as shown by the volume spike (1). Subsequent accumulation began (2) which led to a noticeable upturn in the trend line (3), which was trending up before, just not that much. Some technicians believe that for a trendline to be valid it should be at a 45°angle. Anything steeper is not sustainable; anything flatter isn't a true trend.

PRICE ENVELOPES

A price or percentage envelope is an enhancement of a simple moving average. Traders will surround a moving average with *percentage bands* that indicate a certain

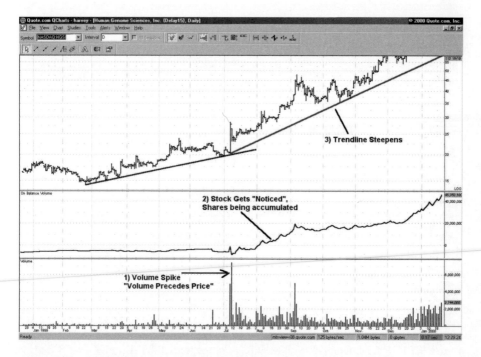

Figure 9.11   On Balance Volume with Daily Bar Chart (Courtesy of QCharts (www.qcharts.com))

percentage above and below the moving average (see Figure 9.12). This strategy makes it easier to spot when a stock or index has strayed too far from the moving average. This would indicate the stock is overextended in one direction or the other. A typical percentage might be 10% (10% above and below the moving average). A short-term trader might use a 3% envelope on a short moving average such as a 10 DMA or a 21 DMA.

This is another tool used to spot extreme price swings that would identify a good opportunity to employ a contrarian viewpoint as the stock returns to a more normal range. (See Bollinger bands later in this chapter for further variations.)

A WORD ABOUT TIME INTERVALS

The computer has done wonders for technical analysis because it has permitted evaluations to be performed faster than ever before. One mistake that many new (and some seasoned) traders and investors make is noting every single wiggle a stock will go through by looking at graphs with a one-minute time interval. Unless you're an emotionless being like Mr. Spock, this will lead to shattered nerves and ulcers. I like to look close-up from time to time; but I get a better perspective when

Figure 9.12   Price Envelopes with Moving Average for SUNW (Courtesy of QCharts (www.qcharts.com))

I step back to look at things using a broader time horizon. Some savvy traders can *scalp* the smaller price fluctuations and make a good living doing it. You're better off leaving that game to someone else and focusing on bigger, longer-lasting trends. You'll preserve your trading capital as well as keep your sanity (or what's left of it).

TOPS AND BOTTOMS AND VOLUME

Let's face it: institutions move markets; the retail investor does not. If you want a good leading indicator of stock direction, volume is a great place to start. *Investor's Business Daily* goes into great depth identifying stocks with the greatest percentage gain in volume. It's easy to find the most actively traded stocks and options on any given day; but percentage-wise, the biggest gainers can be a good signal of big moves (up or down) to come.

Capitulation

Capitulation is a word used to describe an extreme display of a market bottom (most often) and occasionally a market top. The words *top* and *bottom* are those points where buyers and sellers, respectively, exhaust themselves. The guns they're using begin to click-click instead of fire. (The reason this happens is explained further, in Chapter 10, on sentiment analysis.) Basically, the crowd is wrong at range extremes. If everybody is in who wants in, who's left to buy? If everyone's out

---

Capitulation: A point in time when investors, en masse, finally give in during a market decline. That is, some investors will hold fully to their bullish views on the market during a bear market until a certain point. At the height of selling, however, the few remaining bullish investors will finally yield (sell their stocks); when everyone seems to have given up hope, the market has experienced capitulation.

---

who's going to be out, who's left to sell?

An increase in volume is typically a good sign of reversals in the trend or the beginning of a new trend (especially when the volume increases dramatically from the previous day's trading). If the volume triples, that's a healthy sign that the market is about to turn around.

The identification of capitulation is critical because it is the technical equivalent of an all-clear siren following a tornado. The odd thing about capitulation is that it seems to catch almost everyone off-guard. Figure 9.13 features a good example of a chart that looks like it's going down the drain, but instead goes on to rally big time! Remember back in the summer and fall of 1998? There was a tremendous amount of concern about Russia being insolvent, Brazil defaulting on about 600 trillion-million dollars of debt, and interest rates had been going up ad nauseum. There was a dramatic sell-off in September, followed by a rally some would refer to as a bear

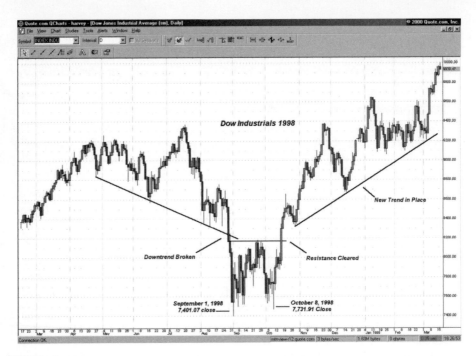

Figure 9.13   Dow Industrials 1998 Bottom (Courtesy of QCharts (www.qcharts.com))

trap. A bear trap is a rally attempt in a bear market that typically fools many traders, and significantly contributes to the overall cynical attitude of investors. Many will argue that this extreme pessimism/cynicism is a requirement for a true market bottom. In the case of capitulation, and trend reversals in general, the technicians sometimes will grudgingly seek out some other indicator (*gasp!*) from a different analysis technique—most often sentiment analysis.

> *Some technical analysts feel that capitulation has to occur in order for the market to move from a bear market back to a bull market.*

TRENDS

A *trend* is the general direction in which a stock or index is headed. In a bull market the trend is up; in a bear market, it's down. Going back to Figure 9.7 for a moment, the trend for PMCS was definitely up before it peaked around $255 a share. It was at this peak that the trend reversed. Wall Street is plastered with clichés, so here's another one: "The trend is your friend until the trend ends." That's true. Physics teaches us that an object in motion will continue in motion until an outside force affects it. A stock going up will continue to go up until it stops, just like a stock going down will continue going down until it stops. To the technical analysts' way of thinking, it's that last part about the outside force affecting it that they're interested in. It's these points in a chart where directions (trends) change that everyone gets all excited about; and you should, too.

Trend: A constant movement of a variable over the course of time. Depending on the time frame, it can be considered a short-term or a long-term trend. For example, the movement upward in a stock price over the course of a few days or weeks is considered a short-term uptrend. A constant, upward move in the price of a security over months or years is considered a long-term uptrend.

When a stock goes up, at a certain point the buyers evaporate, stalling the up move. That point is called the resistance level. A stock or index is said to hit resistance when the sellers (bears) outnumber the buyers (bulls), sending the stock back down. The flip side of the equation is when the stock or index is going down: The point at which the buyers overpower the sellers and the stock begins heading back up is called the support level (see Figure 9.14)

Technical analysis revolves around these two terms: support and resistance. Understanding these concepts will be of tremendous value as we move forward. Let's look at a real chart and see if we can determine support and resistance levels.

Figure 9.15 shows a bar chart that reveals the recent trading action of Microsoft (MSFT). It's easy to see when buyers stepped in, although they couldn't seem to get the stock to rise. Up top, the bulls just couldn't seem to overcome the bears, as the supply was greater than demand. You'll notice in the center of the resistance line there was an attempted *breakout* of the stock, but it couldn't follow through and collapsed. This chart has examples of several different things occurring, such as *consolidation*, *trend reversals*, and a *failed rally*.

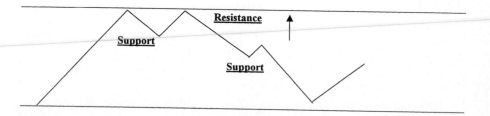

Figure 9.14 Support and Resistance (Courtesy of QCharts (www.qcharts.com))

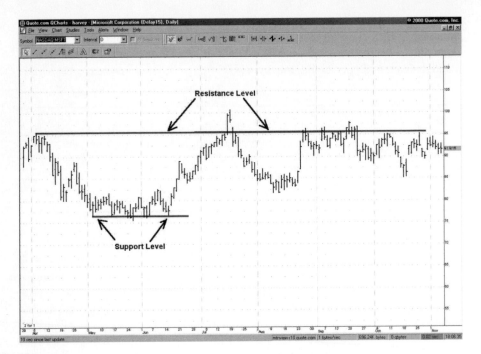

Figure 9.15   MSFT Bar Chart with Support and Resistance Levels (Courtesy of QCharts (www.qcharts.com))

Breakout: When a stock rises above a resistance level or falls below a support level. A resistance level is a price that a stock has risen to on multiple occasions but has failed to exceed, or penetrate. When a stock breaks through that resistance level, especially when volume is high, the stock is likely to make a major advance, according to technical analysts. A breakout on the downside occurs when a stock falls through a support level. A support level is the inverse of a resistance level. It represents a price that a stock has dropped to on more than one occasion, but hasn't been able to penetrate.

Consolidation: The behavior of a stock price after a major advance or decline. Specifically, it is a period of time that sees a stock price trading within a narrow range. Some technical analysts argue that intermittent consolidation periods are necessary for a sustained advance in a stock price.

Trend reversal: Trends are sustained periods of rising or falling prices. When a stock price is moving up, it is an uptrend. If a security's price is moving lower, it is considered a downtrend. Reversals occur when stock prices go from uptrends to downtrends or downtrends to uptrends.

Failed rally: A short-term rise in a stock's price during a predominant downtrend that is quickly met with selling pressure.

Using Figure 9.15, in the center of the resistance line, do you notice the bar that poked its way through but didn't hold? Microsoft tried to break out of its trading range, but couldn't. This is known as a failed rally attempt. Traders look for these situations constantly, since, if it had been able to continue upward, it would have been making new highs. This would have been great news because it would have meant that everyone was making money. In other words, every single person long the stock up to this point had a profit in it. But then the supply of stock dried up because, after all, who wants to sell a winner? However, this was not the case here, and down it came. Traders saw this as a failed rally, and either dumped the stock they owned, taking a profit on the nice run it had just had, or began shorting the stock. Either way, supply began to flood the market and there wasn't enough buying power to keep the price up. In this instance, the bears won the battle.

---

*"Cut your losses, and let your winners run" is yet
another popular axiom in the investment world.*

An interesting thing happens when a stock breaks out: What used to be a resistance line now becomes support! Figure 9.16 demonstrates these dynamics. Once the breakout is confirmed, sometimes there's a new round of buyers at the breakout price with follow-through the next day. Then, if later on the stock sells off and returns to this new support level, traders will first look to see if this support holds, then start buying again! Think of it as climbing the stairs—what was once the ceiling (resistance) now becomes the floor (support).

The opposite is true heading south, as shown in Figure 9.17. The floor now becomes the ceiling. Traders look at this very carefully, too, because if a stock breaks through support, everyone starts looking for the next support level. The chances are pretty good the next stop in a falling price will be there. The art of determining when this fall is over (i.e., something happens to make it stop going down) is sometimes called "picking a bottom," or my favorite, "catching a falling knife." I like the

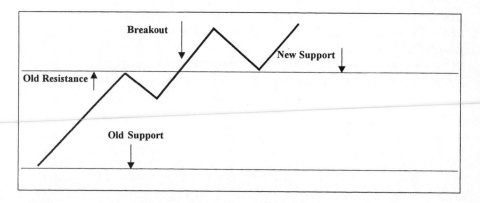

Figure 9.16　Old Resistance Becomes New Support

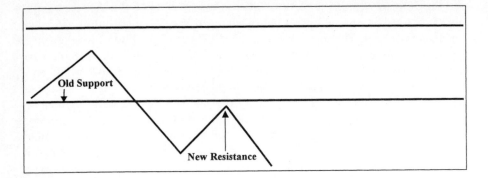

Figure 9.17   Old Support Becomes New Resistance

"falling knife" term because it illustrates how you can get hurt, big time, trying to predict with cash when the exact reversal will occur. Bears do the same thing on a breakout. If they begin shorting too soon, they get what's known as a short squeeze: when they begin to cover, it will often push a stock still higher. That's why traders often prefer to wait until a stock or index hits the next support level and holds. This is one reason it's so easy to lose money: you seldom see panic buying, only panic selling. So watch those support and resistance levels carefully!

Figure 9.18 is a good example of a stock that first broke out above a stubborn resistance level. This particular move looks more like a Roman candle, though, because it soon came tumbling down. The left-hand arrow under "Break Down" shows the first breach of the new support level (old resistance level). The bulls made a valiant attempt to save this stock, but in the end they got butchered as the stock went on to take out even the lower support level—not a good sign.

TREND LINES

A *trend line* is simply the support and resistance lines turned at an angle. A stock or index will follow this trend line as in the previous examples, but this time the lines will not be horizontal. Figure 9.19 shows a stock in an upward or bullish trend line. It's trading in a channel (as did previous examples), but the support line (lows) keep getting higher, as does the resistance line. A technician would look at this and see higher lows and higher highs—hallmarks of an upward trend.

> **Trend lines:** A term used in technical analysis to indicate the direction of a stock price over a period of time. On a stock chart, it can be seen as a straight line along the bottom of an upward-moving stock (market) price or along the top of a downward-trending stock (market) price. Technical analysts believe that the longer the trend line, the more likely it is the stock price will continue in that direction. A break in the trend line indicates a change in trend.

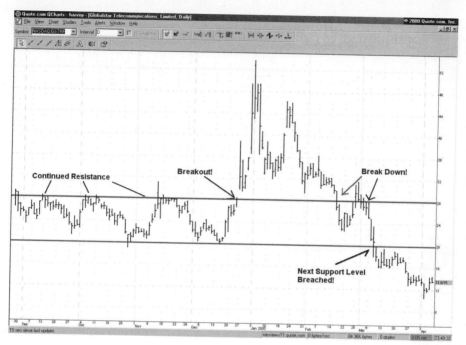

Figure 9.18   Breakout and Break Down (Courtesy of QCharts (www.qcharts.com))

To draw these lines, just take a ruler and pencil, then place the ruler on the lowest points on the zigzag price points. If it is a good example of a trend line, these points will line up. The length of it will vary. Some trend up (or down) for long periods, as in weeks or even months. Others will trend for a few hours. What the technical analyst looks for is this trend to be broken, up or down. Remember that axiom, "The trend is your friend until the trend ends"? In the case of Figure 9.19, the trend went from friend to best buddy when it broke out to the upside, signaling a major breakout. If the support line had been broken, it would have meant a reversal had occurred—a bearish indicator signaling a trader to either close out the position or go short. The *Wall Street Journal*, *Investor's Business Daily*, and *Barron's* are ideal sources to look for trend lines.

When charting a stock or index, sometimes all you'll get is a support or resistance line, as in Figure 9.20. This stock was trending up very nicely, thank you, until it (obviously) fell way out of favor with Wall Street. Figure 9.20 is one ugly scene. Each unit in the bar chart above represents one day, so you can see that this particular stock was doing pretty well. Over the course of three trading days, however, it dropped like a rock, sending a very strong sell signal. You'll notice a gap in the bar figures just below the support trend line. If the violation of the support line didn't get your attention, the gap down certainly did. Remember what I said earlier about a stock going down until something happens to make it stop going down (i.e., the "falling knife" comment)? It's very important *not* to get into the mind-set of "ICGAL" (it can't go any

Figure 9.19   Bullish Trend Line (Courtesy of QCharts (www.qcharts.com))

lower)! It can and it will—and it did. It would appear this stock had some bad news of some sort, and that means it's a cockroach situation (to me, anyway). You know if you see one cockroach, there's sure to be more. One item of bad news means there's a good chance more is on the way. This chart certainly confirms that saying!

The opposite is also true. Figure 9.21 shows the OEX on a slippery slope headed south. But when it does regain its footing and breaks the upper range of the trend line, it's Rally City! This example uses a candlestick chart to illustrate a reversal in a pattern.

There are two varieties of trend lines: *continuation* and *reversal* trend lines. A continuation trend is like a highway in western Kansas: It just keeps on going. But when that highway reaches a "Bridge Out" sign, you have to turn around and reverse your course. A continuation may increase its gradient, or begin to flatten out. It's still continuing. But when there's a break down in the trend line, or break up (as in Figure 9.21), that's called a *reversal* and is very important.

When you look at charts, you're looking for patterns that will help you to forecast the future movement of the stock. There are a variety of patterns that analysts categorize as continuation or reversal patterns. A continuation pattern in a stock chart is an area of consolidation, prior to a stock resuming a trend. For instance, a stock with a strong uptrend will sometimes pause and move sideways for a period of time. When the stock breaks out of that sideways pattern and back in the direction of the previous trend, that period of sideways movement, or consolidation, is

Figure 9.20 Support Line Violated (Courtesy of QCharts (www.qcharts.com))

considered a continuation pattern. Examples of continuation patterns are triangles, rectangles, scallops, and pennants (which will be described in more detail in Chapter 12). A reversal pattern is the area on a chart before a stock breaks out in a direction opposite to the previous trend. For instance, if a stock makes a yearlong advance and reaches $100, falls back down to $80, advances up to $100 again, and then begins a yearlong decline, the reversal pattern on the chart is known as a double top (it has risen to $100 twice and changed direction). Chart patterns considered reversal patterns by technical analysts include double bottom or top, triple bottom or top, broadening top, and head and shoulders.

This is just a thumbnail sketch of charts, volume analysis, and their application in technical analysis. These are by no means the only tools used, just the easier ones to begin with. Next, let's investigate some other tools you can utilize to determine future market direction.

THE USE OF OSCILLATORS

There are two basic kinds of indicators: *lagging indicators* and *oscillators*. Lagging indicators are those techniques that confirm a trend divergence after it has happened. Oscillators are useful in indicating when a market is overbought or oversold by assessing

Figure 9.21   OEX Breaks Downtrend (Courtesy of QCharts (www.qcharts.com))

when a market has reached a high to the upside or a low to the downside. When a market reaches a peak in either direction, it is ripe for a reversal and managed risk strategies can be applied to take advantage of this potential movement.

Oscillators are indicators that help traders to identify a market's momentum by focusing on the rate at which a market is moving. A price oscillator is an indicator that displays the difference between a slow and fast time period, subtracting it from the current interval's price. Utilizing price and volume statistics, oscillators enable traders to predict the strength or weakness of a current market, overbought or oversold conditions, as well as turning points within the market. Momentum charts and rate of change (ROC) oscillators can both be used to help you initiate momentum investing by trading with or against the momentum of the market in hopes of profiting from it. A rate of change oscillator is a percentage indicator that calculates the market's change from the current interval's price versus price *n* intervals ago.

The McClellan Oscillator uses the 19-day and 39-day exponentially smoothed averages of the daily advance/decline values. A move above zero is a signal to buy; and a move below zero is a signal to sell. Oversold conditions exist if this oscillator registers a very negative reading in the vicinity of −100. Overbought conditions exist when this oscillator registers positive readings above 100. This oscillator is primarily used to identify divergences and to confirm trend reversal levels.

Lagging indicators: Often used in reference to economic data, a lagging indicator is a variable that tends to follow changes in overall economic activity. Therefore, a lagging indicator reaches a peak after the peak in economic activity and a bottom after the economy has troughed. Similarly, in reference to some indicators used in technical analysis, a lagging indicator will reach a top or a bottom following the stock or index. Examples of lagging indicators include MACD, MACD-histogram, on-balance volume, and accumulation/distribution.

Oscillators: Leading indicators that identify overbought and oversold conditions. They're shown as a wave of sorts, undulating above and below a midline. When it reaches the lower side of the midline, the market is said to be oversold; when they reach the upper side of the midline, the market is said to be overbought. These extremes signal to a trader that a reversal could be very close. Traders also look for divergences between an oscillator and the price action of a stock or index. These can serve as warning signals, prompting the trader to close out a position and/or initiate a new one, in anticipation of a trend reversal. It should be noted that oscillators work best in nontrending markets. When overall market conditions are obviously bullish or bearish, oscillators will signal overbought and oversold conditions for long periods of time. This makes the oscillator as reliable as a broken fuel gauge. In a strongly trending market, look to other technical analysis instruments such as trend lines and volume for a more accurate reading of conditions. One last thing the trader looks for is when the oscillator crosses the midline, foretelling of a possible change in the trend.

MOMENTUM

The Big "Mo" is an indication of the power behind a stock or index, building and losing momentum. Here's a simple analogy: If your Uncle Wally is running at you full force, he's likely to run you over; but if he's just shuffling along slowly, he'll just bump into you with little or no effect. It's the same way with stocks. If Cisco Systems is barreling ahead and it's about to encounter a former resistance level, chances are decent that it will break through. But if it has the impetus of a death row inmate walking the Green Mile, it probably won't continue on in the same direction without some help.

Momentum is simply the rate of change (the speed or slope) at which a stock or index climbs or drops in value. It is calculated by taking the difference in prices separated by fixed time intervals, such as 5, 10, or 50 days. The intervals you choose depend on your investment time frame. Traders use this indicator as a buy signal when it turns positive, and a sell signal when it turns negative.

In Figure 9.22, the line below the bar chart of Cisco Systems is the momentum indicator. It clearly depicts a momentum shift right after the stock split in March 2000, which was aided in its descent by the April Tech Wreck. The horizontal midline delineates positive and negative momentum. With rising prices

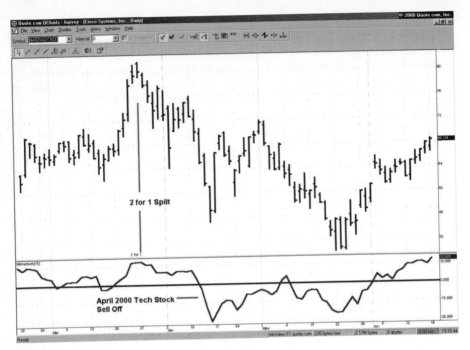

Figure 9.22   Cisco Systems 15-Day Momentum Indicator (Courtesy of QCharts (www.qcharts.com))

(stock heading up), a momentum indicator above zero and heading up indicates upward momentum is increasing. If it's above zero and moving down, upward momentum is decreasing. If a stock or index is declining in price and the momentum indicator is below zero and moving down, downward momentum is increasing. If the momentum indicator is below zero and moving up, downward momentum is decreasing.

Momentum indicator: The momentum indicator is used to identify over-bought/oversold conditions in a stock or index. It is calculated by subtracting the price for a certain number of previous days from the price of the current day. For example, the seven-day momentum indicator equals the most recent closing price minus the closing price seven days ago. If the most recent price is higher, momentum is positive; if it lower, it is negative; and if it is unchanged, it equals zero. Furthermore, if the stock or index has increased by more than a certain number of points (depending on the price of the asset at that time), it is considered overbought. If, on the other hand, it has decreased by more than a certain number of points, the stock or index is oversold. A positive value reflects an overbought market, while a negative value reflects an oversold market.

RELATIVE STRENGTH INDEX (RSI)

The Relative Strength Index was developed by J. Welles Wilder Jr., and subsequently published in his book *New Concepts in Technical Trading Systems* (June 1978). Mr. Wilder discussed two problems with the momentum indicator line. First, there were erratic and sudden changes in the line on days when large price swings were dropped from the average. This created a need for some sort of smoothing mechanism. The second was the necessity of a constant range for the purposes of comparison. The RSI addresses both of these issues.

Relative Strength Index (RSI): The Relative Strength Index indicator, or RSI, is used to identify overbought/oversold situations in a stock or an index. In other words, it is used to identify buying opportunities during short-term market declines and selling opportunities during market rallies. RSI is always between 0 and +100. Higher numbers indicate overbought conditions and opportunities to sell. Lower numbers indicate oversold conditions and opportunities to buy.

The sharp fluctuation problem was corrected by using this formula:

$$RSI = 100 - \frac{100}{(1 + RS)}$$

$$\text{where } RS = \frac{\text{Average of } x \text{ days' up closes}}{\text{Average of } x \text{ days' down closes}}$$

In other words, Wilder utilized averages and not just simple numbers (like the momentum indicator) to calculate and plot his RSI. Traders understand that to make the RSI more pronounced, they use fewer days in the equation. If they're more interested in longer-term price action, more days are used. (Sounds easy enough.) Next, he used a constant range of 0 to 100, and plotted this on a vertical scale. A reading above 70 is considered overbought, while a reading under 30 would indicate an oversold condition. He went on to explain how bear market conditions would push the oversold number to 20, while a bull market would push the overbought reading to 80.

The miracle of hindsight shows that on July 20, 1998, the Nasdaq topped out at 2,022 (see Figure 9.23). The RSI stood at 80, a textbook oversold condition for a bull market. Somewhat prematurely the RSI hit the textbook definition for an oversold bear market on August 31, 1998. Capitulation did not occur for another month or so. October 8 was the day every optimist in the world gave up hope, marking the true bottom at 1,357.09. The RSI stood at slightly more than 29. Either point would have served the long-term investor well, as thereafter the Nasdaq went on a major run.

MOVING AVERAGE CONVERGENCE DIVERGENCE (MACD)

This isn't a refreshment break for burgers at the Golden Arches, but rather a study of the *moving average convergence/divergence (MACD) indicator*. This combines

Figure 9.23 Nasdaq with RSI High and Low Readings (Courtesy of QCharts (www.qcharts.com))

previously discussed oscillator principles with a dual average crossover methodology. (Got all that?) It's derived by dividing one exponential moving average by another, and is plotted on a chart with a midline, or equilibrium line. The exponential aspect, as you recall, gives more weighting to the latest time units, thereby smoothing out sudden gyrations. A buy signal is generated when the faster MACD line crosses above the slower line. A sell signal is generated when the faster line passes under its slower brother.

> **Moving average convergence/divergence (MACD) indicator:** Sometimes pronounced "MAC dee," it is the difference between two moving averages with different time periods. One moving average (MA) will be the average over a relatively short period of time—for example, 11 days. The second moving average is the average price change in a stock over a longer period of time—for instance, 26 days. The first (shorter) MA is referred to as the fast line and the second as the slow line. MACD is the difference between the fast and slow lines. During periods when a stock or index is rising, the fast line will rise faster than the slow line, causing the divergence between the two lines to increase. The fast line will react faster to the most recent data. A signal is generated when the two lines cross over each other. When the fast line is above the slow line and moves lower to cross over, it triggers a sell signal. When the fast line is below the slow line and crosses over it, it gives a buy signal.

But what makes the MACD different from the dual moving average system is that it also fluctuates above and below a zero line, making it resemble an oscillator. When the two MACD lines extend far above the zero line, they represent an overbought condition; if they drop too far below the zero line, they signal an oversold condition.

Another valuable aspect that is often used with the MACD oscillator is the utilization of a *histogram*. A histogram is an illustration of the difference between the two MACD lines. It, too, fluctuates above and below a zero line. The key is to look for when the bars of the histogram grow far above or below the zero line. This indicates the occurrence of a divergence, and a turn is often imminent. Many traders will wait for the histogram to cross the zero line before initiating a new position or trading out of an existing one. Others act as soon as the turn begins—up or down.

MACD histogram: MACD is typically depicted on the bottom of a stock or index chart along a zero line. When the fast line is above the slow line, the MACD histogram will be positive and above the zero line. When the fast line is below the slow line, it will be below the zero line and negative. Therefore, the MACD histogram shows the difference between the long-term and short-term moving averages. When the fast line is moving up more than the slow line, the MACD histogram rises and confirms the move higher in the stock or index. If the stock or index is rallying and the MACD histogram is not moving higher, the rally is not confirmed and likely to prove short-lived. The same analysis is used during market declines. Therefore, the MACD histogram is primarily used to gauge the health of the trend in a stock or index. If it is moving in the same direction of the stock or index, it is considered a healthy trend.

The MACD histogram is a leading indicator. When it turns, it's like a highway sign indicating roadwork ahead. Watch for the orange cones, but keep driving until they steer you around the construction. Watch the MACD lines themselves for the actual turning points (see Figure 9.24).

BOLLINGER BANDS

Bollinger bands are envelopes that surround price bars on a chart and are plotted two *standard deviations* away from a simple moving average. This differentiates the Bollinger bands from price envelopes, because envelopes are plotted by using a fixed percentage above and below a moving average. Standard deviation is a measure of volatility and always changing (according to price fluctuations), so Bollinger bands adjust themselves to the market conditions. They widen during volatile market periods and contract during less volatile periods. I like to look at them as volatility bands.

Figure 9.24   MACD and Histogram Signals (Courtesy of QCharts (www.qcharts.com))

Bollinger bands: Trading bands are a commonly used technical indicator. Basically, bands are two lines drawn at intervals (usually a percentage) around a moving average. Bollinger bands vary in distance from a moving average based on a stock or index's volatility. When the stock or index is exhibiting greater volatility, Bollinger bands will move away from the moving average. During periods of lower volatility, the bands will narrow around the moving average. Furthermore, Bollinger bands are used to indicate overbought and oversold conditions. As prices move closer to the upper band, the more overbought the stock or index is. If prices move toward the lower band, it indicates oversold conditions.

Standard deviation: In financial analysis, an often-used statistical measure. It represents how widely dispersed the individual price values are away from the average (using the same parameters). A large standard deviation in the price of a stock or index suggests higher volatility. A low standard deviation suggests low volatility in the stock or index. Mathematically, it is the square root of the variance.

There is a third line that runs in between the bands, which indicates the moving average. This line can be adjusted, using shorter periods for short-term trading, and extending out to fit your own time preferences and horizons (see Figure 9.25).

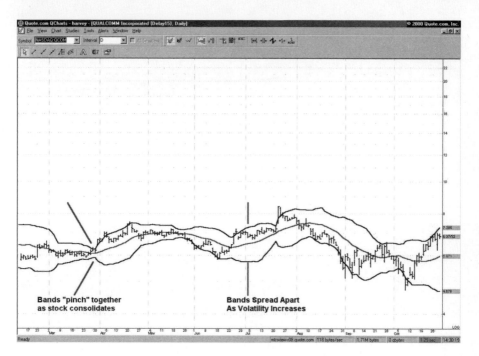

Figure 9.25 Bollinger Bands (Courtesy of QCharts (www.qcharts.com))

The most basic use of the Bollinger bands is to use them as a gauge of over-bought and oversold conditions. But to use this indicator strictly on that basis would be doing yourself an injustice, because Bollinger bands do not generate buy and sell signals alone; that is, they are much more powerful when used in tandem with other technical indicators. Coupled with the RSI indicator, they become extremely useful. For example, if a stock's price hits the upper band, a trader might be tempted to sell. However, if the RSI scale indicates a reading of 70 (80 being the overbought reading), the two together would signal further upside potential.

The possibility exists where the price touches the upper Bollinger band and RSI is 70 or even touching 80, as in Figure 9.26. This could be an indication that the trend may reverse itself and head south. If the price touches the lower band and RSI is in the 20 to 30 range, it might be an indication to start nibbling at the stock, in anticipation of a trend reversal.

> *It's a good idea to limit the number of indicators you decide to work with simultaneously; otherwise, your chart will begin to resemble a bowl of spaghetti with numbers in it.*

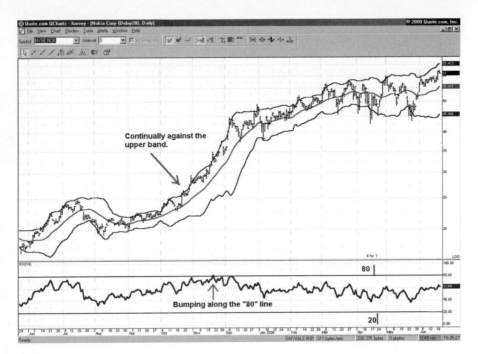

Figure 9.26 Bollinger Bands with RSI (Courtesy of QCharts (www.qcharts.com))

STOCHASTICS

George Lane developed an indicator that relates the closing price to the range in prices for a prior period of time. He called this indicator the *stochastic* and found that 21 days was the optimum time period. The 21-day price range is calculated by taking the lowest price and subtracting it from the highest in the period and then charting it as a percentage on a scale of 0 to 100.

In its most basic terms, *stochastics* are based on the observation that as a stock increases in price, the closing price is higher to the upper part of the price range. As a stock (or index) declines in value, the closing price tends to be near the lower end of the price range. (Okay so far. . . .)

> **Stochastics:** A leading technical indicator designed to pinpoint short- and long-term reversals in trends, by recording closing prices in relation to a recent trading range over a certain period of time.

Stochastics show where the most recent closing price is in relation to the price range for a chosen time period, and use two lines to do it: fast and slow. The fast line, as its name suggests, moves quickly and is used to anticipate price changes. The slower line is calculated by smoothing the fast stochastic line and produces clearer signals. These two lines are labeled *%K* and *%D*. The %D line is the one everyone looks at to provide the clearer signal. Like the RSI, the stochastics indicator often uses 14 days as a chosen time period. Instead of figuring out the equations involved here, let's cut to the chase:

- %K is the fast line.

- %D is the slow line (more reliable and used most often by traders).

These two lines oscillate on a scale from 0 to 100, 20 being really low and 80 being very high. A bearish signal occurs when the %D line is over 80 and forms a divergence from the stock or index price, turning down while the prices continue up. When the %K line crosses the %D line, a signal is generated. If %D follows %K, a change in trend is confirmed. Remember to look for a divergence between price and stochastics. The chart in Figure 9.27 shows PMCS with the stochastics indicators.

Stochastics are best used to locate entry points in major trends especially after a consolidation or to help determine reversals in trading ranges. Although they provide a helpful edge in finding profitable entry points, be careful! Avoid buying when a stock appears overbought and shorting when a stock is oversold—sound advice to all traders.

Figure 9.27   Stochastics for PMCS (Courtesy of QCharts (www.qcharts.com))

A FINAL NOTE ON TECHNICAL ANALYSIS

The study of technical analysis is such an immense subject that I can scarcely do it justice in one short chapter. Each of these discussions is designed to make you a little more aware that this world exists and that you should be aware that it influences the decisions of some very smart people.

Technical analysis is by far the most complex area of learning to trade. However, don't let its complexities overwhelm you. It has its good points, but I never rely on it exclusively 100% of the time. I use other tools and methods to verify what the charts are saying and to acquire the best view possible. Make no mistake—you can overdo any kind of analysis so that you begin to resemble a deer on the highway: wide-eyed and frozen by analysis paralysis. Start out by working with basic charting techniques until you get a feel for how to read a chart. Then start to integrate moving averages into your trading approach. Moving averages are the most popular (and easiest) technical analysis methods used by traders today. Their popularity means that they are a big part of market psychology. From there, you may want to integrate oscillators into your approach. It is very important to be able to recognize overbought and oversold conditions so that you don't throw money down at the wrong time. Just keep trying new techniques and see how they work for you, implementing them one at a time into your decision-making process.

I believe the way to use technical indicators is to look first at weekly indicators to get a basic view of the big picture. Once you have a general understanding you can fine-tune your entry and exit points using daily graphs and figures. The market is too vast to see it all, so decide what sector you can actually understand (or enjoy following), and focus on it. It's like learning to cook. You have to start by boiling water and melting butter before you try to make a five-course meal fit for a king. I discussed only some of the indicators, and then only briefly. All of these techniques take time to get to know. Once again, perseverance will be the key to your success.

If you want to become better acquainted with this field of study, I suggest several books for your review:

- Technical Analysis of the Financial Markets *by John J. Murphy, Prentice Hall Press, January 1999*
- Timing the Market *by Curtis M. Arnold, Probus Pub. Co., June 1993*
- Technical Analysis of Stocks, Options & Futures *by William F. Eng, Probus Pub. Co., May 1998*
- Integrated Technical Analysis *by Ian Copsey, John Wiley & Sons, May 1999*

ROADMAP TO SUCCESS

Objective	Course of Action
Technical Analysis Definition	Technical analysis is the study of market action, primarily through the use of charts, for the purpose of forecasting future price trends, according to *Technical Analysis of the Financial Markets* by John J. Murphy (New York Institute of Finance, June 1999). Technical analysis relies solely on price and volume of the market itself to determine the supply and demand of stocks at various price levels.
Why Use Technical Analysis?	**Trend Identification:** • In which direction is the stock or index going—up, down, or sideways? **Historical Precedents:** • What were the previous points at which trends ended or reversed? **Market Reactions: The Market Discounts Everything** • It's not so much the news, but how the market reacts to it. To understand how the market interprets announcements, economic developments, or any other outside influence, price and volume are all you need to study.
Technical Analysis Tools	There are a variety of tools available in technical analysis. Some you'll want to use, others not. The important thing is to use what you feel comfortable with and what helps you best in determining your investment decisions.

Field Guide to Technical Chart Types	• Charts and Charting
	  –*Line graphs*: Connect the dots by showing the closing price of each time period (hour, day, week, etc.).
	  –*Bar graphs*: Show open, high, low, close.
	  –*Candlestick charts*: Indicate high, low, close, plus they also display more of the emotional intensity between the bulls and bears. Very useful.
	  –*Point-and-figure charts*: Display a series of Xs and Os showing price action, bought and sold. Limited use.

- **Indicators**
  - *Moving averages*: Lagging indicators that confirm a trend's direction.
  - *Oscillators*: These help measure whether the market is overbought or oversold and are anticipatory in nature.
- For more information:
  - www.candleeyes.co.uk/info.htm
  - www.litwick.com/about.html
  - www.stocksurf.net
  - www.candlecharts.com

What to Look For

Three main factors of charting techniques:
Trend lines, support, and resistance.
These will help you to spot:
- Entry and exit points.
- Initial stages of a breakout rally.

Support and Resistance

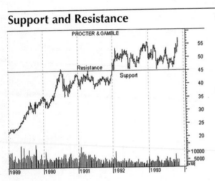
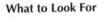
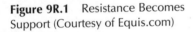

Figure 9R.1 Resistance Becomes Support (Courtesy of Equis.com)

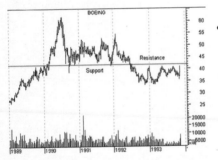

Figure 9R.2 Support Becomes Resistance (Courtesy of Equis.com)

- **Support:** The price level at which a stock or index will receive considerable buying pressure. Technical analysts believe demand at the support level will keep a stock's price from falling lower.
- **Resistance:** The price level at which a stock or index will receive considerable selling pressure. An increasing supply of stock at resistance levels will prevent the stock or index from rising further.
- **Breakout:** When a stock breaks through the resistance level, it's called a breakout, a key component for a major up move. Traders look for this move as a signal to buy, because those with long positions are now making money.
- **Broken Support:** When a stock trades lower than the previous support level, supply (sellers) outstrips demand (buyers), which sends the stock or index lower. Lower prices sometimes create additional selling pressure.

An Easy Way to Remember Support, Resistance, Breakout, and Breakdown

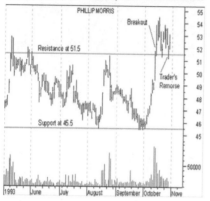

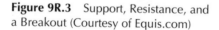

Figure 9R.3 Support, Resistance, and a Breakout (Courtesy of Equis.com)

- **Support:** The floor you're (hopefully) standing on.
- **Resistance:** The ceiling over your head.
- **Breakout:** A stock going up with enough force to punch a hole clean through the ceiling. Old resistance now becomes the new support. *Note:* Sometimes after a trend line is broken, there will be a reversal, albeit a short-term one. This is known as trader's remorse as the price falls (in a breakout) or rises (when a trend line has broken to the downside).
- **Break Down, or Broken Support:** When a stock breaks support, technicians look for the next support level, which usually was, at some time or another, an old resistance level. The support level it just broke through will be a resistance level if and when the stock turns around and heads north again.

Trend Line—A straight line or parallel straight lines indicating the trend in which a stock or index has been moving.

Figure 9R.4 Rising Trend Line (Courtesy of Equis.com)

To draw:

- **Uptrend Line:** Look for two or more low points in the chart, and then connect them with a straight line. This will indicate the support level. Think of this as a ball bouncing up a street. The height may vary, but each time it hits the support level it will head back up; higher highs, higher lows.
- **Downtrend Line:** Look for two or more high points and connect them. This will indicate the resistance line. Think of an enclosed staircase going down. With each step down, the ceiling above you gets lower, too; lower lows and lower highs.
- **Examples:**
  In Figure 9R.6, trend lines A and C are falling trend lines. Note how they were drawn between successive peaks. Trend lines B and D are rising trend lines. They were drawn between successive troughs in the price (from www.equis.com/free/taaz/trendlines.html).

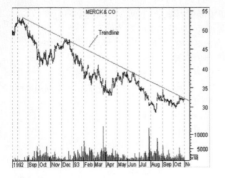

Figure 9R.5 Falling Trend Line (Courtesy of Equis.com)

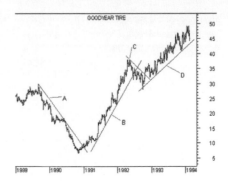

Figure 9R.6 Uptrends and Downtrends (Courtesy of Equis.com)

Good Buying Opportunities—There are definite signals investors look for in technical analysis.

Figure 9R.7 Breakdown (Courtesy of Equis.com)

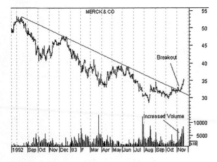

Figure 9R.8 Breakout (Courtesy of Equis.com)

One of the most popular signals is the breakout.

A breakout describes a stock that has moved sideways for a period of time (called basing, or consolidation), then moves to and through a resistance level. For it to be a solid breakout, look for:

- Appreciable increases in volume: Indicates strong conviction.
- Short Covering: If there is a short squeeze, the bears may be forced to buy their stock back, sending the stock up further.
- Momentum Traders: These people pile on when a breakout occurs.

Warning Signs

- Divergence of Price and Volume: A stock moving higher with decreasing volume is a good sign a pullback is near.
- Trader's Remorse: The second-guessing that sometimes accompanies a breakout. The danger is that the breakout becomes a failed rally.

Strong Sell Signals or Shorting Opportunities

Figure 9R.9 Support Broken (Courtesy of Equis.com)

Breaking Support: If a stock cannot hold support and begins to trend below a previous support level, look for the stock or index to trade down.

- If volume accompanies the decline, this is a strong bear signal; people are losing money.
- Sell stops or stop loss orders will kick in, too.
- Traders who specialize in shorting stocks will pile on when a break down occurs.

Watch for buyers to appear, as the break down may be an overreaction to a news event.

Moving Averages

Figure 9R.10 50-Day Moving Average Example (Courtesy of QCharts (www.qcharts.com))

Moving Averages (MAs): Help to confirm a trend by averaging past prices and calculating their average. As a new unit of time passes, the MA drops the previous unit, so that the MA is continually updated.

- It's a lagging indicator. A trend won't show up until well into the new direction. Requires the analyst to anticipate future direction.
- Length can vary. The trader can use shorter MAs if the time horizon is short, or go out longer to get a better sense of overall price history.
- 10, 50, and 200 DMA are the most popular.
  - The shorter the time, the more erratic the movements.
  - Short-term traders use a 10 DMA, while others tend to rely on the 50 and 200 DMA.
- When two or more are used in combination the trader can spot a trend forming sooner.
  - When the shorter MA crosses over the longer MA, an uptrend might be forming.
  - When the shorter MA crosses under the longer MA, a downtrend may be forming.

Figure 9R.11 50 DMA Crosses under 200 DMA (Courtesy of QCharts (www.qcharts.com))

Moving Averages: Simple or Exponential?

Some technical analysis tools call for a simple moving average, while others, like the MACD or RSI, use an exponential average.

- **Simple Moving Averages (SMA)** work well as a lagging indicator, but critics point out that all days receive equal weighting in the calculation.
- **Exponential Moving Averages (EMA)** give increased weighting to the most recent day, thereby making the average react slightly faster than a simple, or arithmetical moving average.

Most traders use the SMA in chart construction. The EMA is utilized in various oscillators.

Oscillators

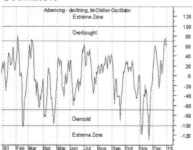

Oscillators are used to anticipate the market's next move. They:
- Utilize a fixed scale (0–100).
- Use a centerline.
- Work very well in a trendless market.
- Are useful in spotting extremes:
    –Overbought and oversold.
        –Use a contrarian approach; the crowd is always wrong at the extremes.

Figure 9R.12
Overbought/Oversold (Courtesy of Equis.com)

RSI Example

Relative Strength Index (RSI)
- RSI measures overbought and oversold extremes on a 0–100 scale; 30 is oversold; 70 is overbought.
- Use these two extremes to employ the contrarian approach; get set for a reversal.
- Divergences are easier to see when RSI doesn't confirm a price move up or down.
- RSI uses an exponential average.
- If RSI surpasses a previous high, it's a bullish sign; if it surpasses a previous low, it's a bearish sign.

Figure 9R.13   RSI Divergence— Micron (MU) Stock Climbs While RSI Deteriorates, Stock Follows Later (Courtesy of QCharts (www.qcharts.com))

Moving Average Convergence/ Divergence (MACD)

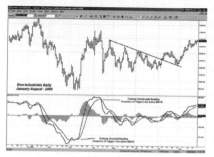

Figure 9R.14 MACD (Courtesy of QCharts (www.qcharts.com))

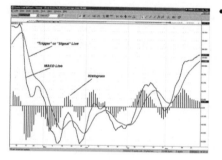

Figure 9R.15 MACD Oscillator (Courtesy of QCharts (www.qcharts.com))

MACD: Combines the two moving average crossover technique with some aspects of the oscillator. (Lagging indicator fused with a forecasting tool.)

- Uses the difference between two exponential moving averages of closing prices (most typically the last 26 and 11 days); this is called the MACD line.
- A 9-day moving average of the MACD line is plotted and laid on top of the MACD. This is called the trigger line (or signal).
- MACD watchers look for the trigger line to move above or below the MACD line, especially when the oscillator is in the overbought or oversold area. (See Figure 9R.14.)
- The MACD serves as a momentum indicator, too, as illustrated by its move either above or below the centerline. Momentum indicators are important to look for as they show the intensity of the emotion behind the move.
    - If the MACD doesn't move below the centerline in a down move, the bears don't have much force.
    - If the uptrend from an oversold position fails to clear the centerline, the bulls don't have the power to climb higher, and the market is likely to fall back.
- A histogram appears as a bar graph that rises and falls on either side of the midline. The histogram is a graphic display of the distance between the MACD and trigger lines, and visually aids the investor in identifying reversals and momentum.
- The MACD will diverge from the price action; the histogram will be the first signal (rising or falling), followed by the actual crossing over/under of the trigger line.

Examples

- In Figure 9R.14, MACD signals reversals in Dow Industrials of a sell-off in the spring of 2000. Look at the far right side of the graph as the Dow breaks through resistance and heads higher. The MACD stayed above the centerline, indicating the downtrend had lost momentum.
- Figure 9R.15 shows a closer look at the components of the MACD oscillator.

Volume: Defined as the number of entities traded during a defined time period. It indicates the intensity of a move (the emotional level) of the market.

Volume: An extremely valuable tool in technical analysis, due to its simplicity and accuracy. Technicians watch volume closely. Low volume indicates hesitation, reluctance to commit. Strong volume shows high demand to either buy or sell. These two traits coupled with price action signal the following:

- **Advancing Price Movement**
  - Volume should increase as a stock rises in price. Failure to do this indicates a lack of buyers' conviction.
  - If price rises and volume declines, this is called a divergence and indicates that the rally is suspect; caution is advised.

- **Declining Prices**
  - If a stock sells off on heavy volume, watch out! This is a signal of institutional selling.
  - If a stock sells off on light or decreasing volume, buyers are waiting for a better entry point.

- **Capitulation**
  - The final, exhaustive effort on the part of buyers or sellers.
  - This is the sign of a top or bottom—the bears (at the top) or the bulls (at the bottom) give up, exiting the market in droves.
  - Capitulation at a top is more difficult to identify than at a bottom.

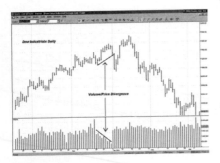

Figure 9R.16 Volume and Divergence (Courtesy of QCharts (www.qcharts.com))

Examples
- Figure 9R.16 shows reluctance on the part of buyers as the stock price rose while volume fell. This is called a divergence and indicates a lack of commitment one way or the other. Also note how the trend line broke support, and the gap down on big volume occurred shortly thereafter.
- In Figure 9R.17, Oracle shows a rising trend line in both price and volume. Even a pullback (shown in the center of the graph) was on reduced volume, and the uptrend resumed for both the stock and the volume.

Figure 9R.17 Increasing Volume (Courtesy of QCharts (www.qcharts.com))

Bollinger Bands and Price Envelopes

Figure 9R.18   Price Envelopes
(Courtesy of QCharts
(www.qcharts.com))

Figure 9R.19   Bollinger Bands
(Courtesy of QCharts
(www.qcharts.com))

Bollinger Bands and Price Envelopes: Similar in that they show a range above and below a moving average line.

- Bollinger bands calculate standard deviations above and below the most recent range of the stock or index.
- When a stock reaches the upper band, it either continues to rally or turns down, signaling a possible reversal and thus a time to sell or go short.
- Bands are another way to view volatility of stock or index—when the bands narrow, the stock has gone quiet. This is a good time to buy options. (You want to buy options when volatility is cheap and sell options when the volatility is expensive—when the Bollinger bands are wide apart.)
- Price envelopes track a moving average as well, but use a fixed percentage added to and subtracted from the moving average to calculate the envelope or price bands.

10

Sentiment Analysis Essentials

For years there have been two main approaches to market research: fundamental and technical analysis. Both schools of analysis offer investors a means of studying the market in terms of present and past performance as reflected by facts. However, these two approaches don't take into account the mass psychology of the investment community. To fill this gap, a third approach—*sentiment analysis*—is slowly gaining in popularity. Sentiment analysis gauges investor sentiment by analyzing the group consciousness in the marketplace, using various market criteria that define the market's state of mind, if you will. Be advised that the meaning of these criteria is subjective. Many market analysts, however, do agree that certain measurements strongly suggest a predominantly bullish or bearish tone to the market.

> **Sentiment analysis:** The process of measuring investor attitudes toward the securities markets. The goal is to determine if investors, or the crowd, are bullish or bearish toward the market. When studying market sentiment, the analyst often takes a contrarian approach. That is, if investors are predominantly bullish, the analyst will be bearish (sell stocks). If, on the other hand, the crowd is bearish, the analyst will turn bullish (buy stocks). Examples of indicators used in sentiment analysis include: survey of newsletter writers, amount of margin debt, mutual fund cash positions, short sales, and others. Sentiment analysis requires the combination of several measurements to reach a conclusion; that is, it requires interpretation!

The stock market is arguably the most graphic example possible of the world's collective consciousness—a never-ending, seesaw battle between buyers and sellers, optimists and pessimists. Some days, it is a raw display of emotion as fear and greed in all their respective glory play themselves out on the battlefields of various exchanges.

Investors and traders can either take advantage of these emotional swings or be swept along with them—buying when they should be selling, and selling at the worst possible times (when smart money is buying). Herd tactics, the notion of buying when everyone else is buying and selling when everyone else is selling, simply doesn't, and cannot, work, especially during extreme highs or lows in the indexes. The axiom of "buying low and selling high" may be easy to understand; but implementing it is another story altogether. When everyone around you is bursting with enthusiasm, as is most often the case in a deliciously profitable bull market, most traders will tell you that getting out runs contrary to what their heart (and net worth) is saying. Conversely, buying when "blood is running in the street" takes nerves of steel. But it's this contrarian way of thinking that can help you to avoid buying the tops and selling the bottoms.

The contrarian investor does the opposite of what the general consensus may be. Even though this may sound suicidal, time has repeatedly proven this strategy's wisdom.

Since emotions often dictate the course of a trader's action, the study of emotion (sentiment analysis) as it pertains to the buying and selling of stocks has produced a number of sentiment indicators. These indicators seek to measure the degrees of levels of fear and greed (optimism and worry) in the marketplace at any given time. The most revered traders are said to act without emotion. This characteristic is considered an ideal, sought and actually attained by some market participants; but the consistency with which these supertraders are able to maintain this ice-water-in-the-veins mind-set varies widely. One thing is certain: It's far easier to make a decision when you're *out* of the market than *in* it!

When this scenario is spread over an entire market, you'll see some people buying and some selling, some at the right time and some at the wrong time—but all at the same time. Hence, market sentiment and psychology offer vital clues when determining the future direction of the market. History has shown time and again that great bull markets have begun when market sentiment is at its nadir. Doomsayers pound their drums as they warn of impending disaster. The problem with this scenario is: If everyone has sold who's going to sell, what would make the market drop any further? Fear keeps many investors on the sidelines as the indexes reverse and power upward until the doomsayers have been silenced. The coast appears clear and the last worrier/pessimist decides it's now safe to invest. This most often signifies the top, as the last of the nervous Nellies enter the market. With everyone happy and fully invested, you'd think the market would spiral ever skyward. The problem with this scenario is: If everyone is invested, who's left to buy?

This case of extreme optimism is the hallmark of a market top. As the media pronounces ever higher highs, new offerings are brought to the table to take advantage of this optimism. Investment dollars are increasingly absorbed until there is no liquidity (relatively speaking), and the erosion begins. Only with the luxury of hindsight can we see that the ensuing downtrend in the market began right after a huge up day—probably the most obvious measure of optimism available. Volume was up sharply, and investors were seemingly buying in at any price. Time and again, this type of *capitulation* is nurtured by extreme exhibitions of fear (shown at market bottoms), and greed (a sign that a top has been reached), and clearly marks major turning points in the market. Beware the panicked trader who can't afford to be left behind at the top or loses any long-term outlook, throwing in the towel at the bottom.

Capitulation: The emotional climax (peak) that ultimately exhausts the momentum of the current trend, signaling either a top or bottom in the market.

SENTIMENT INDICATORS

More often than not, the majority of investors (the crowd) and traders are right in their market analysis—their trend identification is correct. Just about anyone who pays even a modicum of attention to news reports on market activity could tell you things are good (the market's going up) or it's bad (the market's heading south). But when it comes to extreme highs and lows, the majority of people are wrong. Only a minority of money managers and traders have enough savvy to be able to correctly identify true *market tops and bottoms*. I cannot emphasize the power of emotions at these extremes, because facts about earnings or interest rates or the economy confirm the predominant emotion of the time, which makes selling seem like a foolish move or buying an absurd risk.

Market tops: A high point in stock prices generally measured by one or more of the senior averages (i.e., the Dow Jones Industrial Average, the S&P 500, and S&P 100), which is then followed by a period of declining prices. In general, during market tops, investors are optimistic about the future course of stock prices and there is a large amount of public participation in the stock market.

Market bottoms: A low point in stock prices measured by one or more of the senior averages, which is then followed by a period of advancing prices. Traditionally, during market bottoms, public participation in the market is low and there is a large amount of pessimism with respect to stock prices.

How do they determine these turning points? By reviewing a number of technical and sentiment indicators for clues that the trend is shifting from a bullish to a bearish one or vice versa. But the clues are more contrary than coincidental; extremely bullish indicators are actually bearish signals.

In the fall of 1998, the markets were being buffeted by several potentially disastrous events: Russia's default on a bond, fears of financial crises in Asia and Latin America, and the near collapse of a major U.S. hedge fund had sent the markets from a high of 9,368 (DJIA), reached on July 20, to a low of 7,400 on September 1—a

21% haircut. The Dow hit an emotional bottom (a capitulation) a month or so later on October 8, before it turned and headed up in what, in retrospect, was one of the greatest bull runs of all time. It should be noted that the market had rallied a bit through September, so that when it dropped again, the pessimism meter went off the charts.

How was it possible for financial markets, in the face of so much uncertainty and outright fear, to stage such an impressive rally? Let's look at some of the everyday tools (sentiment indicators) traders use to gauge the extent of fear and greed in the market.

The Volatility Index

The measure of volatility in the market is a key factor in determining its state of mind, if you will. In its most basic form, volatility is defined as a statistical measurement of a stock's price change (regardless of direction) represented by a percentage. As mentioned earlier, I prefer to think of it as the speed of change in the market. A stable market moves slowly and a volatile market moves quickly. Implied volatility approximates how much the market thinks an option's price will move. Higher implied volatility (IV) suggests bigger moves, and is also reflective of the degree of optimism or pessimism in a stock, option, or the market in general.

The CBOE Volatility Index (ticker = VIX) computes implied volatility of four S&P 100 (OEX) option contracts in the two front months (in the case of October, the two front months would be October and November), one call and one put contract just out-of-the-money (OTM), and one call and one put just in-the-money (ITM). This index is updated continuously and followed by traders almost as closely as the other major indexes like the Dow Industrials. Since VIX reflects the implied volatility and premium paid for OEX options, it can rise dramatically during periods of uncertainty as investors scramble to hedge portfolios with OEX puts. For example, while VIX fluctuated between 23% and 35% throughout most of 1999, it hit a high of 60% during October 1998's climactic sell-off.

The normal range for the VIX is between 20 and 30. When the VIX either exceeds or drops below this range, a mood of either pessimism (a high VIX), or optimism (a low VIX) prevails. A low VIX is achieved by excessive call contract buying (i.e., the majority of people expect the markets to move higher still); a high VIX reading is indicative of pervasive put buying, or pessimism. Wall Street has many axioms or clichés. However, there's one I consistently live by, and it makes the VIX level easy to understand: When the VIX is low (<20), it's time to go. When the VIX is high (>30), it's time to buy.

CBOE Volatility Index (VIX): The weighted average of the implied volatilities of eight OEX puts and calls with an average time to maturity of 30 days. Updated in real-time using OEX option bid-ask quotes, VIX generates up-to-the-minute estimates of index option volatility.

Figure 10.1 clearly shows the correlation of VIX levels and major turning points in the market. When pessimism was at its highest, an abundance of put buying marked the lowest trading points of the market. People wanted out, period. When there are no more sellers, there's nowhere to go but up. Think about it. If an entire group of stock owners—those with what I'll call weak hands—sell (their fear being so extreme that they want more than anything to be in cash or some other safe haven), and the remaining stockholders are willing to ride the storm out, the selling stops, right? Of course there are still some sellers, naturally; but the number of buyers and the degree with which they buy, dollar-wise, sends the market north. If people weren't selling at 50, for example, after riding XYZ down from its highs around 100, why would they sell when it's going up again? No stock for sale at 50 means higher bids, and voilà! the next bull market leg has begun.

Using the fall of 1998 as an example again, the newspapers were full of stories describing possible consequences of a collapse of Brazil's economy, which would worsen the already shaky footing Russia was dealing with, or perhaps it would work in the opposite direction. Bank stocks with foreign exposure were being dumped at wholesale prices by some very smart people, and who could blame them? There was genuine concern, so that when the final sell-off occurred in October, most investors and traders were prepared to ride the entire U.S. economy right down the drain. The VIX hit an unheard-of high of 60! (Remember, 30+ is generally considered a good entry point!) There was extreme volatility during this period, with the VIX bouncing between 30 and 60. This level of fear when coupled with market volatility and a global economic crisis served as the basis for a move in the Nasdaq from 1,300 to over 5,000 just over a year and a half later! Aggressive call buying, low put/call ratios, and a falling VIX are all symptoms consistent with market-topping activity—theoretically, a prelude to increased volatility. To give you a visual picture, check out Figure 10.2, a chart of the Nasdaq Composite index, and Figure 10.3, a chart of VIX for the same period.

Major Date VIX Turning Points

October 1997	Bottom	54.60
July 20, 1998	Top	16.88
October 8, 1998	Bottom	60.63
January 11, 1999	Top	26.38
March 4, 1999	Bottom	28.15
May 14, 1999	Top	25.01
July 16, 1999	Top	18.13
August 5, 1999	Bottom	32.12
October 15, 1999	Bottom	32.06
January 28, 2000	Bottom	29.09
April 14, 2000	Bottom	41.53

Figure 10.1   Table of VIX Tops and Bottoms

Figure 10.2   Nasdaq Composite 1998 (Courtesy of QCharts (www.qcharts.com))

IMPLIED VOLATILITY AS A MEASURE OF INDIVIDUAL STOCK SENTIMENT

There are three basic dimensions to the value of an option:

1. The price of the underlying stock.

2. The time left to expiration of the contract.

3. The implied volatility of the option itself.

Implied volatility is a computed value that measures an option's premium, rather than the underlying asset. The *fair value* of an option is calculated by entering the historical volatility of the underlying asset into an option pricing model (Black-Scholes for stocks). The computed fair value often differs from the actual market price of the option, depending on the level of interest in the underlying stock.

The best way to analyze whether an option is undervalued or overpriced is to compare its current implied volatility level to its historical volatility levels. The difference between an option's historical volatility and implied volatility provides important clues as to market sentiment. For example, if the implied volatility of an option is higher than the historical volatility, the option is most likely overvalued. In this scenario, if the price of a stock increases, but the implied volatility of the option decreases, you may

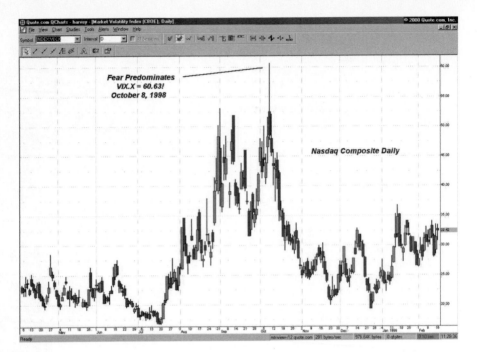

Figure 10.3   Volatility Index 1998 (Courtesy of QCharts (www.qcharts.com))

lose money even though the stock moved in your favor. This is a sign to sell options. If implied volatility falls below historical volatility, the volatility ratios are low and the options are likewise undervalued. If the price of the stock falls and the implied volatility increases, option premiums will increase. This is a good time to buy options.

Without this comparison, the current value of an option's implied volatility tells you very little. For example, let's say a stock's options on a given day have an implied volatility of 100%. Are the options expensive? What if, for the past year, the same stock's options have registered implied volatilities from 110% to 230%? Given that history, I think we would all agree that 100% should rightly be considered small and hence the options cheap.

If the implied volatility of a stock's options moves below or above the actual statistical volatility of the stock, it may create a volatility crush, which, in turn, triggers price movement. Options on stocks often have incredible swings in their implied volatilities. Figure 10.4 shows a six-month price chart for Motorola (MOT) and Figure 10.5 reveals Motorola's implied volatility chart.

Figure 10.5 clearly illustrates the herd mentality of volatility valuations. Peaks and troughs aplenty here, as traders rush in when there's news, unusual price action, or some other force at work. Sometimes traders will jump in just because there *is* unusual price action. There's a group of traders known as *momentum traders* (see

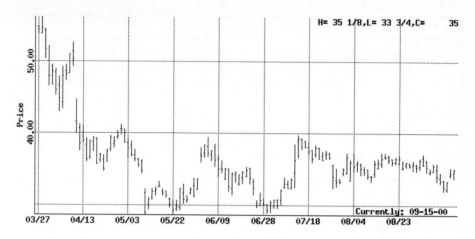

Figure 10.4   Six-month Price Chart for Motorola (MOT) (Courtesy of Optionetics.com)

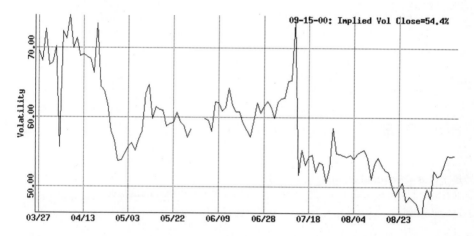

Figure 10.5   MOT Six-Month Implied Volatility Chart (Courtesy of Optionetics.com)

Chapter 12) who look for these kinds of swings. They look for conditions in which pressure begins to build, hoping for an explosive up or down move. It is in this sharp upward move that the premium (IV) of an option goes up as traders rush to participate by using the leverage of options. As momentum begins to subside, they get out. The sell-off not only drops the stock price but also the premium drops, too, a double whammy that causes many option traders to lose money quickly. It's the herd mentality again that creates this high premium. The floor brokers pump up the premium when the buying gets heavy and the stock attracts attention, and then they drop the premium as everyone tries to get out.

> **Momentum traders:** Momentum refers to the tendency for stock prices to move in one direction over time. Momentum traders attempt to capture profits from this tendency by analyzing a stock, not based on fundamental criteria, but on the strength of the stock price movement to the up or downside. If a stock is moving upward rapidly over a long period of time, it has powerful upward momentum, and traders will buy the stock in anticipation of further price appreciation. If, on the other hand, the stock price has been falling over a long period of time, the stock has powerful downward momentum and momentum traders will sell it short to capture profits as the stock price falls further.

By using the contrarian approach, (trading against the majority view), you often can profit by the subsequent decrease in implied volatility by going against the crowd. A good rule of thumb to remember about volatility is: Buy low volatility; sell high volatility.

A good place to find these kinds of stocks is by using the Optionetics.com Platinum service. The Platinum service offers traders an extensive selection of tools including a rank engine (just go to the "Ranker: High/Low IV" section) that sorts through historical data to find stocks that are explosively moving, cheap options, and a variety of implied volatility versus statistical volatility settings. The Platinum service offers a two-week free introductory offer to help you get started on finding explosive trading opportunities.

PSYCHOLOGICAL MARKET INDICATORS

Investor's Business Daily (www.investors.com) offers a variety of sentiment indicators in its "General Market and Sectors" section, currently near the back of the first section. There is a table of psychological indicators printed daily in the *IBD* that can provide some essential numbers of sentiment analysis (see Figure 10.6).

Public/NYSE Specialist Short Sales

A *short sale* is a trade where a person or institution will actually borrow stock to sell, with the idea of buying it back at a lower price. If the number here is above 0.6, it is believed to be bullish; less than 0.35 is bearish. Again, the crowd is considered to be wrong at market extremes, and these two levels would indicate extreme levels of pessimism or optimism.

Ratio of Price Premiums in Puts versus Calls

If put premiums are more expensive than call premiums, puts are most likely experiencing a higher demand, which increases their volatility. A rise in volatility subsequently pumps up the price. A higher demand for puts is a sign that a higher

Psychological Market Indicators	Current 9/28/00	5 Year				12 Month			
		High	Date	Low	Date	High	Date	Low	Date
Public/NYSE Specialist Short Sales	0.99	2.25	6/14/96	0.56	10/31/97	1.37	10/15/99	0.69	6/16/00
Ratio of Price Premiums in Puts versus Calls	0.40	2.57	7/2/97	0.13	5/23/00	1.10	11/8/99	0.13	5/23/00
Mutual Fund Share Purchases/ Redemptions	1.21	2.06	12/1/95	1.06	8/3/98	1.35	2/29/00	1.16	9/30/99
Nasdaq Daily Trading Volume as % NYSE Daily Volume	165%	234%	11/26/99	79.8%	9/4/98	234%	11/26/99	105%	10/27/99
Number of Stock Splits in IBD 6000 (prior 30 days)	75	211	6/18/98	40	11/16/96	124	4/10/00	43	10/22/99
New Issues in Last Year as % of All NYSE Stocks	20.2%	31.7%	11/5/96	12.0%	5/24/99	22.3%	4/14/00	14.2%	9/23/99
Price-to-Book Value of DJIA	6.06	8.29	1/14/00	3.62	10/26/95	8.29	1/14/00	5.63	10/15/99
Price-to-Earnings Ratio of DJIA	20.6	28.7	5/13/99	13.7	10/26/95	26.4	11/22/95	20.2	3/7/00
Current Dividend Yield of DJIA	1.63%	2.44%	10/26/95	1.28%	1/14/00	1.74%	10/15/99	1.28%	1/14/00

Figure 10.6 Psychological Market Indicators (*Source: Investor's Business Daily*, September 28, 2000)

majority of investors have bearish stock positions. From a contrarian perspective, the existence of too many bears brings in the bulls. If the selling strength is played out, buyers may rush in to buoy the market back up. The easiest way to understand this is by applying the law of supply and demand. Heavy put buying is a sign of bearish market bias, while heavy call buying denotes bullish sentiment. However, many professional traders believe that option buyers are usually wrong and apply a contrarian approach to interpret put/call ratios (i.e., if the put/call ratio is high, the contrarian investor takes this as a bullish sign of market strength).

Mutual Fund Share Purchases/Redemptions

Mutual funds are some of the largest players in the stock market. Their size makes them an important sector of sentiment analysis. Analysts study mutual funds by monitoring their cash reserves and tracking their purchase and redemption performance. The *IBD's* fund purchase-redemption ratio compares mutual fund purchases to redemptions. If the ratio of purchases are higher than redemptions, then the funds are cash rich and the general market should be bullish. If there are more redemptions than purchases, then the funds are cash poor and a bearish trend may be developing in the general market.

But the contrarians are always just around the corner. Net redemptions would indicate the general population is feeling pessimistic about the market; and at its extreme measurements, this would be considered a contrarian indicator—that is, bullish. A net purchase paints the opposite picture. When it's at extreme levels on an historical basis, this is a bearish sign (too much optimism).

Institutional investors can also be easily tracked by monitoring a streaming quote screen—specifically watching a stock's *TSize* values which tells you the number of shares in the last trade. TSize is important because a stock moves when an institution or someone who's buying big volume or selling big volume is coming into the marketplace. If you see a stock and it's trading only 100-share lots, there are no really big players in there, so don't expect those stocks to move. You're not going to make a lot of money from those. You have to keep an eye out for block trades—typically defined as 5,000 shares traded at one time. If you start seeing a number of 5,000, 10,000, 15,000 blocks, then you know there are probably some big players who are going to move the market. They're the ones who are going to help you make money.

Nasdaq Daily Trading Volume as % of NYSE Daily Volume

Since the Nasdaq is generally believed to hold more small-cap issues, an increase of Nasdaq volume (more activity in smaller issues), is a typical sign of a late-stage bull market—another way of saying that the party's almost over.

Number of Stock Splits in *Investor's Business Daily* 6,000 (Prior 30 Days)

If the price of a stock rises too high, investors may become wary of investing in it. Many times, companies will choose to orchestrate a stock split to reduce the price. If a stock is selling for $200 a share, they may choose to do a 2:1 stock split, reducing the price of the stock to $100 a share. So if you own 500 shares of a stock at $200 per share before the split, you'll own 1,000 shares of the stock at $100 per share after the split. The market value of the total number of shares remains the same, but the number of the corporation's outstanding shares increases while the price of its stock decreases.

Since stocks split when their prices reach higher levels, an increase would naturally mean higher prices overall, and is a caution sign at best, and a bearish signal at worst.

New Issues in Last Year as % of All Stocks on NYSE

New issues come to market when the getting's good—definitely a bullish sign. Who wants to seek public financing when the market conditions are poor?

Price-to-Book Value Ratio of Dow Jones Industrial Average

Book value is an accounting term used to measure a firm's assets relative to its liabilities. A price-to-book (P/B) ratio is calculated by dividing a company's stock price by its book value. Generally, value investors look for stocks with low price-to-book ratios. Market watchers also follow the price-to-book value of the major averages. The price-to-book ratio of the Dow Jones Industrial Average is the (price-weighted) average P/B of the 30 stocks within the Dow Jones Industrial Average.

If you could buy a dollar for fifty cents, it would be a good deal, right? If a dollar cost $1.50, that's a bad deal. A higher ratio is an indicator of a higher stock price, and is not a sign the Dow Industrials are selling at a cheap price.

Price-to-Earnings (P/E) Ratio of Dow Jones Industrial Average

Price-to-earnings, or P/E, is a company's stock price divided by earnings over the past 12 months. The price-to-earnings ratio of the Dow Jones Industrial Average is the (price-weighted) average P/E of the 30 stocks within the Dow Jones Industrial Average. Higher P/E ratios mean an investor is paying up for earnings. High is bad, and low is good.

Current Dividend Yield of Dow Jones Industrial Average

Dividend yield is the annual dividends of a company divided by its stock price. If, for example, a company pays a $4 annual dividend and the stock price is $50, the dividend yield equals $4 / $50 or 8%. The current dividend yield of the Dow Jones Industrial Average is the annual yield from dividends of the 30 stocks in the Dow Jones Industrial Average if they were purchased at that time. Imagine a teeter-totter; one end is the stock price and the other is the dividend. The higher the yield, the lower the stock price. High yields are a sign of pessimism.

GRAPHIC DISPLAYS OF PSYCHOLOGICAL INDICATORS IN *IBD*

The *IBD* also features a number of excellent graphs that can help investors gauge overall market performance. Let's take a look at some of these clues to market sentiment.

Investment Advisers Bullish and Bearish

Another way to track market sentiment is to survey the opinions of professional advisers. A person can track, in easy-to-read graph form, the percentage of advisers who are bullish and bearish. *IBD* even goes one step further, indicating the overall percentages would tend to indicate sentiment one way or the other. At the risk of repetition, these would be considered contrarian indicators. (*IBD* even tells you that!)

Short Interest Ratio

Short interest ratio is a popular indicator that helps to gauge negative investment sentiment. Shorting a stock is a bearish strategy that involves borrowing shares from a broker in order to receive a credit from their sale. If the price declines, the seller can buy the shares back at a lower price to cover the short and pocket the difference. The short interest ratio indicates the number of trading days required to repurchase all of the shares that have been sold short. A short interest ratio of 1.50 would tell us that, based on the current volume of trading; it would take one and a half days' volume to cover all shorts. Again, using a contrarian view, a high short-interest ratio is usually a sign of a bullish market, while a low short-interest ratio is generally a sign of a bearish market. This is contrarian for two reasons. The first reason is standard, the "If everyone is bearish they must be wrong" analysis from before. The second reason is more subtle, but quite clever: If the short sellers are indeed wrong, and the market is even just neutral or slightly bullish, the short sellers will have to cover their shorts (buy back the stock they have shorted), putting strong buying pressure on the market just as it starts up. This will lead to a multiplying effect to the upside.

Odd-Lot Short Sellers

An odd lot represents any number of stock shares less than 100. Small investors who lack the capital to purchase a round-lot order of 100 shares usually buy odd lots. Hence, odd-lot investors have limited experience and are often wrong. A contrarian interpretation of *odd-lot short sales* is an excellent method of gauging market sentiment. Basic odd-lot psychology assumes that an increase in odd-lot short sales translates as a bullish indicator and a decrease in odd-lot short sales is a bearish indicator.

Odd-lot short sales: The total number of shares sold short in odd lots during a month. In other words, the number of shares sold short in quantities of less than 100 shares. Since investors trading in odd lots are considered less sophisticated, a large number of odd-lot short sales is interpreted as a bullish sign, while a low number is a bearish sign for the market.

ADDITIONAL SENTIMENT INDICATORS

Option Trading Volume

Not to belabor the obvious, but put buyers are typically bearish on a stock, while call buyers are bullish. A comparison of the number of open contracts between these two camps will provide a clue as to how people really feel, and can thereby provide an overall sentiment analysis tool.

When put buying becomes rampant, the majority of people are convinced the stock or index is heading lower. When there's a lopsided proportion of call buyers to put buyers, optimism reigns supreme. A very high percentage of option contracts expire worthless every month, indicating that the majority of options traders are buying at the wrong time. The put/call ratio is a beacon that alerts the astute trader to sentiment extremes—the concentrations of buyers doing the wrong thing. Whenever you see this type of extreme, say to yourself: "The crowd is always wrong."

Put/call ratios are not usually spelled out in detail for the trader; they're forced to figure it out for themselves. (The CBOE provides it for you; go to www.cboe.com.) To calculate it, divide the number of puts by the number of calls. In short, the further the OEX put/call ratio is below 1.00, the more bearish it is; between 1.00 and 1.25 is neutral, and above 1.25 is bullish.

Option Open Interest

Open interest reveals the current number of outstanding option contracts that are available in a specific option series by the end of a trading day. Hence, monitoring the open interest of an option enables traders to track the demand of an option. A rise in an option's open interest means there are additional buyers for the option. Conversely, a decline in the open interest of an option indicates less buyers and more sellers than before. However, comparing the open interest of a call option to the open interest of a put option (with the same strike price and expiration) is a psychological indication of the underlying stock's bullish or bearish bias.

For example, if the open interest in the November 75 calls for Intel (INTC) is 15.1K, then 15,100 contracts have been initiated. If the open interest for November 75 puts is 12.3K, a bullish trend is confirmed. However, to forecast a directional change in the market, it is important to monitor the daily fluctuation of open interest. Since small options investors are consistently on the wrong side of a rally, an abnormal rise or decline in the open interest of puts and/or calls often signals a change in directional bias. Generally speaking, an abnormal rise or decline in open interest once again sends a contrarian signal to the sentiment investor. However, traders must be careful since sometimes a large increase in open interest may only be a large trader or institution hedging a position.

Mutual Fund Sales and Redemptions

The emergence of mutual funds has begun providing useful information as to market sentiment. On-balance volumes (inflow versus redemptions) indicate whether these mutual fund managers will be buying or selling, in simplistic terms. Massive influxes of cash is a strong bullish indicator, the opposite holding true if investors are predominant sellers. This measurement is tough to come by, short of waiting for the media to report it. If you have the inclination and the means, TrimTabs.com (www.trimtabs.com) offers it for a price, although a 30-day free trial is available.

Margin Debt

Another measure of investor sentiment is reflected in the amount of money individuals have been borrowing from their brokers to buy stocks. Margin accounts are brokerage accounts that allow investors to purchase securities on credit and to borrow on securities already in the account. When investors are excessively bullish on the market, *margin debt* will increase. Therefore, as a contrarian indicator, higher levels of margin debt are seen as a negative for the market. Margin debt levels are reported monthly in the *Wall Street Journal*:

> **Margin Debt Falls in July, Following Increase in June**
> *A WSJ.COM News Roundup*
> NEW YORK—Margin debt at member firms of the New York Stock Exchange dropped 0.9% in July, the Big Board said. The NYSE said debit balances in margin accounts of customers of member firms fell to $244.97 billion in July from $247.2 billion in June. Statistics on margin debt, which is accumulated when buying stocks with funds borrowed from a broker, are closely watched for insight into stock-market trends. For example, a steady rise in margin debt, which reached a high of $278.53 billion in March, preceded the spring market sell-off.

> **Margin debt:** Margin debt is accumulated when investors borrow money from their brokers in order to buy stock. The overall levels of margin debt are monitored closely as a gauge of market trends. Specifically, a high level of margin debt is viewed as a negative for the market because investors are borrowing heavily to finance stock purchases.

Advance/Decline Ratio

The A/D ratio shows the number of advancing (gaining in value) stocks versus the number of declining issues. A strong (positive) number is a good indicator the rally underway is solid. A weak number in an advancing market means the advance is limited in its breadth, and the rally is therefore suspect.

A declining market with a lopsided A/D line (more negatives than positives) means there is a widespread retracement in prices occurring, and signals overall weakness in the market. However, a relatively even A/D reading in a down market indicates the bears have control, but by only a narrow margin.

The nightly news reports will often report this figure, but it is difficult to get a graph online (for free, anyway) that shows this over any period of time. To track this on a daily basis, *Investor's Business Daily* has it in its "General Market & Sectors" section.

Rampart Time Index

This indicator (a regular feature in *Barron's*), is shown two ways: the Composite Call Index and the Composite Put Index. Both measure the time premiums on six-month near-the-money option contracts for 1,836 stocks. They show at a glance, on a broad scale, the premiums options traders are willing to pay for a call or put.

Today is May 1, so the Rampart Time Index will look to November contracts. If XYZ Company is selling at $50 per share, and the November 50 Calls are offered at $65, the time premium is $15. News one way or the other on XYZ might send this premium up or down. The more bullish the outlook for XYZ, the bigger this premium will be. So by using 1,836 stocks and measuring the time premiums, the Rampart Time Index provides an investor with another measuring stick of market sentiment.

Closed-End Fund Indicator

This indicator tracks the premiums of closed-end funds, a vehicle utilized primarily by small investors (not institutions). Closed-end funds differ from their open-end cousins because they trade like a stock in the market, complete with bids and offers, and their NAVs (net asset values) may or may not be the same as the market price. This premium or discount of share price to NAV indicates the level of optimism (premium) or pessimism (discount) among retail investors. *Note:* The little guy, being less experienced, is wrong more often than the professionals. Therefore, this sentiment indicator would be a contrary one; a premium might be a bearish signal, while a discount to NAV would show fear among the retail populace, a bullish indicator.

For more information on closed-end fund indicators, check out the Internet Closed-End Fund Investor's web site (www.icefi.com), or write them at The Internet Closed-End Fund Investor, P.O. Box 63042, Colorado Springs, CO 80962-3042.

THE MEDIA

The media is a very easy place to begin testing the waters for market sentiment. Being as objective as possible (tough to do if you're already invested!), what are the talking heads saying on the various financial broadcasts? Are they upbeat and positive, or are they speculating as to how bad it is and when it will be over? One thing to note: Whenever you watch a program that has some market guru or analyst featured, that person's comments about which direction the market will take is stating an *opinion*. If 10 gurus spoke on one day, most likely you'd hear 10 different opinions. But an investor can get some perspective as to the overall consensus (are we going up or are we going down?).

CNBC

CNBC is regarded as the leader in financial news, and that's why I usually keep my television tuned to the station. The content is split into two sections: "Real News" and "Opinions." The "Real News" half is just that: current news headlines for business and nonbusiness news. If a catastrophe has occurred (like an earthquake in California, for example), I want to know about it ASAP. Plus CNBC offers a ticker that's real-time (no 20-minute delays). This is a great way to keep up with stock quotes if you don't have streaming quotes on your computer.

The second half of their programming is opinion. We all have thoughts on where the market is going, what stocks will do well, and how to avoid dogs. It's important to keep in mind that the analysts featured are touting stocks they're already in, or their firm is promoting at that particular time. Don't get me wrong; some of this information is good. But just keep in mind that this content is meant to fill airtime. What do you think they're going to do all day, keep repeating the news on an endless loop like the Weather Channel?

Some of the people they have as guests are extremely well-spoken and knowledgeable (check out Mario Gabelli, John Bollinger, and analyst Dan Niles). Others may be considered tired warhorses by some traders because they tend to call turns in the market so far after the fact as to be almost humorous. However, their stated opinions still have major significance since they are highly regarded at major brokerage firms. It's best to keep your guard up when listening; don't just run out and buy their recommendations willy-nilly.

Here's a list of some of the more popular financial news sites:

- *CNBC: www.cnbc.com*
- *Bloomberg.com: www.bloomberg.com/welcome.html*
- *CNNfn: cnnfn.cnn.com*
- *TheStreet.com: www.thestreet.com*

News Events

Like a day ruined or brightened by an unforeseen occurrence, so too can the prevailing sentiment regarding the market as a whole or a particular stock be influenced by a news event. As mentioned earlier, a gross example of pessimism was prevalent in the fall of 1998 with the financial concerns regarding Brazil and

Russia. These concerns, when coupled with the danger of a hedge fund's crisis, made for unusually high degrees of pessimism. Individual companies can buck the trend of the market as well by announcing some major internal development, or be the subject of an analyst's accusation, the validity of which may be doubtful. Traders and investors vote with their money more times than not, selling faster than butter melts in a hot car, or buying as fast as they can dial up their brokers.

The wisdom of these decisions comes to light only when emotions cool. However, the resulting transitory price swings can and do present beautiful opportunities to buy at a discount or sell into an artificially inflated market.

Figure 10.7 shows a chart of Tyco International that illustrates the power of the media in shifting sentiment. In fall 1999 an obscure research house in the Midwest issued a report stating the company had "cooked the books" and its accounting practices were highly suspect. The SEC followed closely with what it termed a "nonpublic" investigation into Tyco's accounting practices.

What ensued in the next few days can best be described as wholesale dumping by individuals and institutions alike. As you can see, the stock went down sharply. During this sell-off, the company's senior management went on the record (on CNBC, CNNfn, and every other medium they could find) to deny there were irregularities, confirm business was booming, and stress that the outlook remained bright.

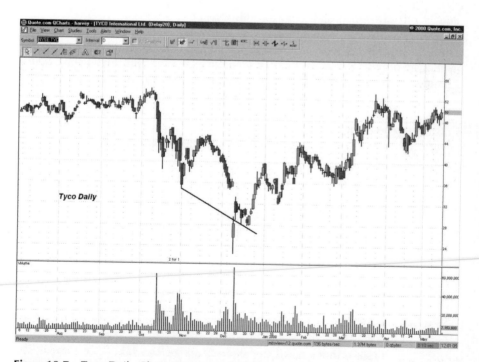

Figure10.7   Tyco Daily Chart (Courtesy of QCharts (www.qcharts.com))

The analysts who covered the company also affirmed Tyco's innocence, with everyone doing their best to question the source of the story.

In the near term, pessimism was high, and the stock sank to yearly lows. However, savvy investors who routinely look for special situations such as this pounced on the temporary dip and bought like crazy. The entire episode turned out to be a tempest in a teacup.

History is full of these kinds of disasters. The market looks at them with short-term horror. But the flip side of the same coin is a tremendous buying and/or trading opportunity as market participants take advantage of excessive pessimism.

Survey of Newsletter Writers

One of the most widely followed measures of investor sentiment is the *survey of newsletter writers* conducted by the editors of *Investors Intelligence* (see Figure 10.8). Each week, a poll is conducted to determine the levels of bullish and bearish sentiment among newsletter writers. The idea is, while some letter writers are quite savvy, taken as a whole, they are no better than average investors. As a result, they become overly bullish at market tops and bearish at major bottoms. Abe Cohen founded *Investors Intelligence* in 1963. Since he passed away in 1983, Michael Burke has served as editor and publisher. Today, *Investors Intelligence* monitors roughly 140 newsletters and conducts polls weekly.

There are differences in opinion regarding how to use *Investors Intelligence* sentiment readings. I look at both the percentage of bulls and bears. When the percentage of bulls exceeds 60%, it is a sign of excessive bullishness and a major negative for the market. If at the same time the percentage of bears falls to 20% or less, we are almost certainly at a major market top. If the percentage of bears rises above 55%, sentiment is excessively negative and the market is probably approaching a bottom. *Investors Intelligence* statistics can be found weekly in *Barron's* or through Chartcraft in New Rochelle, New York (www.chartcraft.com).

Investors Intelligence Sentiment Survey

	Last Week	Two Weeks Ago	Three Weeks Ago
Bulls	43.5%	47.1%	48.6%
Bears	33.7%	31.7%	33.6%
Correction	22.8%	21.2%	17.8%

Figure 10.8 Newsletter Survey (*Source: Investors Intelligence*, 914-632-0422)

> **Survey of newsletter writers:** Statistics on the percentage of bullish or bearish investment newsletter writers used as information about investor sentiment. It is a contrarian indicator. Therefore, high percentages of bullish newsletter writers are considered bearish, while a low percentage is interpreted as bullish.

VOLUME

Veteran traders look to the measurement of volume for verification of a rally or sell-off. Unless big money is in the game, the theory suggests, the strength of any move is suspect. Big money is an affectionate term for the pension fund managers, the mutual funds, and to some extent hedge fund activity. If they're not interested in a stock, the volume is light. If a sector is lagging and volume is light, this indicates that professional money managers are not too keen on the prospects in the near term, at least of that particular group or individual stock.

A good example of institutional involvement occurred in March 2000 when the semiconductor sector began to be the darling du jour of big money (see Figure 10.9). Micron (MU) had traded in a range from around 30 to the low 40s (after adjusting for the 2 for 1 stock split on May 2, 2000), languishing while the rest of the

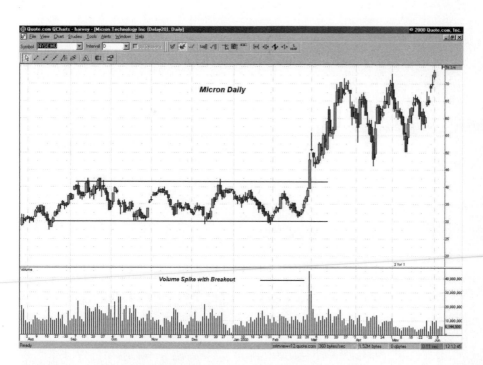

Figure 10.9 Micron Daily Chart (Courtesy of QCharts (www.qcharts.com))

Nasdaq had flourished. Institutional buyers pushed the stock upward and out of its trading range, and alerted investors to a sentiment shift, not just in Micron but the entire semiconductor sector.

MORE VOLUME CLUES

Sometimes volume spikes will tip you off when sentiment in a stock is shifting. Figure 10.10 shows Amazon.com (AMZN), which at the end of April 1998 experienced a major spike in volume although there was no news to speak of. This type of event can be spotted in *Investor's Business Daily* in a feature named "The 'Real' Most Active" that highlights stocks with unusual activity. I like this because it often is an indicator of shifting sentiment. Although trading on insider information is illegal, there's usually a group of people (investors, employees, and vendors) who are close enough to see what's happening. These observations spread like wildfire until the rumor that something big is happening dies down, and the price of the stock sinks in the absence of hard news.

Volume precedes price. The increase in volume indicates some group or groups have taken a position in a seemingly dormant issue, so said issue could then be put on a watch list of your own making. If there is big volume and no price action, the

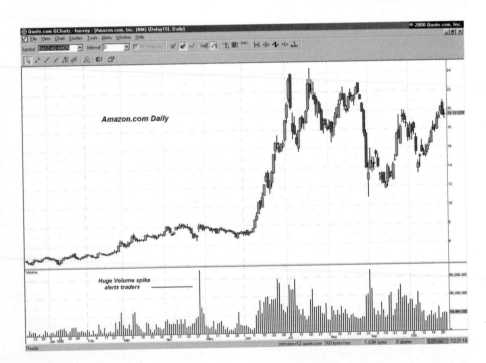

Figure 10.10   Amazon Price/Volume Chart (Courtesy of QCharts (www.qcharts.com))

> **Volume spikes:** A sharp increase in trading activity. When important news concerning a company is disseminated, there will sometimes be abnormally large trading volume in that company's stock. On a stock chart, the increasing volume will be visible along the bottom of the graph—it will appear as a tall vertical bar. That graphical representation of the abnormally large volume is also known as a volume spike.

stock is garnering the attention of institutional investors, and is a good indicator some fundamental shift in sentiment is occurring. The next volume spike with accompanying price action should confirm a definite shift in sentiment. It's like the sound of thunder signaling a storm.

Volume is also one of the tenets of the Dow Theory, in which the initial phase of an upward trend is the accumulation of stock by knowledgeable insiders and astute investors.

There are several places online to look for unusual volume activity.

- *Optionetics.com: www.optionetics.com*
- *Street Index.com: www.streetindex.com/volume_alerts.shtml*
- *Daily Stocks.com: www.dailystocks.com/volume_alerts.htm*

CAPITULATION

Capitulation is an event that signals the bottom in a bear market. Fear and pessimism reach their nadir (or pinnacle, depending on your point of view). Many analysts believe that unless capitulation occurs then a true bottom has not occurred. Capitulation is important, but a bottom can be put in without it. It is important because it rids the market of the overhang of people who wish to sell, but who are waiting for a rise in prices before they do so.

The existence of potential sellers after large declines is not consistent with a bottom. In a capitulation setting, you don't have investors buying at the dip because they have all thrown in the towel. Pessimism is so rampant even a weeklong rally is met with skepticism. At a real bottom genuine fear is in place, and a low-yielding five-year CD looks better than anything. The average investor, having been beaten up pretty badly, has had all the pain and discomfort he or she can tolerate. In the end, the investor is just trying to salvage what is left of his or her investments. When the last of the sellers dries up, only then is the coast clear for a sustainable rally.

Capitulation at the top is tougher to identify because everyone is so darn happy and feeling rich. Good news dominates the airwaves and stock reports, grand vacations are planned, and new goodies have been secured. The top is a triple-digit gain on big volume (usually) and is probably just another great day to be in the market.

The difference between a top and a bottom is that market tops are less precise than bottoms. Whereas the capitulation of bulls is accompanied by heavy selling, the capitulation of the bears may or may not be accompanied by a bout of buying (to cover their short positions). This is why the term capitulation is usually used only for bottoms.

Figure 10.11 shows the capitulation of 1998. Note that a true bottom wasn't hit until October, a month after a massive sell-off. The Volatility Index (VIX), when used in conjunction with this low, signaled investors a true bottom was reached. (It hit 60!)

Figure 10.11 shows what many investors probably would like to forget: the 1998 bear market that began with a July 20 top, and bounced to a painful conclusion, forming a double bottom on September 1 and October 8 before beginning its implausible rally.

COMPARISON INDICATORS

A number of indicators, web sites, and techniques utilize the power of comparison to unveil the strengths and weaknesses of various stocks or economic shifts. Let's take a look at a few of the most popular methods.

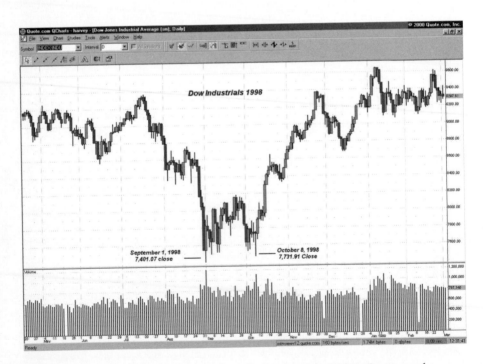

Figure 10.11 Bear Market Capitulation—Dow Industrials (1998) (Courtesy of QCharts (www.qcharts.com))

Gold Prices

Gold is a good sentiment indicator because that's where some investors go to await the End of the World As We Know It. Inflation, wars, and financial instability are the main reasons gold moves up—another way of indicating fear in the minds of investors. Contrarians won't start buying automatically, but by watching this one you can see nervous investors at a glance and judge if anything nasty is on Wall Street's radar screen.

Inflation fears in early May 2000 triggered a big move, as seen in Figure 10.12. Economic reports showed extremely low unemployment just prior to the Fed meeting, escalating concerns about inflation.

THE WALL STREET DETECTIVE

This is a web site with its own sentiment indicators. Since the entire market doesn't move all at once in the same direction, various sectors will be doing well while everything else is cratering. As previously mentioned, sector comparison is an excellent method of ferreting out useful information on specific individual stocks. Go to www.wallstdet.com for more information.

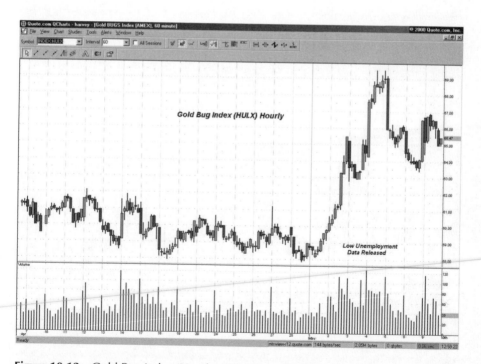

Figure 10.12   Gold Bug Index (Hourly) (Courtesy of QCharts (www.qcharts.com))

INDEX FUTURES

On CNBC every morning before the opening bell, they show on the screen how the S&P 500 *index futures* are behaving. This is an indication of bullish or bearish outlooks by traders on the *Chicago Mercantile Exchange (the Merc)*. Everything from interest rates to the price of orange juice is traded here, including futures prices of various stock indexes. The most widely watched is the S&P 500. When futures are up before the opening, (as compared to fair value), most traders look for an upward bias, at least initially. Figures 10.13 and 10.14 are near mirror images of each other. There are significant nuances, however, subtleties that index traders watch very closely. Traders will take advantage of the disparities between the actual value of the S&P versus the futures prices. In some cases, the futures price will influence the index price, and vice versa. On the right-hand side of the graphs you can see where the futures traded down in a 30-minute period but closed that period with a gain, as illustrated by the long light-colored candlestick. The S&P responded, albeit a bit more conservatively. Traders eventually took the index higher, but only after the futures rose in advance.

FINAL COMMENTS

Sentiment indicators are best viewed broadly and in conjunction with one another. Just as the physician will use various tests to measure the health of a patient, so too

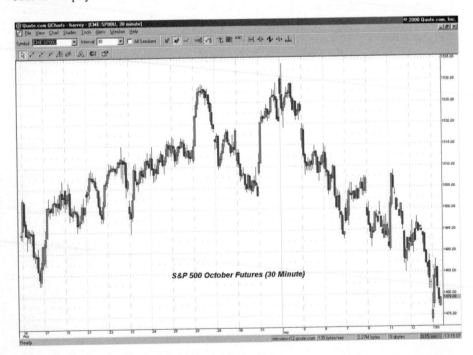

Figure 10.13   S&P Futures (October 2000) (Courtesy of QCharts (www.qcharts.com))

> **Index futures:** A futures contract is an agreement to take or make delivery of a specific commodity on a particular date. An index futures contract is an agreement to take delivery on an index (by the buyer of the futures contract) or make delivery of an index (by the seller) at a predetermined date. Since, unlike most physical commodities, there is no tangible good to take or make delivery of, index futures settle for cash.
>
> **Chicago Mercantile Exchange (the Merc):** Established in 1919, the CME is an organized exchange for the trading in futures of various agricultural commodities, interest rate products, indexes, and currencies.

must the sentiment indicators be used when measuring the degree of fear and greed present at any particular time.

While the snapshot picture will reveal certain characteristics about the market, I get a better sense of things when I track them over a period of time. I also like to overlay these measurements with the sector I'm interested in, because I know that not all sectors rise and fall together. By utilizing sentiment analysis, you've given yourself a third method to assist you in making profitable investment decisions. It represents the final piece of the analysis puzzle and should be part of an investor's daily review of the marketplace. It bridges the gap between fundamental and technical analysis.

Sentiment analysis is also useful in confirming a specific stock's trends and recognizing reversals. Since it gauges the mass psychology of the marketplace, your

Figure 10.14 S&P 500 Index (30-Minute) (Courtesy of QCharts (www.qcharts.com))

interpretation of the findings is the key to whether you are successful. Experience is the missing link in this picture. You may want to keep a journal detailing your interpretations and how they eventually pan out. Every step you take is an important lesson—especially your mistakes.

ROADMAP TO SUCCESS

Objective	Course of Action
Sentiment analysis fills the gap between technical and fundamental analysis.	**Technical Analysis** • No emotion involved. • No news accounts. • No fundamental influence. • 100% charts interpretation. **Fundamental Analysis** • Numbers-driven; financial analysis. • Almost purely subjective measurements.

Sentiment analysis factors in the human element in investing.	Emotions play a large role in the everyday market.
	• Fear and greed create fluctuations in supply and demand.
	• Herd mentality never works at the extremes of the market.
	  –Contrarian approach assumes the crowd is always wrong.
	  –Takes advantage of price swings caused by high levels of fear and greed.
	• Measuring the market's mood is necessary to identify these swings.

Tools Used in Sentiment Analysis	Emotions (sentiment) can be identified by observing investor behavior as measured by how they're investing.
	• Optimism measurements:
	  –Excessive call option buying: low put/call ratio.
	  –Volatility Index (VIX) is at the low end of its range.
	  –The retail investor becomes very active.
	  –Net purchases of mutual funds versus redemptions.
	  –Low liquidity (cash) is on sidelines.
	  –Advance/decline ratio is very strong, near historical highs.
	  –Closed-end funds trading at a premium to their NAVs.
	  –Technical indicators signal overbought condition.
	• Pessimism measurements:
	  –Volatility Index (VIX) is at high end of its range.
	  –Excessive put option buying: high put/call ratio.
	  –Retail investor leaves the market.
	  –Net redemptions of mutual funds versus purchases.
	  –Advance/decline line is weak, near historical lows.

–Closed-end funds trading at a discount to their NAVs.

–Technical indicators signal oversold condition.

Contrarian Approach	**The contrarian approach assumes the "crowd" is always wrong, especially at market extremes.** • A strong bullish sentiment by the majority of investors is a bearish signal. If everyone's already invested, who's left to buy? • A strong bearish sentiment by the majority of investors is a bearish signal. If everyone's already sold that's going to sell and if everyone's already out, what's going to cause the market to drop further? • The crowd is usually correct in the middle of a trend. As the market gets overbought or oversold, near-term or at the ends of a trend, the crowd will become increasingly bullish or bearish, an incorrect stance. • The majority cannot be correct. Betting against the crowd is what the contrarian approach calls for.
Assessing the Market's Mood	**The Volatility Index (VIX)** • Measures call and put buying in the two front months (the current month and the one following). • Calculates the difference in their volumes. • This number has a typical range of between 20 and 30. A low number (low 20s and below) indicates strong bullish sentiment; contrarian indicator—bearish implication. • High number (upper 20s and above) indicates growing bearish sentiment; contrarian indicator—bullish implication. • "When the VIX is high it's time to buy; when the VIX is low it's time to go."

Implied volatility as a measure of stock and index sentiment.	**Implied volatility measures the premium of an option against what it should be trading at.** (Based on the Black-Scholes model of options pricing.)
	• Three dimensions of an option (how it is valued by the market):
	    –Price of the underlying stock.
	    –The time remaining in the contract itself.
	    –The implied volatility (IV) of the option.
	• The demand (or lack thereof) causes the IV to fluctuate in value.
	• Compare the IV to its historical range (historical volatility).
	• A high IV indicates high premium is in the option pricing due to high demand (greed or fear is growing). IV is not sustainable.
	• A low IV indicates low demand, indifference.
	• A below-average or above-average IV will eventually correct itself; the emotional aspects of its price will return to a more balanced level.
	• Buy low IV, sell high IV!

Published sentiment (psychological) indicators indicate daily and/or weekly fluctuations in the mood of the market.

Investor's Business Daily **lists a number of indicators daily in the "General Markets and Sectors" section (located at the back of the first section).**

- *Public/NYSE Specialist Short Sales:* Research indicates specialists to be accurate barometers of future market direction.

    –When ratio is high (>.6) (specialists not short selling), market likely to move higher.

    –When ratio is low (<.35) (specialists short selling), market likely to move lower.

- *Ratio of Price Premiums in Puts versus Calls:* The higher the premium (IV) the higher the greed (or fear). Look for a trend.

- *Mutual Fund Share Purchases/Redemptions:* The more purchases, the more cash mutual fund managers have to work with. A number that drops means people are pulling cash out of the market and is a bearish sign. Contrary indicators are when the ratio is extremely low (majority of investors want out, period) is a good time to put cash to work.

- *Nasdaq Daily Trading Volume as % of NYSE Daily Volume:* The OTC (Nasdaq) used to be referred to as the secondary market, because it was comprised more of lower-cap issues that moved after the NYSE and AMEX had climbed. Not so anymore. Questionable ratio these days.

- *Number of Stock Splits in Investor's Business Daily 6,000 (prior 30 days):* The higher the market, the more stock splits is the basic premise behind this reading. More splits amounts to greater supply, but if the demand doesn't keep pace, this is a bearish condition. Not always a reliable one either.

- *New Issues in Last Year as % of All Stocks on NYSE:* A hot new issue market usually goes with a more speculative environment, which is often associated with a market top.

- *Price-to-Book Value of Dow Jones Industrial Average and the Price to Earnings (P/E) Ratio of Dow Jones Industrial Average:*
    These two fundamental methods for stock valuation are best taken in a historical perspective. When these readings are at relatively high levels, the fundamentalist sees this as an overpriced market, another signal of a pending correction/bear market. Low readings, of course indicate fire-sale prices.

- *Current Dividend Yield of Dow Jones Industrial Average:* A low current dividend yield equates to a high stock price . A high dividend yield means the stock price (the divisor in the equation) is low.

Graphic Displays of Psychological Indicators in *IBD*.	• *% of Investment Advisors Bullish or Bearish:* These indicators are derived from a poll taken by Investors Intelligence, a New Rochelle, New York–based advisory service that publishes a newsletter that surveys 130 advisory firms and then publishes the results. They discovered that most advisory firms are wrong (when measured as a group) due to the fact that they're trend followers. They precede the market, and are considered to be leading indicators. –Bullish chart: Above 55% = Bearish; below 35% = Bullish –Bearish chart: Above 50% = Bullish; below 20% = Bullish • *Short Interest Ratio:* This represents short interest as compared (percentage-wise) to total volume of all exchanges. Look for the trend in this percentage. Increasing percentages is a bullish indicator, as fear is rising. A move up by the market would create a short squeeze. Rising prices would force the short sellers to buy their stock back, pushing stocks even higher. • *Odd-Lot Short Sellers:* This is the ratio of short sells by odd-lotters to total odd lot volume. (Odd lot is less than 100 shares, and is an indication of the retail investor.) Odd-lot activity is a very reliable contrary indicator due to their knack for selling at the bottom and buying at the top.
Put/Call Ratios	Measures the difference between put and call buyers. • When put buying becomes rampant, the majority of people are convinced the stock or index is heading lower; the opposite is true if call buying is increasing. • The put/call ratio is a beacon that alerts the astute trader to sentiment extremes, the concentrations of buyers doing the wrong thing. • The further the OEX put/call ratio is below 1.00, the more bearish it is; between 1.00 and 1.25 is neutral, and above 1.25 is bullish. • The CBOE lists these numbers (www.cboe.com). The *Wall Street Journal*, *IBD*, and *Barron's* are good sources.
Mutual Fund Sales and Redemptions	The more purchases the more cash mutual fund managers have to work with. A number that drops means people are pulling cash out of the market and is a bearish sign. Contrary indicators are when the ratio is extremely low (majority of investors want out, period), is a good time to put cash to work.
Advance/ Decline Ratio	**Shows the number of advancing (gaining in value) stocks versus the number of declining issues.** • A strong (positive) number is a good indicator a rally is solid. • A weak number in an advancing market means the advance is limited in its breadth, and the rally is therefore suspect.

	• A declining market with a lopsided A/D line (more negatives than positive) means there is a widespread retracement in prices occurring, and signals overall weakness in the market. • A number that's almost even shows that bears and bulls are nearly even—a sign of a choppy (trendless) market.
Rampart Time Index	**This indicator (a regular feature in *Barron's*) is indicated two ways:** • The Composite Call Index: The higher the number the greater the optimism. The higher the number the more bearish the signal. • The Composite Put Index: The higher the number the greater the pessimism. The higher the number the more bullish the signal.
Closed-End Fund Indicator	**An excellent barometer of the retail investor's sentiment. It is a contrary indicator.** • A premium to the NAV signals optimism, and is a bearish signal. • A discount to the NAV signals pessimism, and is bullish.
The Media	This is a difficult indicator to assess. Listening to the content of the media (print and broadcast) can help you ascertain the mood of the public at large. This is a tenet in Dow Theory, and signals a top or bottom, depending on whether the tone is optimistic or pessimistic, respectively.
News Events	An adverse event or announcement can cause an overreaction in the market, sending a stock abnormally high or low. Carefully evaluating the real impact on the long-term prospects of the event/announcement can sometimes indicate a good buying (or shorting) opportunity. Various option strategies that assume a contrary stance can take advantage of a return to reason by the market.
Volume	This is best summed up by stating: "Volume precedes price." • Volume can indicate a shift in sentiment, even without a price movement, as insiders and astute investors begin to either accumulate or distribute stock. • If volume accompanies a big move up or down, there is conviction being shown and it should be followed by the investor; "don't fight the tape." • Rising prices and decreasing volumes indicates a lack of conviction; weak conviction. • Receding prices with decreasing volumes indicates a lack of sellers; a good time to buy at the dips. • Volume should increase with prices to confirm advance. • If volume increases with a retracement, it is a sign of further weakness.

Capitulation	The last remaining bull has thrown in the towel. Capitulation is the hallmark of investor resignation, when pessimism and fear are at their highest.

- A good sign of a bottom in a bear market.
- Tough to see clearly in a bull market.
- Short covering?
- Not as dramatic as a major sell-off.

Comparison Indicators	There are a number of indicators sites and techniques that utilize the power of comparison to unveil the strengths and weaknesses of various stocks or economic shifts.

- **Gold Prices**—Gold rises in price when uncertainty and fear increase. Wars, inflation, political events can all send gold higher. The CBOE has gold index options ($GOX).
- **Index Futures**—Commodity and futures traders actually make a market for the future value of various indexes. To track these, head to the Chicago Mercantile Exchange (www.cme.com). Futures are an excellent way to watch emotions, as they are swayed intraday by news events and so on.

Useful Web Sites	**ICEFI Market Sentiment Indicator:** (www.linkindia.com/icefi/index.htm) This web site provides a background of sentiment analysis as well as their proprietary model that utilizes closed-end funds as an indicator.

American Association of Individual Investors: (www.aaii.com) Content on this site deals with "Behavioral Finance" including:

- Overconfidence
- Fear of Regret
- Myopic Risk Aversion

Quick Term Timing: (qtt.com) Uses sentiment analysis in short-term trading. Caveat Emptor.

The Wall Street Detective: (www.wallstdet.com) Joe Duarte has put together a nice site for sentiment analysis, and will send you daily updates via e-mail, using his own models. The price is right too.

Investor's Business Daily: (investors.com) *IBD* provides the greatest psychological indicators in their daily paper, but as of this writing, they do not provide it online. Worth a serious look.

Optionetics.com Platinum: (optionsanalysis.com) For option prices, the measurement of implied volatility (IV) is a tremendous tool for measuring the "expectation" of price movement. This site offers a multitude of option tools, volatility charts, and helpful portfolio management.

11

Studying the Masters

One of the most important things I learned at the Harvard Business School was how to attack a problem when I knew very little about the subject. This ability has served me well, especially when I first decided to try my luck as an investor. My first task was to read as much as I could about the greatest investors and businessmen of all time. Just as each civilization builds upon the mistakes and triumphs of past empires, I knew that I needed to trace the footsteps of these innovative tycoons. Exactly how had they climbed the ladders to success? What kind of approach did they use to divine order in the investment universe?

I can honestly say that it was well worth the many hours I spent in the library reading their books and studying their accomplishments. Each historical figure provided an important piece of the puzzle. However, since time is of the essence and in incredibly short supply these days, what follows is a brief synopsis of some of the brightest stars in the evolution of the markets and the most prominent business-people and industrialists. This list is not meant in any way to be comprehensive. It is simply a list of some of the most successful role models and effective teachers in the business. I hope that they will give you additional insights into what it takes to learn how to trade profitably and spot rising stars in the business world.

MARKET MAGICIANS

Benjamin Graham

London born, Graham graduated from Columbia University with a B.S. in 1914 and immediately began a career on Wall Street as a messenger for a brokerage firm. Within five years, he was made a partner of the firm earning a six-digit yearly salary. In 1926, he teamed up with Jerome Newman to create a successful investment partnership. Three years later, Graham lost most of his fortune in the stock market crash of 1929.

Although the investment partnership of Graham-Newman survived, he returned to the halls of Columbia University to be a professor. With help from colleague David Dodd, Graham completed the first edition of *Security Analysis* in 1934—now considered the bible of fundamental analysis. Two-thirds of a century and five editions later, Graham's timeless wisdom still commands attention and attracts a loyal following among investors worldwide.

Considered the pioneer of fundamental analysis, Graham is most remembered as the author of two very important books, Security Analysis *(1934) and* The Intelligent Investor *(1949).*

Graham began by clearly defining the word *investment* and setting it apart from the word *speculative*. To this end, Graham wrote, "An investment operation is one which, upon thorough analysis, promises safety of principal and a satisfactory return. Operations not meeting these requirements are speculative." (Benjamim Graham and David Dodd, *Security Analysis*, McGraw-Hill, 1934.) This definition enabled Graham to include stocks in the category of investments, a category formerly thought to be the primary domain of bonds. Graham worked to empower his students and clients by teaching them a systematic approach to finding undervalued stocks and bonds through quantitative analysis. In short, *Security Analysis* was the first book to advocate a system for the useful analysis of quantitative factors to methodically select a diverse portfolio of investment instruments.

Diversification is also one of Graham's major doctrines. Graham thought that all stocks have a similar life cycle composed of four basic stages:

1. *Development:* In the earliest stages, increased sales lead to accelerated earnings. These earnings are systematically reinvested into the company to promote growth.

2. *Expansion:* The company grows in leaps and bounds while increasing profits and earnings simultaneously. The sky's the limit.

3. *Maturity:* Revenues stabilize and expansion hits a plateau.

4. *Decline:* Revenues decline and the company's profits and earning start to diminish. Jump ship.

Although buying a stock in its rapid-expansion phase is the most favorable time to invest, Graham noted that determining exactly where a stock is in its life cycle can be quite difficult. In addition, the price of a stock can be pumped up when earnings and profits run high, slowing its continued growth. Instead, Graham advocated a systematic approach for finding stocks that are selling below their intrinsic value. He encouraged investors to analyze a variety of factors including earnings, dividends, net worth, and future prospects to determine a company's intrinsic value. Graham argued that if the gap between the stock's price and the company's intrinsic value were large enough, this margin of safety would preclude the stock from unexpected losses.

Finally, Graham eschewed market optimism because he believed it allowed human emotions to enter the market decision-making process. Graham sought to keep himself beyond the emotions of greed and fear by arming himself with the facts and following a systematic analysis of a stock's accomplishments. I admire his tenacity.

Philip Fisher

After graduating from Stanford University in the early 1920s, Philip Fisher began his illustrious investment career as a bank analyst. In 1931, he became his own boss at Fisher & Company, an investment-counseling firm he owned and operated. Fisher knew that for a company to succeed, it had to grow by manufacturing products, or through providing services that would serve the needs of consumers into the decades ahead. In other words, it had to be ready and able to change with the times. To this end, Fisher avidly watched a company's management team and questioned their integrity and style. He reviewed how the company passed on difficult information to shareholders, how they treated employees, and their turnover rate. He also found it important to compare different companies in the same industry. He valued a company's idiosyncrasies because those factors often made one company stand out from the others.

Fisher was a great believer in the qualitative analysis of companies over the long term, and this became the mainstay of his investment approach. He looked for investments that could maintain higher growth levels than industry averages and honed his ability to size up a stock's capacity to reproduce cash.

Fisher believed that you had to immerse yourself in as much information as you could find out about a company to be able to judge it as a possible stock investment. But listening to what a company had to say about itself wasn't enough. Fisher also paid attention to what the Street had to say about a company. He viewed gossip, rumors, and personal opinions to be an integral part of a stock's character. Fisher knew that a stock's propensity to make or break it on Wall Street was the culmination of a multitude of variables. So although it took an incredible amount of time and energy to complete a thorough investigation of a company, Fisher believed it worthwhile since most of his investments were long-term in nature.

Warren Buffett

As a student at Columbia's Graduate School of Business, Warren Buffett studied under Benjamin Graham. In 1954, Buffett joined Graham's investment firm and became deeply engrossed in Graham's investing techniques. When Graham retired in 1956, Buffett returned to his hometown in Omaha, Nebraska. In 1957, his friends and family invested $105,000 in his investment limited partnership. It blossomed into a billion-dollar empire. If a person had invested $10,000 when Buffett began his career in 1956, and had kept that original amount invested, that person would have been a millionaire by the mid-1990s.

Generally, Buffett risked his capital on the long-term growth of a few select businesses and stuck with those investments through thick and thin. Additionally, it is well known that Buffett avoided the use of leverage, futures, dynamic hedging, modern portfolio analysis, and other convoluted, theoretical models acclaimed by academics. Instead, Buffett drew on his character and his ability to make decisions that were opposite of the prevailing opinion at the time. His patience, discipline, and rational thinking are what separated him from others in the industry, and are certainly qualities that an individual needs to possess in order to succeed in the investment arena.

Buffett's secret to success was a long-term philosophy grounded in buying stock in companies that were undervalued and hanging on to those companies until their hidden value was realized.

Focusing on buying interests in public and private companies, Buffett purchased a controlling interest in a textile company called Berkshire Hathaway in 1962. Eventually, Buffett became the chairman of the company and worked to reinvent the textile manufacturer into a well-diversified, thriving enterprise that deployed its excess capital into different businesses. Following his long-term value philosophy, Buffett searched for and investigated companies that showed potential for long-term appreciation that would help to increase the return on investment of Berkshire Hathaway. The first outside interest that Berkshire Hathaway ventured into was the insurance business, and the up-front cash generation of this business made it very lucrative at the time. Additionally, Berkshire became involved with and plowed capital into the banking and publishing industries. These additional businesses helped to create a diversified company that had significant cash flow and the potential for incredible growth. The rest is history.

Charles Schwab

Charles Schwab started investing in 1957, and in 1974 he became a pioneer in the discount brokerage business. He had the vision to provide average Americans with information, investment tools, and easy, low-cost access to the stock market. Today Charles Schwab & Company is the nation's largest discount brokerage firm. Mr. Schwab has recently been selected by *Money Magazine* as one of the seven people who most influence the United States economy.

There are a couple of fundamental beliefs that have driven Charles Schwab in his personal investing as well as given him the vision to create the largest discount brokerage firm. First, he feels that individuals have the ability to take control of their financial future, and that investing should be a regular part of every household's routine. This stems from the fact that Mr. Schwab feels that no one is going to be more concerned about a person's financial well-being than that individual person. Secondly, Schwab believes that investing is a long-term process that takes time to develop and mature. Therefore, it is critical for the individual to begin that process as soon as possible through investing in common stocks. Over time, stocks have outperformed all other kinds of investments, including bonds, CDs, and U.S. government securities. Schwab feels that of all the many investments that are available, stocks provide the best opportunity for growth over time, and they are the instruments of choice for the long-term investor.

> *Schwab's vision was to provide the common person with access to the moneymaking power of the stock market. His commitment to this vision made his brokerage firm the standard of excellence in the discount brokerage industry.*

The primary reason that Schwab has such a passion for common stock is that there is no other investment vehicle that has the desire to grow like a company, and when an investor purchases the common shares of a company, they are buying directly into that company's growth. He feels that this relationship is unique to equities. It is something that each individual has the ability to benefit from and should take advantage of.

Peter Lynch

Peter Lynch is known for taking a simple approach to investing and finding companies that have the ability to provide superior returns over time. His method is to find companies whose products he knows and understands. He starts out by looking at companies with products the average person uses on a daily basis. Additionally, it is important to understand the economic climate in which these companies are operating. Lynch believes in knowing and comprehending the story behind the company. It's not enough just to track the price of the stock. He thinks investors need to feel comfortable with the companies in their portfolios, truly believing in what they do and/or make. It's simple: If you don't fully know the story behind your investment, then it is more likely you'll be shaken out of a great investment during market corrections. This, in turn, can cause you to miss an opportunity to purchase more shares when the price is low, and the company's doing just fine.

> *Frequently called the #1 money manager of all time, Peter Lynch is the former manager of the Fidelity Magellan Fund and the coauthor of* One Up on Wall Street *and* Beating the Street. *Under Lynch's management, The Magellan Fund went from 20 million in 1977 to 14 billion by his retirement in 1990.*

Mr. Lynch believes investors should be in for the long haul and avoid trying to time the market. Most people who attempt to time the market fail; they are buying when the market is about to drop and selling when the market is putting in a bottom. There was a study done found that illustrates the importance of always being invested in the market. During the years from 1963 to 1993, the market provided an average return on 11.83%. However, if you were not invested during the 10 best days during that period, then your return dropped to 10.17%. If you weren't invested for the best 30 days, then your return decreased to 8%; and lastly, if you were not invested for the best 90 days, then your return fell to 3.28%. Lynch believes that the true way to generate great wealth is to start saving and investing at a young age in good, quality companies and sticking with them through tough market environments.

William O'Neil

It has been said by many that William J. O'Neil, founder of the *Investor's Business Daily* newspaper, has done more to help the individual investor succeed and prosper than any other market guru in the investment community. His main objective was to teach ordinary people how the American economy and market really work, and explain in basic terms how investors can materially benefit.

Mr. O'Neil is the model growth stock investor. His investment philosophy is to invest in thriving companies that are developing and creating new products, new services, and new inventions. He created an acronym—C-A-N-S-L-I-M to help investors remember what they should be looking for when searching for a new company to invest in. The C stands for current quarterly earnings; the A stands for annual earnings increases; the N represents new products, new management, and new highs; the S refers to supply and demand; the L stands for leader or laggard; the I represents institutional sponsorship; and the M refers to the overall current market direction.

Mr. O'Neil is best known for founding the Investor's Business Daily *newspaper and writing the book* How to Make Money in Stocks *(McGraw-Hill, Sept. 1994). His C-A-N-S-L-I-M approach has helped millions of people understand what they need to look for in a promising investment.*

Mr. O'Neil believes that investors should take a longer-term investing approach to the stock market and follow the guidelines that are emphasized in his C-A-N-S-L-I-M formula. He feels that the U.S. economy will continue to grow and remain on its upward path, which will inevitably lead to higher prices in the stock market. What is the formula for this continued economic growth? Mr. O'Neil says that it is "free people, in a free country, with strong desires and the incentives to unceasingly improve their circumstances."

John Neff

A prominent figure in the contemporary world of investments, John Neff recently retired as the manager of the Van Windsor Fund. Under his direction, Windsor became the largest mutual fund and actually surpassed market performance for 22 out of 31 years.

Deemed a contrarian investor by the investment community, Neff preferred to be called a low-P/E investor. Throughout his career, he disregarded the prominent and popular investment philosophies that permeated the investment community and pioneered an innovative investing approach—*Measured Participation*—based on a low-P/E strategy that uses fundamental analysis and common sense to locate undervalued stocks. Eschewing the big growth stocks of his time, Neff found success by placing his bets on the inexpensive, underperforming stocks. This method paid off in huge rewards for both Neff and his investors.

John Neff is the contrarian hero of the contemporary investment community. His investment philosophies are disseminated in his best-selling book, John Neff on Investing *(John Wiley & Sons, Oct. 1999).*

Neff is also a master of knowing when to sell. "Successful stocks don't tell you when to sell," he states. "When you feel like bragging, it's probably time to sell." Time and again, he has proven that his unique approach to investing pays off big and provides huge returns to those who have patience and perseverance.

Linda Bradford Raschke

Raschke initially fell in love with the markets when, as a child, she helped her father look through stock charts for specific patterns. After graduating from college, she unsuccessfully tried to get a job as a stockbroker and eventually took to hanging out on the floor of the Pacific Stock Exchange before starting her job each day as a financial analyst. Eventually a local took her under his wing and introduced her to options trading. She quickly developed her own style by trading options on stocks and indexes before evolving into a futures trader. In 1980, she began her illustrious career as a floor trader on the Pacific Stock Exchange, both as a floor trader and as a money manager, before moving on to the Philadelphia Stock Exchange. In 1986, a serious horse-riding accident forced her to become an off-floor trader specializing in short-term trading. Her phenomenal success in this complex arena gained her the sole woman interview in Jack D. Schwager's best-seller *The New Market Wizards*.

Unlike other buy-and-hold stalwarts, Raschke has made her mark with an aggressive trading style, using methods of technical analysis to point to entry and exit points. Her emphasis on having a plan in place before the trade is opened is a basic doctrine she follows, and apparently it works very well for her style of trading. One pattern that Raschke focuses on is based on finding markets that move from relative lows to relative highs in a matter of days.

As one of the few successful women in the investment business, Raschke encourages women who have the confidence to get involved. She believes that performance is all that counts and that women possess unique qualities that may even help them to acquire and maintain success once it is achieved.

Her worst month of trading set her back just 2%, and her triple-digit returns have made her a sought-after money manager, although she doesn't openly solicit money. She claims that her trades have an approximately 70% profitability rate. She attributes her success in being able to predict market patterns and advises novice traders to immerse themselves in the markets and learn to specialize in one market or pattern before moving on to another.

LEGENDARY INDUSTRIALISTS AND BUSINESSPEOPLE

Andrew Carnegie (1835–1919)

Andrew Carnegie started his first job at age 12, working as a bobbin boy in a cotton factory. He studied hard in night school and eventually got a job as a messenger in a telegraph office. At 18, he became private secretary and personal telegrapher for Thomas Scott, a superintendent of the Pennsylvania Railroad Company. He rose swiftly and succeeded Scott as superintendent of the railroad's Pittsburgh division. At this time, he began investing in the Woodruff Sleeping Car Company. This company was the original holder of the Pullman patents, enabling Carnegie to start his fortune when they launched the first successful sleeping cars on American railroads. He was making $50,000 a year by the time he was 30 years old.

By the time he was 40, Carnegie had consolidated his holdings into his own company, Carnegie Steel. He purchased the coke fields and iron-ore deposits that furnished the raw materials for steelmaking, as well as the ships and railroads that transported these supplies to his mills. Using innovative new British steelmaking processes, plus state-of-the-art assembly production techniques including detailed cost- and production-accounting procedures, the Carnegie Steel Company was able to dominate the American steel industry of the time. A major battle with the unions hurt his reputation and penetrated his seemingly bulletproof business psyche. After years of head-to-head battle with J. P. Morgan, in 1901 Carnegie sold the Carnegie Steel Company to J. P. Morgan's newly formed United States Steel Corporation for $250 million.

Even as a young man Carnegie had always been keen on expressing his opinions regarding political and social matters. The June 1889 issue of the *North American Review* published his most famous article, which came to be called the "Gospel of Wealth." Historians agree that Carnegie would have loved the immediacy of the Internet, especially the fact that his words could be available at any time to millions. In terms of ascertaining how Carnegie's skills could shed a light on picking successful stock tips, he reportedly replied when Mark Twain asked Carnegie his business secrets of success, "Put all your eggs in one basket and then watch that basket!"

Carnegie believed that anyone who accumulates great wealth has a duty to use the surplus wealth for "the improvement of mankind" in philanthropic causes. His greatest and best-remembered philosophical doctrine held that "A man who dies rich dies disgraced."

John D. Rockefeller (1839–1937)

Educated in public schools in his hometown of Richford, New York, John D. Rockefeller started his first job as a bookkeeper at age 16. When he was 23 he went into business with Samuel Andrews, who had invented a new low-cost processing procedure for refining crude oil. By 1865, he had the largest refinery in the area. From then on, Rockefeller concentrated exclusively on making money in the oil business.

In 1870, Rockefeller incorporated his new enterprise with a few associates and called it the Standard Oil Company of Ohio. Since Rockefeller put an emphasis on bottom-line operations, the company was able to acquire pipelines and terminal facilities and negotiated with railroads for favored rates on its shipments of oil. After popular protest, these arrangements were canceled within three months, but most of Rockefeller's competitors in the Cleveland area had already been forced to sell out to his combine. By 1872, Standard Oil controlled nearly all the refineries in Cleveland. By 1882, it had a near monopoly of the oil business in the United States. In 1881, Rockefeller and his associates placed the stock of Standard of Ohio and its affiliates in other states under the control of a board of trustees, with Rockefeller at the head. Thus they established the first major U.S. trust and set a pattern of organization for other monopolies.

Many regarded the aggressive competitive practices of Standard Oil as ruthless. As public hostility toward monopolies grew, some industrialized states began to enact antimonopoly laws, culminating in the passage of the Sherman Antitrust Act of 1890 by the U.S. Congress. In 1892, the Ohio Supreme Court held that the Standard Oil Trust was a monopoly, and in violation of an Ohio law prohibiting monopolies. Rockefeller evaded the decision by dissolving the trust and transferring its properties to companies in other states with interlocking directorates so that his same board of trustees controlled the operations of the affiliated companies. In 1899, these companies were brought back together in a holding company—Standard Oil Company of New Jersey. This company existed until 1911, when the U.S. Supreme Court declared it in violation of the Sherman Antitrust Act, and therefore illegal.

As the father of corporate monopolies, Rockefeller set the standard for outsmarting the competition using any means possible. In response to his Machiavellian techniques, antitrust laws are now in place to undo any attempts by corporations to follow in his illustrious footsteps.

J. Paul Getty (1892–1976)

After graduating from the University of Oxford in 1913, Jean Paul Getty, son of an oil millionaire, worked as an independent wildcatter, buying and selling oil leases near Tulsa, Oklahoma. In the beginning, he worked as his own geologist, legal adviser, drilling superintendent, explosives expert, and roughneck. But J.P. proved to be a gifted entrepreneur and eventually became known as one of the world's richest men.

By 1916, at 24 years old, Getty had to decide what to do with his first million. His father advised him to use his money as an investment in the development and operation of businesses that would provide jobs and wealth for countless employees. He set about turning the world upside down in pursuit of his oil empire.

In the field, the bigger oil companies housed expensive consultants and administrative personnel in fancy digs, while the wildcatters used funky old trucks and muddy cars as their offices. During the 1920s, he moved his base of operations to California and set about gaining control of several large independent oil companies by relying on his own instincts, experiences, and resources learned from his wildcatting days. His most lucrative venture was a 60-year oil concession that he obtained in Saudi Arabia in 1949. The profits from this contract built up his massive financial empire and vaulted him into the billionaire class by the mid-1950s.

In later life, whenever Getty was asked to give advice on gaining and using great wealth, he would always refer back to the lessons he learned earning and investing his first million dollars.

Rupert Murdoch (1931–)

Murdoch received his master's degree at Worcester College, Oxford, England, in 1953 and worked for a while as an editor on Lord Beaverbrook's *London Daily Express*. It was here that he initially acquired real experience in the frontline trenches of sensationalist journalism that would influence his entire career as a publisher. After his father died in 1954, he returned to Australia to claim his inheritance of the *Adelaide Sunday Mail* and the *Adelaide News*. Often writing its banner headlines himself, he quickly transformed the *Adelaide News* into a paper dominated by his trademark style: tabloid reporting of sex and scandal.

In 1969, Murdoch went about obtaining his first British newspaper—the *News of the World of London*. By this time, he had a proven formula for circulation promotion and a relatively conservative editorial signature although his papers continued to feature flashy articles about crime, sex, and scandals along with poignant human-interest stories and sensationalist sports reporting.

In 1985, Murdoch became a naturalized U.S. citizen in New York City. By 1993 he had purchased from the Hearst Corporation and successfully relaunched the tabloids the *New York Post*, the *Star*, and the *Boston Herald*. The 1980s and 1990s saw maximum growth for Murdoch as he bought and sold a slew of American publications. Gradually he adopted the style of each paper he purchased, seeing the value in preserving the styles of his more conventional and respected newspapers and periodicals.

As of January 2000, Rupert Murdoch's News Corporation—now a $28 billion conglomerate—controls 20th Century-Fox, the Fox broadcasting network, the Fox News cable channel, 25 magazines, 132 newspapers (including the *New York Post* and the *London Times*), HarperCollins books, the Los Angeles Dodgers, the National Rugby League in Australia, and an assortment of other business operations.

Murdoch's empire is both respected and feared by his peers. Viacom CEO Sumner Redstone said that Murdoch "basically wants to conquer the world." Both Disney CEO Michael Eisner and Time Warner CEO Gerald Levin mentioned Murdoch as the one media executive whom they respect and fear the most, and whose moves they study incessantly.

Bill Gates (1955–)

By the age of 13, Bill Gates was already starting his career in computers by programming his first software program. At 15, he helped establish a group of programmers in high school, who set up their school's payroll system on computer, and founded Traf-O-Data, a traffic-counting systems company that was successfully marketed to local governments. Later at Harvard University in the early 1970s, Gates developed the programming language BASIC for the first microcomputer programming language used on large computers. At 20 years old, he and Paul Allen dropped out of Harvard and together they cofounded Microsoft in 1975.

In 1981, Microsoft licensed its newly developed operating system called MS-DOS to none other than International Business Machines Corporation (IBM), regarded at the time as the undisputed leader of computer technologies. For the rest of the 1980s, IBM and MS-DOS set the technical standard for the newly emerging personal computer industry. Miraculously, Gates managed to keep Microsoft from being swallowed up by the corporate IBM machine. His independent stance made IBM reliant on the little upstart company for the essential software needed to operate PCs and made Gates a 31-year-old billionaire by 1986. His fortune has increased to the point that by the 1990s Bill Gates was estimated to be the wealthiest private individual in the history of the world.

In 1999, the U.S. Justice Department's antitrust division initiated a lawsuit against Microsoft charging the company with, among other technical fine points, illegally tying its Web browser to its new Windows operating systems. Gates's many rivals, especially those out of California's Silicon Valley, have depicted him as imposing, disingenuous, and intent on making a profit from all the electronic transactions of the world. Meanwhile, his many defenders have long recognized his amazing business genius. I find it quite humorous that in his 1995 best-seller *The Road Ahead* he observed, "Success is a lousy teacher. It seduces smart people into thinking they can't lose." He may have been a bit intuitive of the current antitrust verdict declaring Microsoft to be split in two. He is of course appealing this decision.

Gates is empowered by his ability to think outside the box and discover new ways to make computers more effective through innovative software and indispensable components.

Paul Allen (1953–)

Paul Allen was introduced to computers as a student at Seattle's Lakeside High School in the late 1960s. Frustrated by limited access to mainframes, he and his friend Bill Gates dreamed of a day when there would be a miniature version on every desktop. As a programmer at Honeywell in Boston, Allen read an advertisement for a microcomputer kit in the January 1975 issue of *Popular Electronics*. He convinced Gates to team up with him and create software for it. Intel and Motorola followed with more powerful microprocessors and Radio Shack, Apple, and IBM designed personal computers that used software designed by Allen.

Allen and Bill Gates soon thereafter started a new company called Microsoft. Allen became the head of research and new product development, the company's senior technology position. He championed and helped engineer many of the company's most successful products, including MS-DOS, MS Word, Windows, and the Microsoft

Mouse. He retains his seat on the Microsoft board and remains its second-largest stockholder. He pursues his vision through an array of handpicked, independent companies, each with its own special capabilities and culture. Allen's team looks for established companies with proven management talent, a solid business plan, demonstrated performance, and innovative products or services that can be part of their "Wired World." Synergy can take the form of actual joint projects, or can simply be the exchange of ideas at conferences Allen hosts for his CEOs. The cross-pollination is ad hoc and unforced. Allen believes the companies should be managed independently. "As our strategy evolves, we are pioneering a support structure that the business world hasn't seen before. We're not just breaking ground in specific technologies, but also in the way we invest and our approach to developing these investments."

In place of the typical acquire-merge-rationalize-downsize approach, Allen seeks to add value by contributing his own insights into additional uses for companies' technologies and by exploiting potential synergy between companies.

Richard Branson (1950–)

Richard Branson founded Virgin Records in 1970 as a mail-order record sales company and later opened his first record shop in London. In 1972, he decided to take matters in to his own hands and built a recording studio in Oxfordshire, then started signing his own handpicked artists. In 1977, Richard signed the infamous and groundbreaking punk rock group, the Sex Pistols, after the group was turned down by every other label in Great Britain. They were a phenomenal success and put Virgin Records on the map. Over time, Virgin Records came to represent many music superstars, including Steve Winwood, Paula Abdul, Phil Collins, Peter Gabriel, Bryan Ferry, Janet Jackson, and the legendary Rolling Stones. In 1992, the Virgin Music Group—record labels, music publishing, and recording studios—was sold to Thorn EMI in a $1 billion deal.

In 1984, Branson started a whole new venture—Virgin Atlantic Airways. He founded the airline on the concept of offering a competitive and high-quality upperclass and economy service. These days, it is the second largest international airline in Great Britain.

He is quoted as saying that he dropped out of school at age 15 because he wasn't enjoying the way he was being taught. His lack of enjoyment led him to start a magazine to try to change the world for the better. That choice led him into the world of capitalism and he has succeeded ever since by designing superior services and products and taking chances.

Perhaps the secret to Branson's heroic capital conquests is his innate ability to improve the way businesses are run. His improvements have led to his own success and increased the standards by which his competitors do business.

George Soros (1930–)

Widely known as "the man who broke the Bank of England," he earned international notoriety in 1992 when he speculated that the British pound, would lose
value. When the pound's value did go down, he then repaid his loans at the reduced
value—reaping a cool $1 billion. In its 28-year history, Soros's Quantum invest-
ment fund—started in 1969—is universally recognized as the most successful
hedge fund ever. Soros was one of the first to use the loosely regulated realm of the
island of Curaçao as a base for his operations. He was soon a master of cross-
currency investing, which forced the rest of the investment community to recognize
the developing interdependence of the U.S. economy and geopolitical events.

In early 1997, he was accused of deliberately pursuing the devaluation of Thai-
land's currency, the baht, and Malaysia's ringgit by speculating that the value of
both currencies would drop. Soros excused himself and his company by claiming
that by the time of the devaluations, his funds had already become active buyers of
the currencies, believing that they had already hit bottom. There are widely held
opinions in the financial community that the reason he went after and broke the
Bank of England in 1992 was not because he wanted to make an extra billion dollars, which he did, but mainly because he wanted his social and political positions
to be taken seriously by governments and world leaders.

---

*Since Andrew Carnegie, there hasn't been a more flamboyant and committed
philanthropist than billionaire speculator George Soros. His methods and
morals are often the subject of extreme controversy, especially his most
recent active support for the legalization of medical marijuana.*

Anita Roddick (1943–)

In 1976, a 33-year-old housewife recognized the need for natural beauty products.
With a £12,000 stake, entrepreneur Anita Roddick opened the doors to her first
store, The Body Shop. Her idea quickly took off and her small shop in Brighton,
England, rapidly grew into an international giant as franchising enabled hundreds of
people to open stores all over the world. Today, there are more than a thousand retail outlets in more than 40 countries.

But Roddick's vision was never confined to the making of millions. From the start,
her slogan "Trade Not Aid" has brought her to the forefront of change. Not only has
she fought long and hard to challenge the stereotypes perpetuated by the cosmetics industry, but Roddick also used her company to campaign in favor of animal and human
rights protection. Her devotion to social and environmental causes has helped to define
the new-age concept of corporate responsibility. To this end, The Body Shop initiated a
Community Trade program that creates strategic trade relationships in order to foster
sustainable development in communities around the world. By contracting ingredients
and accessories from socially and economically marginalized communities, she has
been able to generate funding for communities in dire need of support.

The Body Shop's success also lies in Roddick's ability to develop innovative products exclusively found at The Body Shop. She has long sought out natural ways to clean and refresh the human body—long before the rest of the cosmetics industry ever heard of it.

Another part of Roddick's success has been her dedication to including all stakeholders—employees, franchise owners, shareholders, and customers—in her social and environmental efforts. In 1990, The Body Shop Foundation was formed as a way for employees and investors to give something back to the world. Recent projects have included providing medical attention to more than 4,000 Amazonian Indians, as well as renovating orphanages in Romania and Albania. The company even produces an annual "Value Report"—an independently verified audit that reports on how well the company has lived up to its own promises.

Anita Roddick has pioneered a new way of conducting business and has shown the world that a company can make money and support ethical business practices simultaneously.

ROADMAP TO SUCCESS

Objective	Course of Action
Understand the Contributions of Benjamin Graham	• Considered the father of fundamental analysis for penning two books: *Security Analysis* (1934) and *The Intelligent Investor* (1949). • Began by clearly defining the word *investment* and setting it apart from the word *speculative*. This definition enabled Graham to include stocks in the category of investments, a category formerly thought to be the primary domain of bonds. • Worked to empower his students and clients by teaching them a systematic approach to finding undervalued stocks and bonds through quantitative analysis. • Highly recommended diversification as an investment approach.
Understand the Contributions of Philip Fisher	• A great believer in the qualitative analysis of companies over the long term. • Looked for investments that could maintain higher growth levels than industry averages. • Honed his ability to size up a stock's capacity to reproduce cash. • Avidly watched a company's management team and questioned their integrity and style. • Paid close attention to what the Street had to say about a company by listening to gossip, rumors, and personal opinions.
Understand the Contributions of Warren Buffett	• Believed in buying stock in companies that were undervalued and hanging on to those companies until their hidden value was realized.

	• Avoided the use of leveraging, futures, dynamic hedging, modern portfolio analysis, and other popular theoretical models acclaimed by academics. • As chairman of Berkshire Hathaway, Buffett searched for and investigated companies that showed potential for long-term appreciation that would help to increase the return on investment of his star company.
Understand the Contributions of Charles Schwab	• In 1974, Schwab pioneered the nation's largest discount brokerage firm, Charles Schwab & Company. • Recently selected as one of the seven people who most influences the U.S. economy. • Believed that individuals have the ability to take control of their financial futures, and that investing should be a regular part of every household's routine.
Understand the Contributions of Peter Lynch	• Known for taking a simple approach to investing and finding companies that have the ability to provide superior returns over time. • Likes to look at companies whose products you use on a daily basis. • The former manager of the Fidelity Magellan Fund. • Feels that investors should be in for the long haul and avoid trying to time the market.
Understand the Contributions of William O'Neil	• Founded *Investor's Business Daily* newspaper. • Created useful acronym: C-A-N-S-L-I-M. • C stands for current quarterly earnings. • A stands for annual earnings increases. • N represents new products, management, and highs. • S refers to supply and demand. • L stands for leader or laggard. • I represents institutional sponsorship. • M refers to the overall current market direction.
Understand the Contributions of John Neff	• Disregarded popular investment philosophies and pioneered an innovative investing approach—Measured Participation—based on a low-P/E strategy that uses fundamental analysis and common sense to locate undervalued stocks.
Understand the Contributions of Linda Bradford Raschke	• Got her start as a floor trader at the Pacific Stock Exchange before moving on to the Philadelphia Stock Exchange. • Honed her skills as a short-term trader by specializing in pattern recognition and technical analysis detection for optimal entries and exits. • Claims her trades have an approximately 70% profitability rate. • The only woman investor featured in Jack D. Schwager's best-seller *The New Market Wizards*.
Understand the Contributions of Andrew Carnegie	• He began his fortune by investing in the new Woodruff Sleeping Car Company, the original holder of the Pullman patents.

- Using innovative new British steelmaking processes, plus state-of-the-art assembly techniques, Carnegie Steel dominated the American steel industry in the 1890s.
- When asked his business secrets of success, he replied "Put all your eggs in one basket and then watch that basket!"
- He later became a resolute philanthropist, and declared that "A man who dies rich dies disgraced."

Understand the Contributions of John D. Rockefeller	• Rockefeller's Standard Oil Company of Ohio established the first major U.S. trust and set a pattern of organization for other monopolies. • Caused government to enact antimonopoly laws culminating in the passage of the Sherman Antitrust Act of 1890 by the U.S. Congress.
Understand the Contributions of J. Paul Getty	• As an independent wildcatter he worked as his own geologist, legal adviser, drilling superintendent, explosives expert, and roughneck. • He later gained control of several large independent oil companies by relying on his own instincts, experiences, and resources learned from his wildcatting days.
Understand the Contributions of Rupert Murdoch	• Created a media empire, now a $28 billion conglomerate, dominated by his trademark-style news of sex and scandal. • Disney CEO Michael Eisner, and Time Warner CEO Gerald Levin both mentioned Murdoch as the one media executive whom they respect and fear the most and whose moves they study incessantly.
Understand the Contributions of Bill Gates	• Programmed his first software at 13. • Developed BASIC, the first microcomputer programming language at Harvard in the 1970s. • Dropped out of Harvard and cofounded Microsoft in 1975 with Paul Allen. • Became a 31-year-old billionaire by 1986. • Currently appealing the U.S. Justice Department's antitrust verdict declaring Microsoft to be split in two.
Understand the Contributions of Paul Allen	• Dropped out of Harvard and cofounded Microsoft in 1975 with Bill Gates. • He helped engineer and launch MS-DOS, MS Word, Windows, and the Microsoft Mouse. • Now oversees an array of handpicked, independent companies, each with its own special capabilities and culture.
Understand the Contributions of Richard Branson	• Founded Virgin Records in 1970 as a mail-order record company and sold it in 1992 to EMI for $1 billion. • Founded Virgin Atlantic Airways, now the second largest international airline in Great Britain. • Branson says he has succeeded by designing superior services and products and taking chances.

Understand the Contributions of George Soros	• His Quantum investment fund—started in 1969—is universally recognized as the most successful hedge fund ever. • A master of cross-currency investing, he forced the rest of the investment community to recognize the developing interdependence of the U.S. economy and geopolitical events.
Understand the Contributions of Anita Roddick	• Built The Body Shop up from a small shop in Brighton to a successful retail giant with more than 1,000 stores in 40 countries. • Developed the slogan "Trade Not Aid" to pioneer a new way of doing business that forges strategic trade relationships in order to foster sustainable development in communities around the world. • Produced innovative products found exclusively at The Body Shop that focus on natural ways to clean and refresh the human body. • Formed The Body Shop Foundation as a way for employees, investors, and customers to give something back to the world.

12

Taking Advantage
of Market Behavior

Determining the prevailing mood of the market is the essence of successful trading. This is no easy task considering that market conditions reflect the emotions of people—confident, scared, erratic, and unpredictable. But certain basic parameters do exist. You shouldn't short stocks in an up market, and you shouldn't use bullish plays in a down market. "Going with the flow" is a simple way of saying "Don't fight the tape."

In this chapter, I want to focus on providing you with a few insights on how to profit in the markets by assessing market conditions and using the appropriate strategies for these conditions. Since successful trading requires accurate identification of trends and application of the correct strategies to take advantage of these trends, you have to know how to use all the tools in your trading arsenal. Learning how to integrate these various tools will enable you to increase your prowess as an investor or trader.

Generally speaking, the market's going to do one of three things: It's going to go up, down, or sideways. Some studies have indicated it goes sideways roughly one-third of the time. When it reaches extreme levels, the trend will reverse direction. Since there are times when no one really knows which direction the markets are moving, let's take a moment to discuss various market conditions, how to recognize them, and then figure out how to profit from them.

FUSING TWO METHODS: TECHNICAL AND SENTIMENT ANALYSIS

When the only tool you have is a hammer, everything looks like a nail. With no disrespect to fundamental analysis, the best tools to work with when assessing current market conditions are technical analysis and sentiment indicators. Technical analysis provides chart patterns to help traders recognize critical price levels of support and resistance. These levels exert considerable influence on a stock's movement and have a significant effect on how and when a stock should subsequently be traded. Sentiment indicators can help pinpoint extremes in market psychology. Extreme levels of confidence and pessimism will help you identify tops and bottoms, respectively. This approach not only applies to the market overall, but to individual stocks as well.

Fundamental analysis should be used to point out the financial strengths and weaknesses of a field of possible stocks. Even if you're right about buying the stock with the strongest management and the most efficient productivity, if you're wrong about market direction you'll be entering a world of pain, comprised of sell-offs and declining portfolio valuations. So assuming we know what we want to buy, let's figure out when to buy and when to sell.

You need to recognize the trend before you start worrying about how happy or scared everyone is.

MARKET EVALUATION: TRENDS AND MARKET CONDITIONS

The first step in determining a stock's direction is to look at the charts. Do you see a trend of any kind? Up and down trends are comprised of three main phases: major, intermediate, and near-term.

- The major trend lasts a year or more.

- The intermediate trend has a life expectancy of three to four weeks to three to four months

- The near-term trend describes short rallies or pullbacks that last less than three weeks.

Now look at the charts again. Can you spot a long-term trend? If you can't, or need some more hints, there are additional tools you can employ. But the first thing you need to do is look at the market every day. Sometimes there will be a clear picture, sometimes not. Please take note: If the picture is unclear, or you're unsure as to what tack to take, it's best to sit on the sidelines in a cash position. A choppy or trendless market is extremely difficult to make money in, even for the experienced trader.

So if it is a sideways market, it's best to sit it out. That leaves just two directions to look for: up or down trends. Both of these trends can (and do) reverse, or continue on in the same direction after a pause. Therefore, being able to spot reversal or continuation patterns is an invaluable ability. *Reversals* don't occur exclusively at the culmination of a bear or bull market; they happen to individual stocks every day, and in shorter trends as well. When a stock is overextended—up or down—it will reverse. If the market is down seven days in a row, it's probably oversold and you can start looking for a return to the median. The longer a stock or index moves in one direction, the more pressure it builds to reverse direction, even if it's only temporary. For a reversal to occur, some conditions must be present:

- A trend must be in place before it can reverse.
- The breaking of a major line of support or resistance is a strong indicator a trend has reversed.
- A market top is usually shorter and more volatile than a bottom.
- Volume dwindles at the bottom, and the trading range often narrows considerably.

> **Reversal:** The point at which a trend reverses direction, enabling savvy traders who catch the reversal to get in early as the new trend takes off.

The funny thing is, every experienced trader expects a reversal, but many are slow to recognize it when one occurs. This is where the contrarian mind-set is useful, because so much sentiment (positive or negative) can build toward a stock or index. It causes people to react slowly.

Don't try to call the top or bottom precisely. It's better to look for technical signs that show that a reversal is possible, or that the trend will continue in the same direction.

REVERSAL PATTERNS

I want to start with reversal signals because that's where a trend first begins; one dies, and another is born. The biggest profits go to those in at the beginning of a trend. One reason is because knowledgeable investors and experienced traders know enough to go against the prevailing opinion and utilize the contrarian approach to catch the turn. As the trend matures, the makeup of those buying (or shorting) the trend gradually shifts from the knowledgeable investor to the momentum player, and finally to the little guy, whose presence has become synonymous with tops and bottoms (the little guy, like the crowd, is always wrong).

It's a good idea, if you suspect the market is nearing its top or bottom, to review the sentiment indicators. They will offer danger signals before the market's price action will. The following Sentiment Indicators Quick Checklist may come in handy:

- *Check the psychological indicators in Investor's Business Daily for reversal patterns you'll hear about.*
- *Check the Volatility Index (VIX). When the VIX is low, it's time to go! When it's high, it's time to buy! (www.cboe.com).*
- *Check the put/call ratio (www.cboe.com).*
- *Check the A/D line (BigCharts at www.bigcharts.com).*

Compare the Sentiment Indicators to the Averages
Unless your timing is uncanny (coinciding with the exact moment you read this), the sentiment indicators will be somewhere between anguish and exultation, as will the charts. Now look at the charts again, and try to answer these questions:

- Did the stock or index recently finish a move up or down? (Did it break through an old resistance or support level?)
- If it went up, has it leveled off and begun going sideways?
- If it went down, has it reached an old support level? (Draw a horizontal line that connects two old highs that have now turned to support levels.)
- How long was the move up or down? Remember to look at volume, as it helps measure the intensity of the move.

Double Tops and Bottoms

There are two reversal formations that many traders look for to confirm a bottom or top: the *double bottom* (see Figure 12.1) and *double top*. Support at a new low will form before the stock reverses. The subsequent rally sometimes fades, indicating the bulls just couldn't overcome the abundance of sellers. The stock or index either tests the lows again or gets very close to it, and rallies a second time. If this cycle is repeated a third time, it's of course called a *triple bottom* (see Figure 12.2). These are very bullish patterns. The wider (longer) they are, the stronger the ensuing rally. When this formation is applied to a topping out of an index or stock, it's generally not as wide, and will be more volatile. Use extreme caution if the second attempt does not exceed the previous high. What has happened is a lower low, the very definition of a downtrend.

Double bottom: A price pattern or market average that has declined two times to the same approximate level, indicating the existence of a support level and a possibility that the downward trend has ended.

Double top: A pattern that has advanced two times to reach the same resistance level. The first top must be followed by a breakthrough of the support level before climbing back up to the top again. After the second peak, the stock most likely falls back to the support level before continuing to trend or reversing.

Another good pattern to look for a reversal is called a *rounding bottom*. You can see from the chart in Figure 12.3 why it gets that name—there's a wide, curved base. This is a great pattern because it is wide, and as I've said before, the wider (longer) it is, the stronger the move up. It's the timing of it that is frustrating, because this may take a very long time to form. Be patient.

Head and Shoulders

A head and shoulders is a bearish price pattern that has three peaks resembling a head and two shoulders (see Figures 12.4 and 12.5). The stock price moves up to its

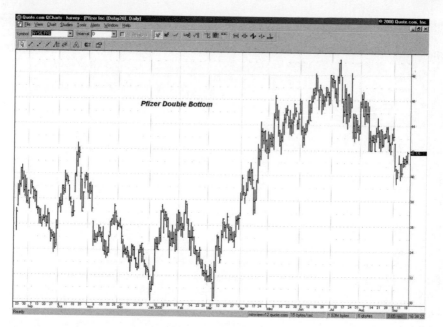

Figure 12.1   Double Bottom Formation (Courtesy of QCharts (www.qcharts.com))

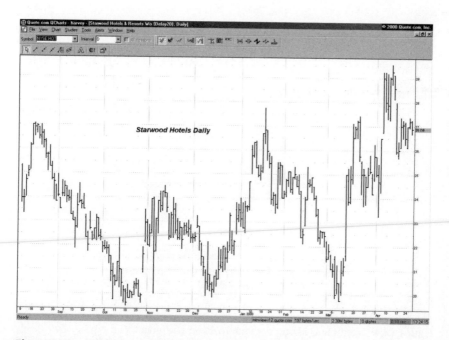

Figure 12.2   Triple Bottom Formation (Courtesy of QCharts (www.qcharts.com))

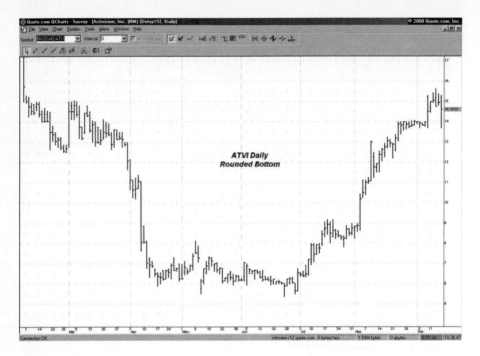

Figure 12.3   Rounding Bottom Formation (Courtesy of QCharts (www.qcharts.com))

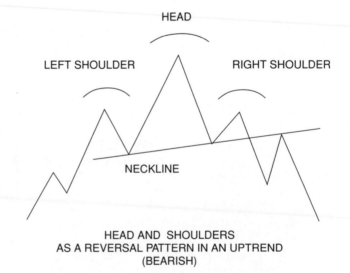

Figure 12.4   Head and Shoulders Pattern in an Uptrend

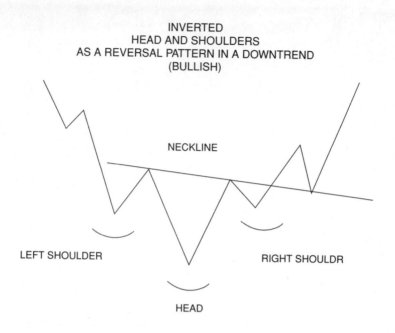

INVERTED
HEAD AND SHOULDERS
AS A REVERSAL PATTERN IN A DOWNTREND
(BULLISH)

NECKLINE

LEFT SHOULDER

RIGHT SHOULDR

HEAD

Figure 12.5   Inverted Head and Shoulders Pattern in a Downtrend

first peak (the left shoulder), drops back, then moves to a higher peak (the top of the head), drops again but recovers to another, lower peak (the right shoulder). A head and shoulders top typically forms after a substantial rise and indicates a market reversal. A head and shoulders bottom (an inverted head and shoulders) indicates a market advance.

CONTINUATION PATTERNS

A sharp rise in price of a stock or index is followed by a resting period, called a *consolidation period*. You might say the market needs to catch its breath while the new price level regains equilibrium. Typically price action narrows and the volume drops off while investors and traders attempt to get a better sense of the next move, up or down. Visually, a consolidating market may resemble a triangle or a rectangle. Experienced traders watch for these consolidations carefully. But tread softly! A relatively short consolidation period should be viewed with caution since not enough of a new base may be in place to support the next thrust up. However, a prolonged consolidation is thought to be a good base for the next trend.

Consolidations have different looks. One such formation is called a *rectangle* because it creates an oblong box. Figure 12.6 shows a daily chart of General Electric

Figure 12.6 Consolidation Pattern (Courtesy of QCharts (www.qcharts.com))

(GE), a good example of how a stock will move, then rest. Although GE was fortunate enough to move up each time, you can see how important it is to watch support and resistance levels. If you want to buy the stock, and you see it clear resistance, that's the time to get in; or if you're in and it breaks support, that's the time to get out.

In Figure 12.6, note that the two consolidation periods are both shaped like a rectangular box. Many traders will lock onto this range, buying at the support level and selling as it nears resistance. The obvious drawback to this strategy is selling before the breakout. Many other investors will wait for the breakout to occur before getting in. Their buying begets more buyers, namely the momentum traders. If there is a large short position held by bears and they begin to cover, the stock can really take off.

> *Once you see the stock has broken out of its recent trading range,
> exhibiting strong signs that a new trend has begun, be ready to act quickly.*

TAKING ADVANTAGE OF RECTANGULAR CONSOLIDATIONS

Long call strategies offer limited risk (the amount you paid for the option) with an unlimited upside potential. This is called a *directional* trade and works best if the stock moves up enough to affect an increase in the option contract. But a long call has one drawback: Once a stock has broken out (or down), the premiums on the options become more expensive. Therefore, we can take advantage of the higher premiums by going one step further, by putting on a vertical spread trade.

Vertical spreads offer limited potential profits as well as limited risks by combining long and short options with different strike prices and like expiration dates. The juxtaposition of long and short options results in a net debit or net credit. The net debit of a bull call spread and a bear put spread correlates to the maximum amount of money that can be lost on the trade—welcome to the world of limited risk. However, the net credit of a bull put spread and a bear call spread is the maximum profit potential of the combined position—limited profit. Success in this kind of trading is a balancing act. You have to balance out the risk/reward ratio with the difference between the strikes—the greater the strike difference, the higher the risk, but also the higher the potential reward.

One of the keys to understanding these vertical spreads comes from grasping the concepts of intrinsic value and time value—variables that provide major contributions to the fluctuating price of an option. Although changes in the underlying asset of an option may be hard to forecast, there are a few constants that influence the values of options premiums. The following constants provide the key to why vertical spreads offer a healthy alternative to traditional bullish and bearish stock trading techniques:

- Time value continually evaporates as an option approaches expiration.

- OTM and ATM options have no intrinsic value; they are all time value and therefore lose more premium as expiration approaches than ITM options.

- The premiums of ITM options have minimum values that change at a slower pace than OTM and ATM options.

- Vertical spreads take advantage of these differing rates of changes in the values of options premiums.

The four vertical spreads that we use can be broken down into two kinds of categories: debit and credit spreads, each with a bullish or bearish bias. The success of these strategies depends on being able to use options to exploit an anticipated directional move in a stock. As usual, timing is everything. To get good at forecasting the nature of a directional trend, try monitoring option volatilities and keeping track of support and resistance levels. Remember, a breakout beyond a stock's trading range can happen in either direction at any time. Limiting your risk is a great way to level the playing field.

Vertical spreads are excellent strategies for small investors who are getting their feet wet for the first time. Low risk makes these strategies inviting. Although they combine a short and a long option, the combined margin is usually far less than what it would cost to trade the underlying instrument and provides special advantages in the case of consolidating markets.

For example, in Figure 12.7 you can see how Seagate (SEG) broke out of its trading range but then fell back to support (see the old high from a week or two previous). The stock pulled back to just below its 50 DMA, and stayed there for about a week before moving higher. Strong stocks on pullbacks are good candidates for spread trades,

Figure 12.7   Seagate Price Chart (Courtesy of QCharts (www.qcharts.com))

especially if you believe the market and the stock are going to rebound soon. (You can also do the same kind of trade only with a downward bias if conditions warrant.)

A bull call spread would have been an excellent way to take advantage of Seagate's movement. A bull call spread is a debit spread created by purchasing a lower strike call and selling a higher strike call with the same expiration dates. The total investment is far less than that required to purchase the stock. A bull call spread offers a limited profit potential and limited downside risk. The maximum risk on one of these trades is equal to the net debit of the options. The breakeven is calculated by adding the net debit (divided by 100) to the long call strike price. To calculate the maximum profit, simply multiply the difference in the strike prices of the two options by 100 and then subtract the net debit. The maximum profit occurs when the underlying stock rises above the strike price of the short call hopefully causing it to be assigned. You can then exercise the long call, thereby purchasing the underlying stock at the lower strike price and delivering those shares to the option holder at the higher short price.

Bull call spread: A strategy in which a trader buys a lower strike call and sells a higher strike call to create a trade with limited profit and limited risk. A rise in the price of the underlying increases the value of the spread. Net debit transaction: Maximum loss = debit; Maximum gain = difference between strike prices less the net debit. No margin is required to place this kind of spread.

Using Seagate, let's say we created a bull call spread by purchasing 1 SEG January 2002 50 Call and selling 1 SEG January 2002 80 Call for a debit spread of 9 or better. Risk on this trade is 9 points, while maximum reward is 21 points. Since it is always a good idea to confirm direction of the stock before entering a trade, the ideal time to put this spread in place was after the bullish trend was confirmed. In this case, the stock sold off on Monday following an uptrend on a Friday. When the stock turned back up midweek, and began to show strength, this was the perfect time to enter the spread.

It's a good idea to work out your strategy the night before, or sometime when the market's not open, so you can coolly evaluate conditions and pricing. Then you're ready to watch and wait for the best entry point.

Figure 12.8 shows the risk graph of this trade. It indicates the potential loss and profit. On a spread trade, you sacrifice a little of the upside potential and really limit the amount you could possibly lose. In this case, if the stock closes below $50 (horizontal axis) there is a total loss of capital. However, $59 is the approximate breakeven point, and you profit whenever the stock goes above that price.

Bull Call Spread

Strategy = Buy a lower strike call and sell a higher strike call with the same expiration dates.

Market Opportunity = Look for a moderately bullish market where you anticipate a modest increase in the price of the underlying above the price of the short call option.

Maximum Risk = Limited to the net debit paid for the spread.

Maximum Profit = Limited [(difference in strike prices × value per point) – net debit paid].

Breakeven = Lower call strike price + net debit paid.

Seagate Technology Inc.
Theoretical Gross Out P&L

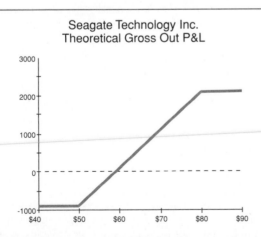

Figure 12.8 Bull Call Spread Risk Graph (Courtesy of Optionetics.com)

ANOTHER CONSOLIDATION PATTERN: NARROWING FORMATIONS

A *narrowing formation* differs from a rectangle consolidation pattern because the support and resistance lines begin to converge toward a focal point somewhere a few days or weeks out. During this period the stock or index will experience a drop in volume and a narrowing of the trading range. This period of consolidation will test resistance levels and support, forming what appears to be a three-sided figure. Essentially what the trader will look for is a triangle of some sort. It can have higher lows and an even level of resistance (see Figure 12.9), or just the opposite, as shown in the Amazon.com chart in Figure 12.10. Think of this type of pattern as a spring coiling before it jumps— the longer the pattern, the bigger the move. To technicians, triangular consolidations come in three forms: flags, pennants, and triangles. Ascending triangles are considered bullish because of the series of higher lows and resistance remaining level. The pressure is building from the bottom, the interpretation being it will spring up. Descending triangles are considered bearish because of the series of lower highs and support remaining level. The pressure is building from the top, the interpretation being it will spring down. Bearish strategies work best for descending triangles; and bullish strategies work best for ascending triangles. Figures 12.9 and 12.10 show examples of ascending and descending triangular patterns, and their classic results.

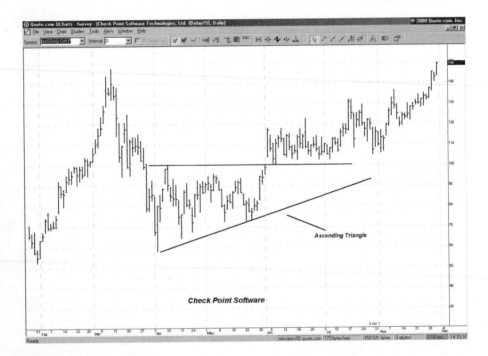

Figure 12.9   Ascending Triangle—Check Point Software (CHKP) (Courtesy of QCharts (www.qcharts.com))

Figure 12.10 Descendinig Triangle—Amazon.com (AMZN) (Courtesy of QCharts (www.qcharts.com))

The pennant is another type of triangular pattern to watch out for. When this type of pattern begins forming, the likelihood of correctly determining the direction of the break is slim. Like other consolidation formations, the volume drops and the range narrows, only this time it's with a higher low and a lower high. This quieting creates the perfect setting for a straddle (the simultaneous purchase of a call and put, at the same strike and for the same month). In this strategy, you don't care which direction the underlying stock moves in, just as long as it moves beyond the upside or downside breakevens. Figure 12.11 shows an example of a pennant formation.

> **Straddle:** A nondirectional option strategy that combines the simultaneous purchase of the same number of puts and calls with the identical strike prices and expirations. The maximum loss is limited to the net debit of the options. The upside breakeven is equal to the net debit (divided by 100) plus the ATM strike price and the downside breakeven is calculated by subtracting the net debit (divided by 100) from the ATM strike price. The maximum profit is unlimited in both directions beyond the breakevens.

In this kind of formation, the volatility of the stock and hence the option premiums fall sharply. This is the beauty of the straddle. Extrinsic value drops considerably, so you're not paying for a lot of time value. When the stock and options come

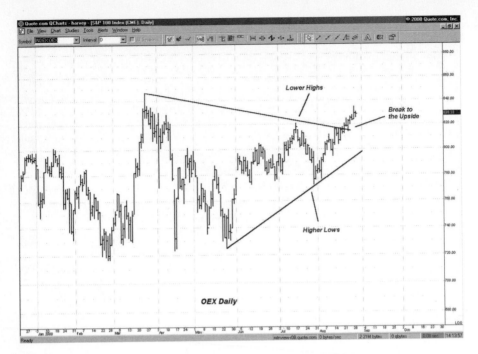

Figure 12.11   OEX Pennant Pattern (Courtesy of QCharts (www.qcharts.com))

alive again, you benefit from the move in the underlying stock as well as an increase in the extrinsic value (implied volatility) of the option!

PULLING THE TRIGGER: ORDER ENTRY

Perhaps no other factor when investing or trading is as critical to a successful trade as the order entry. Think about it. You could buy the most successful stock of all time, but if you got in at the wrong time, the pain factor would probably take you out of the trade. If you buy too high, it's going to be a long haul to break even. The most destructive thing about a bad entry isn't the resulting bad trade; it's the subsequent agonizing over your mistake. Focusing on a bad trade makes you lose sight of other more profitable opportunities, not to mention the psychological trauma of riding a loser back to break even so you can exit without incurring a loss. (Then it goes up and you're on the sidelines.)

Finding one trading strategy that works is the optimal approach. There is no need to learn firsthand every single option strategy known to man to be successful. Like learning about sectors, you start with one strategy at a time, and practice getting good at it. This is important! Do one trade well, and eventually you'll be successful with it. Fortunes are made doing this. It may not be sexy or glamorous or even exciting, but the object of all this work is to make money, not sound like a genius in front of your friends.

Here's a methodology I've used to find a system that works:

First, I look for stocks that have recently made 52-week highs and that then pull back to some area of support but do not break below their 200-day moving average.

I use an oscillator called stochastics to help me enter the trade. Stochastics is a *leading indicator* that records closing prices relative to a recent trading range over a specified period of time (see Figure 12.12). The general idea behind stochastics is quite simple. A stock trending upward tends to close near its high of the day and a stock trending downward tends to close near its low of the day. The indicator attempts to spot reversals in recent trends. For example, if a stock is in a primary uptrend, but is in the process of pulling back and its closing prices begin clustering around the highs of its daily trading range, there is a high probability that a rise in price will follow. Conversely, in an upward-trending market, if a stock begins closing near its daily lows, the upward trend is likely to reverse. This indicator can help to improve entry points and pinpoint when the primary trend is going to resume.

To learn more about technical indicators and how to use them, go to:

- *Bridge News: www.bridge.com*
- *Trading-Ideas.com: www.trading-ideas.com/guide/technical.html*

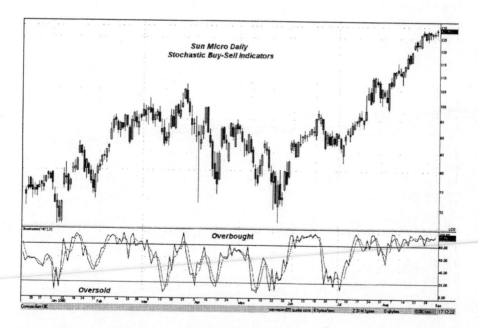

Figure 12.12   Sun Microsystems (SUNW) Stochastics Example (Courtesy of QCharts (www.qcharts.com))

USING SENTIMENT TO CONFIRM THE CHARTS

In the chart formations I've shown you, interpretation is required. We've had the luxury of seeing what happens over a time period, and determining what trade would have worked. Not so in real life. This is where sentiment indicators can help sharpen the picture. It won't always help, but they certainly won't hurt either. Sometimes you'll call it correctly, and sometime you'll miss. Such is life.

What does a good trade idea look like? Technically the charts look good. Fundamentally, it's a stock you'd like to own, and the sector is performing well (i.e., it's going up overall or appears to be turning). The only item left can be easily overlooked: sentiment. It only takes a few extra minutes of preparation, but these minutes can be vital to your success. Here's a quick checklist of sentiment indicators:

- **Put/Call Ratio:** A lopsided ratio can indicate extreme bullish or bearish traders. Contrary indicator. (E*Trade has a great feature for this, and it's free at www.etrade.com.
- **Short Interest:** What's the short position? This is stated in "days to cover." Basically, the longer it takes to cover, the more pessimistic the sentiment; but if you're a contrarian, the more bullish the sign. Check with Zacks (www.zacks.com) or Allstocks.com (www.allstocks.com).
- **MACD and/or RSI Oscillators:** Check for overbought or oversold extremes.
- **On-Balance Volume:** Is the stock trending more toward accumulation or distribution?
- **Volume versus Price:** Is volume trending with or diverging from the price? Increasing price and decreasing volume is not good.
- **Insider Buying/Selling:** Always a telltale sign. Check out insiderSCORES.com (www.insiderscores.com/index.asp).

TERMINOLOGY REGARDING MARKET BEHAVIOR

Commentators or guests on financial programs discuss various terms that might be unclear to you as to their meanings, not to mention their implications. Listed next are popular indicators of conditions, their meanings and significance.

Market Breadth

Everyone hears about the Dow being up or down on any given day, but the market breadth data provides deeper insight into the general direction for the day, week, or year. Here are listed the most commonly used market breadth indicators you'll see. (These numbers are "per exchange.")

- **Advances:** Total number of issues gaining in price.
- **Declines:** Total number of issues declining in price.
- **Unchanged:** Total number of issues whose prices did not change.

The *advance/decline line* compares the number of advancing issues (those increasing in price) against those that declined. Calculations are based on the opening trade of normal market hours as compared to the closing price. It doesn't take into account after-hours trading. A strong A/D is a more in-depth indicator of the breadth or strength of the market. A market whose main index (like the Dow Industrials) is up big on the day, but whose A/D line is negative, signals that the rally was selective—not a very bullish overall indicator. All it takes for the Dow to be up or down is a strong movement by a few of the Dow components. The overall market may be down for the day, but if Microsoft or IBM had a huge day, the Dow indicates a gain for the day.

The same holds true for the Nasdaq Composite index. Big days in either direction for the big-cap names like Cisco or Dell may distort what really occurred that day.

- *New Highs:* Stocks making new 52-week highs.

- *New Lows:* Stocks making 52-week lows.

The number of new highs and lows is significant because in order for the market to advance, a good number of stocks need to break out of their recent trading ranges into new territory (see Chapter 9 on technical indicators). When a stock is making new highs, it's bullish because everyone is making money (except of course the short sellers), regardless of their purchase price. Investors hang onto their winners, so supply dries up, and if demand stays constant or increases, the stock or stocks will run further.

The opposite is also true for the new lows. Although most people are underwater, there are groups that are not—those that are selling the stock short, and those that have owed the stock for a very long time. By definition, the new lows are usually defined as 52-week lows. For those firms that have been around for a long time, the 52-week low may not be anywhere near the all-time lows. For instance, Coca-Cola (KO) reached a 52-week low in March 2000 when it dropped to almost $42 per share. However, that was not the all-time low—$42 per share was the all-time high back in March 1996, and thus anyone who had purchased it prior to March 1996 would still be in a profitable position. For all practical purposes, though, most KO stockholders were underwater, or those with a really low basis fell underwater as they looked back on the $40 drop their stock had taken over the previous 18 months. In many cases, you can expect more selling if it stays down as investors cut their losses.

- *Advancing volume:* The combined volume of all advancing stocks.

- *Declining volume:* The combined volume of all declining stocks.

- *Total volume:* Trading volume all stocks traded.

Volume

A/D volume and total volume are good indicators of strength. If the market is up big, but volume is poor, the rally's credibility is uncertain; that is, it doesn't do much to inspire further buying, as investors are sitting on the sidelines to get a better idea of market direction. Large volume days are better indicators of market psychology; if it's down or up on big volume, that's your cue as to sentiment and the trend.

The TRIN ($TRIN) is a good way to observe volume differences between buyers and sellers intraday. The TRIN, or Trader's Index, is the difference between advancing and declining volume. Think of this in terms of a teeter-totter; a reading above 1 means the market is selling off; below 1 the balance of volume is buying volume. The TRIN is useful intraday to act as a contrary indicator, signaling overbought or oversold conditions. A TRIN of 1.5 would indicate incredible selling pressure, and, according to the contrarian, a reversal is due. (The duration or magnitude of the reversal is not so easily spotted.) A TRIN of .35 indicates confidence levels are high, and is thus considered to be a bearish indicator. During the trading day, most traders watch the direction the TRIN is going more than the levels themselves. Only at the extremes is the number itself truly important.

Figures 12.13 and 12.14 show the interesting relationship between TRIN and the Dow on one of the most volatile days ever experienced by investors. The TRIN reached as low as .47 while the Dow went up 77 before a massive sell-off occurred sending the TRIN to +1.77 and the Dow off 506.

Tick ($TICK)

This figure is derived by taking the number of stocks heading up and then subtracting the number of stocks headed down. The typical tick will range anywhere from +500

Figure 12.13   TRIN on April 4, 2000 (Courtesy of QCharts (www.qcharts.com))

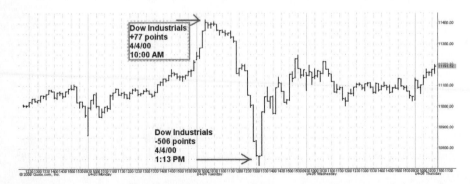

Figure 12.14   DOW on April 4, 2000 (Courtesy of QCharts (www.qcharts.com))

to –500, give or take. However, the extreme readings of +1,000 or –1,000 serve as excellent contrary indicators, because this type of a reading cannot be sustained; it must return to the normal trading range. It's also a good idea to track the direction the tick is going. Direction is more important most times than the actual reading.

Volatility Levels

We've discussed volatility previously, but since it is a key factor in determining current stock or market conditions, let's do a quick review. Volatility can be defined as a measure of the amount by which a stock price is expected to change. It's no mystery that a stock that has fallen into a narrow trading pattern (directionless) has low volatility. These stocks are not hard to find and it can be very profitable to spot them because when they do come alive (as they often do), the only question is which way will they move: up or down?

Markets that move erratically have higher volatility than markets that are range-bound (i.e., directionless). That's why it's important to keep an eye on the volatility of the stocks you may want to trade. If the stock is already all over the map, trending up or down, at least you can determine the trend it's in and employ a suitable strategy. A stock in such a trend might possibly warrant a spread to capture some of the volatility.

MARKET PRICING INEFFICIENCIES

The market may efficiently process information, but option pricing doesn't work that way. We learned in Chapter 6 about the Black-Scholes option pricing formula. Sometimes the actual market price will fall way above or below this line, but has a way of returning to normal pricing as time goes on. Calendar spreads take advantage of one of these scenarios, when close-in option contracts are priced well above what the Black-Scholes model indicates the price *should* be. By looking at the Optionetics.com Platinum site, you can quickly determine the feasibility of putting on a calendar spread.

Volatility skews in the option prices occur when the volatility is higher in some months than others, or in the higher (or lower) strike prices. Certain option spreads provide the perfect dynamic to take advantage of specific skews.

I like to focus on calendar spreads since volatile markets make these trades so attractive. A calendar is a spread that combines the purchase and sale of options with the same strike price but different expiration dates. The longer-term option is purchased and the shorter-term option is sold simultaneously. Calendar spreads can be created with a bullish, bearish, or neutral bias, and the maximum risk on the trade is the net debit paid to establish the position. The objective of this position is to have time eat away at the short option while the long option retains its value. Usually, there are additional adjustments that can be made to the position in order to increase its profitability. Here's the way a calendar spread order would be entered when the XYZ October 35 puts are selling at $4 and the XYZ July 35 puts are selling for $2$1/2$:

Buy 1 XYZ October 35 put (XYZVG) and sell 1 XYZ July 35 put (XYZSG) for a debit of $1^1/_2$ or better, opening both sides.

The trick to finding great calendar spreads is finding options with unusually high implied volatility in the front months and low to normal implied volatility in the back months. This difference in implied volatility across expiration months is referred to as *volatility skew*. Wild market fluctuations make this a relatively simple task to accomplish; implied volatility will normally skyrocket when fear and uncertainty hit investors. Actually, sometimes it is possible to get a net credit for a calendar spread, which means that you would have a no risk position! These are the types of trades that traders should be looking for in uncertain environments with an emphasis on risk management. Before any trade is placed, the question that should always be answered is, "What are the consequences if I am wrong?" Never let any one trade put you out of business. There are so many different opportunities the market provides that it is not necessary to place an inordinate amount of risk in any one position.

DETERMINING VOLATILITY LEVELS

In Chapter 10, we discussed the Volatility Index or VIX. It's the easiest place to start, because all it takes is punching in the ticker "$VIX," or "VIX.X" depending on your quote delivery source. Recently the VIX has faded in terms of accuracy for determining the market's sentiment, simply because of the decline in OEX call and put buying—the determinants of the VIX. It still is a good indicator of fear (when the reading is above 30 or so); but the summer of 2000 saw the VIX trade down to the low 20s, even the teens, and it stayed there. But I still watch it and take its level into consideration when assessing the current market mood.

Assessing volatility levels of individual stocks isn't quite as easy, but it's still not very difficult. There are several methods available, but they do require a computer to get the most accurate results. The fastest method is to use Bollinger bands, a tool we learned about in Chapter 9, on technical analysis. The bands are a measurement using standard deviations above and below a moving average, which is a long way of saying recent price swings. If the bands are wide apart, volatility is high. This means the stock has experienced a wide degree of price swings when compared to its moving average (usually 20 days). That's not a good signal to be buying options, as a rule of thumb. You want to buy options when the volatility is low; the bands are narrow (close together), indicating the premiums on the underlying options are low.

Figure 12.15 shows a daily chart of JDS-Uniphase in its meteoric rise in the second half of 1999. The stock moved sideways and was quiet for several weeks. The Bollinger bands narrowed, indicating low volatility. But once it began to run, the bands expanded due to the increased demand (and expectations) for the stock. Those that purchased options when the implied volatility (IV) was low did well two ways: The price of the stock increased as well as the IV (extrinsic value). Just because the bands narrow doesn't automatically indicate a stock or index will climb. Lower IV means the stock might move decisively one way or the other; there's no accurate way to tell.

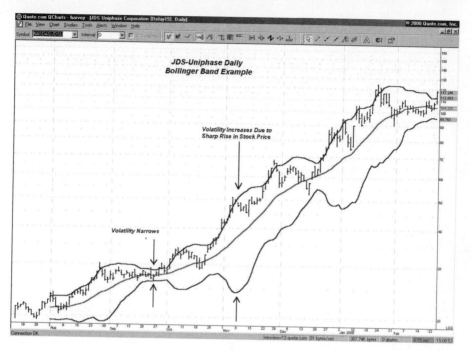

Figure 12.15   JDS-Uniphase Bollinger Bands—Depicts Volatility Swings in the Stock (Courtesy of QCharts (www.qcharts.com))

Another avenue is to go to Optionetics.com and using the free Platinum site just type in the stock symbol, then select Charts on the pull-down menu. A six-month chart of the stock and its implied volatility (IV) will be displayed, as well as a two-year chart and the options tables as well. The six-month chart will show the level of current volatility. This is a good first step, and an important one as well.

Just remember: Buy low volatility; sell high volatility.

ADDITIONAL TERMINOLOGY REGARDING MARKET BEHAVIOR

- ***Stock Price Cycles:*** There exists a group of technicians that closely follow price patterns. Since patterns repeat themselves, cycles become observable. Probably the most notorious and well-known cycle is the *Elliott Wave theory*. Based on repetitive wave patterns and the Fibonacci ratio, Elliott Wave analysis enables traders to determine where the market is currently in comparison to the overall market movement. There are three major aspects of wave analysis: pattern, time, and ratio. The basic Elliott pattern consists of a five-wave up-trend followed by a three-wave correction. Cycles are discerned by combining the application of moving averages and oscillators over extended periods.

- *Declining Stock Behavior:* A stock that changes direction, shifting from an uptrend to a down one, tends to exhibit similar chart patterns, although not every stock reverses the same way every time. Some important indicators will flash warnings beforehand, in most cases. Some of these include:

  Price/Volume Divergence: The stock keeps going up, but on declining volume.

  A Series of Lower Highs and Lower Lows: This occurs in a stock where there are increasing amounts of supply earlier on in each rally. Trend lines can easily illustrate this scenario.

  A "Gap Down" Opening: This one is tough to miss, especially if you own it. A stock will open lower than the previous day's close, creating a gap in the chart. If it's on heavy volume, this could spell trouble.

  On-Balance Volume (OBV) Is Negative: OBV tracks the volume of buyers and sellers, and clearly illustrates on charts whether a stock is under accumulation or distribution. The OBV line will trend downward in a distribution circumstance while the stock price is still increasing.

  Analyst Downgrades a Stock: This kind of event will likely cause the above signals to show. Brokerage firm analysts can exert a lot of influence over a stock's performance. A downgrade can mean just an adjustment, or an obscure signal to the firm's clients to get out.

  Earnings Warning: A warning from a company announcing it will miss Street expectations for the current quarter is enough to send a stock to the doghouse for a long time. Sometimes it's a timing issue, sales being pushed back or didn't get booked in time. Nonetheless, pay attention to any corresponding downgrades from analysts. Cut losses sooner rather than later.

- *Averaging Down:* If you are long stock and it takes a significant drop in price, many traders buy more shares of the stock at the lower price to reduce the breakeven of all of the shares. The concept of averaging down on a stock that moves against you sounds okay at face value, but in reality is discouraged. The theory is that a lower cost basis will mean profitability sooner when the stock turns back up. The fact remains you were wrong in the first place as to the stock's direction. Averaging down is throwing good money after a bad trade and should be avoided.

- *Rallies and Sell-Offs:* The markets experience exaggerated displays of confidence and fear as shown by rallies and sell-offs. A rally can mean the beginning of an extended up move, or a retracement back to where it fell from. A sell-off could mean profit taking or a serious correction. In both cases it's hard to tell without getting some confirmation from other indicators. Volume, market breadth as discussed earlier, and the evaluation of technical and sentiment indicators all provide pieces to what is a very big puzzle.

- *Buybacks:* Corporations do their best to continually boost their profitability, and sometimes the market just doesn't appreciate it. It's at these times a company will announce that they will go into the open market and buy back or repurchase shares they have previously sold to the public. For a company to do this, it is in effect stating that the best use of capital is to invest in them. This is a bullish sign and a strong display of confidence.

- *Stock Splits:* Stock splits occur when a company decides its stock price is (usually) too high in price, making it beyond the reach of most noninstitutional investors. A common form is a 2:1 split, in which a shareholder receives two shares for every one owned. If you owned 100 shares at $200 in a 2:1 split, you'd end up owning 200 shares at $100. A *reverse split* works the other way. If it was a 1:2 reverse split and you had 100 shares at $50, originally, you'd own 50 shares at $100 afterward. Stock splits increase as a market goes up, and they work as an indicator of market sentiment.

- *Advancing Stock Behavior:* Stocks in a bullish mode will exhibit similar patterns. Fundamentally, demand will begin to outweigh supply, but before then volume will increase. There's an old saying: "Volume precedes price." Volume changes are a good way to spot a stock before it begins a move up. Technically, an advancing stock will have higher highs and higher lows. Each advance is progressively higher before selling moves it back, and even then it doesn't go back as far as before. This trend is easily identified by using trend lines (as discussed in Chapter 9, on technical analysis). Volume should continue strong as the price increases, and pullbacks should be seen as buying opportunities. If volume tapers off as the price advances, this is known as a *divergence*, a serious sign that the advance is not sustainable.

- *Divergence:* Divergence is a term applied to any two indicators that begin to generate conflicting signals. Popular divergence signals include price and volume (as discussed earlier); MACD lines and the histogram; the advance/decline line moving down while the index rises. Divergences represent an early warning sign of a reversal in the current trend of an index or stock, and are of great significance to traders.

- *Correction:* A correction is a mild down move in an up leg of the market, and lasts a relatively short time. A correction turns into a bear market at 20% of a down move from its recent high.

- *Capitulation:* A capitulation occurs most often in bear markets. It's that point where the last optimist says, "I've had enough," throws in the towel, and quits the market. Signs of capitulation occurring are a huge down move on big volume, with market sentiment indicators turning extremely pessimistic. From a contrarian viewpoint, the majority is wrong at market extremes, so if everyone has sold, it can't go any lower.

- *Market Tops and Bottoms:* Spotting a bottom is almost easier than a top, due to the near-cataclysmic cave-in of a bottom (as discussed in *capitulation* above). A top is marked by an impressive display of confidence and wanton disregard of fear—big up day, impressive volume, low VIX, and every indicator flashing buy. A top may look like a flagpole in a parking lot, sticking way up and giving the impression it looks overextended, as it probably is. The luxury of hindsight can identify a top; but when everything seems to be going your way, a downturn is probably looming in the not too distant future.

SELECTING A PROFITABLE STOCK

Finding a profitable stock is the question of the ages. Even Will Rogers advised investors to "just buy stocks that go up." But since it is a lot easier said than done, here's a process to follow to help identify stocks on the rise.

- *Find a Promising Stock:* To find one stock to buy requires looking at a number of them. I like to be in the right sector—one that is either already strong or is showing signs of turning. Sector selection has a lot to do with performance. *Investor's Business Daily* has a complete list each day in the back of the first section, or check out Rabbitt Analytics to see how it ranks the sectors using its own proprietary system (www.rabbittanalytics.com/default.htm).

- *Screen It:* Screens give you the opportunity to narrow your search by filtering out the characteristics you don't want in a stock, and leaving you with the ones you do want. Maybe I'm looking for a mid-cap stock with low volatility in the defense sector with a good debt-to-equity ratio and earnings increasing at a 20% rate the past four quarters. This is where the computer can be a valuable aid. Zacks Investment Research offers excellent screening tools (my.zacks.com/screening/index.php3), and so does HardRightEdge.com (www.hardrightedge.com).

- *Rank It:* Once you've found a good candidate, how does it stack up against its peer group, or similar companies in the same industry group? *Investor's Business Daily* ranks virtually every stock that's traded according to profitability and its comparative rank in the industry group.

- *Consult Fundamental and Sentiment Analysis:* There's nothing that compares with studying the balance sheet to dig out those tidbits of information that help identify a stock that's ready to move. While you're at it, see how the Street looks at it and try to assess the way they feel. Is it out of favor? Is it the current darling of institutions? Optionetics.com (www.optionetics.com) has a ranking system that indicates implied volatility, which is another way to check sentiment. Also take a look at Bollinger bands for a quick read on a stock's volatility as a gauge of sentiment.

- *Watch Technicals for Perfect Timing:* Break out the charts and start drawing lines. How do you know what a good entry point is without a chart? Look for a stock that has retreated back to a 50-day MA support line and shows signs of turning, or a stock that is breaking out (or down) to a new high or low. Perhaps it's a surge in volume for several days but the stock hasn't moved. New highs, support and resistance, and volume increases should be a part of your criteria.

SCREENING METHODS

Today's technology has provided any person with access to a computer and the Internet the ability to search the entire universe of stocks and stock options in order to find and create profitable trades. If you actually think about this fact for a moment it is mind-boggling. The average investor now has access to information that in years past was only available to professional firms. In the old days, an investor's research was limited to *Value Line Investment Survey*, *Standard & Poor's Stock Reports*, and the occasional analyst report from the investor's brokerage firm. Unfortunately, these reports were usually months behind and outdated when the investors received them. Technology has now provided direct access to all the information investors and traders need to make informed and intelligent decisions regarding their investments almost instantaneously. This places the individual investor in a position to research his (or her) own ideas more efficiently and effectively while substantially increasing returns over the course of time.

There are countless combinations of criteria that investors and traders have come up with in order to find companies that demonstrate the characteristics that they are seeking. Value investors have different criteria they are searching for than have the growth and momentum investors. It is important to note that as the market changes, the types of criteria that you, the investor, will be screening for is going to change as well. Nothing ever stays the same in the stock market and your stock screening should continue to evolve with what is currently working in the market. The most important quality of a great investor is to be able to discern what is working in the current market environment and find trades that profit from that market insight. Here are lists of different screens for value, growth, and momentum investors.

The value screen searches for stocks that meet these parameters:

1. Stocks whose P/E ratios are among the lowest 40% of all firms.

2. A market price to book value calculation could be built into the screen.

3. Minimum compound annual growth rate for sales and earnings could be specified.

4. A minimum dividend payout ratio or dividend yield could be specified.

5. A minimum return on total assets or owners' equity could be required to reflect the profitability of the firm.

The growth screen searches for stocks that meet these parameters:

1. Current quarterly earnings are exploding.

2. Annual earnings growth rate is greater than the overall market's earnings growth rate.

3. Close to or making new highs.

4. Has a smaller number of shares outstanding.

5. Price is greater than $30 per share.

The momentum screen searches for stocks that meet these parameters:

1. Stocks that are in the strongest industry groups.

2. Stocks that have recently made new highs and pulled back off those highs.

3. Stocks that have given a technical signal that they are ready to resume their upward trend (e.g., stochastic positive breakout).

This is by no means an exhaustive listing of potential screens; however, it should give you a good idea on how you may want to create your own screens and adjust them to suit your own personal trading style.

Screening Sites: Here's a list of sites that offer screening tools.
- *Morningstar.com: (screen.morningstar.com/StockSelector.html)*
- *Wall Street Research: (www.wsrn.com/home/dataset/search.html)*
- *Zacks: (my.zacks.com/index.php3)*
- *Silicon Investor: (www.siliconinvestor.com/stockscreen/simplescreen.gsp)*
- *Quicken Stock Screen: (www.quicken.com/investments/stocks/search)*
- *ClearStation Technical Events: (www.clearstation.com/cgi-bin/events?Cmd =techev)*
- *Hoover's Advanced Stock Screener: (www.hoovers.com/search/forms/ stockscreener/0,2221,71,00.html)*

SELLING SIGNALS

One of the most difficult disciplines that traders and investors must incorporate into their trading routine is taking profits. Until a position has been exited, any profits are only paper profits and are at risk to be taken away by the market at any moment. How do you know when to get into another stock? How do you know when to let your profits run? When do you sell? I always analyze a stock's risk-to-reward relationship when answering these questions for myself. When I go long a stock, the anticipation is that the potential upside is substantially greater than the potential downside. However, once I am in that position, if that favorable risk-to-reward relationship changes, then I begin looking to exit the position. Theoretically, this is an easy thing to say; however, in reality it is a discipline that needs to be cultivated.

There are different warning signs that a stock will give signaling to the investor that a change in the risk-to-reward relationship has occurred. Again, I like to keep my analysis as simple as possible, and there are three primary events that will trigger me to sell or exit a long position. First, if there is something that has negatively impacted the fundamentals of the company then I will sell it, no questions asked. This could include a multitude of factors such as, a change in management, a less optimistic view of future performance than originally expected by the company, or products that have the possibility of becoming obsolete.

The second event that will cause me to exit a long position is if the stock breaks the support of where I originally entered. Remember, I am trying to get into the stock when its primary uptrend has resumed. If the stock breaks down at that entry point, then there is a high probability that the up trend is not intact. Lastly, I will use the stochastics indicator to help exit a trade when profits have already been accrued. Just as stochastics can help pinpoint when to enter a stock, it can also help the trader to exit a position. When the stochastic indicates that there is a high probability that the stock in an upward trend is going to reverse direction, I will go ahead and take my profits, because the risk-to-reward relationship has changed from when I originally entered the position.

Figure 12.16 summarizes the buy and sell indicators.

TRADING SOFTWARE

There are a multitude of software programs available that make technical analysis, fundamental analysis, and all of the searches and screens discussed above extremely simple to complete. In many cases, all you will need to do is click your mouse, and *bingo*, your reports are generated in a matter of seconds. Every trader and investor has their own opinions about software for their own personal reasons; therefore, it is really not possible to claim that one program is greater than another. However, I will review a few of the primary software packages that I use to perform the above functions.

Omega Research offers some of the finest software products on the market. I can personally recommend TradeStation, OptionStation, and SuperCharts. TradeStation is one of the most advanced charting programs on the market today. It literally transforms your computer into an intelligent trading assistant that scans the market for you, instantly alerting you to profitable buy/sell opportunities based on the guidelines of your trading system. It has all the bells and whistles to help you make the most of your time and money.

OptionStation is a software program designed to help options traders make educated trade decisions. After Omega Research's initial development, the company asked me to review it to make sure that everything that I needed as an options trader

Buy Signals	*Sell Signals*
• New highs	• New lows
• Trend line support	• Trend line resistance
• Divergence in technicals	• Divergence in technicals
• Volume spikes	• Support level broken
• OBV (on-balance volume) turns positive	• OBV trends negative
• Higher highs, higher lows in trend line	• Lower highs, lower lows in trend line
• Gaps up on heavy volume	• "Gap down" opening
• Closes at high of day	• Closing at the lows of the day
• Option volume increases (open interest)	• Option volume increases (open interest)
• Sentiment indicators flash very strong pessimism	• Sentiment indicators flash very strong confidence

Figure 12.16 Buy and Sell Indicators

was accessible (which I did with gusto). It enables you to manage and analyze risk and reward potentials for your market positions, works with real-time and/or end-of-day data, delayed quotes, and manual input. All the important options strategies are available as well as such key analysis criteria as implied volatility, risk curves, and the ability to evaluate option prices to determine fair value.

SuperCharts Real-Time is an excellent charting program that works with Option-Station to enhance your ability to watch the markets that you are interested in and then carry that information right into OptionStation. As a comprehensive technical analysis software, it has real-time capabilities built into all of its analysis and charting features. You can use the live quote window to get quick and easy access to up-to-date information. It keeps track of trading volumes and fundamental data, or takes advantage of 80 technical indicators, 15 drawing tools, real-time alerts on trend lines and prices, automatic candlestick patterning, and real-time news updates. Both SuperCharts and TradeStation make it easy to know your P&L on a tick-by-tick basis so that you can accurately make adjustments, maximize profits, and minimize losses. Go to www.omegaresearch.com for more information on on these excellent software programs.

Another excellent tool is Telescan Investor's Platform, otherwise known as TIP. This system offers a wealth of statistical and textual information on more than 300,000 securities, market indexes, currencies, and commodities. The Telescan database contains online quotes delayed by 20 minutes, historical price and volume data dating back to 1973, more than 80 technical and fundamental indicators that can be charted, insider trading information, and news from Reuters and PR Newswire. The most powerful tool of the TIP software is its stock searching/screening capabilities. This program offers over 200 fundamental and technical indicators for defining a search request that enables investors to customize their searches and apply them to their own trading methods. For more information on the products offered by Telescan, please visit the web site: www.telescan.com.

There is also software that can be downloaded off the Internet for free that is called BigEasyInvestor. This software package has many of the same features as Telescan and has extremely powerful searching/screening capabilities as well. Any type of technical criteria can be typed in and the software will search the entire universe of stocks and list the securities that meet your request. For more information on this software visit the web site: www.bigeasyinvestor.com.

Investor's Business Daily has an excellent online program called Daily Graphs Online. This program is an interactive, financial information service that offers graphs for equities traded on the NYSE, Nasdaq, and AMEX. The service also provides technical and fundamental data for over 11,000 companies as well as individual databases on mutual funds, bonds, economic variables, industries, sectors, and market indicators that are tracked by their proprietary database. Additionally, there are weekly reports that are generated based on William J. O'Neil's investment philosophy and his proprietary performance criteria. Please visit www.dailygraphs.com for more information on this service.

AIQ (Artificial Intelligence Quotient) has an options program, Option Expert, that generates real-time quotes, ranks the options according to volatility, and offers strategies to trade based on current premiums and time remaining before expiration date. It's fast and easy to use, and has another, separate program for stocks (Trading Expert Pro), too. You pay a low price for both programs (or you can purchase them separately), then pay a monthly charge for the data feed. For more information, go to www.aiq.systems.com.

Some software programs have very steep learning curves that discourage many a trader. The Omega program can be a little tough at first, but it's what I use. People who do utilize it could not imagine trading without it. Many programs have their own proprietary indicators and signals. This is an area I feel chat rooms can really help. Pose the question to a virtual room of investors, and you'll get plenty of feedback. Look for the ones mentioned most to get an idea of what works for the average trader.

CONCLUSION

This chapter pulled together many of the concepts you've learned, and showed you how to utilize them to make money in the stock market. Like any market, the stock market is firmly rooted in the principles of supply and demand. If you keep this in mind, it will help you in assessing market conditions.

If you see greed forming as fear is being erased, you can:

- Buy the stock.
- Buy a call option.
- Buy a bull call spread.

If you see fear forming as greed is being erased, you can:

- Sell your stock and take a profit.
- Sell the stock short.
- Buy a put option or bear put spread.

If the market is trendless, and you determine that the volatility levels have dropped, you can buy a straddle using LEAPS options and go on vacation until things heat back up. If you determine volatility is high, check the options tables and look for pricing discrepancies, which could offer calendar spread opportunities.

Like I said before, try to get good at one trading strategy. Look for the breakout or the range-bound chart pattern. Study a sector and look for possible situations to utilize your trade specialty. This is somewhat like considering a new car; you never notice Dodge Vipers until you consider buying one. Then, suddenly, you begin seeing them all over town. The same holds true with bull call spreads, or straddles. Look for that formation that has been profitable for you in the past. You'll be surprised how often they occur and you'll be astounded at the money you can make by specializing in one trading strategy at a time.

ROADMAP TO SUCCESS

Objective	Course of Action
Trading approaches: When and how do I begin trading?	Determining current conditions requires looking at a number of different things: • Market sentiment utilizing sentiment analysis techniques. • Technical outlook utilizing various technical analysis tools. A conclusion is drawn from these readings. It should be assumed that no matter how carefully you study market conditions or how careful you are, you will make mistakes along with your successes. Human beings are unpredictable and therefore so are the markets. • Cut your losses early. • Let your profits ride.
To begin, look at a graph of the market. • Dow Industrial ($INDU) • Nasdaq Composite ($COMPX) • S&P 100 ($OEX)	*Wall Street Journal* and *Investor's Business Daily* publish daily charts, or go online to any number of financial home pages. • Yahoo! Finance • MSN MoneyCentral • Optionetics.com (www.optionetics.com) • CNNfn • CNBC
There are three things that the market does: Goes up, down, or sideways (trendless).  **Figure 12R.1** Qualcomm's Three Trends (Courtesy of QCharts (www.qcharts.com))	Look to see if a trend exists. It is estimated that the market trades in a flat range (sideways) about one-third of the time. • Consolidation phase in which sellers and buyers (supply and demand) are in equilibrium. • Technical analysis tools that help identify trends are of little use in this phase. • This type of market is very difficult to make money in. Traders usually wait for the next trend to develop, whether it is in an index or an individual stock. In Figure 12R.1 QCOM heads up, steepens, tops out, consolidates, then goes into a downtrend.

A trend can be viewed in three distinct sections:
- Primary
- Intermediate
- Short-term

The long-term trend lasts a year or more. It is interrupted by the intermediate trend, known as a correction.
- If the primary trend is up, the intermediate trend will be down.
- If the primary trend is down, the intermediate trend will be up. Many analysts and traders call it a bear market rally or a bear trap.

When an uptrend begins, in either a stock or an index, the early stages are typically the most profitable.

Early trend identification yields the most profits.
- Investor sentiment may still be extreme—bullish or bearish—as the new trend begins.
- Contrarian views are very useful at this stage, because the crowd is always wrong.
- Therefore, identification not only of trend, but also of sentiment indicators is critical.
- There are definite chart patterns that can forecast (to a certain extent) the beginning of a new trend.

In Figure 12R.2, AMD shows how profitable a new trend can be as it breaks out of a consolidation pattern and turns north with a vengeance.

Figure 12R.2 AMD Breaks Out (Courtesy of QCharts (www.qcharts.com))

A new trend begins as the result of a reversal of the old trend.

"The trend is your friend until the trend ends."

The Bottom: What It Looks Like
The launch pad for a new bull market.

A market bottom sometimes takes a long time to put in place, certainly longer than a top. Here are some common characteristics of a market bottom.
- If pessimism is high, it will be indicated by:
    - A high VIX (above 30).
    - Put/call ratio indicates the crowd has a downward bias.
    - There are plenty of good reasons why the market shouldn't go up.
- Rallies have stalled; as the stock or index climbs, volume drops off. People are taking their profits quickly and leaving the market.
    - The market reacts negatively to news, good or bad.
    - Interest rates have risen, and remain high.

Figure 12R.3 Triple Bottom—Starwood Hotels & Resorts (Courtesy of QCharts (www.qcharts.com))

–Odd-lot short sales spike up (*IBD*) (The small investor buys and sells at the exact wrong time).

Stocks can put in bottoms without the market.

- The entire market doesn't go up or down at the same time.
- Some sectors will bottom (and top) before or after the market as a whole.

Many of the signals that apply to an index or the broader market don't apply exactly to individual stocks. However, you can still look at these sentiment indicators:

- Large short positions: There's a good amount of open short positions, which would need to be covered if the stock began making a solid move up (www.trading-ideas.com).
- Put/call ratio: Indicates a bearish bias.
    - –E*Trade (www.etrade.com)
    - –CBOE (www.cboe.com)
- Volume has dried up, and the stock has gone sideways for an extended period.

Figure 12R.4   Global Crossing September 1999 Bottom (Courtesy of QCharts (www.qcharts.com))

Technical indicators to watch for:

- Chart formations
- Volume increases

In Figure 12R.5, support is broken, higher lows and good volume mark the low, and stock breaks through resistance.

A stock or index will produce similar chart patterns. Technicians place a great deal of credence in these, even if you don't, because they show how the balance of supply and demand fluctuates. Here's a list of chart patterns that would indicate a bottom has been reached:

- **A double or even a triple "bottom."** When you look at a stock chart it appears the lowest points look like legs sticking down, like table legs. When there are two, it's a double; three, of course, is a triple bottom.
- The wider the legs are apart, the more solid the base is. This means that a new up trend could really go a long way. This is why so many traders like to see these double and triple bottoms.

The consolidation period indicates stock is changing hands, from weak ones to strong ones. Dow Theory states that this is the first stage of a bull market—the accumulation of a stock by insiders and astute investors.

Figure 12R.5   JNJ Daily (Courtesy of QCharts (www.qcharts.com))

Figure 12R.6 GE Daily—Support, Then Resistance, Then Uptrend (Courtesy of QCharts (www.qcharts.com))

Figure 12R.7 Cup and Handle Formation—Trying to Rally about Support/Resistance Line at Right (Courtesy of QCharts (www.qcharts.com))

- **The rounding bottom** chart pattern resembles the bottom of a bowl, the stock's consolidation gradually shifting from distribution to accumulation. Remember: Insiders (and some institutions) know best what the outlook is for their company. If you see them buying, it's a very positive sign.
- **The Cup and Handle** chart gets its name because of its appearance (www.stocktables.com).
- **The Inverted Head and Shoulders:** A stock or index on a downtrend will have lower lows and lower highs. The final two lows will form the left shoulder. When the chart hits the second low and rallies back, it hits the resistance line of the left shoulder and drops, but not as far. (A higher low marks the right shoulder.) Should the stock clear resistance on the next rally attempt, the inverted head and shoulders is completed, and is a very strong bullish (reversal) pattern (www.hardrightedge.com).

The Market Top: An Agonizing Decision to Sell

Figure 12R.8 Conceptus (CPTS)— Breaks Resistance, but Is Looking Top-Heavy (Courtesy of QCharts (www.qcharts.com))

When everything is going your way, and investor confidence is at its greatest, the top is near. (The crowd is always wrong at the extreme highs and lows.)

Sentiment indicators that suggest the market is headed higher include:

- Put/call ratio is bullish.
- VIX is in low 20's or even the teens. (This indicator is more reliable for indicating a bottom rather than a top.)
- Investors Intelligence survey (*IBD*) percent of bullish advisers is 55% or higher.

Watch for other signals, too.

- Specialist short sales are a very good indicator. These are the people on the

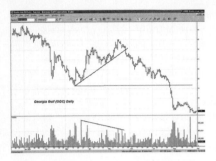

Figure 12R.9   Georgia Gulf (GGC)
(Courtesy of QCharts
(www.qcharts.com))

NYSE floor and are usually accurate in
their assessment of market direction.

- Advance/decline line begins to
  deteriorate.
- A rally attempt following a big rally fails,
  and on lower volume.
- Odd-lot transactions are up. I sound like a
  broken record: The little guy, like the
  crowd, is always wrong.

In Figure 12R.9, GGC makes a nice rally
attempt, but cannot sustain it as buyers
disappear; goes on to break support as
massive selling appears.

Continuation patterns: resting or retreating?

Figure 12R.10   Amazon.com (AMZN)
(Courtesy of QCharts
(www.qcharts.com))

Figure 12R.11   Applied Materials
(AMAT) (Courtesy of QCharts
(www.qcharts.com))

You watch a stock climb and you want to
own it, but don't want to chase it. When it
stops for a rest, will it continue or reverse?

- Watch for continuation pattern to form:
  - Ascending triangle
  - Pennant
  - Trendless range

- A short consolidation is a weak one. Be
  careful for a reversal if the stock tries to
  climb too soon.
- Long consolidation is what to look for.
  Watch volume; breakouts on big volume
  are the ideal situations to look for.
- Bearish plays are possible if support is
  broken; there's no such thing as panic
  buying, which is why stocks drop faster
  than they climb.

In Figure 12R.10 Amazon.com breaks
through a key support level after a
descending triangle.

In Figure 12R.11 Applied Materials has a
short narrowing consolidation period and
breaks to the downside on big volume—a
very bearish sign.

Pulling the trigger; he who hesitates is lost.

When a consolidation ends and a new trend
is forming, don't be caught by analysis
paralysis. Make your decision and go for it.

- Watch for trader's remorse, which could take you out quickly. Give it some wiggle room.
- If it falls back into range, get out. You can always buy it back.
- Keep an eye on volume. Volume should trend up (overall). If volume dries up as price increases, be on the lookout for a quick reversal.
- Use stochastics or another oscillator to help determine entry and exit points.

Use sentiment analysis for reversals.

Contrary indicators will help alert you to overbought and oversold conditions. Look at stochastics, MACD, or RSI for overbought/oversold readings.

- Watch the put/call ratios for lopsided sentiment.
- On-balance volume indicators will alert you to shifts in accumulation or distribution. (This is the first phase of a new trend according to Dow Theorists.)
- Insider buying or selling is a solid indicator of the company's fortunes by those closest to the information. They will bet with their pocketbooks (www.insiderscores.com/index.asp).

Market Information Terminology: Overcoming the language barrier for a better picture of market activity.

- **Market Breadth:** Readings of how the overall market performed. This will provide you with a more accurate picture of the underlying strength (or weakness) of the market.
    - –**Advances**—Total number of issues gaining in price.
    - –**Declines**—Total number of issues declining in price.
    - –**Unchanged**—Total number of issues whose prices did not change.
- **Advance/Decline Line**—Compares the number of advancing issues (those increasing in price) against those that declined. Calculations are based on the opening trade of normal market hours as compared to the closing price.
- **New Highs**—Stocks making new 52-week highs. The number of new highs is significant because in order for the market to advance, a good number of stocks need to break out of their recent trading ranges into new territory.

- **New Lows**—Stocks making 52-week lows. The opposite is also true for the new lows. Everyone, regardless of the purchase price, is underwater. Expect more selling if it stays down, because investors cut their losses.
- **Advancing Volume**—The combined volume of all advancing stocks.
- **Declining Volume**—The combined volume of all declining stocks.
- **Total Volume**—Trading volume of all stocks traded.
- **A/D Volume** (and total volume)—A good indicator of market strength. If the market is up big, but volume is poor, the rally's credibility is uncertain; that is, it doesn't do much to inspire further buying, as investors are sitting on the sidelines to get a better idea of market direction. Large-volume days are better indicators of market psychology; if it's down or up on big volume, that's your cue as to sentiment and the trend.

TRIN—An overview of volume difference between advancing issues and declining issues.

The TRIN, or Trader's Index, is the difference between advancing and declining volume. A reading above 1 means the market is selling off; below 1 the balance of volume is buying volume. The TRIN is useful intraday to act as a contrary indicator, signaling overbought or oversold conditions. A TRIN of 1.5 would indicate incredible selling pressure, and, according to the contrarian, a reversal is due. (The duration or magnitude of the reversal is not so easily spotted.) A TRIN of .35 indicates confidence levels are high, and is thus considered to be a bearish indicator. During the trading day, most traders watch the *direction* the TRIN is going more than the levels themselves. Only at the extremes is the number truly important.

Tick—This figure is derived by the number of stocks heading up and then subtracting the number of stocks headed down.

The typical tick will range anywhere from +500 to –500. However, the extreme readings of +1,000 or –1,000 serve as excellent contrary indicators, because this type of a reading cannot be sustained; it must return to the normal trading range. It's also a good idea to track the direction the tick is going. Direction is more important most times than the actual reading.

Volatility levels can be defined as a measure of the amount by which a stock price is expected to change.

Market pricing inefficiencies make certain trades feasible.

Calendar spreads: A calendar spread is created by using long and short options with the same strike price but different expiration dates.

- The objective of this position is to have time eat away at the short option while the long option retains its value.
- Look for options with unusually high implied volatility in the front months and low to normal implied volatility in the back months.

Determining Volatility Levels

The overall volatility in the market is most easily seen by the Volatility Index ($VIX). When the VIX is high (+30) it's time to buy; when the VIX is low, it's time to go.

- More reliable for high readings than when it gets low.
- Bollinger bands are often used to determine volatility of individual stocks.
  - –www.equitytrader.com
  - –www.clearstation.com spotlights stocks experiencing high volatility readings.
- Price envelopes are also used, but they work for measuring extreme highs and lows by using a set average above and below the previous 20 days or so moving average of the stock.

More Terminology Regarding Market Behavior

- **Stock Price Cycles**—There exists a group of technicians who closely follow price patterns. Since patterns repeat themselves, cycles become observable. Probably the most notorious and well-known cycle is the Elliott Wave theory. Cycles are discerned by combining the application of moving averages and oscillators over extended periods. For more information, go to:

  –**Mr. P. C. Wong's Presentation** (home. netvigator.com/~pcwonghk/ewt.htm)

  –**The Investment FAQ** (www.invest-faq. com/articles/tech-an-elliot.html)

- **Declining Stock Behavior**—A stock that changes direction, shifting from an uptrend to a down one, tends to exhibit similar chart patterns, although not every stock reverses the same way every time. Some important indicators will flash

More Terminology Regarding Market Behavior

warnings beforehand, in most cases. Some of these include:

-*Price Volume Divergence*: The stock keeps going up, but on declining volume.

-*A "Gap Down" Opening*: This one is tough to miss, especially if you own it. A stock will open lower than the previous day's close, creating a gap in the chart. If it's on heavy volume, this could spell trouble.

-*OBV Is Negative*: On-balance volume or OBV tracks the volume of buyers and sellers, and clearly illustrates on charts whether a stock is under accumulation or distribution. The OBV line will trend downward in a distribution circumstance.

-*Analyst Downgrades a Stock*: This kind of event will likely cause the above signals to show. Brokerage firm analysts can exert a lot of influence over a stock's performance. A downgrade can mean just an adjustment, or an obscure signal to the firm's clients to get out.

-*Earnings Warning*: A warning from a company, announcing they will miss Street expectations for the current quarter is enough to send a stock to the doghouse for a long time. Sometimes it's a timing issue, sales being pushed back or didn't get booked in time. Nonetheless, pay attention to any corresponding downgrades from analysts.

- **Averaging Down**—The concept of averaging down on a stock that moves against you sounds okay at face value, but in reality is discouraged. Perhaps a lower cost basis might mean profitability sooner, but usually not.

- **Rallies and Sell-Offs**—The markets experience exaggerated displays of confidence and fear as shown by rallies and sell-offs. A rally can mean the beginning of an extended up move, or a retracement back from whence it came. A sell-off could mean profit taking or a serious correction. In both cases it's hard to tell without getting some confirmation from other indicators.

- **Buybacks**—Corporations do their best to continually boost their profitability, and sometimes the market just doesn't appreciate it. It's at these times a company will announce it will go into the open market and buy back or repurchase shares it has previously sold to the public. This is a bullish sign and a strong display of confidence.
- **Stock Splits**—Stock splits occur when a company decides its stock price is (usually) too high, making it beyond the reach of most noninstitutional investors. A common form is a 2:1 split, in which a shareholder receives another share for every one owned. If you owned 100 shares in a 2:1 split, you'd end up owning 200 shares, but at half the presplit price. A *reverse split* works the other way. If it was a 2:1 reverse split and you had 100 shares originally, you'd own half that, or 50 shares, afterward, at twice the previous price.
- **Advancing Stock Behavior**—Stocks in a bullish mode will exhibit similar patterns. Fundamentally, demand will begin to outweigh supply, but before then volume will increase. There's an old saying: "Volume precedes price."
- **Divergence**—Divergence is a term applied to any two indicators that begin to generate conflicting signals. Divergences are an early warning sign of a reversal in the current trend of an index or stock, and are of great significance to traders.
- **Correction**—A correction is a mild down move in an up leg of the market, and lasts a relatively short time. A correction turns into a bear market at 20% of a down move from its recent high.
- **Capitulation**—A capitulation occurs most often in bear markets. It's that point where the last optimist says, "I've had enough," throws in the towel, and quits the market. Signs of capitulation occurring are a huge down move on big volume, with market sentiment indicators turning extremely pessimistic.

- **Market Tops and Bottoms**—Spotting a bottom is almost easier than a top, due to the near-cataclysmic cave-in of a bottom. A top is marked by an impressive display of confidence and wanton disregard of fear; big up day, impressive volume, low VIX, and every indicator flashing buy.

Selecting a Profitable Stock Go to the sector that's currently performing well. Here's a list of sites to assist you in determining who's doing well and who's not.	**Rabbitt Analytics** (www.rabbittanalytics.com/default.htm) **StockTables** (www.stocktables.com) **Screen It** • www.radiowallstreet.com • www.hardrightedge.com • www.hoovers.com • www.investors.com • my.zacks.com/screening/index.php3
Find the best-performing stocks within that sector.	*Investor's Business Daily* ranks them daily (www.investors.com). **EquityTrader.com** has a more limited listing, but it's very good, too (www.equitytrader.com). **Zacks** has a terrific list, too (www.zacks.com).
Consult Fundamental and Sentiment Analysis	• Use the sites listed in Chapters 7 and 8 to review fundamental analysis. • Compare and contrast to other companies within the same sector. • Use *IBD* to get a snapshot report card of the stock's performance, ranking, and whether it's under net accumulation or distribution.
Watch Technicals for Perfect Timing	Look for the formations we've discussed previously. Look for volume changes, breakouts, and break downs. Ask yourself: "What trend is this stock in? Up, down, or is it trendless?"
Value Screening Methods	**The Value Screen** • P/E ratios. • Market price to book value. • Minimum earnings growth rate. • A minimum dividend payout ratio or dividend yield could be specified. • A minimum return on total assets or owners' equity could be required to reflect the profitability of the firm.
Growth Screening Methods	**The Growth Screen** • Current quarterly earnings are exploding. • Annual earnings growth rate is greater than the overall market's earnings growth rate.

	• Close to or making new highs. • Have a smaller number of shares outstanding. • Price is greater than $30 per share.
Momentum Screening Methods	**The Momentum Screen** • Stocks that are in the strongest industry groups. • Stocks that have recently made new highs and pulled back off those highs. • Stocks that have given a technical signal that they are ready to resume their upward trend (i.e., stochastic positive breakout).
Screening Sites	• **Morningstar.com** (screen.morningstar.com/stockSelector.html) • **Wall Street Research** (www.wsrn.com/home/dataset/search.html) • **Zacks** (my.zacks.com/index.php3) • **Silicon Investor** (www.siliconinvestor.com/stockscreen/simplescreen.gsp) • **Quicken Stock Screen** (www.quicken.com/investments/stocks/search) • **Clear Station Technical Events** (www.clearstation.com/cgi-bin/events?Cmd=techev) • **Hoover's Advanced Stock Screener** (www.hoovers.com/search/forms/stockscreener/0,2221,71,00.html)
Buy/Sell Signals	Figure 12.16 has a list of indicators that offer clues as to when to buy and sell a stock. In addition, other indicators include: • Oscillator extremes. • MACD (watch the histogram). • RSI. • Stochastics. • Insider buying or selling: The assumption here is that if the people that know the most are buyers or sellers, shouldn't that mean something to you? • Watch out for people just selling for liquidity purposes only. • When restricted stock becomes unrestricted, this is called the lock-up date. Many employees and directors will jump to realize their gains. Watch for price gyrations as this date nears (www.ipolockup.com).

- Candlestick charts have some very reliable buy and sell formations. For a list of 11 reliable bullish candlestick patterns: www.geocities.com:0080/WallStreet/Market/1078/surfport.html.
- Or Steve Nison's page; this guy literally wrote the book on candlestick charting (www.candlecharts.com).

| **Trading Software** | Trading software requires overcoming a learning curve. These programs take advantage of the ever-increasing power of computers to screen and spot for various chart formations, volume alerts, even for option risk characteristics. I have a terrific program on my site: www.optionsanalysis.com. Other good ones include: |

- **Telescan** (www.telescan.com)
- **Big Easy Investor** (www.bigeasyinvestor.com)
- **Omega Research** (www.omegaresearch.com)
- *Investor's Business Daily* has an excellent online program called Daily Graphs Online (www.dailygraphs.com).
- **AIQ** (www.aiqsystems.com)

| **Some Final Thoughts** | You can know everything in this book and then some, and still the market will humble you. Even the odds by following these hard-earned words of wisdom: |

- If you have something major on your mind, some event or condition that prevents you from focusing on the market 100%, don't trade. Period.
- If you experience a string of losses and your confidence is shaken, wait a few days before entering the market, then trade small. Get your swing back before you start trading in earnest.
- Do your homework. Know what your entry and exit points are before you enter a trade.

13

The Path to Trading Success

Fortitudine vincimus.
("By endurance we conquer.")
—Ernest Shackleton, Antarctic explorer

Learning the rules of trading and investing in the stock market is a long and arduous journey. It is a road which took me many years to master. Even now, I know there is still a great deal more to be learned. The day that I think I have learned all I need to know to be successful in the markets is the day that I retire. I will then know there is nowhere to go but downhill. One thing I have learned is that the market is the greatest equalizer of education. Whether you are a Harvard MBA or a high school dropout, the market provides each individual with the same risks and rewards. Each day you will be evaluated by your successes and failures in the market. Hopefully, you will have a great many more successes than failures.

The objective in writing this book has been to provide a path to trading success. In this final chapter, I would like to summarize the steps that I like to use. You may want to integrate these steps into your own trading style or modify them to better meet your own trading needs. Your personality and your personal risk profile should always guide you to engage the types of trading or investment that best fit your lifestyle. In the end, if you find a path that fits your personality and one that you enjoy, you will surely be more successful in the long run.

THE BASIC RULES OF THE GAME

Rule 1: Understand the Psychology of the Trade

First and foremost, you need to get your head straight as to how to win. You have taken the very first step by reading this book and can follow it up by practicing what we have been preaching here. I hope this first step places you on the path to success. Just remember that each and every day is a learning process with the markets. Never believe that you are smarter than the markets, as the markets will always win. Get your head on straight—practice humility; but be aggressive enough to jump into promising opportunities. Your psychological makeup will be as much a factor in your success as your knowledge of and execution in the markets.

Rule 2: Acquire the Knowledge on How the Markets Truly Work

Just because you read a book on the markets doesn't necessarily mean that everything will work for you as a trader. If you like an idea or a concept, test it. Then test it again and retest it. Until you feel comfortable with a trade idea or concept you will not be able to properly implement the strategy. The market is a complex animal. You will need to experience firsthand how the market reacts to market information such as interest rate changes or how individual stocks react to earnings reports. You must remember that the market is notorious for giving false signals to everyone who participates. The noise in the market can sometimes be like the thunderous roar of a tornado. Just be careful and don't be swept away by it.

Rule 3: Develop a Working Knowledge of Entry and Exit Orders

You may have knowledge of the markets, but until you know how to place your idea in the market properly your knowledge cannot be put to work. The types of orders you use both for the entry of the order as well as the exit of the order will greatly affect your trading profits. You must learn when to use limit orders as well as market orders. Test these orders in the market when you start to place your trades. You will see a big difference on how quickly you get filled as well as how you react to the trade. Sometimes the most frustrating thing is to place an order in the market and have to wait around wondering if it's ever going to get filled. You may be amazed at how your nerves react to just waiting for a trade to be executed.

Rule 4: Understand How to Manage Risk

If you want to survive as a trader or investor, you must develop a healthy respect for risk and how to manage it. Most people enter a trade dreaming about how much money they can make. I worry about how much I can lose. So before you place a trade, make sure you ask yourself two questions: What if I am right and what if I am wrong? It may be more fun thinking about what will happen if you're right, but you'll play the game much better if you spend more time concentrating on the ramifications of being wrong. It is absolutely critical to know how much you can lose or accept as risk before you place a trade. You must accept risk as a daily part of your trading. Learning to manage the risk will enable you to stay in the game and reap more rewards. I like to have a visual picture of risk and reward before I place a trade. So I suggest you do the same. There are plenty of software programs specifically designed to help traders accomplish this feat, or you can use the Platinum program located at the Optionetics.com web site to help you understand exactly what a trade's risk and reward looks like.

Rule 5: Pick a Strategy that Matches the Market Conditions

The market is like a storybook that tells a new story every day. Opening that book each day to read the story demands that you learn to read between the lines in order to forecast market performance and apply the appropriate strategies. When you understand the many strategies you can use, you learn to match the strategy with the market conditions. Markets go up, down, and sideways. No strategy works all the time. If it did, we would all be filthy rich. So you need to learn to read the market conditions and adjust your trading approach accordingly. Since it is important to use all the weapons you have available to you to trade, I strongly urge you to integrate options into your trading arsenal. I believe that options allow you to be much more creative and to place the odds in your favor. But before trading options, you have to make sure that you understand all the risks and rewards associated with options trading.

Rule 6: Manage the Strategy

Once you have placed a trade, you have to manage it effectively. If you buy a stock, when are you going to sell it? If you buy an option, do you want to exercise it or sell it? If you have a profit objective, when will you take it? If you have a trade on, when do you want to adjust it? These are just a few of the questions you need to answer. Sometimes the management of a trade is more difficult than just placing a trade. You should always know what your next reaction will be and what prompts you to take it. Planning ahead is a very important part of the game and will definitely contribute to your success.

HOW TO PICK A STOCK WINNER

To be successful you need to know the rules of the game. Then you need to know where to apply these rules. Every trading day, I wake up trying to figure out how to pick a winner. I have a few guidelines that help me to make the right decisions that I will now share with you.

Watch What Moves

All kinds of media bring us the news of the day and since news moves the markets, I have become a media hound. What follows is a brief synopsis of the main news arteries and how I take advantage of them.

Television
First, I watch TV and lots of it. No, I don't spend my time watching *Barney* or *Who Wants to Be a Millionaire*. I am busy watching the business channels: CNBC and

CNNfn. I basically live and breathe watching CNBC. I have grown up with it as a trader and I get a great deal of useful information listening to it as a constant backdrop to my trading day. After all, if they are talking about it on TV, then the stock is usually moving. They are paid to talk about stocks that move, so I watch what they watch. I like to play the momentum stocks and when they are talked about on TV, they usually have some reason to move. If you can't watch CNBC all day long because you have a day job, then turn it on when you get home so you can catch up on whatever you missed.

When I am unable to watch CNBC then I watch CNNfn (CNN Financial). I have appeared several times on this show and it seems to be almost everywhere including the airports. Watching it will help you to keep an eye on stocks that are in the news. If you are hearing about a stock on CNBC or CNN, so are millions of other traders and investors.

Web Site Surfing

Throughout this book, I have constantly referred you to a host of web sites. Some web sites have become so popular that they are carving their own special niche of influence on market sentiment. Sites like TheStreet.com, Zacks Investment Research, and Yahoo! Finance have taken the bulls by the horns more than once. So bookmark the biggies and surf the Net to find out what other sites can help you maneuver the market obstacle course as best you can. There's a great deal of information out there, so take another look at my recommendations in each of the "Roadmaps" to streamline your surfing and save time.

I have to admit I am very prejudiced about my favorite web site: Optionetics.com. My team of traders and support staff work endless hours to make Optionetics.com the ultimate site for traders. In addition to serving as the primary resource for trading information for our students, we have thousands of people visiting it every day, and we recently received a "Best of the Web" award from *Forbes* magazine. We strive each and every day to provide high-quality information geared to helping you find promising trading ideas and make informed trading decisions.

Newspapers and Magazines

What would a trading and investing career be without the *Wall Street Journal* and *Investor's Business Daily*? These two newspapers should be read daily to help you get a feel for what is happening in the markets. Both have good web sites as well. I also like to read *Red Herring*, which has some great articles and information on one of my favorite markets: the technology sector. Make sure to check out its web site (www.redherring.com). Of course, *Barron's* is another must-read and offers a host of information you can't find anywhere else. These are just a few of the magazines and newspapers you should read; but they should be the ones at the top of any trader's reading list.

REVIEW OF FUNDAMENTAL ANALYSIS AND HOW IT WORKS

In this section, I just want to review and highlight some elements of fundamental analysis to try to simplify your analysis process. Remember that fundamental analysis scrutinizes a stock based upon information, which will likely drive the price of the stock. Let's take a look at the events, which will most likely affect the price of a stock. It is important for you as a trader to understand each and every element that can drive the price of your stocks up or down, or keep the stock in a trading range.

Earnings (Announced and Preannounced)

Earnings are one of the main reasons stocks go up or down—sometimes with a vicious move that can ruin any trader's day. Companies in the United States report earnings every three months. These are referred to as quarterly reports. It is the job of the company to accurately and fairly disclose its financial condition to the public. It does this in two ways: the actual announcement and a "preannouncement." A preannouncement is when the company announces to the public that it will not meet, or it will exceed, earnings expectations. When this happens the stock will usually move quickly if the number is way out of line of what analysts and traders expected. Once a company preannounces, this is a good time to jump in since it is often a great driver of price action.

Analyst Upgrades/Downgrades

Stock prices are very much a function of what the analysts say about a stock. Wall Street is driven by research from many brokerage firms on many stocks. The analysts from these firms stay in touch with the management of the company. It is their job to try to forecast the future growth of the company as well as stock prices for their clients. They are not always right; no one is. But with their ear close to management's voice, they can hopefully put together a smart future plan for their clients. Now, the problem arises when the management has guided the analysts incorrectly and surprises the Wall Street analyst community with information that was unexpected. On many occasions, this can mean a stock price getting chopped in half. How would you like to lose 50% on a stock just because the management was not guiding analysts correctly? If management was guiding for a profit and a loss comes in, watch out. Pay attention to what the analysts say; they can drive a stock in either direction quickly.

New Product Announcements

Let's say you wake up one day and you hear about a company that has developed a cure for cancer. What would happen to the stock price? It skyrockets, right? One company made this exact announcement and the stock went from $11 a share to roughly $85 a share overnight! Although it was exciting to see this kind of price action, you can't believe everything you hear. This same company later stated on CNBC that more tests were needed. Well, the stock fell $30 on that news and continued to fall. This is what a new product announcement can mean: a swift move in either direction. This is especially evident in the areas of human genomics. Watching these stocks move swiftly in either direction can seem incredible. See what happens in the race to build the fastest computer chip between Intel (INTC) and Advanced Micro Devices (AMD), and watch Rambus (RMBS), also. These stocks move and they move big. It is exciting to track stocks after they have announced new products, but you may want to use nondirectional option strategies to take advantage of them.

Management Changes

If a well-known company is sluggish or moving down, management changes may be imminent. When a new CEO comes in, watch to see how the market reacts. You can make a great deal of money by following these companies when they make a big change. The big investors, the institutions, will drive the stock up if they like it and down if they don't. Just look at what happened when IBM brought in Lou Gerstner, or when Hewlett Packard or AT&T made changes at the top of the management chain. These stocks all made robust moves to the upside. Keeping an ear out for changes in management can earn you a great deal of money.

Stock Splits

If there is a system that helps a trader make money (at least in the past few years), it comes from focusing on stocks that have already announced a stock split or are projected to announce a split. Many momentum traders love jumping into these stocks. A company will announce a stock split usually when the stock has made a big run-up in price. The board of directors votes on a split to make the shares more affordable to more investors (at least this is the theory) as well as to promote another stock run-up (this is not supposed to be the main objective). Splits are usually announced right around the same time as earnings reports. How do you find these stocks? Just look for companies that have exhibited this pattern before. For example, if you look at a stock like Yahoo! (YHOO), you will see a distinct pattern. Also, companies should have enough shares authorized to make the split possible. There are some great stock split services on the Internet (check out www.splitmaster.com, www.stocksplits.net, and www.tradingday.com). As a trader, this can be a very lucrative way to look for opportunity. A word of caution: Stocks typically run up in the anticipation of the split and the announcement. They may sell off in the short run after the split; but they are usually good companies, ready to go up again.

Accounting Irregularities

What is an accounting irregularity? Well, another way to put it is a potential that the company has "cooked the books." Some would call this fraud. What if a company has overstated sales or overstated earnings, and then its overstatements are subsequently discovered? Well, it has to report this to the investment community. The investment community then gets a chance to react to the information. In most cases, the stock will quickly fall in price. I have seen stocks decline as much as 90% in price when information hits announcing that the previous information provided was false. This kills investor confidence, and everyone bails out as quickly as possible. Sometimes the accounting irregularity is not a big problem and the company will rebound. Most of the time, it is real and the stock price will plummet like Niagara Falls. In some cases, the irregularity is so severe the company has to file for bankruptcy, as it will have to restate earnings, may have defaulted on bank loans, and may be besieged by investor lawsuits. It is hard to come back from all this adversity. Just do some research on Bre-X Minerals and you will see what I mean. Even the hint of an accounting irregularity creates a bad situation for any company.

Takeovers

Takeovers are another area that can really drive price action. There are two kinds of takeovers: friendly and unfriendly. You don't make much money with friendly takeovers. This is a kiss-and-hug situation when everyone agrees to the transaction. I like the unfriendly takeover, as this is where money can be made. If a company wants to buy another company without the target company's blessing, then the first company must make a hostile bid. This means that it tries to accumulate enough shares to make its presence known. Then it starts a proxy fight to buy a controlling share of the stocks of the target company in order to have control of the board of directors. If the target company does not want to be acquired, it may put into place defense tactics, or demand that the price be increased to expand shareholder value. In many cases, the price will be bid up not only by the first company that made the offer, but also by other companies now interested in the target company. This is a very interesting process. Just watch the movie *Barbarians at the Gate* and you will find a very humorous view of the RJR Nabisco bidding war. It is well worth the time.

No News

When you see a stock make a big move up or down and there is no news to be found, it usually means that some news has leaked and it will be evident in the short term. Keep an eye on these stocks. I can't tell you how many times I have seen the stocks that I am watching make a major move only to find out that information (that was supposed to be made available to everyone at a later date) somehow already leaked out. This happens in many cases when a big brokerage firm's analysts may have received information that they are able to provide to their clients first. This is not what the rules say should happen, but it has happened in the past. In fact, the Securities and Exchange Commission has just issued new guidelines for the release of information making it wrong to have "selective disclosure." Now companies have to make information available to everyone, including the public trader, at the same time. With the proliferation of the Internet, you now can listen to company conference calls that provide access to the same information the large institutional investors get.

UNDERSTANDING TECHNICAL ANALYSIS AND HOW IT WORKS

One of the problems I had when I first started my trading career was that I read every book on trading I could find and then focused on learning each and every technical analysis tool. In many cases, I would try to combine too many tools and each would give me a different opinion. A multitude of technical analysis tools have been developed over the years. In this section, I will review my two favorite tools that I work with daily due to their simplicity and trading validity. For more information, please review the information in Chapter 9.

Volume

First, I like to look at the volume trading on a stock. How do you do this? Easy, just put a stock chart together using a daily bar graph and put a volume indicator on it. Almost all software programs which do charts will give you volume. I like volume because it's usually a great indicator for discerning the beginning or the reversal of a stock price move. This is especially evident when a stock has moved up or down quickly in a short period of time—referred to as a volume spike. This means that the volume of shares traded on the stock have spiked up from previous periods. You can even get an average trading volume each day; and if you see volume at least double, then this may be a precondition to a move or reversal. Remember that for every buyer there will be a seller. So if someone is giving up on a stock or taking profits, someone else is initiating a position. If you buy good companies when they get hit hard on a fast move down and the volume spikes, this may be a great time to place a long strategy on the stock.

Moving Averages

I like to look at two very simple moving averages to give me an idea as to where the stock price will be: the 50-day moving average and the 200-day moving average. Remember that a moving average is an average of the closing price of the stock over the period of time you choose as the analysis period. So if you wanted to look at a 50-day moving average of IBM you would take the closing price for the last 50 days, add them up, and divide by 50. This would be the average price close for the last 50 days. You would calculate the 200-day moving average (MA) the same way. Luckily, these days all programs have an ability to put moving average lines on your charts, including multiple moving averages. How do you use this information? Well, a good company will usually have its stock price trading above both its 200- and 50-day moving averages. Usually when the stock price falls below its 50-day moving average you need to see if it will fall further to the 200-day MA. It should bounce from the 200-day MA. If it does not bounce and breaks below the 200-day MA, then the stock will likely fall more. Just practice by looking at a large number of charts with a 50-day and 200-day MA. You will eventually build a good feel as to how to trade using this method.

Don't Overanalyze—Avoid Analysis Paralysis

As stated earlier, the problem with technical analysis is that an individual trader when first introduced to the concepts will try to use too many tools at the same time. This may cause analysis paralysis, as novice traders have a tendency to overanalyze. I don't know anyone who overanalyzes who makes a great living as a trader or investor. You need to take action to make money in the markets. Without action, there will be no profits. In the beginning you have to learn as much as you can about technical analysis. But as you progress, concentrate on the tools you like and understand best. Make sure to test them first by using any of a number of computer programs that allow you to back-test a system. Don't waste a great deal of time on any system that doesn't work for you. There is no holy grail. More than likely, you will find out that you will make more money using the same principle I use: the KISS principle (keep it simple, stupid).

PUTTING IT TOGETHER: HOW TO FIND A GREAT TRADE

Now that you have lots of great knowledge, how do you find that great trade? Well, I like to look at stocks that move—the bigger they move the more they excite me. I like to trade technology stocks because that is where the action has been. Someday the excitement (and movement) will be in another sector and I will change my focus to that sector. As a market player, you have to be able to adjust quickly to the market conditions. Start by getting to know one sector very well. Get to know the top stocks in it very well. If you live in Texas, maybe the oil sector is best. If you live in Silicon Valley, then you are in the capital of the technology world. If you feel competent in one sector, go ahead and move into another and then another until you amass as much information as you can. But take the time to do your homework in each sector before you start trading the stocks in it.

Step 1: Analyze Your Personality

What kind of stocks do you like? How much risk can you afford to take? How much are you willing to risk on one trade? How much time do you have to manage the trade? It is absolutely vital to assess how a stock fits your personal trading approach and lifestyle.

Step 2: Pick a Stock

Integrate the techniques explained in this book to find a promising opportunity. Make sure that any stock you choose is one that you want to follow. Look at the fundamental news to analyze the stock and then use technical analysis to analyze the timing of the trade. If you don't know where to start, just pick a great company with great earnings prospects. Talk to other investors and watch CNBC. If you still don't know where to start, look at Sun Microsystems (SUNW), Cisco (CSCO), and Intel (INTC). These have been favorites of many individual traders and institutions over the years.

Step 3: Analyze a Trade Strategy

What kind of trade do you want to place? Is it an options or a stock trade? What kind of time frame does it require: short-term or long-term? What is the trade's risk-to-reward profile? What happens if you're right? What will you do if you are wrong? These may seem like simple questions, but you'd be amazed at how many people never ask these kinds of questions before placing a trade. Cover your bases as best you can, and you'll be prepared for whatever the future brings.

Step 4: Place the Trade

Before placing the trade with your stockbroker, write it down on paper so that you don't make a mistake placing it. All orders called in by phone are recorded, and it's very easy to get nervous and place the wrong order (which can be disastrous). If you are using an online brokerage, make sure you are absolutely comfortable with the process. If you have any questions, call and ask a live broker to help you. There is no shame in asking for help, and it's their job to help you make money—not lose it. If you still don't feel confident placing a trade, paper trade it. Just track your positions on paper until you find you feel comfortable with the process. There's always another good trade just around the corner, so don't worry about missed opportunities. The key is to be comfortable with the ordering process. If you can't find a good trade, or you feel uncomfortable with the trade, go back to Step 1 and keep trying until you get it right. Perseverance is vital to your success.

Step 5: Manage the Trade

Managing the trade is what makes or breaks a trader. If you're right, what actions will you take to capitalize on the situation? If you're wrong, when will you get out? If it's a long stock position, have you placed a stop loss? Do you know how to adjust your trade? Did you get out as the stock did not do as well as you thought it would? These are all great questions to ask. Set your profit and loss objectives in advance and follow your own rules to the letter.

Step 6: Monitor Your Progress

It is important to monitor your progress as a trader or investor to learn from your mistakes and your triumphs. What portfolio management system do you use? Have you been achieving the results you expected? If not, do you need more education or experience? Are you habitually making the same mistake? What can you do to improve yourself as a trader or investor? Be bold in your efforts at self-assessment.

Keep your head out of the sand. Accept your losses gracefully by using them as opportunities for personal growth. Remember that financial security is often the product of small but consistent gains coupled with huge once-in-a-while profits.

GIVE YOURSELF THE WINNER'S EDGE

This book is my attempt to help people take their first step on the path to success in the stock market. I only wish I had been given this kind of a foundation when I started out. It would have saved me many years of hardships and many lost dollars. By reading this book, you should now have a clear understanding of what it takes to pursue what I believe is the ultimate profession and lifestyle. The techniques in this book are many of the same principles of risk management used by professional brokers. Before you make any decisions with respect to a particular stock, ask yourself not only "What if I'm right?" but also "What if I'm wrong?" Only by being keenly aware of market volatility, taking steps to mitigate risk, and filtering out unimportant information does it become possible for investors to avoid the school of hard knocks, sleep well at night, and enjoy trading for what it ought to be—fun.

Although it may seem difficult at times, try to enjoy yourself while you take this journey. Undoubtedly the urge to quit may bear down upon you when times get tough. But winners don't quit; they just keep persisting until they get it right. If you don't enter, you can't win—it's as simple as that. It takes knowledge and experience to master the markets. By reading this book, you now have the basics of stock trading; it's up to you to gain the experience in slow increments that add up to a successful journey.

I truly hope this book empowers you to become a successful trader or investor. If you find enjoyment and success in the markets, then we have completed our original goal: to help people who simply didn't know where to start find their way into the heart of the stock market. I wish you all the luck in the world. Welcome to the stock market!

Appendixes

APPENDIX A. FINANCIAL PROFILE TEMPLATES

PERSONAL BALANCE SHEET

Assets	Amount	Liabilities	Amount
Finances		**Short-Term Debt**	
• Cash	_____	• Credit card debt	_____
• Checking account	_____	• Medical/dental debt	_____
• Savings account	_____	• Vehicles debt	_____
• Trading account	_____	• Short-term loans	_____
• Mutual funds	_____	• Miscellaneous debt	_____
• 401(k)	_____		
• IRAs	_____		
SUBTOTALS			
Long-Term Assets		**Long-Term Debts**	
• House (mortgage)	_____	• Mortgage	_____
• Vehicles	_____	• Tuition loans	_____
• Fixtures	_____	• Long-term loans	_____
• Recreation	_____		
• Equipment	_____		
• Miscellaneous	_____		
SUBTOTALS			
NET TOTALS			
ASSETS – LIABILITIES =			

MONTHLY INCOME STATEMENT

Monthly Income	Amount	Monthly Expenses	Amount
Cash Received		**Basic Living Expenses**	
• Wages after taxes	_____	• Rent/mortgage	_____
• Alimony income	_____	• Food	_____
• Child support	_____	• Utilities	_____
• Rental income	_____	• Phone/ISP bill	_____
• Business income	_____	• Heating	_____
• Additional income	_____	• Transportation	_____
		• Clothes	_____
		• Entertainment	_____
		• Miscellaneous	_____
		Insurance Payments	
		• House/renter's insurance	_____
		• Health insurance	_____
		• Dental insurance	_____
		• Car insurance	_____
		• Life insurance	_____
		• Long-term care insurance	_____
Totals		**Debt Payments**	
Income Total – Exprenses Total =		• Credit card (minimum payment)	_____
		• Alimony	_____
		• Child support	_____
		• Tuition loan	_____
		• Miscellaneous loans	_____

RISK TOLERANCE AND INVESTMENT GOALS

Risk Tolerance		*Investment Goals*	
Monthly Income	_____	Investment Goal ÷	_____
– Monthly Expenses	_____	Years until Retirement	_____
Net Profit/Loss	_____	Annual Return Goal	_____
Total Assets	_____	**Financial Potential**	
– Total Liabilities	_____	• Tax bracket	_____
Net Worth	_____	• Utilities	_____
		• Phone/ISP bill	_____
3 × monthly expenses		• Heating	_____
(aggressive)	_____	• Transportation	_____
		• Clothes	_____
6 × monthly expenses	_____	• Entertainment	_____
(moderately aggressive)		• Miscellaneous	_____
		Insurance Payments	
9 × monthly expenses	_____	• House/renter's	
(conservative)		insurance	_____
		• Health insurance	_____
		• Dental insurance	_____
		• Car insurance	_____
		• Life insurance	_____
		• Long-term care insurance	_____
		Debt Payments	
		• Credit card (minimum	
		payment)	_____
		• Alimony	_____
		• Child support	_____
		• Tuition loan	_____
		• Miscellaneous loans	_____

Totals
Income Total – Expenses Total =

APPENDIX B. STOCK ANALYSIS TEMPLATE

Company:	Entry Date:
Industry Sector:	Capitalization:
Present Price:	52-Week High:
Target Exit Price:	52-Week Low:

Quarterly Figures

Quarter	Earnings per Share	Sales
Latest Quarter		
Previous Year Quarter		
% Change (Latest Quarter—Previous Year Quarter)		

Five-Year Price-Earnings Figures

Year	Price 52-Week High	Price 52-Week Low	Earnings per Share	P/E Ratio High	EPS	P/E Ratio Low	EPS
Total							
Average							
Is the current 52-Week High or Low higher or lower than the average?			Is the current P/E ratio higher or lower than the average P/E ratio?				

Growth Rate

Current EPS		Next Year's Projected EPS		Growth Rate = Projected EPS Current EPS	
Current EPS		Projected EPS Two Years from Now		Growth Rate = Projected EPS Current EPS	

Five-Year Sales/Expenses Performance

Year	Annual Sales	Annual Exprenses	Net Profit
% Change (Last Year—two years ago)			

Price to Sales Ratio
(Every $1 of sales = "X" amount of investing value)

Year	Market Capitalization (# Outstanding Shares × Price per Share)	Annual Sales	Price to Sales Ratio (Capitalization—Sales)
% Change (Last Year—two years ago)			

APPENDIX C. MARKET TIME LINE

YEAR	HISTORICAL FACT

1273   Kublai Khan issued the first paper notes made out of mulberry bark and fixed with his seal.

1368   The first official paper money—the Kwan—was created by the Ming dynasty of China.

1531   The first official stock exchange opened its doors in Belgium (although the Romans are credited with the earliest history of traded securities).

1602   Amsterdam opened the second securities market.

1661   Sweden took credit for issuing the first European paper money.

1688   London hosted its first trading of securities.

1690   British Empire first used promissory notes to finance their siege of Quebec.

1773   The first official London exchange opened its doors.

1790   Trading of securities emerged in the United States when the federal government issued $80 million in bonds to refinance all federal and state Revolutionary War debt. The bonds were the first shares of public securities to be traded at the first American stock exchange established in Philadelphia.

1792   New York City's prominent merchants and brokers signed the Buttonwood Agreement formalizing the trading of securities at a regular commission basis and marking the unofficial birth of the New York Stock Exchange (NYSE). The NYSE began by trading five securities—three government bonds and two bank stocks.

1830   The first railroad stock was listed. From that point on, railroad stocks consistently dominated the markets for the rest of the century.

1842   The second exchange, the American Stock Exchange (AMEX), emerged and is still referred to as the "curb market" because originally trading actually took place on the street.

1871   The NYSE switched to a system of continuous trading which replaced the trading of certain stocks at specific times. This major revision, in turn, created precise fixed locations to trade each particular stock eventually known as trading pits.

1921   The AMEX finally moved indoors.

1929   Stock market crashed ushering in a decade of severe depression.

1971   Designed by the Securities and Exchange Commission (SEC), the Nasdaq, the world's first electronic exchange, hits the airwaves.

APPENDIX D. BASIC STRATEGY REVIEWS AND RISK GRAPHS

Long Stock

Strategy = Buy shares of stock.

Market Opportunity = Look for a bullish market where a rise in the price of the stock is anticipated.

Maximum Risk = Limited to the price of the stock as it approaches zero.

Maximum Profit = Unlimited as the price of the stock rises.

Breakeven = Price of the stock at initiation.

Margin = Required. Usually 50% of the total cost of the shares.

Short Stock

Strategy = Sell shares of stock.

Market Opportunity = Look for a bearish market where a fall in the price of the stock is anticipated.

Maximum Risk = Unlimited to the upside.

Maximum Profit = Limited to the full price of the stock shares as they fall to zero.

Breakeven = Price of the stock at initiation.

Margin = Required. Usually 150% of the total cost of the shares.

Long Call

Strategy = Buy a call option.

Market Opportunity = Look for a bullish market where a rise above the breakeven is anticipated.

Maximum Risk = Limited to the amount paid for the call.

Maximum Profit = Unlimited as the price of the underlying instrument rises above the breakeven.

Breakeven = Call strike price + call option premium.

Margin = None.

Short Call

Strategy = Sell a call option.

Market Opportunity = Look for a bearish or stable market where you anticipate a fall in the price of the underlying stock below the breakeven.

Maximum Risk = Unlimited to the upside beyond the breakeven.

Maximum Profit = Limited to the credit received from the call option premium.

Breakeven = Call strike price + call option premium.

Margin = Required. Amount subject to broker's discretion.

Long Put

Strategy = Buy a put option.

Market Opportunity = Look for a bearish market where you anticipate a fall in the price of the underlying stock below the breakeven.

Maximum Risk = Limited to the price paid for the put option premium.

Maximum Profit = Unlimited to the downside beyond the breakeven.

Breakeven = Put strike price – put option premium.

Margin = None.

Short Put

Strategy = Sell a put option.

Market Opportunity = Look for a bullish or stable market where a rise above the breakeven is anticipated.

Maximum Risk = Unlimited to the downside beyond the breakeven.

Maximum Profit = Limited to the credit received from the put option premium.

Breakeven = Put strike price – put option premium.

Margin = Required. Amount subject to broker's discretion.

Covered Call

Strategy = Buy the underlying security and sell an OTM call option.

Market Opportunity = Look for a bullish to neutral market where a slow rise in the price of the underlying stock is anticipated with little risk of decline.

Maximum Risk = Virtually unlimited to the downside below the breakeven all the way to zero.

Maximum Profit = Limited to the credit received from the short call option + (short call strike price – price of long underlying asset) × value per point.

Breakeven = Price of the underlying asset at initiation – short call premium received.

Margin = Required. Amount subject to broker's discretion.

Covered Put

Strategy = Sell the underlying security and sell an OTM put option.

Market Opportunity = Look for a bearish or stable market where a decline in the price of the underlying stock is anticipated with little risk of the market rising.

Maximum Risk = Unlimited to the upside beyond the breakeven.

Maximum Profit = Limited to the credit received on the short put option + (price of the short underlying asset – put option strike price) × the value per point.

Breakeven = Price of the underlying asset + short put premium received.

Margin = Required. Amount subject to broker's discretion.

Bull Call Spread

Strategy = Buy a lower strike call and sell a higher strike call with the same expiration dates.

Market Opportunity = Look for a moderately bullish market where you anticipate a modest increase in the price of the underlying above the price of the short call option.

Maximum Risk = Limited to the net debit paid for the spread.

Maximum Profit = Limited [(difference in strike prices × value per point) – net debit paid].

Breakeven = Lower call strike price + net debit paid.

Margin = Required. Amount subject to broker's discretion.

Bull Put Spread

Strategy = Buy a lower strike put and sell a higher strike put with the same expiration date.

Market Opportunity = Look for a moderately bullish market where you anticipate a modest increase in the price of the underlying asset above the strike price of the short put option.

Maximum Risk = Limited [(difference in strike prices × value per point) – net credit].

Maximum Profit = Limited to the net credit received when the market closes above the short put option.

Breakeven = Higher put strike price – net credit received.

Margin = Required. Amount subject to broker's discretion.

Bear Put Spread

Strategy = Buy a higher strike put and sell a lower strike put with the same expiration date.

Market Opportunity = Look for a bearish market where you anticipate a modest decrease in the price of the underlying asset below the strike price of the short put option.

Maximum Risk = Limited to the net debit paid.

Maximum Profit = Limited [(difference in strike prices × value per point) – net debit paid].

Breakeven = Higher put strike price – net debit paid.

Margin = Required. Amount subject to broker's discretion.

Bear Call Spread

Strategy = Buy a higher strike call and sell a lower strike call with the same expiration date.

Market Opportunity = Look for a moderately bearish market where you anticipate a slight decrease in the price of the underlying asset below the strike price of the short call option.

Maximum Risk = Limited [(difference in strike prices × value per point) – net credit].

Maximum Profit = Limited to the net credit received.

Breakeven = Lower call strike price + net credit received.

Margin = Required. Amount subject to broker's discretion.

Long Straddle

Strategy = Purchase an ATM call and an ATM put with the same strike price and the same expiration.

Market Opportunity = Look for a market with low volatility where you anticipate a sharp volatility increase.

Maximum Risk = Limited to the net debit paid.

Maximum Profit = Unlimited to the upside and downside beyond the breakevens. Profit requires sufficient market movement but does not depend on market direction.

Upside Breakeven = ATM strike price + net debit paid.

Downside Breakeven = ATM strike price – net debit paid.

Margin = None.

Short Straddle

Strategy = Sell an ATM call and an ATM put with the same strike price and the same expiration date.

Market Opportunity = Look for a wildly volatile market where you anticipate a period of low volatility.

Maximum Risk = Unlimited to the upside and the downside beyond the breakevens.

Maximum Profit = Limited to the net credit received. Profit is possible if the market stays between the breakevens.

Upside Breakeven = ATM strike price + net credit received.

Downside Breakeven = ATM strike price – net credit received.

Margin = Required. Amount subject to broker's discretion.

APPENDIX E. OPTION EXPIRATION MONTH CODES

	Jan	Feb	Mar	Apr	May	Jun
Calls	A	B	C	D	E	F
Puts	M	N	O	P	Q	R

	Jul	Aug	Sep	Oct	Nov	Dec
Calls	G	H	I	J	K	L
Puts	S	T	U	V	W	X

APPENDIX F. STRIKE PRICE CODES

A	B	C	D	E	F	G	H	I
5	10	15	20	25	30	35	40	45
105	110	115	120	125	130	135	140	145
205	210	215	220	225	230	235	240	245
305	310	315	320	325	330	335	340	345
405	410	415	420	425	430	435	440	445
505	510	515	520	525	530	535	540	545
605	610	615	620	625	630	635	640	645
705	710	715	720	725	730	735	740	745

J	K	L	M	N	O	P	Q	R
50	55	60	65	70	75	80	85	90
150	155	160	165	170	175	180	185	190
250	255	260	265	270	275	280	285	290
350	355	360	365	370	375	380	385	390
450	455	460	465	470	475	480	485	490
550	555	560	565	570	575	580	585	590
650	655	660	665	670	675	680	685	690
750	755	760	765	770	775	780	785	790

S	T	U	V	W	X	Y	Z
95	100	$7^{1}/_{2}$	$12^{1}/_{2}$	$17^{1}/_{2}$	$22^{1}/_{2}$	$27^{1}/_{2}$	$32^{1}/_{2}$
195	200	$37^{1}/_{2}$	$42^{1}/_{2}$	$47^{1}/_{2}$	$52^{1}/_{2}$	$57^{1}/_{2}$	$62^{1}/_{2}$
295	300	$67^{1}/_{2}$	$72^{1}/_{2}$	$77^{1}/_{2}$	$82^{1}/_{2}$	$87^{1}/_{2}$	$92^{1}/_{2}$
395	400	$97^{1}/_{2}$	$102^{1}/_{2}$	$107^{1}/_{2}$	$112^{1}/_{2}$	$117^{1}/_{2}$	$122^{1}/_{2}$
495	500	$127^{1}/_{2}$	$132^{1}/_{2}$	$137^{1}/_{2}$	$142^{1}/_{2}$	$147^{1}/_{2}$	$152^{1}/_{2}$
595	600	$157^{1}/_{2}$	$162^{1}/_{2}$	$167^{1}/_{2}$	$172^{1}/_{2}$	$177^{1}/_{2}$	$182^{1}/_{2}$
695	700	$187^{1}/_{2}$	$192^{1}/_{2}$	$197^{1}/_{2}$	$202^{1}/_{2}$	$207^{1}/_{2}$	$212^{1}/_{2}$
795	800	$217^{1}/_{2}$	$222^{1}/_{2}$	$227^{1}/_{2}$	$232^{1}/_{2}$	$237^{1}/_{2}$	$242^{1}/_{2}$

APPENDIX G. VARIABLE OPTION DELTAS

All options are provided a delta relative to the 100 deltas of the underlying security. If 100 shares of stock are equal to 100 deltas, then the corresponding options must have delta values of less than 100. You can estimate an options delta as follows depending on the movement of the underlying stock.

OPTION DELTAS	CALLS		PUTS	
	Long	**Short**	**Long**	**Short**
ATM	+50	−50	−50	+50
ITM				
1 Strike	+60 to +65	−60 to −65	−60 to −65	+60 to +65
2 Strikes	+70 to +75	−70 to −75	−70 to −75	+70 to +75
3 Strikes	+80 to +85	−80 to −85	−80 to −85	+80 to +85
OTM				
1 Strike	+35 to +40	−35 to −40	−35 to −40	+35 to +40
2 Strikes	+25 to +30	−25 to −30	−25 to −30	+25 to +30
3 Strikes	+15 to +20	−15 to −20	−15 to −20	+15 to +20

APPENDIX H. INTERMARKET RELATIONSHIPS

Interest Rates	Bonds	Stocks	Dollar
Rising	Falling	Falling	Rising
Falling	Rising	Rising	Falling
Stable	Stable	Up/Stable	Stable

Note: If these relationships do not hold, then there is said to be a divergence. A good trader will look for reasons for a divergence and look for opportunities to make money under the circumstances.

APPENDIX I. LISTS AND TABLES

The following tables are a source of information regarding the largest companies along with their standings in the major indexes and sectors.

Largest NYSE Companies

Company	Symbol	May 2000 Market Cap ($bil.)	May 2000 NYSE Average Daily Volume	May 1999 Market Cap ($bil.)
General Electric	GE	509.5	13,625,153	322.7
Exxon Mobil Corp.	XOM	290.7	4,368,871	193.9
Wal-Mart Stores	WMT	263.1	6,511,786	189.6
Citigroup Inc.	C	203.5	8,258,420	149.6
International Business Machines Corp.	IBM	196.7	5,706,291	214.8
Lucent Technologies	LU	187.7	9,303,896	149.7
American International Group	AIG	176.3	2,839,834	120.0
Merck & Co.	MRK	172.5	4,381,762	159.6
Pfizer Inc.	PFE	170.6	9,655,066	138.5
SBC Communications Inc.	SBC	150.5	4,860,943	100.2

Source: NYSE.

Largest Computer Companies

Company	Symbol
Microsoft Corp.	MSFT
Apple Computer Inc.	AAPL
Alph Microsystems	ALMI
Intel Corp.	INTC
AmerUs Life Holdings, Inc.	AMH
Concurrent Computer Corp.	CCUR
Convex Computer Corp.	CNX
Compaq Computer Corp.	CPQ
Dell Computer Corp.	DELL
Gateway 2000 Inc.	GTW
Hewlett Packard Co.	HWP
International Business Machines	IBM
Micron Electronics	MUEI
Silicon Graphics	SGI
Scientific Technologies	STIZ
Sun Microsystems	SUNW

Nasdaq Companies by Sector

Sector	Number of Companies
Computer Programming and Data Processing	569
Finance, Insurance, and Real Estate	963
Services	511
Retail/Wholesale Trade	547
Manufacturing	1,324
Transportation and Communications	345
Drugs	275
Computers and Office Equipment	161
Other	199

Nasdaq Non-U.S. Companies by Global Market Cap

Company	Symbol	Country	($Millions)
Toyota Motor Corp.	TOYOY	Japan	$129,316
Ericsson Telephone Co.	ERICY	Sweden	$61,920
Lvmh Moet Hennessy	LVMHY	France	$27,209
Canon, Inc.	CANNY	Japan	$27,034
NEC Corp.	NIPNY	Japan	$24,730
Reuters Group PLC	RTRSY	United Kingdom	$19,606
Fuji Photo Film	FUJIY	Japan	$19,041
Orange PLC	ORNGY	United Kingdom	$18,723
Tokio Marine and Fire Insurance	TKIOY	Japan	$17,608
Global Crossing	GLBX	Bermuda	$17,316
Nissan Motor Co. Ltd.	NSANY	Japan	$15,235
AB Electrolux	ELUX	Sweden	$14,968
Volvo AB SWE	VOLVY	Sweden	$13,742
Colt Telecom Group Plc	COLTY	United Kingdom	$13,370
Kirin Brewery Ltd	KNBWY	Japan	$12,867
ABB Ab-Spon Adr	ABBBY	Sweden	$12,955
Akzo Nobel NV	AKZOY	Netherlands	$12,236
Anglo AM CP So. Africa	ANGLY	South Africa	$12,158
Mitsui & Co. Ltd.	MITSY	Japan	$10,492
De Beers Cons. Mines	DBRSY	South Africa	$9,362

Top 10 Initial Public Offerings—January–June 1999

Company	Symbol	Sector	Offering	Country	Underwriter
United Pan-Europe Communications NV	UPCOY	Broadband communications	$576,928,000	Netherlands	Goldman Sachs/Morgan Stanley
Barnsandnoble.com	BNBN	Internet bookstore	$517,500,000	United States	Goldman Sachs
Northpoint Communications	NPNT	Internet access	$414,000,000	United States	Goldman Sachs/Merrill Lynch
Pinnacle Holdings, Inc.	BIGT	Wireless equipment	$308,364,000	United States	BT Alex. Brown
Time Warner Telecom	YWYC	Telecom services	$289,800,000	United States	Morgan Stanley/Lehman Brothers
TC Pipelines	TCLPZ	Pipelines	$235,750,000	United States	Goldman Sachs
Rhythms NetConnections	RTHM	Internet access	$226,406,000	United States	Merrill Lynch/Salomon Brothers
Onemain.com	ONEM	Internet services	$215,050,000	United States	BT Alex. Brown
EToys Inc.	ETYS	Internet retailer	$191,360,000	United States	Goldman Sachs
MIH Ltd	MIHL	Cable television	$187,830,000	B.V.I.	Merrill Lynch

Source: Securities Data Corp.

Top Mutual Fund Companies—One Year (1999)

Fund	Symbol	Return (%)
PBGH New Opportunities	PBNOX	294.27
Ivy: European Opport/Adv	IEOVX	250.47
Ivy: European Opport/A	IEOAX	248.08
Ivy: European Opport/B	IEOBX	246.99
Dreihaus European Opport	DREOX	188.33
Deutsche Eur Eqty Gr/lst	MEUEX	184.16
Dreihaus Intl Discovery	DRIDX	180.37
Dresdner RCM Biotech/N	DRBNX	165.84
Nicholas-App Glbl Tech/I	NGTIX	158.49
PBHG Select Equity	PBHEX	154.27
Kopp Emerging Grth/Inst	KEGIX	151.02
Kopp Emerging Grth/A	KOPPX	150.21
Kopp Emerging Grth/C	KEGCX	148.71
Black Rock Itl Sm Cp/Ist	BISIX	145.19
Franklin Biotech Disc/A	FBDIX	144.61

Top Mutual Fund Companies—Five Years (1995–1999)

Fund	Symbol	Return (%)
Firsthand: Tech Value	TVFQX	56.83
Fidelity Sel: Electronics	FSELX	49.26
Rydex:OTC/Inv	RYOCX	47.49
PIMCO:Innovation/A	PIVAX	45.77
PIMCO:Innovation/B	PIVBX	45.23
PIMCO:Innovation/C	PIVCX	45.22
PBHG Select Equity	PBHEX	42.79
Fidelity Sel:Technology	FSPTX	41.97
Fidelity Sel:Computers	FDCPX	41.58
INVESCO Telcom/Inv	ISWCX	41.52
Calamos Growth Fund/A	CVGRX	41.03
First Amer:Tech Fd/Y	FATCX	40.69
Bridgeway: Aggressive Grth	BRAGX	40.63
First Amer:Tech Fd/RA	FATAX	40.33
INVESCO Tech/Inv	FTCHX	39.32

Largest Nasdaq Companies as of June 30, 1999

Company	Net Worth
Microsoft Corporation	$460,301,731,633
Cisco Systems	$205,836,908,430
Intel Corporation	$197,421,000,000
MCI WorldCom Inc.	$160,131,862,734
Dell Computer Corporation	$ 94,012,301,000
Oracle Corporation	$ 54,122,978,250
Sun Microsystems Inc.	$ 53,114,058,250
Yahoo!	$ 39,196,176,500
Amgen	$ 31,167,817,375
Comcast	$ 28,019,451,439

World Market Dollar Volume Growth 1990–1998

Nasdaq	89
NYSE	33
London	26
Paris	24
German Stock Exchanges	12

Top Indexes

Index	Symbol
Dow Jones Industrial Average	$INDU
Dow Jones Transportation Average	$TRAN
Dow Jones Utilities Average	$UTIL
Nasdaq 100 Index	$NDX
Nasdaq Composite Index	$COMPQ
NYSE Composite Index	$NYA
S&P 500 Stock Index	$SPX
S&P 400 MidCap Stock Index	$MID
S&P 100 Stock Index	$OEX
Nasdaq High Technology Index	$IXCO
PSE High Technology Index	$PSE
Morgan Stanley High Tech Index	$MSH
Semiconductor Index	$SOX
AMEX Major Market Index	$XMI
AMEX Composite Index	$XAX
Wilshire Composite Index	$WSX
Toronto 35 Index	$TSE-TC
TSE 100 Index	$TOP-TC
TSE 300 Composite Index	$TT-TC
Mexico Index	$MEX
10-Year T-Note Interest Rate (x.10)	$TNX
30-Year T-Bond Interest Rate (x.10)	$TYX
PHLX Gold and Silver Index	$XAU
AMEX Oil & Gas	$XOI
Value Line Index (Geometric)	$XVG
Russell 1000	$RUI
Russell 2000	$RUT
Russell 3000	$RUA

APPENDIX J. TYPES OF ORDERS

Type of Order	Description
At-Even Orders	Should be placed without a debit or a credit to the account. That means that you may have to wait until the market gets to the right prices for your trade to be placed.
At-the-Opening Orders	Should be executed at the opening of the market or should be canceled.
Day Orders	Remain good only for the duration of the trading day that it is entered. It is canceled at the end of the trading day, if not executed.
Good till Canceled Orders	Remain in effect until executed, explicitly canceled, or the contract expires.
Immediate or Cancel Orders	Must be executed immediately in whole or part as soon as it is entered. Any part not executed is automatically canceled.
Fill-or-Kill Orders	Must be executed immediately or by a specific date as a whole order. If not, the order is canceled.
Limit Orders	Specify a maximum buying price or a minimum selling price.
Limit Buy Orders	Must be executed below the current market price.
Limit Sell Orders	Must be executed above the current market price.
Market-on-Open Orders	Must be executed during the opening of trading.
Market-on-Close Orders	Must be executed during the closing of trading.
Market Orders	The most common type of order. Buying or selling securities at the price given at the time the order reaches the market. This can be different from the price on your broker's screen. A market order must be executed at the best price the market has to offer. It is the only order that guarantees execution.
Market-if-Touched Orders	Combine market and limit orders, whereby the order becomes a market order when the options or stock reach a specified price.
Market-if-Touched Buy Orders	Become a buy market order when the options or underlying fall below the current market price.
Market-if-Touched Sell Orders	Become a sell market order when the options or underlying rise above the current market price.
Stop Orders	Used to limit risk. They become market orders when the options or stock reaches a certain price.
Buy Stop Orders	Become a market buy order upon a trade at or above the specified price.
Sell Stop Orders	Become a market sell order upon a trade at or below the specified price.
Stop Limit Orders	An extension of stop orders where the activated order becomes a limit order instead of a market order.

APPENDIX K. EXCHANGES AND SEC

American Stock Exchange

www.amex.com

The American Stock Exchange is comprised of companies that were too small to be listed on the New York Stock Exchange. Requirements include a pretax income of $750,000 in two of the last three years, stockholders equity of $4,000,000 and a minimum market capitalization of $3,000,000. The AMEX web site is quite extensive and offers quotes, news, and exchange information as well as excellent educational materials.

Chicago Board of Trade

www.cbot.com.

The Chicago Board of Trade is primarily a futures and options exchange, where the Dow Jones Industrial Averages (DJIA) futures trade. The CBOT also has a trading simulation through the Auditrade system. There is a charge of $10.00/month to participate in Auditrade's simulated trading. This will allow you to practice trading using a fake account and real prices, until you get comfortable with the strategies and their results.

Chicago Board Options Exchange

www.cboe.com

The Chicago Board Options Exchange is the largest options exchange in the United States. Its web site offers news, new option listings, and exchange information on equities, options, and LEAPS. Specialization includes calls and puts on NYSE stocks, the S&P 500, U.S. Treasury bonds, and other indexes.

Nasdaq

www.nasdaq.com

The National Association of Securities Dealers Automated Quotations (Nasdaq) system is also known as the over-the-counter market where, via online computer transactions, OTC, and specific New York Stock Exchange–listed securities can be bought and sold through licensed securities brokers and dealers. It features the internationally acclaimed Nasdaq overview and the worldwide Nasdaq network of Nasdaq performance data. There are quotes, charts, graphs, ticker search services, and features such as the 10 most active share volumes, polling volumes, and most active advanced performances. A good site to set up portfolio tracking and stock screening. An excellent site tour helps you get started.

New York Stock Exchange

www.nyse.com

The New York Stock Exchange (NYSE), or the Big Board, is the world's largest equities market with a capitalization of over $12 trillion. A tremendous amount of information is available about new and previously listed companies, with annual reports, research, publications, and news.

Pacific Stock Exchange

www.pacificex.com

The Pacific Stock Exchange (PCX) is the third most active stock exchange in the country and the third largest stock options exchange in the world. More than 2,600 stocks, bonds, and other securities issued by publicly traded companies, as well as options on more than 550 stocks are traded on the PCX, along with a variety of indexes. Quotes on equities and options are delayed 20 minutes.

Philadelphia Stock Exchange

www.phlx.com

The Philadelphia Stock Exchange (PHLX) was founded in 1790 as the first organized stock exchange in the United States. The PHLX trades more than 2,800 stocks, 700 equity options, 12 index options, and 100 currency options; 15-minute delayed quotes and volatility charts are available, along with news, research, and daily market analysis.

Securities and Exchange Commission

www.sec.com

The Securities and Exchange Commission (SEC) has a lot of detailed securities-related information. SEC reports of listed companies, investor guides, and EDGAR. The EDGAR database performs automated collection of corporate information and reports required to be filed with the SEC. In 1998, the SEC's web site received a Webby award for Best Money/Business site.

APPENDIX L. MEDIA SOURCES AND WEB SITES GUIDES

Magazines

Barron's: This outstanding magazine offers breaking and scheduled financial news and commentary from the *Wall Street Journal Interactive Edition*, plus exclusive, weekday coverage from industry giant and pioneer *Barron's.*

Business 2.0: This insightful business magazine offers readers a host of market info and data from the cyber world's cutting edge.

Business Week: This popular magazine has been around for a long time offering a great selection of business news and commentary.

Fortune 500 Magazine: This well-written magazine site offers lists of top company performers, industry medians, and of course the famous Fortune 500. Top analysts give an inclusive analysis of the unique Fortune 500 macro view of financial events.

Investor's Business Daily—Option Guide: Another exceptional biweekly publication to spot stocks with options which can make a big move. This periodical reviews every stock that has options complete with pertinent charts and graphs. Worth its weight in gold many times over once you understand the risks and rewards associated with options strategies, and techniques used to maximize gain and minimize risk.

Online Investing: An excellent magazine specifically focusing on the needs of the online investor. This monthly magazine offers the latest reviews of financial web sites as well as snappy news and insightful trading articles. Great writers and unique perspectives keep this relative newcomer a definite up-and-comer.

Technical Analysis of Stocks & Commodities: Good cross section of stock and commodity information. More technical than other periodicals, but a very good source of interesting trading ideas designed to foster trader success by offering information on technical trading strategies, charting patterns, indicators, and computerized trading methods through well-researched feature articles.

Wired: Well-known for its cutting edge style and lively commentary, *Wired* magazine provides plenty of interesting news, articles, commentary, and market analysis with an inclination for high-technology subjects and online dot-com companies.

Worth: This magazine offers a variety of investment articles, feature stories, and archived stories from previous editions. There is also an online link to the complete Peter Lynch archives, a section for investor resources, and Investing 101 for beginners.

Useful Web Sites

Free information about stocks and options on the Internet abounds. Please keep in mind that many new internet web sites are created daily, and the information on individual sites is dynamic and ever changing. This is just a small selection of sites that we have found to be well-designed, user-friendly, and useful.

Education
Final Bell
www.sandbox.net/finalbell/pub-doc/home.html
CNN Financial Network hosts the Final Bell, which is a place you can join free stock trading simulations, master the basics of online investing, and compete for great prizes.

Motley Fool
www.fool.com
The Motley Fool site was created to educate, amuse, and enrich. This popular and entertaining site has a vast amount of information including quotes, charts, financials, education, portfolios, news, and ideas.

Options Industry Council
www.optionscentral.com
The Options Industry Council (OIC) is the educational arm of several exchanges, including the American Stock Exchange (AMEX), Chicago Board Options Exchange (CBOE), Pacific Stock Exchange (PSE), the Philadelphia Stock Exchange (PHLX), and the Options Clearing Corporation (OCC). The site offers free educational material to help you learn about trading options.

Stock Track
www.stocktrak.com
Stock Track provides portfolio simulations featuring stocks, options, futures, bonds, and more. Over 10,000 college students use this terrific educational site each semester in their finance and investment courses. Stock Track is now available to anyone, allowing you to manage a fake brokerage account of $100,000 in order to test strategies, place trades, and learn about the financial markets.

Virtual Stock Exchange
www.virtualstockexchange.com
The Virtual Stock Exchange is a simulation web site utilized by over 65 colleges and investment clubs, managing portfolios through free simulations. Their investment guide contains a glossary, online resources, and market strategies.

Charts and Quotes
BigCharts
www.bigcharts.com
Bigcharts is sure to become one of your favorite sites with intraday charts, historical quotes, and quotes on over 34,000 stocks, mutual funds, and indices. Great info on the big movers and losers in the main markets, momentum charts, and other goodies.

BMI

www.bmiquotes.com

Bonneville Market Information (BMI) has free 20-minute delayed quotes, a link to CBS MarketWatch, and end-of-day global market information, including exchange rates and American depositary receipts (ADR) prices. Real-time quotes are available for a fee.

ClearStation

www.clearstation.com

This site focuses on technical information including customized charts, graphs, and company profiles. Enjoy custom portfolios, quotes, charts, message boards, and daily e-mail alerts plus recommendations that are actually worthwhile.

CyberInvest

www.cyberinvest.com

CyberInvest is an excellent guide for the focusing on investor education, portfolio tracking, market monitors, Zacks research, global investing, portfolio tracking, and a round-up of the coolest tools on the Web.

DBC Online

www.dbc.com

A comprehensive site that includes delayed and real-time quote services, news, movers and shakers, charts, portfolios, and alerts. Many trading software programs are compatible with DBC (also known as Signal) to run their analysis systems.

Financial Web

www.financialweb.com

This extensive site is one of our favorites for reviewing fundamental data and historical prices of options and stocks, and for researching mutual funds.

PC Quote

www.pcquote.com

PC Quote has delayed quotes and access to real-time quotes on stocks, options and futures, as well as a multitude of insightful articles and pertinent data.

Quicken.com

www.quicken.com

The Quicken site has quotes, advanced charting, portfolio information, news, analysis, profiles, SEC filings, and reports in addition to its turbo tax products.

Quote.com

www.quote.com

One of the best sites on the Net, Quote.com offers a full web page of useful information, including delayed and real-time quotes, charts, earnings estimates and reports, top business stories, NYSE most active gainers and losers, and a market guide with in-depth information on individual companies. You can also register for hourly updates; dynamic quote service, and timely news feeds.

StockMaster

www.stockmaster.com

StockMaster is another excellent site with quotes and clear daily price charts with separate volume charts. Check out their investor sentiment surveys.

StockTools

www.stocktools.com

The StockTools site has delayed quotes on all the major U.S. and Canadian exchanges. Nice features include a wide variety of industry groupings for selecting quotes. Customizable graphs, and extensive historical quotes are also available.

Timely.com

www.timely.com

Timely.com is a friendly little site with 15 to 20-minute delayed quotes, charts, and indicators on over 17,000 different securities. Lists most actives, biggest gainers and losers also.

Yahoo! Finance

quote.yahoo.com

The Yahoo financial site has quotes, financial news, features, a reference section with calendars, the latest market news, and a portfolio feature to track your favorite stocks.

News Sources

Bloomberg

www.bloomberg.com

Bloomberg's site has a staggering array of financial information including headlines, market updates, and equity indexes. Currency calculators and cross-currency rates are useful bonuses. Real audio sound bites are available for up-to-the-minute updates.

Business Week

www.businessweek.com

Business Week online has daily briefings, quotes, and portfolio information. Many interesting and well-written articles make this a worthwhile site, while the banking, technology, and education centers are interesting. The searchable archive dates back to January 1991.

CBS MarketWatch

www.marketwatch.com

CBS MarketWatch is sure to be on everyone's bookmark list, with comprehensive coverage of news, headlines, and market data. Delayed quotes are supplied by DBC.

CNBC

www.cnbc.com

The CNBC television news channel is the leader in business news. The CNBC site has programming information for CNBC in the U.S., Europe, and Asia. Biographies for the CNBC staff are also online. Extensive executive and job search Web listings and phone numbers are available.

CNNfn

cnnfn.cnn.com

The CNN television news channel has successfully spun off their online Financial News site, with the hot stories of the day, market updates, quotes, resources, and briefings.

Dow Jones

www.dowjones.com

The Dow Jones site has global market updates, economic indicators, the quotes, and the newswire. Access to other business publications is also available.

Dun & Bradstreet

www.dnb.com

Dun & Bradstreet specializes in press releases and company profiles, focusing on news, views, and trends.

The Economist

www.economist.com

The *Economist* is the international journal of news, ideas, and opinions. Thought-provoking analysis and articles abound in the current issue, as well as access to archived editions.

Financial Times

www.ft.com

The *Financial Times'* online newspaper requires free registration to access headlines and financial information. Free search of archived articles is available.

Forbes

www.forbes.com

Forbes Digital Toolbox is an intriguing site with many of the *Forbes* lists, interesting commentary, and delayed quotes.

Investor's Business Daily

www.investors.com

The *IBD* site has incorporated many topical daily news articles from sections such as Inside Today, Front Page, Computers & Tech, the Economy, the Markets, and Vital Signs.

Kiplinger

www.kiplinger.com

Kiplinger online is an excellent source of business forecasts and personal financial advice. The PAWWS Financial Network provides 20-minute delayed quotes.

MoneyNet

www.moneynet.com

Reuters MoneyNet has market briefs, indexes updates, the market snapshot, business news, company news, quotes, and top stories.

Moody's

www.moodys.com

Moody's Investors Service is the leading provider of credit ratings, research, and financial information to the capital markets.

Nasdaq Trader
www.nasdaqtrader.com
The Nasdaq Trader has trading and market data services, volume reports on shares, lists of share volume leaders, trading halts, and access to Nasdaq news.

Reuters
www.reuters.com
Reuters news service has an impressive array of financial information; especially useful are the world market indices and information on the foreign exchange (ForEx) markets.

Standard & Poor's
www.stockinfo.standardpoor.com
The Standard & Poor's site contains interesting, updated headlines and market commentary, and a wealth of information on the S&P 500.

Technical Analysis of Stocks and Commodities
www.traders.com
The online site of *Technical Analysis of Stocks and Commodities* magazine has monthly featured articles and excellent educational information for the novice trader. A wide variety of links and resources make this a useful site.

Wall Street Journal
www.wsj.com
Wall Street Journal Interactive Edition requires a small fee for online subscription. There are some interesting free features such as top business news in Spanish and Portuguese, annual reports from selected companies, the Small Business Suite, and Shareholder Scorecard. There is also an updated job and career search section with technical, professional, and management positions listed.

Worth
www.worth.com
Worth Online has a variety of stories and archived stories from previous editions. Check out the complete Peter Lynch archives, the investor resource section, and Investing 101 for beginners.

Zacks Investment Research
www.zacks.com
Zacks Investment Research site has a nice variety of research, emerging stock picks with potential for explosive growth, analysis, quotes, and balance sheets. It also has a subscription service that delivers news and quotes regarding your personal portfolio picks directly to your desktop.

Search Engines
HotBot
www.hotbot.com
HotBot is a superb search engine with fast access to business and financial information.

Infoseek

www.infoseek.com

Infoseek has both business and personal finance sections, with quotes, charts, market research, DRIPs, shareholder reports, and a section on stock market basics. They have an excellent free subscription service that delivers market information directly to your desktop.

Lycos

www.lycos.com/money

The Lycos site is an excellent source for stock and other financial information. They have access to quotes, headlines, stock alerts, and a link for the top 10 investment sites.

Yahoo!

www.yahoo.com/business

The Yahoo! site for business and the economy has a wealth of information from business headlines and indexes to economic indicators and the international economy.

Informative Sites

Briefing.com

www.briefing.com

The Briefing.com site has live market commentary, stock analysis, quotes and charts, sector ratings, and an economic calendar. Other premium services are available.

COOP

www.coop-options.com

The Committee on Options Proposals is comprised of respected options industry professionals and marketing personnel from 40 stock exchange member firms, the four options exchanges, and the OCC.

Daytraders

www.daytraders.com

This site is a daytrader's paradise, full of news and resources. Delayed quotes are supplied by Quote.com. The trading strategies section has some wonderful common sense information for all traders.

Direct Stock Market

www.dsm.com

Direct Stock Market provides investors, entrepreneurs, and securities industry professionals with current, complete, and immediate information about public and private offerings.

Economagic

www.economagic.com

One of the most comprehensive free economic sites on the Net with access to more than 100,000 core U.S. macroeconomic documents and government reports. A must for any broad market analyst trying to keep track of government reports and economic events.

EDGAR-Online

www.edgar-online.com

This first-rate site is truly a valuable financial resource. It allows you to access EDGAR filings using an electronic data-gathering analysis retrieval tool (now, that's impressive) to locate the SEC filings that interest you. Check out the exclusive drill-down tools, "IPO Express" feature, and insider trading updates. Program an alert to let you know when a company you are watching files a new document. Although this is a subscription-based site, they do offer a few free services including custom portfolios.

FINweb

www.finweb.com

FINWeb is a highly concentrated financial economics web site dedicated to listing internet resources providing substantive information concerning economics and finance-related topics. Sections include Electronic Publishing (Journals), Working Papers, Databases and Research Tools, and of course extensive links. Very highbrow—check out the jokes about economists, too.

Individual Investor

www.individualinvestor.com

The Individual Investor online site has access to quotes, strategies, the Magic 25, hot stocks, analysis, portfolio and mutual fund information.

InfoBeat

www.infobeat.com

InfoBeat is an easy-to-use, one-stop shopping site for getting information delivered right to your PC. Just click on Finance to set up portfolios of stocks and receive daily e-mail messages containing closing prices and pertinent news. Click on Select and then Business and Finance to browse their extensive selection of e-mail newsletters and columnists from leading publishers that you can receive free.

Info Space

quotes.infospace.com

Info Space has access to 50 real-time stock quotes per day and unlimited delayed quotes. Company research and market updates such as movers and performers are available. Links to the Yellow and White Pages let you search for financial Advisers. Stock news is available by ticker symbol.

Investorama

www.investorama.com

Doug Gerlach's Investorama is a wonderfully comprehensive directory for investors. Researching a stock is especially easy as there is a huge variety of research, company background and analysis available including several types of quotes and charts from BigCharts. A great site.

Investor Guide

investorguide.com

The Investor Guide is a tremendous resource for personal investing on the Web; in addition to quotes and news, they have over 1,000 responses to investment questions. This excellent, comprehensive site focuses on investing, personal finance, and education. They also run the hedge hog investment competition. Have you ever wanted to create and manage your own $1,000,000 hedge fund? Here's your chance.

Investor Home

www.investorhome.com

The Investor Home page is a treasure trove of links, quotes, charts, research, profiles, and earnings estimates. This site has won five awards the last time we checked.

Money Club

moneyclub.com

The MoneyClub has information on all aspects of money. In addition to the info center and news room there is basic stock and quote information. A wide variety of topics, such as, IPOs, real estate, credit and debt collection, banking, insurance, retirement, and taxes are also covered.

Optionetics.com

www.optionetics.com

The Optionetics.com site has comprehensive information available on all financial markets. It offers quotes, market analysis, and a multitude of daily articles by insightful investment journalists. Make sure to check out the Platinum area, a comprehensive options analysis program designed to fit the needs of the active option trader.

Stocks.com

www.stocks.com

The Stocks.com site is a financial resources guide with access to quotes and research and a ton of excellent links.

StockSecrets

www.stocksecrets.com

The Stock Secrets site claims to be the most complete financial library on the Internet. Use its search engine to scroll through more than 3,000 pages of financial books.

Silicon Investor

www.siliconinvestor.com

The Silicon Investor site claims to be the largest discussion community on the Web with over 3,500,000 messages in its database. This haven for tech stock investors specializes in computers, software, communication, semis, biotechnology and medical devices, and much more. Quotes and charts are supplied by North American Quotations, Inc., and are delayed 15 to 20 minutes.

TheStreet.com.

www.thestreet.com

Controversial analyst Jim Cramer hosts this site. Most active, and percentage gainers and losers are prominent features here. Two weeks free at sign-on, with interesting articles and insights. Excellent commentary and market analysis can be delivered to your desktop (available by subscription).

Thomson Investors Network

www.thomsoninvest.net

The Thomson Invest site allows you to access news from their newsroom and retrieve selected articles in from the Market Monitor. Research, news, and intraday quotes are nice features.

WallStreetCity

www.wallstreetcity.com

The Wall Street City site has it all, from market analysis, commentary, and consensus reports to news, quotes, charts, reports, and the S&P Marketscope.

Wall Street Research Net

www.wsrn.com

The Wall Street Research Net has over 500,000 links to help professional and private investors perform fundamental research on actively traded companies and mutual funds, and locates important economic data that moves markets.

World Wide Financial Network

www.wwfn.com

The World Wide Financial Network has an excellent variety of investor resources—from indexes, point and figure charts, and quotes to extensive research, feature articles, and access to online brokers. Overall a great site.

APPENDIX M. ONLINE BROKERAGE DIRECTORY

Online Brokerage	Web Site	Phone
A.B. Watley	www.abwatley.com	888-229-2853
Accutrade	www.accutrade.com	800-494-8939
American First Associates	www.aftrader.com	888-682-6973
American Express Financial Direct	www.americanexpress.com/direct	800-297-5300
Ameritrade	www.ameritrade.com	800-454-9272
BCL Online	www.bclnet.com	800-621-0392
Benjamin & Jerold Discount Brokerage	www.stockoptions.com	800-446-5112
BOSC Online Brokerage	www.oneinvest.com	888-843-6382
Brown & Co.	www.brownco.com	800-225-6707
Bull & Bear Online	www.bullbear.com	800-285-5232
Bush Burns Securities	www.bushburns.com	800-821-4803
Castle Securities	www.castleonline.com	800-891-1003
Charles Schwab Online	www.eschwab.com	800-225-8570
Citicorp Investment	www.citicorp.com/us/investments	800-846-5200
CompuTEL Securities	www.computel.com	800-432-0327
CyBerBroker, Inc.	www.cybercorp.com	877-729-2379
Datek Online	www.datek.com	800-823-2835
Discover Direct	www.discoverbrokerage.com	800-584-6837
DLJ Direct	www.dljdirect.com	800-825-5723
Dreyfus BrokerageService	www.edreyfus.com	800-421-8395
Empire Financial Group	www.lowfees.com	800-569-3337
E*Trade	www.etrade.com	800-786-2575
FarSight Financial	www.farsight.com	800-830-7483
Fidelity Web Xpress	www.fidelity.com	800-544-5555
Firstrade.com	www.firstrade.com	800-869-8800
ForbesNet	www.forbesnet.com	800-488-0090
Freedom Investments	www.freedominvestments.com	800-944-4033
Frontier	www.ffutures.com	800-777-2438
InternetTrading.Com	www.internettrading.com	800-696-2811
InvestEXpress Online	www.investexpress.com	800-392-7192
InvestIN.com Securities	www.investinsecs.com	800-327-1883
InvesTrade	www.investrade.com	800-498-7120
J.B. Oxford & Company	www.jboxford.com	800-799-8870
Lexit Capital	www.lexitcapital.com	888-778-4998
Main Street Market	www.mainstmarket.com	800-710-7160
MB Trading	www.mbtrading.com	888-790-4800
Mr. Stock	www.mrstock.com	800-470-1896
Muriel Siebert & Co.	www.siebertnet.com	800-995-7880
MyDiscountBroker.com	www.mydiscountbroker.com	888-882-5600

National Discount Brokers	www.ndb.com	800-888-3999
The Net Investor	www.netinvestor.com	800-NET-4250
Online Trading.com	www.onlinetrading.com	800-995-1076
Peremel Online	www.peremel.com	800-737-3635
Preferred Trade	www.preferredtrade.com	800-889-9178
Quick & Reilly	www.quick-reilly.com	800-793-8050
Scottsdale Securities	www.scottrade.com	800-619-7283
Sunlogic	www.sunlogic.com	800-556-4600
Suretrade.com	www.suretrade.com	800-394-1452
Trade4Less	www.trade4less.com	800-780-3543
Tradewell Discount Investing	www.trade-well.com	888-907-9797
Trading Direct	www.tradingdirect.com	212-766-0241
TruTrade	www.trutrade.com	800-328-8600
Vision Trade	www.visiontrade.com	800-374-1940
Wall Street Access	www.wsaccess.com	800-925-5781
Wall Street Discount Corporation	www.wsdc.com	888-492-5578
WallStreet Electronica	www.wallstreete.com	888-925-5783
Wang Investments	www.wangvest.com	800-353-9264
Waterhouse Webroker	www.tdwaterhouse.com	888-687-0984
Web Street.com	www.webstreetsecurities.com	800-932-8723
Wilshire Capital	www.wilshirecm.com	800-926-9991
Wyse Securities	www.wysesecurities.com	800-640-8668

APPENDIX N. FORMULAS

Call Options: Intrinsic value = Underlying asset(UA)'s Current price
$\qquad$ − Call strike price

Put Options: Intrinsic value = Put strike price − Underlying Asset's Current price

Time Value = Option premium − Intrinsic value

$$\text{TRIN} = \frac{\text{Volume declining/Number declining}}{\text{Volume advancing/Number advancing}}$$

Current Ratio = Current assets/Current liabilities

$$\text{Debt to Equity} = \frac{\text{Total liabilities}}{\text{Shareholder's equity}}$$

P/E Ratio: Stock price divided by Earnings per share − P = Price/E
$\qquad$ = Earnings per share

Peg Ratio = P/E ratio/EPS growth rate

Relative Strength Index (RSI)

$$\text{RSI} = 100 - \frac{100}{1 + \text{RS}}$$

$$\text{RS} = \frac{\text{Average of } x \text{ days' up closes}}{\text{Average of } x \text{ days' down closes}}$$

Index

FREE TRADING PACKAGE
From George Fontanills and Tom Gentile

$100 FREE GIFT

Now that you've read George and Tom's book, wouldn't you like to keep up with their day-to-day trading strategies? We're going to make it easy to do by sending you a FREE Trading Package worth $100.

Their company, Global Investment Research Corp., is one of the leading investment publishing companies in the trading industry today. Global has grown to provide dozens of vital resources for stock and stock options traders. Using a simple yet effective philosophy of continued education and personal attention, George and Tom and their team of traders strive for excellence in all their trading products and services.

To receive your free trading package, complete and mail (or fax) the coupon below to:

Global Investment Research Corp.
P.O. Box 620238
Woodside, CA 94062-0238
Or Fax to: 650-378-8320

You may also reach us by phone at (888) 366-8264, or (650) 378-8333 outside the U.S., e-mail the authors at george@optionetics.com or tom@optionetics.com. You can also visit our web site at www.optionetics.com.

George Fontanills and Tom Gentile Trading Package

❏ I would like to learn more about George and Tom's trading secrets and strategies. Please send me the FREE trading package mentioned in the Stock Market Course.

Name: _____

Address: _____

City, State, Zip:_____

Phone: _____ **Fax:**_____

E-mail:_____

I purchased this book from:_____